Creative Industries in Turkey

Tolga Hepdinçler and Hasan Kemal Suher (Eds.)

Creative Industries in Turkey

PETER LANG

Bibliographic Information published by the Deutsche Nationalbibliothek

The Deutsche Nationalbibliothek lists this publication in the Deutsche Nationalbibliografie; detailed bibliographic data is available online at http://dnb.d-nb.de.

Library of Congress Cataloging-in-Publication Data

A CIP catalog record for this book has been applied for at the Library of Congress.

Book published with the support of the Bahcesehir University

Printed by CPI books GmbH, Leck

ISBN 978-3-631-81176-4 (Print)
E-ISBN 978-3-631-82389-7 (E-PDF)
E-ISBN 978-3-631-82390-3 (EPUB)
E-ISBN 978-3-631-82391-0 (MOBI)
DOI 10.3726/b17040

Peter Lang – Berlin · Bern · Bruxelles · New York · Oxford · Warszawa · Wien

This publication has been peer reviewed.

www.peterlang.com

Dedicated to our beloved friend Tanzer Ercanpolat (1971-2019)…

Table of Contents

List of Abbreviations

2D:	Two dimensional
3D:	Three dimensional
AI:	Artificial Intelligence
API:	Application Programming Interface
AR:	Augmented reality
ASVOFF:	A Shaded View on Fashion Film
AVOD:	Audio/Video on Demand
AWAL:	Artists Without a Label
B2B:	Business to Business
BAU:	Bahçeşehir University
BFF:	Boğaziçi Film Festival
BKM:	Beşiktaş Cultural Center
CAVE:	Cave Automatic Virtual Environment
CEO:	Chief Executive Officer
CNN:	Cable News Network
DAW:	Digital Audio Workstation
DCMS:	Department for Culture, Media, and Sport
DJ:	Disc Jokey
DM:	Dungeon Master
DMC:	Doğan Music Company
DVD:	Digital Versatile Disc
CNBC-e:	Consumer New and Business Channel-Entertainment
EWA:	European Women's Audiovisual Network
FF:	Film Festival
FIAPF:	International Federation of Film Producers Associations
FIFA:	International Federation of Association Football
FIPRESCI:	International Federation of Film Critics
FPS:	Frame-per-second
FRP:	Fantasy Role Playing
GM:	Game Master
GWA:	Golden Awards Excellence
HMD:	Head-Mounted Display
HR:	Human Resources
HTC:	Huawei Technologies, Co.
IAAF:	International Association of Athletics Federations

IDA:	Communication Consultancies Association of Turkey
IFPI:	International Federation of the Phonographic Industry
IIFF:	International Istanbul Film Festival
IKSV:	Istanbul Foundation for Culture and Arts
IPRA:	International Public Relations Association
ITFA:	International Documentary Film Festival Amsterdam
KRS-ONE:	Knowledge Reigns Supreme over Nearly Everyone
LAN:	Local Area Network
LP:	Long Play
M4NM:	Music for Non-musicians
MC:	A Master Of Ceremonies
MESAM:	Musical Work Owners' Society of Turkey
MIAM:	Centre for Advance Studies in Music
MR:	Mixed reality
MSG:	Musical Work Owners' League of Turkey
MTV:	Music Television
MÜYAP:	Turkish Phonographic Industry Society
MÜYORBİR:	Association of Music Interpreters
NGO:	Nongovernmental Organization
NLTR:	News Lab Turkey
NTV:	Nergis Television
P2P:	Peer-to-Peer
PC:	Personal Computer
PCM:	Pulse Code Modulation
PR:	Public Relations
PSA:	Public Service Announcement
RIAA:	Recording Industry Association of America
RPG:	Role-Playing Game
RTÜK:	The Supreme Board of Radio and Television
SIYAD:	Film Critics Association
SPSS:	Statistical Package for the Social Sciences
SVOD:	Subscription Video on Demand
TRT:	Turkish Radio Television
TÜBİTAK:	Scientific and Technological Research Council of Turkey
TUHID:	Turkish Association of Public Relations
TURSAK:	Turkish Cinema and Audiovisual Culture Foundation
TV:	Television
UGC:	User-Generated Content
UIP:	United International Pictures

UK:	United Kingdom
UNCTAD:	United Nations Conference on Trade and Development
UNDP:	United Nations Development Programme
UNESCO:	United Nations Educational, Scientific and Cultural Organization
USA:	United States of America
VFX:	Visual Effects
VMVPD:	Virtual Multi-channel Video Programming Distributors
VOD:	Video on Demand
VR:	Virtual Reality
VR1:	Virtual Reality First
WB:	Warner Bros.
WIA:	Women in Animation
WIPO:	World Intellectual Property Organization
YÖK:	Council of Higher Education
ZORLU PSM:	Zorlu Performing Arts Center

Tolga Hepdinçler

Foreword

Creative industries have become frequently expressed in academic studies in recent years. In the 2000s, new fields of study added to traditional media studies seem to require the adoption of the concept. In particular, the media transformed by new media technologies and the newly emerging areas of media applications difficult to define within the framework of the traditional media or cultural industries have required the use of creative industries as a new concept. On the other hand, cultural and artistic activities that are not included in the definitions of media have led to the use of the concept effectively in the last two decades. It is viable to say that the definitions of the creative industry are evaluated in different frameworks. If we make an evaluation in academic circles, Tab. 01 represents how creative industries are defined in different research areas such as creativity and content production (Pratt, 2004, 2008; Florida, 2010; Drake, 2003; Lazetti et al., 2008; Banks, 2010, McKinley & Smith 2009; Eikhof & Haunschild, 2006), creative economies (Howkins, 2001; Cave, 2002; Cunningham, 2002, 2008; Potts et al., 2008, Banks & Hesmondhalgh, 2009) and consumption of the creative contents (Deuze, 2007; Gill & Pratt, 2008; Evans, 2009; Shorthose, 2004). In this book, we tried to redefine and develop current definitions and debates in this framework.

Creative industries encompass a wide range of industrial activities covering film, television, broadcasting and advertising which are also traditional sectors of the media industries, as well as video games, design, music, visual arts, the UK's Department of Culture, Media and Sport (DCMS), who first defined the field, added industrial areas such as architecture, the art and antiques market, crafts, interactive leisure software and fashion (DCMS, 2001). More recently, United Nations Development Programme and United Nations Conference on Trade and Development report on Creative Industries in 2010 defined a classification relies on enlarging the concept of "creativity" from activities having a strong artistic component to "any economic activity" producing symbolic products with a heavy reliance on intellectual property and for as wide a market as possible (UNDP & UNCTAD, 2010, p. 7). In this context, the report defines a classification of creative industries with their distinctive characteristics such as heritage, arts, media and functional creations.

Heritage	Arts	Media	Functional Creations
• **Traditional cultural Expressions** • art crafts, festivals and celebrations • **Cultural sites** • archaeological sites, museums, libraries, exhibitions, etc.	• **Visual Arts** • painting, sculpture, photography and antiques • **Performing Arts** • live music, theatre, dance, opera, circus, puppetry	• **Publishing and printed media** • books, press and other publictions • **Audiovisuals** • film, television, radio and other broadcasting	• **Design** • Interior, graphic, fashion, jewellery, toys • **New Media** • architectural, advertising, cultural and recreational, creative research and develop- ment (R&D), digital and other related creative services

Tab. 0.1: Classification of creative industries (UNDP & UNCTAD, 2011)

UNDP and UNCTAD have also set the benchmarks that are effective in identifying creative industries. The framework cited by the report is an important step in defining the boundaries of creative industries. Thus, it is a basic framework for understanding potential creative industries:

> The creative industries are the cycles of creation, production and distribution of goods and services that use creativity and intellectual capital as primary inputs; constitute a set of knowledge-based activities, focused on but not limited to arts, potentially generating revenues from trade and intellectual property rights; comprise tangible products and intangible intellectual or artistic services with creative content, economic value and market objectives; stand at the crossroads of the artisan, services and industrial sectors; and constitute a new dynamic sector in world trade (2010, p. 8).

According to Bartley, the "creative industries" idea itself is a product not of industry but of history, both immediate and long-term. In the long term, the concept evolved from the old conceptualizations of the cultural industries and creative arts, and immediately the idea of the creative industries arose from recent changes in technology and the world economy, especially during the 1990s (Hartley, 2009, p.5). According to this definition, while creative industries are shaped by the Frankfurt School conceptualizations of cultural industries, they also define a new idea that incorporates the profound artistic and aesthetic experience of creative arts. On the other hand, it is positioned in an economic landscape that is being reshaped with new technologies. Even if creative industries are primarily tested on the political economy axis, interdisciplinary approaches such as media studies, communication, cultural studies, visual studies, sociology, film studies, audience studies, aesthetics and art theory have expanded the boundary of the concept. The inclusion of interdisciplinary trends around or within the concept of creative industries seems inevitable within the boundaries of which the concept is defined. It is necessary to establish a framework that requires not only the circulation and transformation of creative content as a commodity but also the identification of the processes inherent in production and consumption of creative industrial products.

According to Hartley et al., the sectors within creative industries – the creative arts (visual and performing arts, dance, theatre, etc.); the established media (broadcasting, film, television, radio and music); new media (software, games, e-commerce and e-content) – together with architecture and design move from the resolutely non-commercial to the high-tech and commercial (Hartley, et al., 2013). This growth seems to be largely related to the quantitative increase observed in the production, circulation and consumption of creative products and the increasing speed of these processes along with the digitization. The technological developments that have led to the growth of the market have not only limited to national industries but also led to the formation of a new and dynamic market on an international scale. In addition, the exchange of creative experiences on a transnational scale influences local content production styles and forms. With this transformation, the formation, diversification and hybridization of a global language is observed in creative content production. Thus, local creative experiences are diversified with global practices, not only with local creative sources. At the other end of the industry, the audience of creative products has emerged from new consumption trends that differ from the traditional audience, and technological advances have created new perceptions and consumption habits in using creative products.

Here, it is possible to say that creative industries evolved into a framework that differs from the definitions of cultural industries in terms of produce, creative product and audience. As observed in examples such as video games and virtual reality applications, it is not possible to talk about the exchange value of the traditionally defined commodity. The emergence of industries independent of space and infrastructure in the traditional sense is open to debate that it will be inadequate to measure the impact on mass culture and creative production. Here, we are not talking about the culture industry but focusing on how creativity became a part of the culture industries and how it shapes along with the convergence culture.

This book proposes to define the creative industry in Turkey with different aspects, which have created surplus value with the contribution of innovative initiatives and technological developments in recent years. For this purpose, new media and alternative industries emerging with technological developments, as well as traditional media industries transformed by technological developments, have formed the limits of the study. Especially in the academic circle of Turkey, the limited literature of creative and cultural industry discussions increase the importance of this study. The book concentrates on video games, cinema, animation and creative activities that have gained economic and cultural activity in recent years. Also, it focuses on the unique cases of the core creative industries, such as new media. In more detail, it provides a critical and alternative approach to the production, distribution and use of creative industry content beyond an overview of these industries.

Thus, the chapters of this book are organized as per five effective industries in Turkey: game, film, music, public relations and new media. The first three chapters of this book focus on the game industry, one of the growing industries in recent years. While Aker's chapter of this book aims to define the concept of gamification, one that shows the application of game-based ideas and elements to be applied in non-game environments including business processes, the other two chapters on the game industry investigate emerging communities such as gamer communities and role-playing communities. While Şengün, Çatak and Sonbudak's chapter explores the relationship between local creative industries and the local audiences by using Turkish video game producers and gamers as a case study, Sungu and Bostan's chapter explores foundation role-playing communities and their effects on gamer communities and local game industry.

Chapters from 4 to 9 focus on the film industry. Özkaracalar's chapter investigates horror film boom has been effectively ruled the Turkish film industry last decade. The chapter takes a close look at this relatively recent phenomenon. After a brief overview of the earlier Turkish horror movies, how the horror genre managed to make a more definite inroad into Turkish cinema after 2004 is recounted. Hepdinçler and Tetik's chapter investigates the current landscape of distribution in the Turkish film industry while it focuses on drastically transforming and changing distribution ownerships in the Turkish film industry since millennia. Kaya's chapter on festivals defines an alternative path for independent filmmakers. It discusses the contributions of the international film festivals of İstanbul to the industry, while briefly reviewing the difficulties they face. Ulusoy's chapter focuses on a convergent industry of fashion and video that is commercially effective. The chapter also focuses on the brief historical background of the creative processes becoming significant in content production. Noyan's chapter on the animation film industry reflects a critical perspective on representation of women labor in the animation film business. The chapter includes an in-depth investigation about gender equality regarding issues of discrimination and inequality. The chapter of Vatanarttıran defines a discussion and historical perspective on the dubbing industry that is historically attached to the film industry. Other than being a secondary industry, the chapter investigates evolution of dubbing to one of the concerning industries in relation to the film and advertisement industries.

Chapters 10 and 11 focus on emergent genres of the Turkish music industry, such as alternative music and hip-hop. Tamer and Engin's chapter presents a survey on the current status of the Turkish independent music industry, taking into consideration the effects of technological advancements during the last decade. On the other hand, Ömerbaş focuses on a relatively new boom in the Turkish music industry. The chapter explores the changing scene of Turkish language hip-hop music and more particularly the alternative discourse defined by the industry.

Chapters 12 and 13 concentrate on the public relations industry. Suher, Sohodol and Geysi frame concepts of creativity in the industry based on perception, quality, influences, barriers, and approach of managers and clients. The survey conducted with 170 professionals working in public relations agencies in Turkey shows that creativity in the industry is in progress, and there are several problems about client perspectives and structures of agencies in terms of creative execution. Eker and Engin focus on a special PR event. The chapter explains the features of hallmark events and the contributions of cultural heritage to the city of Konya. The International Commemoration of the 745th Anniversary of Mawlana-Rumi's Reunion 2018 analyzed with its contribution to tourism, culture, and people living in the city.

The last two chapters focus on creativity in terms of new media. The first chapter introduces a unique approach to news content by defining creative production in the culture of post-industrial journalism. Filibeli, Aşçı, and Cerrahoğlu introduce the new form of news media by using both theoretical and practical implications on the integration of journalistic production, constraints of social media, fundraising, and audience expectations. The last chapter of the book by Çatak, Köknar and Akan focuses on a virtual reality industry that is one of the prospecting industries in Turkey. The chapter utilizes beneficial information on the first steps of an emerging creative industry. The chapter defines an industrial landscape with a chronological view on university research projects and master and doctoral theses written. Interviews conducted with the pioneers of this industry in Turkey will provide a special insight into a creative industry founded, funded, developed and matured in Turkey.

References

Banks, M. (2010). Craft labour and creative industries. *International Journal of Cultural Policy*, *16*(3), 305–321.

Banks, M., & Hesmondhalgh, D. (2009). Looking for work in creative industries policy. *International Journal of Cultural Policy*, *15*(4), 415–430.

Caves, R. E. (2002). *Creative industries: Contracts between art and commerce.* Cambridge: Harvard University.

Cunningham, S. (2002). From cultural to creative industries: Theory, Industry and Policy Implications. *Media International Australia Incorporating Culture and Policy*, *102*(1), 54–65.

Cunningham, S. (2008). Four models of the creative industries. *International Journal of Cultural Policy* , *14*(3), 233–247.

Deuze, M. (2007). Convergence culture in the creative industries. *International Journal of Cultural Studies*, *10*(2), 243–263.

Department for Culture, Media and Sports /DCMS. (2001). *Creative industries mapping documents 2001*. Retrieved from https://www.gov.uk/government/publications/creative-industries-mapping-documents-2001

Drake, G. (2003). This place gives me space: Place and creativity in the creative industries. *Geoforum*, *34*(4), 511–524.

Eikhof, D. R., & Haunschild, A. (2006). Lifestyle meets market: Bohemian entrepreneurs in creative industries. *Creativity and Innovation Management*, *15*(3), 234–241.

Evans, G. (2009). Creative cities, creative spaces and urban policy. *Urban Studies*, *46*(5–6), 1003–1040.

Florida, R. (2010). *The flight of the creative class: The new global competition for talent*. New York: Harper Collins e-books.

Gill, R., & Pratt, A. (2008). In the social factory? Theory. *Culture & Society*, *25*(7–8), 1–30.

Hartley, J. (2009). *Creative industries*. Malden, MA: Blackwell

Hartley, J., Potts, J., Cunningham, S., Flew, T., Kane, M., & Banks, J. (2013). *Key concepts in creative industries*. Thousand Oaks, CA: SAGE Publications.

Howkins, J. (2001). *The creative economy: How people make money from ideas.* London: Allen Lane.

Lazzeretti, L., Boix, R., & Capone, F. (2008). Do creative industries cluster? Mapping creative local production systems in Italy and Spain. *Industry & Innovation*, *15*(5), 549–567.

McKinlay, A., & Smith, C. (2009). *Creative labour: Working in the creative industries. Houndmills*, Basingstoke, Hampshire: Palgrave Macmillan.

Potts, J., Cunningham, S., Hartley, J., & Ormerod, P. (2008). Social network markets: A new definition of the creative industries. *Journal of Cultural Economics*, *32*(3), 167–185.

Pratt, A. C. (2004). Creative clusters: Towards the governance of the creative industries production system. *Media International Australia Incorporating Culture and Policy*, *112*(1), 50–66.

Pratt, A. C. (2008). Creative cities: The cultural industries and the creative class. Geografiska Annaler: Series B, *Human Geography*, *90*(2), 107–117.

Shorthose, J. (2004). A more critical view of the creative industries: Production, consumption and resistance. *Capital & Class*, *28*(3), 1–9.

UNDP & UNCTAD (2010). *Creative Economy*. Report 2010, Geneva and New York, NY: UNDP and UNCTAD.

Şafak Şahin

An Introduction to the Main Concepts of Creative Industries

The creative industries enabling information and technology–based new areas provide opportunities as one of the newest and dynamic factors, especially for developing countries. Creative industries have opportunities to bring prosperity and income by processing the intellectual property as a raw material. These industries and sectors, generally positioned in the service sectors, constitute a strong link between itself and production industries by the added value of design and automation technologies. As a concept, "creative industries" was firstly mentioned by Adorno and Horkeim (1972) who are the essential intellectuals of the Frankfurt School. The creative industries, which started to become prominent at Australia and England in the middle of the 1990s, stood out of developing/industrialized countries by the added value on efficiency, export, modernization, and employment (Hartley, 2005). The term "creative industry" basically points out the markets formed by the creative entities. These entities also stimuli economic growth and development.

The owner of the explanation above is DCMS (United Kingdom Department of Culture, Media & Sport). Especially at the end of the 1990s, and after the establishment of a unit for creative industries by DCMS (DCMS, 2001), the initiatives on creative industries has changed the definition and categorization of it (Lazzaretti, Capone & Seçilmiş, 2014). Besides the definition and studies of DCMS, there are different explanations and concepts about this field. In the literature, which researched about cultural products and outputs, such terms can be seen as; "creative economy-creative sectors," "cultural economy-cultural industries," "content industries," and "creative class." But among these concepts and/or terms, "creative economy-creative industries" and "cultural economy-cultural industries" are more prevalent and more commonly used (Şimşek & Güven, 2017). The prominent definitions about creative industries and cultural economies are mentioned by the organizations such as DCMS, UNCTAD, and WIPO (2001, 2007, 2008, 2003).

Although it is relatively a new concept for the social era, creative industries have studied and explained from different point of views and different approaches. In literacy, it is possible to find various arguments about creative industries, culture industries, and creative economy.

Approaches to Creative Industries

The arguments about the concept of creative industries generally take place between the supporters who claim that the individual creativity results in the positive economic-social outputs and the skeptics who criticize these claims (Lovink and Rossiter, 2007). Even though it contains several points of view, the first approach generally relies on liberal and the second on Marksist theories. Economic and political approaches generally prefer the term "cultural industries" instead of creative industries (Flew, 2011).

According to Howkings (2005), the emphasis of producing welfare relying on intellectual property is the key feature of creative industries in the definition of DCMS which is generally accepted. The understanding of intellectual property made the artistic and cultural field expeditiously narrow. Thus, it is claimed that this approach could not go beyond to extend the definition of cultural industries to copyright industries (Potts et al., 2008). In spite of this, it is claimed that creative industries contain artistic products which are seen as traditionally sophisticated and indirect contributors such as distribution, publication, and sales channels (UNCTAD, 2010; Howkins, 2005). Thus, creative industries, which was a new category for academic, economic, and political fields, placed in both a deeper and wider position. This category is while extending to more widen field via containing indirect commercial factors and old high arts. On the other hand, it is getting deeper by opening space to the entrepreneurs of the flexible capitalism. Creative industries literature, which can be accepted as mainstream, does not hesitate to find the production of the cultural products as commodities (Demir, 2014). On the contrary, it accepts the transformation of creativity to commercial value as the basic characteristic of creative industries (Hartley, 2005). In the literature, it's claimed that creative industries contain the entrepreneurs of new economy which art, media or cultural industries kept them out of the scope (Cunningham, 2002). It can be analyzed well if the concept of creative industries is explained as the transformation from human capital theory to creative capital theory. The basics of creative capital theory actually relies on human capital theory which was generated by a group of evolutionary finance researchers. Florida (2002) argues his own approach based on human capital theory.

Garry Becker (1962, 1964, 1993), Nobel awarded theorist who made the most essential contributions to human capital theory, excluded it from material or standard capital such as bank accounts, stocks, factories, and machines. He emphasizes the importance of education and essentialness of investment on intellectuality. And he points out education as the measurement dynamics of the human capital. Human capital theory gained a place among the theories of development, especially in the light of endogenous growth theory. Especially Lucas (1988) accepts human capital as a basic criterion in his own development model. Before the endogenous theory, also Schumpeter (1947) gives the initial basics to creative capital theory by using the terms "creativity," "innovation," and "creative destruction." As mentioned above, Richard Florida (2002, 2009) has created his own approach from these points of view and initial theories.

The political and scientific interest paid to creativity and its impact on economic and territorial development increased with the 2002 publication of Richard Florida's book on the social ascension of the "creative class." The focus is no longer simply on an economic sector, but also addresses occupations. Moreover, he expands the concept of creative economy to a significant degree. For Richard Florida, advanced industrial societies have entered a new economic era in which the primary motor of growth is innovation, not only its artistic dimensions, but also the (techno)scientific and entrepreneurial arenas. According to this mindset, the creative class, as the new productive class under formation, is above all defined on an economic basis (function). It refers to a vast group of socioprofessional categories: artists, engineers, programmers, entrepreneurs, inventive managers, lawyers, and health and finance professionals.

From all these initial and essential approaches about creative industries, the point views and explanations become more related to economy- and marketing-based definitions. There are several new studies and approaches for creative industries which are not only related also rely on basics of economics. One of these approaches can be considered as a supportive explanation of commercial commodity which claims by Vardar (2017). According to him, there are six characteristic features of creative industries:

1. It is not completely possible to determine the quality and quantity of demand or product. Even if it can be named the outputs of the creative industries as "experience products". Because the marginal benefit and marginal price are depending on the abstract needs of the consumers.
2. Just as the demand cannot be determined, the quality and quantity of supply also cannot financially be determined.
3. Creative industries are dependent on other service sectors such as registering/patent, sales/marketing, and accounting.
4. Production can be collective or individual. Thus, coordination is required in collective production and complementarity of other services in individual production.

5. The producers who work in the creative industries, classified as their abilities such as differentiating capability. Supply is not stable because the production depends on human capital or traits of groups who have strong coordination.
6. Most of the cultural products obtained as the result of the creative industrial activities are profitable sectors which belong to intellectual property rights like copyright, patent, etc., in long term.

Before Vardar's (2017) ranking of the features of creative industries, Caves (2000) has also another explanation and detailed approached to characteristics of creative industries. Caves propounds seven economic activities of creative industries:

1. Uncertain demand or "nobody knows." It is very difficult to predict consumer reaction and therefore consumer demand to a new cultural work. This implies that the risk of any creative output is high and perhaps unquantifiable. The method of risk-sharing in the organization of productive process will be important. The asymmetric nature of information is a problem. Because the output is ultimately a result of experience.
2. Creative workers' bond with their creation or "art for art's sake." Unlike the standard construct that workers do not necessarily care about the characteristics of the output they produce, creators of creative output care deeply about the quality and integrity of their work, even if it may be unnoticed by most consumers, and even it its achievement requires a sacrifice in terms of income. The difficult problems faced by an entrepreneur who wishes to organize creative activities are on both sides of the transaction: production and sales. The creator does not know and cannot predict whether his creation will elicit the same reactions from others as from the creator himself.
3. Creative outputs need diverse skills or "motley crew." Many creative outputs require a diverse crew of skilled practitioners who must meet some threshold level of competence. The more complex the creative output, the more diverse, superior, and proficient the skills. This is most visible in performing arts or in fine print-making or in bronze sculpture-making. The output is the work of an ensemble whose members must be present and must contribute to the success of the output. This is beyond the standard team work, so beloved of industrial organization theorists.
4. Differentiated products or "infinite variety." A creative artist can choose to express himself from an endless number of possibilities. The outputs or products a creator produces are both vertically and horizontally differentiated from similar products. Say, two similar products can provide similar experience; yet the consumers assess one better than the other. This is an example of "vertical differentiation." Likewise, two similar products can

provide similar experience; neither the products nor the experience is identical, and some consumers prefer one while other consumers prefer the other. This is an example of "horizontal differentiation." This differentiation gives rise to intractable problems of pricing faced by the organizer of creative activities: the aggregate price consumers are willing to pay for a creative output that might not be sufficient for the success of the organized activity.

5. Vertically differentiated skills or "A list/B list." Creators who supply their own individual creative inputs in the production of a creative product or service differ vastly in their talents. Thus, the creative inputs are vertically differentiated. An analogy is the "A list" and "B list" of film actors, directors, screenwriters, etc. This ranking of inputting creators typically resonates with consumers; consumers willingly pay more for A-listers than B-listers. The phenomenon of the differential rents extracted by A-listers exists in almost all creative endeavors.
6. Time is of the essence or "time flies." A close temporal coordination in production and distribution of creative activity is often essential to bring to fruition the creative product or service. All investment projects, creative or otherwise, are likely to suffer diminution of prospective cash flows.
7. Durable products and durable rents or "Ars longa." The durability of creative outputs invites patent and/or copyright protection permitting the creator or owner to collect rent in the form of royalties or licensing fees. This has at least two effects: (1) The streams of rents are lumpy over time. This requires contracting and collecting agents or organizations. (2) Durable products remain durable if they stored properly and remain retrievable promptly. This requires contracting and warehousing and curating agents or organizations.

According to these explanations, approaches, and definitions above, it is understood that creative industries are mostly associated with the term "economy." Thus, the models and especially the key concepts of creative economy should be analyzed in detailed.

Creative Economies

The basic economy of modern industrial society is industry based, whereas the basic economy of postmodern society is evolving to sector of services. Especially in the basic economical classifications, sector of services turned into the dominant area of activity. With their added values, creative industries create connection between service and industrial sectors. From this point, creative industries are not only a contribution to the social and artistic area, but also are the basic inputs of the development process – R&D development, IT, communication, and traditional industries.

The income elasticity of creative industries provides revenue growth because it is above the unit value according to spending. Besides, it enhances the quality of human capital because of the factor of compulsory specialization input and also naturally gives importance to technology and intellect- based production. Thus, it is one of the basic dynamics of development and endogenous growth.

According to Gouvea and Vora (2018), countries that are not addressing R&D and innovation requirements for the further expansion of their creative economies could fall victim to the creative divide. Countries that do not properly address the foundations for the creation and development of a dynamic and globally competitive creative industry will fall behind other countries that are addressing these basic requirements. The creative economy also presents the potential for circular causation effects, leading to a virtuous cycle of economic development and also holds the potential for spillover effects throughout economies resulting in higher growth. These economies show higher levels of economic complexity and also are more competitive in global markets. Moreover, a dynamic creative economy may also have positive impacts on a country's ability to address the "middle-income trap" phenomena.

For the United Nations Conference on Trade and Development (UNCTAD), the creative economy is an evolving concept based on creative assets potentially generating economic growth and development (2008):

- It can foster income generation, job creation and export earnings while promoting social inclusion, cultural diversity, and human development.
- It embraces economic, cultural, and social aspects interacting with technology, intellectual property, and tourism objectives.
- It is a set of knowledge-based economic activities with a development dimension and crosscutting linkages at macro and microlevels to the overall economy.
- It is a feasible development option for innovation, multidisciplinary policy responses, and interministerial action.
- At the heart of the creative economy are the creative industries.

And also, in UNCTAD's next report (2010), it is explained that the creative industries were relatively less effected from the 2008 economic crises. Creative industries are essential to realize the economic bounce which the developing countries want. The countries should do required legal and administrative regulations and support capital accumulation with the long-term policies.

It is easily understood from the explanation above that creative industries can support and foster the economies via its unique features such as creating values. According to the report of creative industries in Switzerland (Weckerle, Page &

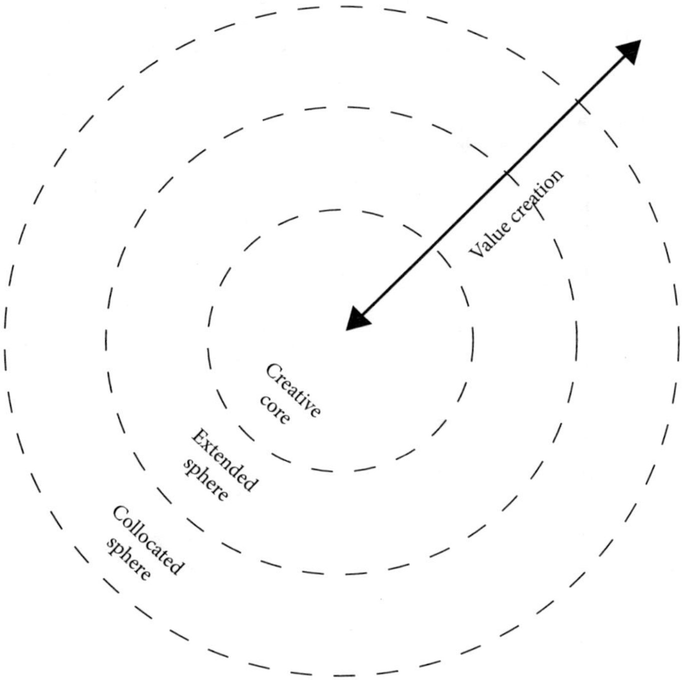

The creative economies model. The figure illustrates the three spheres of the creative economies – "creative core," "extended sphere," and "collocated sphere" – and defines value creation as a transversal process

Fig. 0.1: Value creation in the creative economies (Weckerle, Page & Grand, 2016)

Grand, 2016), the value of creative industries is explained with a model of value creation (Fig. 0.1).

According to the report, authors explain the model via symbolizing the main issues of creative industries with the concept of "core" and "spheres." Creative economies are determined by the interaction between a "core" area, in which original creation occurs, and an "extended sphere," which consists of other creative and innovative actors and a multitude of other organizations in the "collocated sphere" (Weckerle, Page & Grand, 2016):

— A given element of the "creative core" is a concept of creativity that is closely related to artistic creation and the creative industry, i.e., the creative economies.

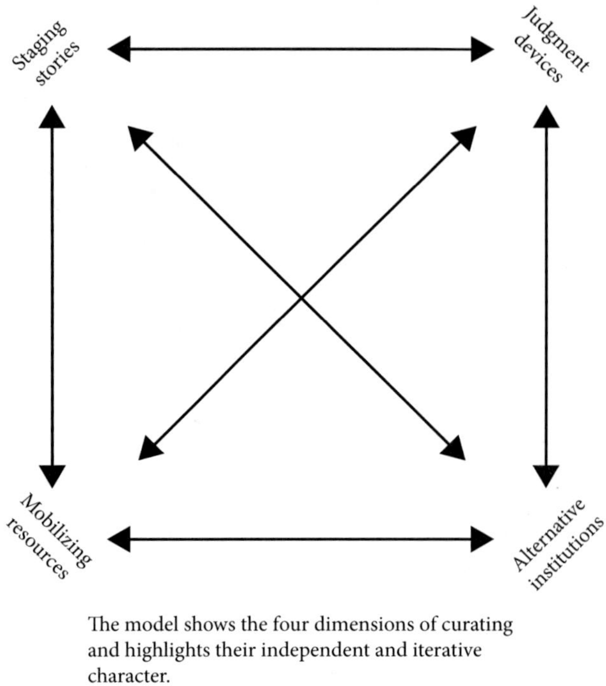

Fig. 0.2: Action field of curating (Weckerle, Page & Grand, 2016)

In the same report, authors demonstrate another model about creative economies. In this model, different than the "core" concept, it is explained by emphasizing the processes (Fig. 0.2).

In this model above, instead of meaning to organizing an exhibition, curating refers to processes and actors active in the most diverse cultural, social, economic, or scientific fields – as a rule under different designations, such as director, producer, broker, or entrepreneur.

As it can be understood from the evolution of the models, creative economies started to be more linked to the creators. All these processes need creative groups, and these groups are named in various concepts such as talent groups, creative class, and creative employees. The main explanations and references about creative industries are connected with economies of countries but in recent years, studies turn to emphasize the cities rather than the countries. There can be several reasons for that, but the most possible reason is the relationship between the creative class and the metropole cities. And the other possible reason can be the economic power of the big cities which can drive the whole economy of the developed and the developing countries.

Creative Class in Creative Cities

In creative economies, as mentioned above, there are three main concepts. These are "creative industries"; Florida's (2011) "creative class" which means artists, researchers, and creative professionals; and Charles Landry's (2004) "creative city."

Richard Florida (2011), in his study, researches as to why some cities in the world are richer than the others and when compared, he found that it arises from the creative class who live in these cities. The term "creative class" also points out the transformation from industrial production to creative production. Thus, this approach of Florida who claims that creativity is an economic value and human creativity is a limitless source, also points out the main source of the economy. These people are architects, artists, musicians, advertising professionals, researchers, authors, entrepreneurs, engineers, and scientists; and all of them are economically value creator individuals. Florida (2011) says that at the beginning of the 21st century, this class represents one-third percent of all labor and the value of creative sector's revenue equals to half of all income and salaries of US.

In the basics of creative industries exists the individual creativity and talented-creative individuals are the propulsive force of the successful cities. This new class of the new economy consist of the people who keep this rising economic field. This class is the main factor of creative economy and the main indicator of the city capital. Florida summarizes the features which this class demands from the cities where they live with 3T (talent, tolerant, technology). These are all necessary for economic growth; 3T can be explained briefly like this: To generate creative value for creative class, talent is necessary.

Besides, technology is not only the power of creative industries, but also the new economies. With the development of digital technologies, it is said that the whole future economies will digitalize and thus there will be globally digitalized culture. But in these cities where the creative people live and add values, there are some features which these people seek. To gain these features and so to attract creative class and human capital, cities are in hard competition. Also, to be an attractive city for these people, these regions have to own intense and wide labor market, there has to be cafes and other meeting points to provide business movement, there has to be tolerance for different thoughts, cultures, ethnic diversity, and requirements to carry on its own culture that has to be authentic (Westlund & Calidoni-Lundberg, 2007).

New Issues in Creative Industries

According to the meetings about creative industries under the leadership of Istanbul Development Agency, the professionals and the related responsible share their comments to create more effective results in this field. There are four main and possible issues which may affect directly or indirectly the creative industries. And these issues can be seen as thematic areas which related researchers and professionals may contribute to and add value to each of them. These issues are: (a) ecosystem, (b) demand for design and creative good and services, (c) design and value added, and (d) data and knowledge.

Ecosystem

Creative industries and cultural sectors have various actors representing public, academic, business, civil society sectors, or professions, which, as whole, constitute the backbone of a vast ecosystem. In fact, depending on the definition, the umbrella term "cultural and creative industries" may encompass a wide range of classical and modern sectors, which share some commonalities as well as having many unique features. That signifies also a variety of actor types, services, infrastructures, and links. Compared to innovation and entrepreneurship ecosystems, despite its economic potential, ecosystem of creative industries appears less structured, under subsidized, and under supported by governments. Ecosystem actors need to be empowered with improved access to finance and government grants, technical support, and skilled human resources. Networking and collaboration are also key factors which enable mutual learning and innovation, improving awareness on contemporary trends and opportunities. Therefore, both quality and quantity of links between actors should be increased through effective networking structures and creative/design hubs.

Demand for design and creative good and services

Demand is a key factor to actualize the potential of design and other creative sectors in fostering prosperity. Yet, both general public awareness as final consumers and the awareness of those using design service as an input for production of services and goods remain relatively low. That highlights the need for exploring means to stimulate demand and to provide better links between customer needs and supply. In addition to improving local demand, creative industries should be encouraged towards and be enabled to benefit from opportunities presented by other markets and tourism specifically. Cities with their economic, social, and cultural dynamism; cosmopolitan fabric; and strong connectivity play key roles in fostering design and other creative sectors. In return, creative industries and particularly design have strong prospects to lead the postindustrial transformation of cities and to improve their external and internal images.

Design and value added

Design is a very strategical creative sector with regard to its cross-sectoral links and huge potential it offers for increasing value added. Within a broader perspective, design culture implies a more extensive use and therefore has even a larger potential to foster economic and social change and to improve quality of life by allowing policies, products, services, processes, and infrastructures to better match human needs and to meet societal and environmental concerns.

Recent technological developments especially in ICT sector and strong digital transformation trends once more underline the significance of design along with creative content. While boosting productivity and cost minimization, Industry 4.0 opens vast frontiers for the use of design through immense data about production and consumer needs and also by intensifying user experience. More collaborative works are needed to reveal the potential of design and to examine successful cases within this new context.

Data and knowledge

Though research on creative industries and cultural sectors demonstrate their significance in terms of economic development and social life, further research is needed to identify common dynamics, peculiarities, interconnections, and challenges facing their development. Above all, policy makers need operational data and working knowledge to develop better policies and tools to address the needs of these sectors and to help them achieve their economic and social potential.

References

Adorno,T., & Horkheimer, M. (1972). *Dialectic of enlightenment.* London: Verso.

Becker, G. (1962). Investment in human capital: A theoretical analysis. *Journal of Political Economy Part 2: Investment in Human Beings*, *70*(5), 9–49.

Becker, G. (1964). *Human capital.* New York: Columbia University Press for the National Bureau of Economic Research,.

Becker, G. (1993). *A theoretical and empirical analysis, with special reference to education*. Chicago: The University Press of Chicago,.

Caves, R. E. (2000). *Creative industries: Contracts between art and commerce.* Cambridge, MA: Harvard University Press.

Cunningham, S. D. (2002). From cultural to creative industries: Theory, industry and policy implications. *Media International Australia Incorporating Culture and Policy, 102*(1), 54–65.

Demir, E. (2014). Creative industries. *Ilef Journal, 1*(2), 87–107.

Department for Culture, Media and Sports /DCMS. (2001). *Creative industries mapping documents 2001.* Retrieved from https://www.gov.uk/government/publications/creative-industries-mapping-documents-2001

Flew, T. (2011). *The creative industries: Culture and policy.* London: SAGE Publications.

Florida, R. (2002). The rise of the creative class cities without gays and rock bands are losing the economic development race. *Washington Monthly, 34*(5), 15–26.

Florida, R. (2011). *The rise of creative class and how it is transforming work, leisure, community, and everyday life.* New York: Basic Books.

Florida, R. & Mellander, C. (2009). Human capital, the creative class, and tolerance: effects on regional wages and income. *Special issue of the Annals of Regional Science, 10*(1007), 1–24.

Gouvea, R., & Vora, G. (2018). Creative industries and economic growth: Stability of creative products exports earnings. *Creative Industries Journal, 11*(1), 22–53.

Hartley, J. (2005). *Creative industries.* Oxford: Blackwell Publishing.

Howkins, J. (2005). The Mayor's commission on the creative industries. In J. Hartley (Ed.), *Creative industries.* (pp. 117–125). Oxford: Wiley-Blackwell.

Landry, C. (2004). *A creative city a toolkit for urban innovators.* Comedia London Sterling: Earthscan Publications,

Lazzaretti, L., Capone, F., & Seçilmiş, İ. E. (2014). The structure of the creative and cultural sectors in Turkey, *Maliye Dergisi, 166*, 195–220.

Lovink, G., & Rossister, N. (2007). Proposals for creative research introduction to the my creativity reader. In G. Lovink & N. Rossister (Eds.), *My creativity reader.* (pp. 9–16). Amsterdam: Institute of Network Cultures.

Lucas, R. E. (1988). On the mechanics of economic development. *Journal of Monetary Economics, 22*, 3–42.

Potts, J. D., Cunningham, S. D., Hartley, J., & Ormerod, P. (2008). Social network markets: A new definition of the creative industries. *Journal of Cultural Economics, 32*(3),67–185.

Schumpeter, J. A. (1947). The creative response in economic history. *The Journal of Economic History, 7*(2), 149–159.

Şimşek, G., & Güven, A. (2017). A new momentum for Turkey in creative sectors: Midwood Istanbul Film Studio. *The Journal of International Social Research*, *10*(51), 1131–1146.

UNDP & UNCTAD. (2008). *Creative economy report 2008*. Geneva & New York, NY: UNDP and UNCTAD.

UNDP & UNCTAD. (2010). *Creative economy report 2010*. Geneva & New York, NY: UNDP and UNCTAD.

Vardar, S. (2017). Yaratıcı endüstriler. *Kalkınmada Anahtar Verimlilik*, *338*, 40–48.

Weckerle, C., Page, R., & Grand, S. (2016). *The Swiss creative industry report: From the creative industry to the creative economies*. Retrieved from http://www.creativeeconomies.com/downloads/eng_creative-economy-report-2016.pdf

Westlund, H., & Calidoni-Lundberg, F. (2007). The creative class and social capital. CESIS Electronic Working Paper Series. Retrieved from https://static.sys.kth.se/itm/wp/cesis/cesiswp112.pdf

WIPO-World Intellectual Property Organization. (2003). *Guide on surveying the economic contribution of the creative industries*, Geneva. Retrieved from https://sic.cultura.gob.mx/documentos/825.pdf

Çakır Aker

Chapter 1 Investigation of Gamification and Its Effects on Marketing in Turkey

Introduction

In the last decade, technological developments have started to shift towards a direction which puts the users and their experiences in its core. This shift in understanding users has naturally brought much interest on user engagement and enjoyment. The developments in technology have also enabled the creation of new forms of participation in problem solving and value creation. The ever-increasing importance of user preferences led to an industry in which the user and user experience as an emerging term play a crucial role. As Aker and Öztürk (2015) mention, in today's world, the new uses of communication technology should be able to offer its user a better usability and user experience to a wider market in order to succeed. Consequently, this shift in understanding technological and communicational developments has increased the interest towards games, since in their essence, games involve user engagement and mostly rely on it. Moreover, games that were only played through game consoles and computers in the past have now become available for every age group, regardless of time and place, through mobile technologies, spreading its potential for user engagement and increase in motivation. As a result, video games have become one of the major components of entertainment industry in the last three decades (Korhonen, Montola & Arrasvuori, 2009).

Games are essentially created and developed with the notion of providing fun and enjoyment. Consequently, the nature of games requires the engagement of a user. Games can provide this engagement by combining appropriate game elements while utilizing different aspects rather than focusing directly on being fun. An example regarding this kind of an approach could be "serious games", in which the goal of the game is not solely enjoyment but also involves a "serious" goal or message such as a political perspective and/or an educational purpose. As a definition, serious games are computer-based actionable systems that are designed to teach and inform while utilizing game elements such as rules, challenge, or fantasy (Carmody, 2012). Meanwhile "educational games" or "edugames" are described as fun and interactive alternative to the education process, which may bring a brand new perspective to the context of education (Barbosa, 2015). Both these interlacing perspectives through games and the field of game studies offer a sense of commonality on definitions and their distinctive characteristics which position games as a multipurpose digital tool in general because of their great potential of incorporating knowledge and information within the foundations and exposing it in an entertaining and engaging form (Allery, 2014; Barbosa, 2015; Carmody, 2012). These game genres could be given as examples of games that are considered as one of the most common applications in terms of games being utilized out of the context of games, as we know it. Similar uses of game mechanics in non-game environments have also started to emerge in parallel with developing technologies which are embedded in our daily lives. Although the idea that game elements can be applied in various fields for increasing engagement and participation in nearly any subject from education, marketing and/or political means; not until the 2000s the term "gamification" has started to be used. Similarly, video games have increasingly become a part of our everyday lives during the last decade. In this notion, the novel age is considered to be the conceptual age in which games are integrated to our everyday lives (Pink, 2006), embedding game design techniques and mechanics ubiquitous to us. As Johnson et al. (2013) also stated, in the last decade, games are being utilized for much more than recreational purposes. Following this notion, the term "gamification" has become popular not only as an innovative and effective tool to motivate and engage people but also for holding the potential to motivate co-creation while being utilized. After the year 2010, gamification became a frequently used term within the literature, shedding new light on the path of using game-based elements and their application.

In this study, I will discuss both the theoretical definition and application of gamification in the context of marketing in Turkey. Although the field of game studies has conducted various researches on gamified experiences, regardless of the attention over the term "gamification" which quickly gained popularity within the industry, academia has been slow to react. Therefore, this study aims to anchor a relation between the field of game studies via inspecting the use of game elements in non-game environments and the industry's perspective in the context of gamification with a focus on Turkey. As defined by industry experts and academia, gamification can be applied to any problem that can be solved by influencing the human behavior and motivation with its strong and flexible structure (Zichermann & Cunnigham, 2011). Thus, the main objective of this study is to investigate the versatile concept of gamification while explaining and examining various marketing applications utilizing gamification and to provide better understanding of the term and its use in the industry for future researchers and professionals. In this respect, it is suggested that gamification will be used by the practitioners in the future in Turkey. Thus, this research would also potentially provide contribution to the future of gamification in Turkey.

Gamification

Gamification is an emerging phenomenon that is receiving increasing attention from both practitioners and researchers. As a term, gamification originated in the digital media industry. Current industry refers to the term between several concepts such as the institutionalization and ubiquity of games in everyday life (Schell, 2010; Chatfieldi 2005; Helgason, 2010) or the application of game elements to make other non-game products and services more enjoyable and engaging (Zichermann, 2011; Zichermann & Cunningham, 2011). The increase in the number of scientific studies published in recent years about the role of gamification shows that the issue has become a popular field of study as well (e.g. Hamari et.al., 2014; Werbach & Hunter, 2012; Deterding, 2011; Zichermann & Cunningham, 2011). Furthermore, with the potential to enhance and improve the user experience via offering motivating and engaging game experiences, gamification is considered to be a novel and effective way among marketing techniques in our era (Hamari, 2017). In order to comprehend the importance and significance of gamified experiences, several researchers and professionals from the industry have attempted to define the term "gamification". From one perspective, gamification is defined as the use of game elements in non-game activity areas (Deterding et al., 2011, p.2) in order to enhance the user's experience or to connect to the game platform. Huotari and Hamari (2012) have narrowed the framework of the concept of gamification and brought it closer to the business perspective. Accordingly, gamification can be understood as a service development process with game experience gained to support the total value creation of the user. A more extensive and much more accepted definition by both the professionals and researchers is that the gamification is an approach which can be applied to any problem that can be solved by influencing the human behavior and motivation with its strong and flexible structure (Zichermann & Cunnigham, 2011). However, there are no commonly accepted affordances that explain how gamification stems from games.

One of the rather specific perspective for inspecting the relation between games and gamification is that games (and video games primarily) are designed with the purpose of entertainment, while motivating users to engage in the act with strong intensity and for a really long time without interruption. Hence, as a basis for defining gamification, this study will follow the latter definition which defines the concept as game elements potentially being able to make non-game services and products more engaging and entertaining, thus indicating affordances of gamification. Moreover, the literature does not clearly indicate that the affordances implemented in gamification have to be the same as the ones used in games. A rather distinctive criticism towards the field of gamification is that empirical studies which define gamification elements seem to be lacking (Hamari, Koivisto & Sarsa, 2014) as well as the lack of empirical studies providing evidence of gamification's impact on consumer behavior and marketing (Deterding et al., 2011; Hamari, 2017).

Whereas serious games would imply the design of games for non-entertainment purposes and contexts, gamified applications harbor elements of games (Deterding et al., 2011). Therefore, it is crucial to understand the game elements for the intrinsic mechanisms and affordances of gamification. These elements of games are interconnected with each other and to game mechanics and dynamics, and affordances such as points, badges, or leaderboards which are often applied in gamified design (Matsubara & Da Silva, 2017). Moreover, in theory, gamification depends on game elements and motivational models (Çağlar & Kocadere, 2015). To apply gamification, firstly, industry developers and researchers need a list of game design elements, and then secondly, they need to integrate these elements into their intervention (Cugelman, 2013). However, gamification researchers do not always agree on what these ingredients are. Considering all of these perspectives, to gain better understanding on the term "gamification" and its affordances in the first place, game elements which provide affordances for gamification must be inspected.

Gamification Affordances

Fundamentally, games are artifacts that are created to deliver engaging and entertaining experiences to their users. Although the field of game studies does not have a clear definition of the elements that cover the term "game" in a holistic manner, one solution is to identify distinctive set of properties which are shared by games and that are characteristic to games. Accordingly, Werbach and Hunter (2012) laid out the game elements in three distinct categories; dynamics, mechanics, and components. These categories are also defined according to their level of abstraction, components being the least and dynamics being the most abstract. Werbach and Hunter (2012) have proposed a hierarchical model for these three game element categories.

Accordingly, dynamics represent the highest abstraction level. Dynamics include constraints, emotions, narrative, progression, and relationships. Mechanics category represents the way to push interactions and engagements.

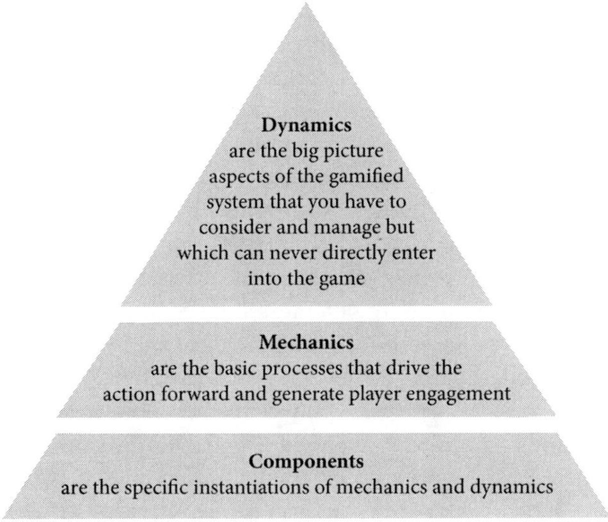

Fig. 1.1: The hierarchy of game elements (Werbach & Hunter, 2012)

They include elements such as challenge, chance, competition, cooperation, feedback, resource acquisition, rewards, and win states. Components represent the least abstract level of game elements which include achievements, avatars, badges, collection of objects, combat, content unlocking, gifting, leader boards, levels, points, quests, social graphs, teams, and virtual goods. These categories are depicted in order to address the levels of influence to the overall game experience in Fig. 1.1.

Nevertheless, as Cheong et al. (2014) clearly noted in their study, gamification cannot simply be about the use of game elements in non-game environments. It also includes aspects such as the utilization of game design and game thinking. Additionally, the overall gamified experience cannot be considered to be solely affected by game elements, but the interdependencies and interactions between them.

Whereas games and the sub elements that define a game were being debated in the literature, with the expansion and development in the field of gaming and the rise of the importance for user experience research within the field of game studies, more researchers began to study "motivational affordances" (Zhang, 2008) in order to inspect games and gamified experiences. The term "affordance" refers to the actionable properties between an object and an actor

(Gibson, 1977; Norman, 1999) and is mostly used in resemblance to game elements within the field of game studies. Several scholars (e.g. He, Greenberg & Huang, 2010; Brynjarsdottir et.al. 2012; Huber & Hilty, 2014) have argued that taking user's motivational needs into account is one of the most crucial but often neglected design aspects for communication technologies. Although these motivational affordances are identified for the field of design and information and communication technologies at mind (Zhang, 2008), Hamari, Koivisto and Sarsa (2014) have managed to adopt the notion and have conducted a comprehensive literature review indicating the affordances of gamification according to empirical studies in the literature. Accordingly, they have identified 10 different affordances based on the terminology that is used in the reviewed papers – points, leaderboards, achievements/badges, levels, story/theme, clear goals, feedback, rewards, progress, and challenge. Points, leaderboards, and badges are the most commonly analyzed affordances in gamified experiences and are considered to be "goal metrics" as all three are used to keep track of and provide feedback on player performance in games (Zagal et al., 2007). It should also be noted that these affordances do not directly refer to successful gamified experiences and hence should not be always considered as necessary at all times. Sailer et al. (2014) mention this as "single elements can help to enhance certain feelings, like feelings of competence, autonomy and social relatedness, but these feelings tend to refer to an overall experience within the gamification environment". Nevertheless, it is crucial to address each one of them and to analyze their relations to understand the concept of gamification.

Points

As one of the commonly applied game elements, points are often employed in gamification projects and have a direct impact on user's behavior (Jia et.al, 2016). Points are utilized as affordances for assessing the performance of the user during interaction while providing a foundation for other game components such as leaderboards, badges, rewards, or levels. Although the use of points can differ between gamified applications, they are mostly considered helpful in goal setting, habit tracking, and providing a feeling of accumulation towards the goal (Werbach & Hunter, 2012).

Leaderboards

Among various examples of games and gamified experiences, leaderboards are often used and refer to accumulated points of the user. This affordance is defined as typically providing multiple goals and not giving specific instructions

"…on which of the presented goals is a worthwhile target" (Landers, Bauer & Callan, 2017). Similar to casual video games or the old arcade machines in which the leaderboards were utilized to provide a social reward for high-scorers, the leaderboards in gamified experiences allow the users to feel competent about their performance in a social manner. On the other hand, leaderboards provide a sense of competition, which might motivate the user to achieve even more. Since the basic notion of leaderboards is dependent on the social motivations, it is commonly implemented as if it would be publicly visible. Users may vary in their motivations to achieve a place on leaderboards (Hamari et al., 2014). But it was also indicated in the literature that, although an effective tool for directing behavior, goal-setting or leaderboards in our case has significant downsides. As Landers et al. (2017) indicated; "by focusing effort narrowly, other desirable outcomes are often deprioritized". As a result, leaderboards are considered to be used carefully in gamification design and mostly to provide a sense of competition and achievement since the affordance could also be harmful for the overall experience, overshadowing the other affordances.

Badges/Achievements

Badges are also considered to be one of most common affordances investigated in gamification studies and employed in a variety of contexts (Hamari et al., 2014). Hamari (2013) states that "badges have been considered as the blueprint of gamification and have been the primary game mechanism in popular gamified applications". Following the implementation of leaderboards and often based on points, badges or achievements are utilized to provide indication of success in a gamified experience. From a systematic point of view, badges represent significant visual elements, rewards, and the fulfillment conditions which determine how the badge can be earned (Hamari, 2013; Hamari & Eranti, 2011; Jakobsson, 2011; Montola et al., 2009). Furthermore, because of the visual property of the affordance, badges can additionally enhance the narrative by either accompanying the story or supporting it. Badges are commonly implemented to provide a sense of accomplishment for the user, thus providing intrinsic motivation (Malone, 1981). Because of this trait, they are often employed for increasing the motivation throughout the experience. Although badges may provide the sense of success to the user, they are not always considered to be social or related to competition, hence cannot be considered equivalent to leaderboards. Another use of badges refers and indicates clear goals affordance since they are identified to guide user behavior and set goals (Montola et al., 2009). Badges consist of optional rewards and goals whose fulfillment is stored outside the scope of the core activities of a service (Montola et al., 2009; Jakobsson, 2011). In other words, badges can be used for affirmation symbols as well as identifiers for the users with a group that works towards the same goals. Thus, by utilizing badges, players could be motivated to earn them and thus certain sub-goals could be pointed out.

Levels

In most games, levels indicate progress. Levels serve as a marker for players to know where they stand in a gaming experience over time (Zichermann. & Cunningham, 2011). Similar to points and leaderboards, levels are also used in order to keep track of the game stage and provide feedback to the player on games (Zagal et al., 2007). Moreover, levels are not specifically referred to the notion of increase in difficulty of tasks as the case mostly on video games. They are utilized to enhance the sense of accomplishment and progress in gamification. Levels could be implemented to adhere a sense of achievement and competence whereas the user could relate his/her level with other users on a social level, in this context referring to leaderboards. Moreover, levels could be utilized for indicating specific badges and the overall progress, thus guiding the user towards clear goals.

Story/Theme

Story/theme is considered to be an emotional motivational source (Jia et al., 2016) as in this affordance it can provide the sense of autonomy to the user within the system. Meaningful stories are often wrapped around certain activities. According to Malone (1982), "Fantasy is probably the most important feature of computer games that can be usefully included in other user interfaces". In his definition, he indicates that the use of theme/fantasy makes the experience emotionally more appealing to users. In its core, the element of fantasy depends on the story and narrative of the game. For the user to get emotionally involved with the points, badges, or any other success indicators, the story or theme should be meaningful in a gamified design. Kapp (2012) mentions that a storyline can help learners to achieve an ideal interest curve – the interest of the players' peak around the beginning, at the end of the learning process, and to stay motivated throughout the experience. From the industry point of view, this affordance is usually employed to create an engaging gamified experience by providing an escape from the reality of work-related tasks and offers an alternative reality to the user for motivating them to be engaged.

Clear goals

One important aspect of games is that clear goals have been correlated with its popularity (Malone, 1982; Sweetser & Wyeth, 2005). Goals are objectives that a person or a system desires to achieve (Oxford Dictionaries, 2014). The affordance is crucial so that the players can understand the task at hand which they are trying to succeed, and as a result they would stay engaged with the gamified system (Csikszentmihalyi, 1988). Similar to games, clear goals affect the users in gamification systems by indicating tasks whether on a short or long term. Thus, clear goals are essential for engaging the users at the first place. Moreover, clear goals can provide the necessary motivational drive for the users to engage with the system. Goals can set the tone in a game and/or gamified system and can be modified for generating particular behaviors and feelings in a game (Fullerton, 2007). It is important to understand that the goals also refer to rules of the game at hand since the players are expected to reach their goals only by the rules of the game.

Feedback

Feedback is the one of the main affordances in terms of interaction; yet in a gamified system, it often refers to meaningful feedback to create meaningful interaction. The player will typically know if the goals are reached through feedback in the game. For instance, the feedback can be communicated using rewards, badges, points, or unlocking new challenges and goals. The players are expected to follow the rules of the gamified system in order to achieve the goal that is set in front of them, but they would not understand if the goal has been reached unless they receive any sort of feedback. It is important to note that the feedback mechanisms can be directly included to those affordances, but in terms of behavioral perspective, as Sailer et al. mention (2014), "Players are likely to be motivated if gamification provides immediate feedback in form of positive and negative reinforcement". In other words, the instantaneous feedback is considered to be the main reason for users to feel motivated and engaged in their actions (Kiryakova, Angelova & Yordanova, 2013).

Rewards

As mentioned before, points or trophies can be seen as virtual rewards in gamified experiences. Rewards fulfill the general sense of achievement and success for the player by providing constructs of conflict. Reward systems are employed to provide and increase a feeling which could give immediate feedback to the players' success, awarding them with various virtual objects such as points, trophies, or items on task completion. Although they seem to be very simple at a first glance, rewards and points can address motivational mechanisms (Sailer et al., 2014).

Progress

Several researchers (e.g.: Berkling. & Thoma, 2013; O'Donovan et al., 2013; Raymer, 2011) have used progress indicators for educational means and found that they are useful for gamifying education. The progress affordance focuses on individual players and their progress. The implication of the affordance often takes place in the form of progress bars and indicate the players' distance for reaching a goal. It also provides feedback regarding the players' competence while providing the necessary information of players' current position in the game. It is important to differentiate other metric elements such as badges and levels from progress affordance since while these elements indicate a result within the game in terms of short-term goals, progress indicators deliver the necessary information on where the player is at the game in the current state as well. Nah et al. (2014) put the difference between badges and progress bars clearly by indicating "While badges demonstrate achievements towards a particular level/goal, progress bars are used to track and display the overall goal progression".

Challenge

Challenges are tasks that users perform and progress towards defined objectives. In its core, challenges represent the obstacles ranging from decision-making and problem-solving strategies through to action reflexes (Kosmadoudi, et al. 2013). In gamified experiences, the challenges must also follow a similar notion, such as in games, providing sufficient challenges is not just to engage with the player but to test the skills of the player throughout the experience (e.g. variable difficulty level). Fundamentally, challenges are interconnected with the affordances of rewards, achievements, points, and goals. It should be noted that essentially challenges are one of the most crucial elements of a gamified system since they allow players to move towards a given goal while artificial difficulties and decisions are experienced during the journey. Yet the challenges must be considered carefully before application in order to not provoke negative emotions instead of positive ones via progression, utilizing both knowledge and challenge in balance (Sweetser & Wyeth, 2005). This balance between play knowledge or skill and challenges would help ensure that the challenges in the game match the player's skill levels, providing the sense of flow (Csikszentmihalyi, 1988).

Although these elements/affordances have their unique definitions in terms of defining a gamified experience, they all are correlated with each other and thus provide parts of the overall gamified experience regarding their employment. As Sailer et al. (2014) put it; "Single elements fulfill different functions, but in interaction with each other they can have varying and complex motivational effects."

Methodology

Qualitative research is applied in the explanation and understanding of a phenomenon. Unlike quantitative data, qualitative data are not measured in terms of quantity or frequency, yet are inspected to gather in-depth meanings and processes (Labuschagne, 2003). Moreover, the flexibility of semi-structured interviews allows to pursue a series of less-structured questioning and enables exploration of issues raised by the interviewee. Since the focus of this study was also to identify industry insights as well as the utilization of gamification approach within the industry in Turkey, semi-structured interviews were conducted with industry professionals and experts. The interviews were conducted via surveys and face-to-face discussions focusing on project development processes and gamification affordances that are employed during gamification projects in Turkey. In order to analyze the current position that gamification holds in the industry, the framework of the survey included open-ended questions to generate some general answers. The interview questions included 10 questions about the current application of gamification methods in the industry such as the utilization of game elements/gamification affordances employed during projects, the overall process insights and the general tendency of the industry towards gamification, and interpretation of future objectives of the application of the method throughout the industry.

A total of five gamification specialists working in the industry have been interviewed for the study, who have experience varying between 4 and 7 years and have already worked in several gamification projects. An in-depth analyses on the answers from the semi-structured interviews have been conducted to gain a deeper understanding in regard to the related topic. All the interviews were conducted individually to prevent experts from affecting each other while a common subject was on debate.

Gamification in Turkey

The results suggest that most of the gamification projects in which the experts took an active role were aimed to utilize nearly all the gamification affordances while points, badges, and leaderboard affordances were being the most used. Even though the participants indicated that all of the affordances were effective in their own way, specific motivational affordances, such as challenges, depend on the goal and the context of the gamification projects at hand.

The results from the interviews suggest that the term "gamification" has started to gain traction among some of the industry leaders and entrepreneurs, thus becoming increasingly popular in the industry of banking and service in Turkey. The experts mentioned that employing gamified experiences for businesses involve not only marketing but also educative means. It was highlighted that gamification was applied not as a part of a marketing strategy but as a fundamental core of the whole design process of an experience. Although the term "gamification" has recently became popular, it was mentioned that the benefits of embedding gamified experiences to services have started to be understood with each passing day. One of the participants mentioned the increasing awareness regarding the term "gamification" in Turkey by indicating: "Even though the term is new to the industry in Turkey, many services and applications started to adapt towards these novel approaches and benefit from it", while adding that the clients who applied gamification to their businesses clearly received positive feedbacks from users. The same expert also indicated that the application of gamification techniques within the industry quickly affected the market and caused the term to become a trending topic in the industry in recent years. Another expert underlined the increasing popularity of the term by mentioning the increase in number of successful gamification projects in various industries including education, marketing, and service businesses. Moreover, he also mentioned that the ubiquity of the game elements embedded in gamification projects also potentially provide hidden benefits such as the betterment of user experiences and providing solutions for design-related problems. Lastly, all of the participants have agreed on the notion of gamification being applicable to nearly every aspect which relates to user experience by enhancing and/or solving problems while increasing engagement regardless of the industry.

However, according to the interview results, most of the participants mentioned that the overall expertise on the field of gamification is still dearth and the field has to be recognized more. Additionally, all of the participants have indicated that gamification methods have recently been started to be utilized in the marketing industry but are considered to be effective only when applied. An expert from the educational games department of a well-known bank from Turkey indicated that, "For instance, it was quite clear that, for the municipality of İstanbul, a gamification project in which the users were awarded with extra transportation ticket quotas, was successful in terms of being popular when it was released and was influencing for further projects". By mentioning so, the expert indicated the fact that the novel capabilities of gamified systems and them being more interesting and engaging for general population of service users makes the whole process of interaction more enjoyable. On the other hand, the same expert mentioned that gamification would prove more useful for short-termed marketing goals, stating that the main weakness regarding the current situation of gamification was its insufficient utilization in the industry. Another expert mentioned the issue by saying that popular use of gamification affordances, such as the use of rewards to provide motivation, are insufficiently positioned in general. This expert who worked in the field of gamification not only as a professional but also as a lecturer indicated that, "Gamification is being used as if it is only about giving rewards for promoting a specific behavior, rather than creating engaging experiences throughout a project". Moreover, he highlighted that this current short-term perspective towards gamification is possibly harmful for the sake of gamification and its utilization in the industry since the basic affordances would only help if the gamification is employed in a long-term strategy for providing feasible results. As a result, he mentioned that "the scarcity on the use of other affordance types result in gamification being understood as only a short-term solution". Similarly, yet another expert who has been working in the field for over seven years as a gamification professional indicated that the overall expectancy of the industry from gamification projects was mostly about enhancing the short-term motivations, thus leading to unsuccessful projects, scarring the reputation of gamification within the industry. These comments were all pointing out the importance of the perception of the industry towards gamification since they underline a problem about the application of gamification which would affect the perception towards gamification in Turkey negatively. These answers also revealed that experts may have conflicting predictions on how gamification should be utilized, as one participant thought it was effective being used as a short-term tool whereas the other experts thought it otherwise.

According to the qualitative analysis of the semi-structured interviews, it has been identified that nearly all of the gamification experts mentioned that they have utilized only a number of gamification affordances throughout their gamification designs while points, badges leaderboards, and rewards being most used since they were easy to apply to projects. It was additionally identified that the experts have specifically mentioned utilizing these common affordances the most, while adding the elements of story the least. Furthermore, all of the participants indicated that the notion of gamified experience became dull for the users after some amount of time since the industry has the tendency for affording short-term strategies. One participant pointed out this issue by saying,

"The greatest problem about gamification is that the continuation of the project could not be sustained", indicating that the "applications which provide great expectations and the feeling of engagement" fade after a short amount of time and become a routine for the user. Hence all the participants of the study highlighted the importance of the renewal of gamification motivations and elements over time either by developing the gamification design at hand or producing a new one in order to achieve a sustained and engaging experience in a holistic perspective.

Because of the exponentially developing technological advancements, similar to other fields focusing on users, gamification is an evolving term in Turkey as well. But the term has been conceived differently in terms of its application. Thus, one of the experts mentioned that the importance of personas that are also being utilized in the field of user experience should be considered and embedded in the makings of gamification projects to further improve the effectiveness of gamification. He added, "without thinking about the target audience and their personas, and only by focusing on potential technological advancement, it would not be possible to think a successful gamification project". Moreover, another expert indicated that the "lack of expertise in the professional workforce" designing and developing gamification projects for the industry is one of the main reasons that many of them fail initially. To increase the potential effectiveness of these projects, both participants suggested that the gamified experiences should be considered as long-term strategies and would require sustainable design which would withhold the wrong conception of gamification projects being used for bursts of engagements and enjoyment only as a "phase". Nevertheless, as mentioned before, another expert pointed out that the success of gamification in short-term goals is effective and these strategies would benefit seasonal services. Moreover, the same expert mentioned that the problem about gamification and its application in the business of service is "the insufficiency in the number of projects" and not their longevity in general. As for the future predictions, all of the experts indicated that there is a strong need for gamification to become fully understood as an interaction strategy by businesses and decision makers since there is much more to learn about how this would improve and solve potential user–related problems. One expert who works for the service industry expressed the importance of the conception of gamification being a "process related framework" as applying the idea of gamification is possible to nearly any field including not only the service or marketing industry but also to education, products, or even government institutions for enhancing performance both for the users and the employees. While one expert indicated the importance of the terms' ubiquitous nature and how it is improving our daily lives, another expert indicated that the ubiquity of gamification is still not here but will be achieved in the near future by telling; "I believe that the focus would be on behavioral and sustainable gamification applications for the products in the near future such as the retweets that the user can get in twitter". Thus, indicating a commonality between promotional elements that are being used in social mediums today and gamification. Two of the experts stated that gamification will be following the footsteps of terms such as "blockchain" or "internet of things", as being well accepted and greeted in recent years. One expert among those two especially point out that, "the increase of importance regarding the terms artificial intelligence or big data would be beneficial for gamification since these terms could further improve the applicability of gamification such as them being designed procedurally for the individual rather than a group of people as is done right now". Moreover, one expert mentioned the importance on the necessity of interdisciplinary perspective which would allow for success since the term "gamification" has its roots from different fields that are used both in games and in marketing business. He indicated that "interface, experience, interactivity or gamification could not be thought separated and hence should be thought to work together, joining people to work on projects from different professions". Lastly, three of the experts mentioned about the much needed academic research in the field of gamification. They indicated that future research about the term would shed light on the experiences gained via gamification projects and their exact outputs meanwhile increasing its potential area of use within the marketing industry in Turkey.

Conclusion

Although these remarks from three different professionals from the field of gamification seem to resemble each other in terms of the necessity of gamification being used more often, or generally for long-term strategies, a difference in approach was also observed in terms of applicability of gamification and its future. All the experts came from different disciplines and backgrounds. Perhaps because of that, none of them has agreed upon the definitions on gamification affordances exactly, even providing conflicting explanations for some of the affordances which are based on basic game elements. Moreover, instead of the common working field, the experts have imposed disparate perspectives towards the current state of gamification in Turkey. This is observed to be a result referring to the differences between the expertise of the participants and their various project goals. Even though the experts have indicated that they have known gamification affordances and their specific points of influence which vary between project goals, they also expressed that they have been trying to use nearly all of them.

Fundamentally, these findings have identified some of the most profound gamification affordances that are understood dividedly throughout different gamification projects. An example would be the affordance of challenge for which participants indicated conflicting aims regarding the term. While two participants were stating that using the challenge affordance would be crucial for the overall motivation for engagement, the other experts highlighted the importance of increasing the emotional satisfaction and longevity of the gamification project via using all the elements associatively. In this context, for example, an expert mentioned that he only uses the challenge element to provide immersion in the game, while another expert mentions that he aims to use the challenge to provide emotional long-term satisfaction. As another example, while one of the experts was emphasizing the importance of using badges, another expert mentioned that this affordance would not be of much importance. The affordances are observed to be not understood similarly in terms of definitions and application in the industry. It is determined that these terms also imply different meanings between experts and professionals.

As stated by several researchers in the field; points, levels, and leaderboards form three of the most common patterns. Similarly, Zagal et al. (2007) categorize them as goal metrics. Due to the apparent connection to games and to the practical implications to various non-game contexts, these goal metrics have been perceived as corner stones of gamification. Von Ahn and Dabbish (2008) consider them essential for increasing enjoyment in human computation tasks. Similar to those, the interview results indicated a tendency towards the employment of these affordances the most. Yet, as stated by Mekler et al. (2013), research on the effectiveness of goal metrics in non-game contexts is still limited and differential. They also state the importance of game elements for the success of gamification by mentioning, "…However, if the aim of gamification is to facilitate intrinsic motivation, then the mere addition of points, levels and leaderboards is not sufficient to make non-game contexts more engaging". The results have pointed out that although dividend in perspective, all of the experts were able to identify the importance in the use of gamification affordances in a holistic manner and their relations during their application. Cugelman (2013) mentions that the most important risk about gamification is "becoming overconfident in the ability of the method to exert massive influence across all contexts", which then can cause the term to be understood as the only measure for persuading users. As for the use of gamification in Turkey, it is inspected that the experts were aware of the risk of the term being understood as an easy and effective way of influencing masses. The term is still increasing its popularity because of various events both academic and professional. Meanwhile the industry is slowly but steadily discovering its potential. When inspected, it was identified that most of the cases in Turkey were related to user awareness or user engagement. Moreover, the experts mostly refer to short-term gamification strategies and campaigns while the story of affordance was applied the least because of the limited amount of time investment that is expected from the user.

Gamification is a method capable of being used for marketing strategies as it would prove most useful when it is implemented in long-term strategies and goals, providing sustainable engagements. The understanding over gamification affordances separately would allow more experts and researchers to investigate its effects while identifying the relations between those elements can provide for better engaging experiences. Although the term is an emerging one, the industry in Turkey is realizing the potential of engaging experiences, thus paving a path for gamification applications with each passing day. Nevertheless, it is important to note that the research and application of gamification projects is still scarce, and the drawbacks should be discussed and clearly defined among gamification experts to provide generalized and successful projects.

References

Aker, Ç., & Öztürk, Ö. (2015). Social media interactions and the use of third-party management applications on effectiveness and perception of information. In *DUXU: International Conference of Design, User Experience, and Usability* (Vol. 9188, pp. 3–12). Los Angeles, CA: Springer.

Allery, L. (2014). Make use of educational games. *Education for Primary Care, 25*(1), 65–66.

Berkling, K., & Thomas, C. (2013). Gamification of a Software Engineering course and a detailed analysis of the factors that lead to it's failure. In *2013 International Conference on Interactive Collaborative Learning (ICL)*, pp. 525–530.

Brynjarsdottir, H., Håkansson, M., Pierce, J., Baumer, E., DiSalvo, C., & Sengers, P. (2012). Sustainably unpersuaded: How persuasion narrows our vision of sustainability. In *Proceedings of the SIGCHI Conference on Human Factors in Computing Systems*, 947–956.

Carmody, K. W. (2012). *Exploring serious game design heuristics: a delphi study* (Doctoral dissertation), Northeastern University.

Cheong, C., Filippou, J., & Cheong, F. (2014). Towards the gamification of learning: Investigating student perceptions of game elements. *Journal of Information Systems Education, 25*(3), 233–244.

Csikszentmihalyi, M. (1988). The flow experience and its significance for human psychology. In M. Csikszentmihalyi & I. S. Csikszentmihalyi (Eds.), *Optimal experience: Psychological studies of flow in consciousness* (pp. 15–35). Cambridge: Cambridge University Press

Cugelman, B. (2013). Gamification: What it is and why it matters to digital health behavior change developers. *JMIR Serious Games*, *1*(1). 2–7.

Çağlar, Ş., & Arkün-Kocadere, S. (2015). Gamification in online learning Environments. *Journal of Educational Sciences and Practices*, *14*(27), 83–102.

Deterding, S., Sicart, M., Nacke, L., O'Hara, K., & Dixon, D. (2011). Gamification. Using game-design elements in non-gaming contexts. In *CHI'11 extended abstracts on human factors in computing systems*, pp. 2425–2428.

Fullerton, T. (2007). *Game design workshop: A playcentric approach to creating innovative games*. Boca Raton, FL: AK Peters/CRC Press.

Gibson, J. J. (1977). *The theory of affordances*. Hilldale, USA, 1(2).

Hamari, J. (2013). Transforming homo economicus into homo ludens: A field experiment on gamification in a utilitarian peer-to-peer trading service. *Electronic Commerce Research and Applications*, *12*(4), 236–245.

Hamari, J. (2017). Do badges increase user activity? A field experiment on the effects of gamification. *Computers in Human Behavior*, *71*, 469–478.

Hamari, J., & Eranti, V. (2011). Framework for designing and evaluating game achievements. In *Digra 2011 Conference*.

Hamari, J., Koivisto, J., & Sarsa, H. (2014). Does gamification work? A literature review of empirical studies on gamification. *HICSS 14*, 3025–3034.

He, H. A., Greenberg, S., & Huang, E. M. (2010). One size does not fit all. In *Proceedings of the 28th International Conference on Human Factors in Computing Systems – CHI 10*, pp. 927–936.

Helgason, D. (2010, January 14). *Trends: Unity technologies* [Blog post]. Retrieved from: https://blogs.unity3d.com/2010/01/14/2010-trends/

Huber, M. Z., & Hilty, L. M. (2014). Gamification and sustainable consumption: Overcoming the limitations of persuasive technologies. In Advances in *i*ntelligent *s*ystems and *c*omputing ICT *i*nnovations for *s*ustainability, pp. 367–385.

Jakobsson, M. (2011). The achievement machine: Understanding Xbox 360 achievements in gaming practices. *Game Studies*, *11*(1), 1–22.

Jia, Y., Xu, B., Karanam, Y., & Voida, S. (2016). Personality-targeted gamification. In *Proceedings of the 2016 CHI Conference on Human Factors in Computing Systems – CHI 16*.

Johnson, D., Jones, C., Scholes, L., & Carras, M. C. (2013). Videogames and wellbeing: A comprehensive review. In *Young and Well CRC*.

Kapp, K. M. (2012). *The gamification of learning and instruction*. San Francisco: Wiley.

Kiryakova, G., Angelova, N., & Yordanova, L. (2013). QR codes in the business world. *Trakia Journal of Sciences*, *11*(1), 370–376.

Koivisto, J., & Hamari, J. (2019). The rise of motivational information systems: A review of gamification research. *International Journal of Information Management*, 45, 191–210.

Kosmadoudi, Z., Lim, T., Ritchie, J., Louchart, S., Liu, Y., & Sung, R. (2013). Engineering design using game-enhanced CAD: The potential to augment the user experience with game elements. *Computer-Aided Design*, *45*(3), 777–795.

Landers, R. N., Bauer, K. N., and Callan, R. C. (2017). Gamification of task performance with leaderboards: A goal setting experiment. *Computers in Human Behavior*, *71*, 508–515.

Malone, T. W. (1981). *What makes computer games fun*. Palo Alto, CA: Xerox Palo Alto research center.

Malone, T. W. (1982). Heuristics for designing enjoyable user interfaces: Lessons from computer games. In *Proceedings of the 1982 conference on Human factors in computing systems* (pp. 63–68). ACM.

Mekler, E. D., Brühlmann, F., Opwis, K., & Tuch, A. N. (2013, October). Do points, levels and leaderboards harm intrinsic motivation?: An empirical analysis of common gamification elements. In *Proceedings of the First International Conference on Gameful Design, Research, and Applications* (pp. 66–73). ACM.

Montola, M., Stenros, J., & Waern, A. (2009). *Pervasive games: Theory and design*. CRC Press.

Nah, F. F. H., Zeng, Q., Telaprolu, V. R., Ayyappa, A. P., & Eschenbrenner, B. (2014, June). Gamification of education: A review of literature. In *International Conference on HCI in Business* (pp. 401–409). Cham: Springer.

Norman, D. A. (1999). Affordance, conventions, and design. *Interactions*, *6*(3), 38–43.

O'Donovan, S., Gain, J., & Marais, P. (2013). A case study in the gamification of a university-level games development course. In *Proceedings of the South African Institute for Computer Scientists and Information Technologists Conference* (pp. 242–251). ACM.

Raymer, R. (2011). Gamification: Using game mechanics to enhance eLearning. *ELearn, 2011*(9), 3.

Sailer, M., Hense, J., Mandl, J., & Klevers, M. (2014). Psychological perspectives on motivation through gamification. *Interaction Design and Architecture Journal*, (19), 28–37.

Schell, J. (2010). *Visions of the Gamepocalypse.* [Online]. Retrieved from: http://bit.ly/bT62k3

Sweetser, P., & Wyeth, P. (2005). GameFlow: A model for evaluating player enjoyment in games. *Computers in Entertainment (CIE)*, *3*(3), 3–3.

Von Ahn, L., & Dabbish, L. (2008). Designing games with a purpose. *Communications of the ACM, 51*(8), 58–67.

Werbach, K., & Hunter, D. (2012). *For the win: How game thinking can revolutionize your business*. Philadelphia: Wharton Digital Press.

Zagal, J. P., Mateas, M., Fernández-Vara, C., Hochhalter, B., & Lichti, N. (2007). Towards an ontological language for game analysis. In S. de Castell & J. Jenson (Eds.), *Worlds in play: International perspectives on digital games research* (pp. 21–36). New York: Peter Lang.

Zhang, P. (2008). Motivational affordances: reasons for ICT design and use. *Communications of the ACM, 51*(11), 145–147.

Zichermann, G., & Cunningham, C. (2011). *Gamification by design: Implementing game mechanics in web and mobile apps*. Sebastopol, CA: OReilly Media.

Sercan Şengün, Güven Çatak, and Mustafa Feyyaz Sonbudak

Chapter 2 It Is So Good, It Cannot Be Turkish: A Case Study of Local Video Game Producers versus Local Gamer Communities

Introduction

Jenkins (2012; Jenkins & Deuze, 2008) proposes that today's media cultural scene is a participatory one. This defines both the consumption of the media and the processes of production. Especially for the video games industry, it is seemingly less and less possible for gamers to consume a video game without actually participating in its extended media presence (e.g., social media content and interactions, gaming news, review videos, playthrough videos, fan fiction, fan art, forums, walkthroughs, leaderboards, internet memes, transmedia practices, etc.). Postigo (2007) asserts that "the fan culture for digital games is deeply embedded in shared practices and experiences among fan communities, and their active consumption contributes economically and culturally to broader society." (p. 300) Video game producers begin this communication and participation process during the production of a game, and an increasing number of video games rely on prerelease marketing or communication to be successful. Preview copies, demos, crowd-source funding, developer blogs, and alpha and beta tests constitute some of the methods mobilized for this aim. Equally useful are do-it-yourself tools and media kits released along with the video games to promote fan production and modding.

A contemporary discussion focusing on gamers, however, underlines that excessive critique and exercise of power in production of games from the perspective of gamers can easily become a disruptive element in the industry (Rumphol-Janc, 2013; Chu, 2014; Şengün, 2014). Consequently, it could be argued that while participatory culture enriches the industry of video games—which is frequently cited as a part of the creative industries (Tschang, 2007, 2009)—it can also translate into barriers in production and marketing.

In this study, we aim to determine how these dynamics work for Turkish gamers and their participatory relationship with games produced by Turkish developers. Using secondary analysis of online sources, we also intend to create a snapshot of the cultural atmosphere that Turkish video game developers enjoy and/or suffer currently and determine some bullet points on how to improve it.

Background

According to Klevjer's (2002) interpretation of Eskelinen (2001), video games form configurative processes as opposed to movies and literature which are dominantly interpretative forms. This contrast results in players' "need to participate in the construction of [video games'] material structure" (p. 192) that may occasionally situate the players at odds with the design decisions in video games and effectuate an ongoing tension between them and the developers. The need to participate in the video game's production, development, or management can manifest pre- or postrelease in various ways which are briefly outlined below.

Gamer Postrelease Participation in Video Game Production

Mittell (2013) cites one prominent method of postrelease fan participation in video games as creating, populating, updating, and using fan wikis and underscores that these wikis "mirror [the game's] online storyworlds with comprehensive analysis and discussion of how games work." (p. 41) Searching for knowledge about the game online, commenting, sharing, and creating one's own version of guides or how-tos do not require specialized knowledge such as programming or art skills. Additionally, some video games initiate a wide range of fan programming cultures. According to Postigo (2008), fan programming has different varieties: (1) modders use a video game's code to make extensive changes or create a new video game entirely (e.g., *Enderal: Forgotten Stories* created from *The Elder Scrolls V: Skyrim*); (2) mappers create new locations and maps for video games; and (3) skinners create new in-game commodities like characters, items, vehicles, etc. Another classification is provided by Tavares and Roque (2007) as: (1) actors (players who self-produce content without the specific aim of disseminating it); (2) reconfigurators (players with less technical skills who dominantly mobilize the tools provided by the game developers to make adjustments on the games); and (3) coders (players with better technical skills who produce complementary tools to change the game experience and game code). Arakji and Lang (2007) define this process as some video game companies opening "a portion of their proprietary content for transformation by consumers and [allowing] the development of consumer-designed and consumer-implemented derivative products." (p. 195) Naturally, these productions might have their own issues of copyright tensions. While some first-person shooter games like *Quake, Battlefield 1942, Unreal Tournament, Counter-Strike*, and some open world role-playing games like *The Elder Scrolls V: Skyrim* facilitate fan programming tools for their player base and do not interfere with the distribution of results, other video games might restrict and regulate certain aspects of these processes.

Fans can also produce fan arts (illustrations of in-game locales or characters), fan fiction (unofficial stories that expand or replace game scenarios), cosplay (creating costumes and items as well as dressing up and being photographed as characters from the game), and producing machinimas. Machinima is defined as "3D computer animation gameplay recorded in real time as video footage and then used to produce traditional video narratives" (Berkeley, 2006, p. 66). According to Nitsche (2005) "in a repetition of early cinema's history, many of Machinima's milestones are formulated not as artistic expressions of carefully developed ideas but as technical breakthroughs." (p. 214)

Other methods of note are player-created tiers in alternate reality games (Dena, 2008) and streaming/watching cultures such as Twitch, YouTube, etc. (Gandolfi, 2016).

Gamer Prerelease Participation in Video Game Production

Apart from joining the fan production postrelease, fans of the game can join in the discussions around the game prerelease and during development. Marchand and Hennig-Thurau (2013) present a conceptual framework about how the game content can reach the game consumer through a complex value chain (see Fig. 2.1). Within this framework; communication channels (traditional and social media), other consumers and fanbase around the game, and related content (official or fan production) play an as important role as the platforms and the distribution channels. In fact, a study by Mathews and Wearn (2016) highlights that gamers trust the opinions of YouTubers and friends and family more than the traditional marketing channels. Another previous research underscores the importance of social media channels and word-of-mouth for Turkish developers in promoting their games as compared to traditional channels (Şengün, 2018). An analysis by Xiong and Bharadwaj (2014) revealed how prerelease online buzz patterns can actually predict the sales and performance of a new product.

Crowdfunding and prosumer-investor relationships are also effectively mobilized by game developer's prerelease to both fund and presell their games (Planells, 2017). By participating in crowdfunding, the players become a small-scale investor for the game and may become a part of the discussion on how the game development should progress by voting, deciding, and commenting on features.

Another value chain is presented by Jöckel, Will, and Schwarzer (2008) that outlines the nuance in games with online services, servers, and persistent worlds

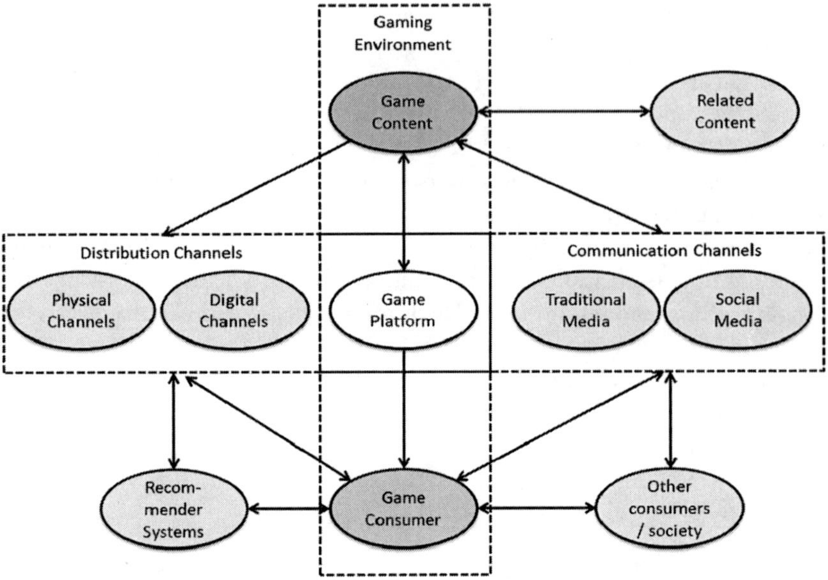

Fig. 2.1: Conceptual framework of value creation for video games by Marchand and Hennig-Thurau (2013)

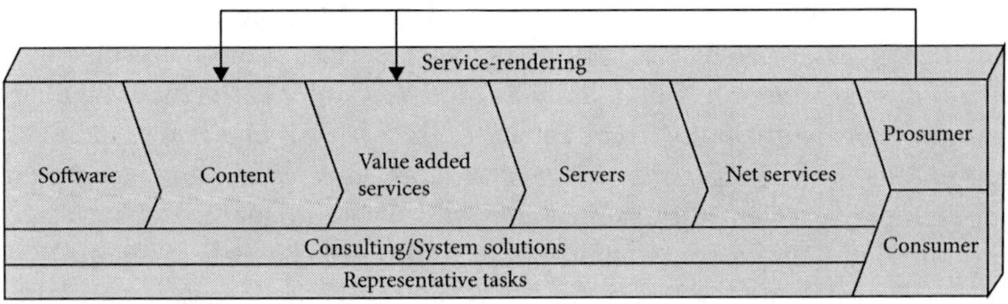

Fig. 2.2: Value chain of online-distributed digital games by Jöckel, Will, and Schwarzer (2008)

(see Fig. 2.2). In this model, the online games not only feed the content produced by prosumers back into game itself, but also expand on their value-added services (e.g., social, aggregation, security, etc.) according to the feedback provided by the community. Early access has also become a popular release strategy for games with online services (Lin et al., 2018). Early access games refer to players purchasing access to unfinished software in order to "influence the software development process by giving developers early feedback." (ibid., p. 771) Active players in early access can provide feedback to the developers in order to effect the final content of a release game as well as how the mechanics should work.

Burger-Helmchen and Cohendet (2011) underline that "firms manufacturing video games and player communities enjoying the games are closely related, not only in a producer-user way, but also in co-development, testing and diffusion activities." (p. 317) Some of the player types they define that have a strong impact on the game production cycles are: (1) content builders (players who produce additional content for the games in the shape of previously outlined mods); (2) gamer organizers (players who voluntarily or in official capacity answer questions about the games in social channels, organize in-game events, etc.); (3) open players (players who produce FAQs, blogs, websites, and social media groups about the game); (4) beta testers (players who play the demo, alpha, or beta versions of the game and disseminate content related to these versions to create negative or positive attention); (5) creative testers (players who create artwork or creative content around the game); and (6) the previously mentioned crowd-sourcers.

Dahlander and Magnusson (2008) define this symbiotic relationship as "harnessing the community" and define three phases: access, alignment, and assimilation. Adapting to the video game industry, the access phase refers to the developer company providing access to some of the content and tools around the game to the community, so that the gamers can direct their creative skills and time toward the game. In the alignment phase, the company must clearly communicate what kind of game that they want to make and what the gamers should expect from that particular game, so that what the community produces and the company wants to make are aligned. Finally, in the assimilation phase, the company elicits good ideas, feedback, and even products from the community and makes them a part of their game.

All these participation methods point to a fragile relationship between the developer companies and the players. On the one hand, video games as media products need the participation of players to become alive and functioning. On the other hand, the players constantly test, force, criticize, and attempt to change the boundaries of their freedoms within the management of the game. The outcome may enrich the game experience for themselves and others as well as having the potential to nurture toxic relationships between the players and developers. This marks a learning process for both sides since improper conduct from either the developers or the players have the potential to damage the culture of the particular video game product.

Methodology

In order to illustrate how a participatory culture between Turkish game producers and Turkish gamers is constructed, we have employed a two-step analysis of secondary data. We have selected 12 video games (*Conarium, Dark Inside, Dark Raid, Monochroma, No:70 Eye of Basir, Oddmar, Overfall, Reclaim, Recontact Istanbul: Eyes of Sky, Roots of Insanity, Solarix*, and *Stygian: Reign of the Old Ones*) produced and released within the last five years (in fact, *Dark Inside* and *Stygian: Reign of the Old Ones* are unreleased) and collected user comments from platforms like Steam (only Turkish reviews) and prominent Turkish gaming news sources (Merlin'in Kazanı, Bölüm Sonu Canavarı, and Oyungezer) that published preview, prerelease, and postrelease news, videos, and interviews about the games.

Initially, one of the researchers read all the comments for 3 games (*Dark Raid, Monochroma*, and *Reclaim*) out of 12 and created a codebook (MacQueen et al., 1998) for systematic coding of the textual data (Strauss and Corbin, 1990). These 3 games were the most dated among the 12 in terms of their release dates. The codebook was created by eliminating all comments that did not correspond to relevant discussions and isolating the ones that were about the game being a local production. Then, all the remaining comments were read to produce general themes and codes to construct a codebook. This codebook (see Tab. 2.1) was given to the two other researchers to analyze the comments from the remaining nine games and distill code segments. Each code segment was marked as having positive, negative, or mixed sentiments. Code segments with mixed sentiments typically had positive and negative sentiments packed together in the same sentence (e.g., "it is good that the game has Turkish subtitles but it lacks Turkish voice-overs").[1] The code segments were also noted whether they were made pre- or postrelease. Prerelease comments are usually made based on preview videos, trailers, or demos of the game—without access to the full game. As a result, prerelease sentiments present a good representation of the impressions or opinions of the local industry as well as the game itself.

Results

We present our results in three sections: the main data set (that includes nine games), the automated valence analysis performed by an API, and the pilot

---

1 All the translations of the comments in this chapter are made by the authors from Turkish.

Tab. 2.1: The codebook used in analyzing the data

Code	Description
Originality	This code encapsulates the discussions regarding how unique the game idea, story, mechanics, etc., are.
Quality	This code encapsulates the discussions regarding the overall quality of the product based on visuals, music, playability, etc.
Opinions about Local Game Developers and Industry	This code encapsulates the discussions stemming from the fact that the game was produced by a Turkish company or a team.
Turkish Language	This code encapsulates the discussions regarding whether the game has a Turkish language—be it in subtitles or voice-overs. In some rare cases, even the names of the development group were drawn into the discussions.
Turkish Culture	This code encapsulates the discussions regarding whether the content of the game reflects or is informed by the Turkish culture.
Price	This code encapsulates the discussions regarding the pricing structure of the game.

study (that includes three games). Our findings and coding are fine tuned in the analysis of the main data set; however, we decided to include the pilot study separately for more insights.

Main Data Set

The nine games in the main data set are: *Conarium, Dark Inside, No:70 Eye of Basir, Oddmar, Overfall, Recontact Istanbul: Eyes of Sky, Roots of Insanity, Solarix, and Stygian: Reign of the Old Ones.* Out of these nine games, *Dark Inside and Stygian: Reign of the Old Ones* are unreleased.

Our analysis resulted in 596 code segments. The distribution of the code segments depending on the game and their pre- or postrelease status is given in Fig. 2.3. The mean of the prerelease segments was $x=19.44$ ($\mu=18.71$; $R=0–62$), and for postrelease it was $x=46.67$ ($\mu=49.07$; $R=0–135$). The game that produced the most number of codes was *Roots of Insanity* (n=160; %26.8) and the least was *Oddmar* (n=7; %1.2; all postrelease).

Almost half of our code segments were produced by Steam (n=309; %51.8), followed by Merlin'in Kazanı (n=179; %30), Bölüm Sonu Canavarı (n=64; %10.7), and Oyungezer (n=44; %7.4). The distribution of the valence of these codes are given in Fig. 2.4.

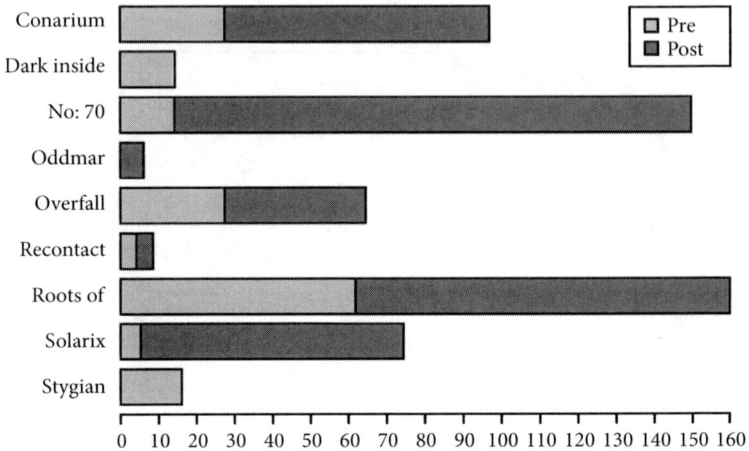

Fig. 2.3: Distribution of the code segments depending on the game and the segment's pre- or postrelease status. (Game pre/post: *Conarium* 28/70; *Dark Inside* 15/0; *Eye of Basir* 15/135; *Oddmar* 0/7; *Overfall* 28/36; *Recontact Istanbul: Eyes of Sky* 4/5; *Roots of Insanity* 62/98; *Solarix* 6/69; *Stygian: Reign of the Old Ones* 17/0)

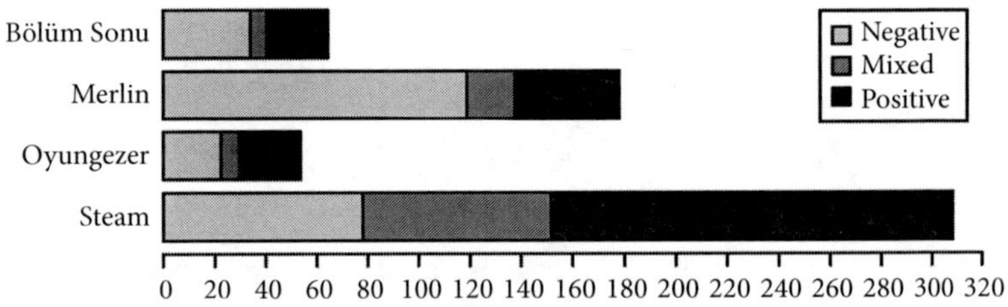

Fig. 2.4: Distribution of the code segments depending on the source platform and the segment's sentiment. (Source negative/mixed/positive: Bölüm Sonu Canavarı 34/6/24; Merlin'in Kazanı 119/18/41; Oyungezer 22/8/15; Steam 78/75/156)

To test whether the code segment sentiments are independent of the source they come from, we have performed a Pearson's chi-square test of independence which indicated a very strong correlation between the source and the sentiments ($p<.05$ [2.2e-16]; $x^2=86.38$; df=6). This led us to believe that Steam significantly produced more positive code segments while the remaining three Turkish news sources either produced significantly more negative sentiments or remained on par. This result is relevant for our discussions. Since Steam is an international

Tab. 2.2: Code category distribution per game in pre- and postrelease periods. (Colors are only used for easy reading.)

		Originality			Quality			I. Opinions			Language			Culture			Price		
		N	**M**	**P**	**N**	**M**	**P**	**N**	**M**	**P**	**N**	**M**	**P**	**N**	**M**	**P**	**N**	**M**	**P**
Conarium	**Pre**	5	-	-	1	2	1	2	2	6	7	-	-	-	-	-	2	-	-
	Post	-	-	2	4	4	7	2	3	18	10	4	4	1	1	2	2	2	4
Dark Inside	**Pre**	3	1	-	3	-	-	5	-	3	-	-	-	-	-	-	-	-	-
	Post	-	-	-	-	-	-	-	-	-	-	-	-	-	-	-	-	-	-
No 70: Eye	**Pre**	5	-	-	2	-	-	3	-	2	-	-	-	-	-	2	-	1	-
of Basir	**Post**	4	2	5	11	4	7	13	27	15	-	-	11	-	-	9	18	-	9
Oddmar	**Pre**	-	-	-	-	-	-	-	-	-	-	-	-	-	-	-	-	-	-
	Post	-	-	-	-	-	-	-	1	1	-	-	-	2	1	-	1	1	-
Overfall	**Pre**	2	1	1	1	-	3	1	2	6	5	2	1	-	-	-	1	-	2
	Post	-	-	-	1	-	-	-	-	-	29	1	5	-	-	-	-	-	-
Recontact:	**Pre**	-	1	2	-	-	1	-	-	-	-	-	-	-	-	-	-	-	-
Istanbul	**Post**	1	-	-	1	-	1	1	-	-	-	-	-	-	-	-	1	-	-
Roots of	**Pre**	30	5	-	4	-	3	6	-	10	1	-	-	1	1	-	-	-	1
Insanity	**Post**	15	3	2	9	5	3	4	12	16	2	3	14	2	-	-	2	2	4
Solarix	**Pre**	-	-	-	-	-	-	1	-	2	2	-	1	-	-	-	-	-	-
	Post	1	2	1	1	1	2	5	8	25	7	-	13	-	-	-	-	1	2
Stygian	**Pre**	-	-	-	-	-	-	-	1	5	7	-	1	1	-	-	1	-	1
	Post	-	-	-	-	-	-	-	-	-	-	-	-	-	-	-	-	-	-

platform wherein the players from all over the world can access reviews and scores, Turkish users were seemingly less critical of the Turkish games with positive or mixed sentiments outperforming the negative ones. Although, these reviews are in Turkish, international users would still be able to understand the recommended/not recommended selection and might use tools like Google Translate or browser automatic translation tools to read the comments. However, since the three news outlets attract only Turkish users, the discussions made here proved to be more critical and unforgiving.

Next, we present the code category distributions in Tab. 2.2. This table is outlined per game and per pre- and postrelease periods.

According to the results in Tab. 2.2, several interesting points emerge:

- To test whether the code segment sentiments are independent of the pre- and postrelease period they are found at, we have performed a Pearson's chi-square test of independence which indicated a very strong correlation ($p<.05$

[1.157e-06]; x^2=27.34; df=2). According to the result, prerelease sentiments were significantly more negative while postrelease sentiments were more distributed across negative-positive categories.

- Some sentiments can change drastically between pre- and postrelease times (e.g., originality and industry opinions about *Conarium*, language use and price about *Roots of Insanity*) while some can be reinforced (e.g., language use of *Overfall*) or diminished (e.g., originality of *Roots of Insanity*).
- Generally, we see a rise in the trust and opinions on what the Turkish developers can do between the pre- and postrelease periods. While Turkish gamers are more skeptical and dismissive of Turkish-produced games during prerelease, they become more supportive postrelease. This is an interesting result as it puts the Turkish developers in a weird situation where their prerelease efforts are met with more negativity and they have to take some extra measures to appeal to the local communities.
- In fact, in some pre- vs. postrelease examples, it is possible to see that even when the sentiments about the quality and originality of the game stayed negative, the trust and support to Turkish game development were increased to a more positive viewpoint (e.g., *Roots of Insanity*). This is another interesting result which underscores that even subpar Turkish games can garner some support and attention in spite of failing to meet the expectations.
- Finally, we calculate the correlation coefficients between a game's pre- and postrelease sentiment counts per category and find that four out of six games (excluding two games that are not released yet, so they do not have postrelease data, and *Oddmar* that had no prerelease data) displayed significance: *Conarium* ($p<.01$ [0.005138], t=3.24), *Overfall* ($p<.05$ [0.0372], t=2.27), *Roots of Insanity* ($p<0.05$ [0.01427], t=2.75), and *Solarix* ($p<.01$ [7.419e-05], t=5.28). This mirrors Xiong and Bharadwaj's (2014) previous assertion that prerelease buzz can predict postrelease sentiments and performance.

Valence Analysis

To augment our qualitative coding, we have also run our code segments through Cognitus API which is a Turkish valence analysis application.[2] The API created a polarity score for each code segment that ranges between -1 and +1 depending on how negative or positive the sentiment in the segment was.

2 Cognitus AI http://cognitus.ai/.

Tab. 2.3: Means of valence scores per game per category as calculated by Cognitus API. (Light gray cells indicate an increase from pre- to postrelease, dark gray cells indicate a decrease from pre- to postrelease, and colorless cells indicate no change or missing values.)

x̄		Originality	Quality	I. Opinion	Language	Culture	Price
Conarium	**Pre**	-0,576	0,110	0,058	-0,311	-	0,332
	Post	0,028	0,134	-0,062	0,044	-0,015	0,130
Dark Inside	**Pre**	-0,363	-0,348	-0,344	-	-	-
	Post	-	-	-	-	-	-
No 70: Eye of Basir	**Pre**	0,116	-0,434	-0,723	-	0,020	0
	Post	-0,252	0,223	-0,291	0,640	0,100	-0,068
Oddmar	**Pre**	-	-	-	-	-	-
	Post	-	-	-0,654	-	-0294	0,056
Overfall	**Pre**	-0,348	0,061	-0,305	-0,202	-	-0,185
	Post	-	-0,821	-	-0,453	-	-
Recontact: Istanbul	**Pre**	0,166	0,553	-	-	-	-
	Post	0	0,163	0,379	-	-	-0,810
Roots of Insanity	**Pre**	-0,094	0,049	-0,094	0	-0,637	-0,371
	Post	-0,502	-0,308	-0,060	-0,051	-0,751	-0,047
Solarix	**Pre**	-	-	-0,610	-0,273	-	-
	Post	0,366	-0,069	-0,139	0,225	-	0,014
Sytgian	**Pre**	-	-	0,357	-0,669	-0,723	-0,270
	Post	-	-	-	-	-	-

We assume that 108 mixed codings were all in agreement between the API and the researchers. The API disagreed in 46 out of 252 negative (%18.25) and 78 out of 236 positive (%33.05) segment coding. We removed the disagreed segments from the data set to create the results in Tab. 2.3.

Pilot Data Set

In our pilot study to construct the codebook, we have looked at three games that were the most dated (*Monochroma, Dark Raid*, and *Reclaim*) and only within the previously mentioned three Turkish news websites.

Although, this pilot analysis was more qualitative and collected less categorical data (e.g., sentiments), we have seen that the prerelease criticism was focused on originality and distrust in Turkish development scene. After the release, the criticism shifted toward quality and pricing. Discussions around Turkish language and culture were prominent during either period.

Discussions

As a rising creative industry, video games development practices rely on pre-release marketing and communication more than ever. Especially companies with smaller teams and limited access to development and marketing funds (commonly referred to as indie developers) rely on player support and buzz for their games to be successful. Previous research shows that in this kind of small team, indie formation is very characteristic of Turkish video game development scene (Şengün, 2018).

In this study, we aimed at illustrating the current dynamics between Turkish video game developers and Turkish gamer communities as a case study of local prosumer relationship. An emerging industry like Turkey would present a useful testbed to understand how local support could affect the growth of local developers. Using secondary analysis of online sources, our research yielded interesting themes where the discussions coalesced.

First, originality was an important factor to gain the support of the local community. Possibly due to our sample, we have consistently met with comments like: "for once [Turkish developers] should create something other than horror games," "I feel revolted from seeing military equipment and stereotypes," "I feel bored from this horror game glut," and "this feels like a one-on-one copy from [another game]". Turkish gamers felt that indie characteristics and resources were no excuse for copycat games that feel low-fidelity versions of existing projects and expected to see the realization of original ideas and concepts from local developers.

Accordingly, quality was an issue that frequently came up; however, Turkish gamers seemed more forgiving on low-quality games from local developers as long as they felt that the games were original and displayed effort. A good amount of reviews started with sentiments like "I will evaluate this game within the league of Turkish games [as opposed to industry standards]," "if this was a foreign game I would not recommend it but because it is Turkish I cannot criticize it heavily," "if this was not Turkish-made, I would have given it a worse review," and "I am happy to support it—it is not a successful product but close." A country-of-origin (COO) research made in the 1990s asserts that Turkish consumers behave more positively toward foreign-made products (Ger et al., 1993). However, Kaynak and Kara (2002) assert that, after the 2000s, Turkish consumers displayed more ethnocentric behaviors toward local products versus foreign products. Cengiz and Kırkbir (2007) also published a detailed work outlining the perceptions of Turkish consumers toward certain COOs.

One issue to note, in terms of quality, is the issue of optimization, which comes up extensively in Turkish reviews. Seemingly, Turkish gamers are very sensitive about frame-per-second (FPS) issues in 3D games and feel strongly against any game that fails the optimization for the smooth-running of its graphics. On this issue, it is possible to find strong quotes like: "We [Turkish gamers] feel ashamed of this game. […] Do not call yourselves game developers if your game cannot provide us the FPS that contemporary games provide—especially when your game already feels like it belongs to a gaming console of 3 or 4 generations ago." There were several suggestions from gamers that if local developers do not know how to optimize 3D games, they should stick to 2D games or face heavy criticism.

The use of Turkish language is a very passionate and buzz-creating issue. Turkish gamers strongly push toward Turkish language option in any game produced by Turkish developers. In fact, many declare that they are not willing to purchase the game and actively boycott it until the game has a Turkish option. Lack of Turkish can frequently be seen as an insult toward the Turkish gamer community: "The Turkish developers who do not provide Turkish options in their games are belittling us," "I am advanced level in English, so [playing a game in English] is not a problem for me, but what they are doing is disgraceful," and "not having a Turkish option means the developers do not care about the Turkish gamers […] I would never buy their games." The ideal Turkish options that needs to exist in a game are Turkish voice-overs and subtitles. If a game has Turkish subtitles but English voice-overs, it can still be criticized. Turkish gamers also seem reactive toward English game names as well as development studio names. There is a minority of gamers who think that the choice of investing in English first is justified: "If a company feels safe about the amount of sales in Turkey, don't you think that they would release a Turkish version," "it is not shameful that there is no Turkish version [instead] it is illogical to not have an English version and reach masses," and "we already saw the sales performance of games that have Turkish options, very few justifies the Turkish language." Essentially, if a Turkish development company is aiming at getting the support of local gamers, Turkish language option seems to be an indispensable issue.

Our research indicated that there is comparatively little demand or resistance for and against the use of Turkish cultural elements in games. They are recognized when present (e.g., music with Turkish tunes, local characters in game stories, Turkish locales, etc.) and create a positive vibe; however, their lack is not criticized passionately. There were a few calls for game elements that are informed by Turkish mythology (especially within the discussions around *Oddmar* which is a game informed by Norse mythology) which did not gather much support. This has been a surprising result since previous research on video game representations of cultures—especially ethnic and racial—have proved to be impactful on gamer communities such as creating coping mechanism (Harrell et al., 2019) or online toxicity (Şengün, 2019).

Turkish gamers display a price-sensitive characteristic. We have noted when the reviews mentioned a "fair" price and found out that the mean of the voiced fair price for a Turkish indie game was $\bar{x}=17.6$ (R=4–31) Turkish liras.

Finally, when we look at the sentiments directed toward perceptions, trust, and opinions toward the local industry, the results display a generally positive trend. There is a good amount of users who express their discontent with the games but still feel that the games need to be supported so that the local industry can grow: "I give a positive reviews because it is Turkish, they should produce better games," and "in my opinion, we should put aside all the negativity and support this Turkish-made game." Another group expresses controlled criticism in the hopes of improvement: "We should support this game because it is Turkish, but we also need to talk about what is missing so that they can get better," and "if we support something bad because it is locally made, it would hurt us and [the developers]—they should realize their errors so that they can avoid them next time." Last but not the least, a vocal minority seems unconvinced: "it is better to have no local games than having these," "I bought it because it was Turkish, but please do not make games if this is the best you can make," and "[Turkish developers] please do not make games!"

These results highlight some learnings for Turkish game developers in particular, but local game developers in other countries in general. In markets where product consumption is ethnocentric, local indie developers can substitute ambitious projects with smaller games with high quality and high originality to garner attention and support from local gamers. Local language support (a must-have for Turkish players) and cultural elements also contribute toward building positive attention. Again, for ethnocentric markets, since locally produced games represent the culture and ethnicity at large, players may resist products that they deem to be subpar. Even when the developers meet with resistance in local channels (such as local gaming websites), they should be aware that players could act more forgiving, positive, supportive, and protective in channels where international gaming communities are present (such as Steam). This means that local developers would benefit from not creating friction with local gamers over sentiments in locally accessible channels. A player who seems overcritical and unsupportive in local channels could champion a local product in internationally accessible platforms if communicated properly.

References

Arakji, Y., & Lang, K. R. (2007). Digital consumer networks and producer-consumer collaboration: Innovation and product development in the video game industry. *Journal of Management Information Systems, 24*(2), 195–219.

Berkeley, L. (2006). Situating machinima in the new mediascape. *Australian Journal of Emerging Technologies and Society, 4*(2), 65–80.

Burger-Helmchen, T., & Cohendet, P. (2011). User communities and social software in the video game industry. *Long Range Planning, 44*, 317–343.

Cengiz, E., & Kırkbir, F. (2007). Turkish consumers' evaluation of products made in foreign countries: The country of origin effect. *Innovative Marketing, 3*(2), 72–98.

Chu, A. (August 28, 2014). *It's dangerous to go alone: Why are gamers so angry?* Retrieved ftom https://www.thedailybeast.com/its-dangerous-to-go-alone-why-are-gamers-so-angry

Dahlander, L., & Magnusson, M. (2008). How do firms make use of open source communities?. *Long Range Planning, 41*, 629–649.

Dena, C. (2008). Emerging participatory culture practices: Player-created tiers in alternate reality games. *Convergence: The International Journal of Research into New Media Technologies, 14*(1), 41–57.

Eskelinen, M. (2001). The gaming situation. *Game Studies: The International Journal of Computer Game Research, 1*(1).

Gandolfi, E. (2016). To watch or to play, it is in the game: The game culture on Twitch.tv among performers, plays and audiences. *Journal of Gaming and Virtual Worlds, 8*(1), 63–82.

Ger, G., Belk, R. W., & Lascu, D. (1993). The development of consumer desire in marketizing and developing economies: The cases of Romania and Turkey. *Advances in Consumer Research, 20*, 102–107.

Harrell, D. F., Şengün S., & Olson D. (2019). Africa and the avatar dream: Mapping the impacts of videogame representations of Africa. In K. Josephs & R. Risam (Eds.), *Digital black Atlantic*. Minneapolis: University of Minnesota Press.

Jenkins, H. (2012). *Textual poachers: Television fans and participatory culture.* New York, NY: Routledge.

Jenkins, H., & Deuze, M. (2008). Convergence culture. *Convergence: The International Journal of Research into New Media Technologies, 14*(1), 5–12.

Jöckel, S., Will A., & Schwarzer, F. (2008). Participatory media culture and digital online distribution—reconfiguring the value chain in the computer game industry. *The International Journal on Media Management, 10*, 102–111.

Kaynak, E., & Kara, A. (2002). Consumer perceptions of foreign products: An analysis of product-country images and ethnocentrism. *European Journal of Marketing, 36*(7–8), 928–949.

Klevjer, R. (2002). In defense of cut-scenes. In F. Mäyrä (Ed.), *Computer games and digital cultures conference 2002 proceedings*. Tampere: Tampere University Press.

Lin, D., Bezemer, C., & Hassan, A. E. (2018). An empirical study of early access games on the Steam platform. *Empirical Software Engineering, 23*(2), 771–799.

MacQueen, K. M., McLella, E., Kay, K., & Milstein, B. (2009). Codebook development for team-based qualitative analysis. *Cultural Anthropology Methods, 10*(2), 31–36.

Marchand, A., & Hennig-Thurau, T. (2013). Value creation in the video game industry: Industry economics, consumer benefits, and research opportunities. *Journal of Interactive Marketing, 27*, 141–157.

Mathews, C. C., & Wearn, N. (2016). How are modern video games marketed? *The Computer Games Journal, 5*(1–2), 23–37.

Mittell, J. (2013). Wikis and participatory fandom. In A. Delwiche & J. J. Henderson (Eds.), *The participatory cultures handbook* (pp. 35–42). New York: Routledge.

Nitsche, M. (2005). Film live: An excursion into machinima. In B. Brunhild (Ed.), *Developing interactive narrative content* (pp. 210–243). Munich: High Text.

Planells, J. A. (2017). Video games and the crowdfunding ideology: From the gamer-buyer to the prosumer-investor. *Journal of Consumer Culture, 17*(3), 620–638.

Postigo, H. (2007). Of mods and modders: Chasing down the value of fan-based digital game modifications. *Games and Culture, 2*(4), 300–313.

Postigo, H. (2008). Video game appropriation through modifications: Attitudes concerning intellectual property among modders and fans. *Convergence: The International Journal of Research into New Media Technologies, 14*(1), 59–74.

Rumphol-Janc, N. (2013). *Why are gamers on the internet so angry?*. Retreived from https://www.gamnesia.com/articles/why-are-gamers-on-the-internet-so-angry.

Şengün, S. (2014). *Türkler yaptıysa bi cacık olmaz… 'vs 'Türkler cin ali bile yapsa desteklerim*. Retrieved from http://sercansengun.com/vot/turkler-yaptiysa-bi-cacik-olmaz-vs-turkler-cin-ali-bile-yapsa-desteklerim.

Şengün, S. (2018). A survey of marketing management for the video games industry in Turkey. In S. Öztürkcan & E. Yolbulan Okan (Eds.), *Marketing management in Turkey* (pp. 353–387). Bingley, UK: Emerald Publishing Limited.

Şengün, S., Salminen, J., Jung, S., Mawhorter, P., & Jansen, B. J. (2019). Analyzing hate speech toward players from the MENA in league of legends. In Extended abstracts of the 2019 CHI conference on human factors in computing systems (p. LBW0173). New York, NY: ACM.

Strauss, A., & Juliet C. (1990). *Basics of qualitative research: Grounded theory procedures and techniques*. Newbury Park, CA: Sage Publications.

Tavares, J. P., & Licínio, R. (2007). Games 2.0: Participatory game creation. In: *Proceedings of the 6th symposium on computer games and digital entertainment 2007*.

Tschang, F. T. (2007). Balancing the tensions between rationalization and creativity in the video games Industry. *Organizations Science*, *18*(6), 989–1005.

Tschang, F. T. (2009). Creative industries across cultural borders: The case of video games in Asia. In L. Kong & J. O'Connor (Eds.), *Creative economies, creative cities* (pp. 25–42). The Netherlands: Springer.

Xiong, G., & Bharadwaj, S. (2014). Prerelease buzz evolution patterns and new product performance. *Marketing Science*, *33*(3), 315–461.

Ludography

Battlefield 1942 [video game] (2002). Redwood, CA: Electronic Arts.

Conarium [video game]. (2017). Istanbul: Zoetrope Interactive.

Counter-Strike [video game]. (1999). Bellevue: Valve Corporation.

Dark Inside [video game]. (nd.). Istanbul: G-Tech Atolye. Unreleased.

Dark Raid [video game]. (2014). Istanbul: Vector Games.

The Elder Scrolls V: Skyrim [video game]. (2011). Rockville: Bethesda Game Studio.

Enderal: Forgotten Stories [video game]. (2019). Tutzing: SureAI.

Monochroma [video game]. (2014). Istanbul: Nowhere Studios.

No:70 Eye of Basir [video game]. (2017). Istanbul: Oldmoustache Gameworks.

Oddmar [video game]. (2018). Istanbul: Mobge Ltd.

Overfall [video game]. (2016). Istanbul: Pera Games.

Reclaim [video game]. (2014). Istanbul: No-pact Studios.

Recontact Istanbul: Eyes of Sky [video game]. (2017). Istanbul: Recontact Digital Arts.

Roots of Insanity [video game]. (2017). Istanbul: Crania Games.

Solarix [video game]. (2015). KISS Ltd.

Stygian: Reign of the Old Ones [video game]. (nd.). Istanbul: Cultic Games. Unreleased.

Quake [video game]. (1996). Richardson, TX: id Software.

Unreal Tournament. (1999). [video game]. Potamac: Epic Games.

Ertuğrul Süngü, Barbaros Bostan

Chapter 3 The Evolution of Role-Playing Game Communities in Turkey and Their Effects on Creative Industries

The Evolution of Role-Playing Culture in Turkey

From Spacewar to the persistent multiplayer worlds of the 21st century, video games have moved from subculture to mainstream industry and various genres also have emerged. Among the genres, role-playing games (RPGs) require special attention, and readers of this chapter should be familiar with the concept of role-playing. RPGs are interactive worlds where players assume the roles of fictional characters and determine their own actions based on the character they play. Players typically follow a storyline in a fictional world and interact with other player (PCs) or non-player characters (NPCs) to complete missions and achieve various goals. As the player completes quests and overcomes conflicts, his/her character advances in levels and becomes stronger. Tabletop fantasy RPGs have parallels to wargames and educational simulations, but they focus more on the role and player choices are virtually unlimited (Fine, 1983). The key difference between tabletop RPGs (or FRPs) and computer RPGs is that the video game is no longer a collectively produced fantasy and takes place within strictly defined parameters (Apperley, 2006). These games were being played in many cities in Turkey, especially in İstanbul in the mid-1990s. To make a more detailed examination of the evolution and the current state of this subculture, an analysis of the late 1990s' FRP Cafés would be undeniably noteworthy.

Sales of FRP materials in İstanbul began in 1995 with the foundation of Büyük Mavi Company. Aforementioned company imported popular 1990s fantastic fiction novels and essential rulebooks to play FRP games. ADandD 2nd Edition books, which already had an immense fan base abroad, quickly started to meet with the target audiences in bigger cities like İstanbul and Ankara. Before these imports started to arrive in Turkey, different system books were produced and many fantastic fiction books were in print and/or hitting the presses. As a result of this, in a short amount of time, a myriad of FRP games were played. Similarly, books that are still being talked about, such as Margaret Weis and Tracy Hickman's Dragon Lance and R.A. Salvatore's Forgotten Realms series, were printed in this era and reached audiences in Turkey concurrently.

After Büyük Mavi's imports, an ensemble of friends, which had the leading members Özgür Özol, Gökhan San, and Altuğ Öneroğlu, opened the Sihir Café in May 21, 1997, in Beşiktaş, İstanbul. A week later, in May 28, they organized an interactive Dragon Lance tabletop game with 40 players. This event practically banded together the whole FRP community in the same place. After radically changing the theme of FRP Café in 2001, Sihir Café shut down its doors in 2004. Between 1997 and 2001, Sihir Café mostly sold fantastic fiction and RPG system books, materials for the trading card game Magic the Gathering, and tabletop miniature war game Warhammer. Customers could eat and drink or play FRP games or read books they bought in the entrance level or get to the second floor and play digital games on PCs. After 2001, Sihir Café was also being used as a publishing house and turned into a hobby club. Following this change, the café abandoned the second floor and carried on its activities in the entrance and basement floors. The entrance floor was serving customers with different gaming tables that Warhammer players could use, and game materials such as tree, house, fence, and castle miniatures. The basement level had lockers for the members, a big table for painting Warhammer figurines, and two rooms with PCs and sound systems to play FRP games.

Besides the aforementioned services, Sihir Café had a remarkable menu. Even though this menu had ordinary cookies, classical sandwiches, and main courses; every item had an intriguing name that would interest those who experienced the RPG culture. The menu started with drinks. Except for regular orange, carrot, and apple juices there were other items such as: Health Potion, Mana Potion, Swamp Juice, Nature Man, and Deep Blue. The sandwich section had the following items: R2-D2, Cylon, Go Kurt (a "catchphrase" used in the Turkish comic series Tarkan), Drow, Kagonesti, Dimernesti, Kender, and the most expensive item of the whole menu: Dragon Fest. Under the grilled cheese section, another interesting item was "Amcan" (could be translated as "Your Uncle") which was actually another local grilled sandwich type known as "Yengen" (could be translated as "Your Aunt", such as a meal a loving aunt would prepare). Every item in the menu had a little illustration; some of them showed the food and others show what each name represented. Each item showed similarities with the science or fantastic fiction concepts, races, and characters that named them. This was the most compelling part of the menu. For example, if you ordered a Health Potion, a red-colored fizzy drink would show up and if you ordered a Mana Potion, a blue-colored drink would. These names were references to the iconic game Diablo, which was immensely popular at the time. Dimernesti Sandwich is another example. This item had tuna in it and was named after the oceanic elven race in the Dragon Lance series. It was attractively named for anyone who would visit Sihir and was a part of this community. Even more, for a marine food sandwich this name was funny, witty, and a successful choice.

Another similar site was opened in 2000, again in Beşiktaş, on Akaretler. Saklıkent, which opened its doors in 2000, was selling novels, system books, Magic the Gathering, and Warhammer products just like Sihir Café did. In the three-story space, almost all kinds of games, including PC games, could be played. Saklıkent was founded by Yusuf Kemal Vefa and continued to serve customers till 2005. After that, Yusuf Kemal Vefa and Rıfat Levis founded Pegasus Toys Company in 2006. It opened a shop in Beşiktaş Mısırlıbahçe Street in 2011 and became Turkey Distributor of Magic the Gathering, Warhammer, YuGiOh! and Italeri products. This place also became a center for these games' tournaments. In the late 1990s, other than Sihir and Saklıkent FRP Café's, there were many other similarly themed cafés such as Kamer, Geçit, and Tılsım. Around the same time another shop, Oversoul, opened up in Ankara.

These places, more importantly than anything else, were gathering points for people. Places like Sihir and Saklıkent serviced customers with exceptional and diverse gaming spaces; over time many customers became regulars because of this. It should be noted that FRP Cafés' iconic gaming spaces came forth because the games sold in there needed tables to be played, and they were basically social activities. These cafés provided a cultural exchange point for anyone interested with the subculture. More so, Magic the Gathering, with its competitive nature, started to gather a substantial audience. Having a national team that enters international tournaments also helped this. Emre Yavuz, the owner of a publishing company specialized in publishing comic books, summarized his experience in these places as:

> I own a publishing house right now, and the experiences I get from these comic and game shops prove more than useful for me, because most of the books I've published aims to the audience I saw, knew, and talked with in these kind of places. Moreover, I had the chance to gain a lot of friendships in that world. (E. Yavuz, personal communication, March, 23, 2019)

Nevertheless, FRP, Magic the Gathering, and Warhammer games were only the beginning in cafés like Sihir and Saklıkent; people played all kinds of digital games as well. Istanbul at that time did not have DSL or cable internet connection service providers; therefore, only available connection speeds were limited to, at first 36K and sometime later 56K dial-up. Unfortunately, these speeds were too slow for online gaming. As a result, playing games on Local Area Network (LAN) was much more popular. Customers who shared the same kind of hobbies shortly noticed PC adaptations of their beloved RPGs they were accustomed to play on tabletop at aforementioned places. Game series such as *Baldur's Gate*, *Diablo*, and *Fallout* quickly became one of the most popular topics that were being discussed by regulars. At the time, creating a proper LAN connection was not really plausible because of the technical shortcomings and even more players preferred to experience RPG physically and not digitally. The major titles that changed the scene were *Starcraft* released in 1998 and *World of Warcraft* released in 2004. Ceyda Doğan Karaş, a project manager, editor, content manager, and cosplayer consultant, summarized this era as:

> When we look at it on the general cultural level, these great hobbies such as FRP, video games and cosplay already existed in our country. But because Internet usage and social media wasn't prominent as much as it is today, they had a minute presence in the minds of the public. Just because the Internet and social media were not active, it was as if they didn't have them. Nowadays, almost all kinds of fairs and events include some type of FRP activities and allow for, at worst, a few hours of adventures. (C. D. Karaş, personal communication, March, 25, 2019)

In a sense, it can be said that the FRP Café era has been long gone but for those who visited these places; getting together, sharing experiences, and acting as a community was an irreplaceable lifestyle choice. People who are still active in the community most of the time tend to refer to these places as gaming clubhouses; it can be argued that this is more suitable to the spirit of these games. After FRP Cafés started to disappear from the landscape, regulars, in their search for a place to get together and chat with like-minded individuals, started to "migrate" to other establishments. One of the most popular locations was Tophane, which was a well-visited location that was famous in the European side of the city between the start of the millennium and the year 2015 for its hookah cafés. Around the time Tophane rose up in popularity among the RPG fanbase in Turkey, digital communities as a concept started to pick up speed on the Internet, and more and more people started to join them.

FRPNET, which was founded in 2004, was one of the most popular platforms that should be mentioned while exploring this period. At this point, long form discussions on online forums get a more prominent role in the community. These forum discussions became an important part of people's lives, and people who met online started to meet in real life as well. Atmosphere of discussions on the Internet mirrored how it was in the cafés for the most part; everyone kept sharing their knowledge on different kinds of fantastical worlds. FRPNET, especially after the era of FRP Cafés came to an end, in a sense took the role of a digital café, which kept the RPG community together. Kayra Keri Küpçü, who has been the chief editor of FRPNET since the beginning, is closely acquainted with the community and has organized many activities, headed by the site. With its experienced editorial staff FRPNET kept up with the times, and was revised several times and finally reached how it is today.[1] FRPNET's content includes science and fantastical fiction news and articles, and in general anything that has relation with the "subculture." If we look at site statistics we will see, in 2017, it had 1,092,171 visitors and they looked up 2,478,245 pages. In 2017, the total time spent by visitors of FRPNET was 2.6 million minutes; that is, 4.95 years.

The Impact of Fantasy Role-Playing Games on Turkish Youth

It is not surprising to find that some of the people working in the Turkish game industry had a tabletop role-playing background, which may be attributed to the unique skills they develop while playing these games. People practice role-playing in different contexts but they also develop some unique skills defined by Bowman (2010) such as: (1) enhanced communal cohesiveness through the narrative enactment within a ritual framework, (2) improved complex problem-solving skills through the enactment of scenarios, and (3) the ability to develop alternate personas through a process known as identity alteration. It is also claimed that tabletop RPGs have a positive effect on the creative potential and emotional creativity of individuals (Dyson et al., 2016). A qualitative study on why people play tabletop RPGs showed that imaginative creativity, exploring and knowing self, belonging, and interacting are some of the motivational drivers behind these experiences (Coe, 2017). Some other benefits of tabletop RPGs highlighted by similar studies are: positive psychological and social development, enriched learning, identity exploration, and improved empathy (Daniau, 2016; Merilainen, 2013).

The chief editor of FRPNET, Kayra Keri Küpçü, who is now the marketing and communications manager of Monster Notebook, pointed to the fact that these games also have an educational value in people's lives and contributed to personal development through exposure to continuous learning opportunities:

> For example, if you are going to host a FRP game that is set in space, to create a more consistent environment, first you find yourself researching space, then structures of spaceships, then the fuel that spaceship uses to move in space for years on end, then how other planets would be for living conditions wise, how would people live on them; these goes on and you keep researching space and the science behind it for a long time. Or, if you will have a castle siege in one of your games, you will find yourself researching

1 Çatak, Shodan, Yapar, and Küpçü, (n.d.). FRPNET. Retrieved from https://frpnet.net/.

> the history of how sieges were done during the Middle Ages to find out what conditions they were done in. You look up for castle siege weapons, Middle Ages war strategies, and other things such as weapons people used at that time. (K. K. Küpçü, personal communication, March, 4, 2019)

Turkey is a multicultural and multiethnic society and Ahmet Serkan Aydın, who is now working as a user experience researcher, explained how this subculture shaped his worldviews and his understanding of people from different cultures, as well as religions.

> I don't know if these places, as in their physical existence, had an effect on my life. However, the people I met in those cafés and what have shared and done together changed me in a cognitive sense, which is undeniable and permanent. Especially playing role-playing games with hundreds of people, witnessing different story structures, being exposed to thousands of characters; I can say these things helped me analyze the narrative structures we face nowadays in a much comfortable way. Furthermore, communicating and interacting with the many different characters in these stories proves useful while communicating with the people I meet in my personal life. On top of that, my exposure to the worlds and myths that were constructed as part of these stories shaped my world-view and understanding of religions as well. Now I can analyze in a much better manner what people believe in and why do they believe in that particularly. I understand the reasons of the actions of people, who I may have judged in the past. (A. S. Ayan, personal communication, March, 30, 2019)

Another distinctive impact of RPGs in Turkey is how they improved people's language skills. These fantasy RPGs were developed in the United States and therefore the language of the game is English. People were learning English as a foreign language, but it was these games that fired their enthusiasm to develop it. The chief editor of FRPNET, Kayra Keri Küpçü, who also worked as an editor in various publishing houses, pointed to this specific benefit of playing these games:

> Although I studied at private schools for my primary and secondary education, I had a much lower level of English education in high school and if I had not played FRP in those years I could have forgotten English altogether, but I had reinforced my English knowledge thanks to the rule books and fantastic fiction books I have read. FRP offers a rich social environment where lots of information can be absorbed from different sources; it helped me learn English and moreover it let me play games that I had the most joyous moments in. I had never read a book until 1997, but when I met with fantastic novels and rule books, I became a total bookworm. (K. K. Küpçü, personal communication, March, 4, 2019)

People who have played fantasy RPGs also pursued careers in the gaming industry in the upcoming years. The subculture they belonged to also contributed to their careers. Kaan Günay, who worked in Riot Games before, summarized his experiences as:

> To summarize what I have said before in more general terms; I think the effects of FRP and FRP Cafés to my life is just like the relation in 'chicken or the egg' dilemma. It has an impact on my current work life in terms of not just shaping the circles I'm a part of, but making me wonder about new fields of interests, introducing me to new kinds of game mechanics, and many other things as well. It effected my career and it will continue to do so… (K. Günay, personal communication, March, 29, 2019)

The Evolutıon of a Subculture: The Convention Era

Just like many other communities, gatherings are an important part of the gaming world. Physical or digital, as stated before, gaming as a hobby tends to be a social experience. To this day, we see that in the FRP community, the topic of "convention" holds an important place. If we examine the concept from a broader perspective, we will undoubtedly see many different kinds of "models." A myriad of diverse communities get together in these expos. A convention of book lovers would be distinct from a gaming convention, because gaming is an interactive experience and fans will always be interacting with each other. Maybe hacker conventions would be a better example where hackers meet, work together towards a common goal, share their knowledge, and keep up with advancements in their fields of interest. These are also true for gaming communities as well. In time, many different kinds of RPG conventions were organized, which originally have its roots in medieval themes. These conventions can be described as Medieval-Fairs with gaming. People who are interested in RPGs get together and play mostly one session or "one-shot" games. Over time, these events became widely accepted in Turkey; and they became one of the most common types of activity that RPG fans took place in.

Tabletop RPGs create "shared imagined spaces" where players can explore an entity or a concept within it, and it is important to note that these experiences were not augmented by computer graphics but were still fun and meaningful and immersive (Mäkelä et al., 2005). The inclusion of a Game Master (GM) or Dungeon Master (DM) improves the gaming experience; and tabletop RPGs are superior to their computer counterparts in terms of heightened enjoyment, temporal dissociation, and narrative engagement (Tychsen et al., 2007). This also inspired game designers to put GM functionality in multiplayer computer RPGs to give the control of the game world to the players and to encourage a dynamic form of storytelling in games (Tychsen et al., 2005). Dynamically building game plots, which are centered on player actions, is the goal of a story or drama manager in interactive narrative systems. In this regard, tabletop RPGs also inspired researchers of interactive narrative, who attempted to analyze how DM or GM strike a balance between their pre-authored plots and player's freedom to create a well-structured and meaningful experience (Peinado and Gervas, 2004). Delmas et al. (2009) identified the major tasks performed by a game master such as getting and analyzing information from players, collecting information on the player's knowledge and synchronization of the state of the game, and then proposed architecture for interactive storytelling in games.

Because tabletop RPG gaming required four to five people on average, getting together and doing something with others was undoubtedly a difficult thing for the RPG community. Those who were associated with role-playing loved to share their knowledge and were interested in talking about anything that was related to fantastical and science fiction. Even though in the FRP Café era these kinds of discussions were inevitable, after 2005 there was no common space; and talking and discussing with people who shared your hobbies became difficult. The next event in this field was ITUCON'96 held in 1996, Turkey's first known FRP event.

Eventually different university clubs started to cooperatively work on these events. Science Fiction and Fantasy Clubs of universities all around the country started to organize more and more events, and convention organizations gained momentum in 2007. In the same year, nearly the whole RPG fan base and lovers of the culture attended ICON that took place in İstanbul University. Again in the same year, another big convention took place at İstanbul Commerce University Üsküdar campus' gymnasium. Between 2007 and 2008, many different university clubs organized different kinds of conventions.

One of the said conventions was Sabancı University's SUCON, which took place in Minerva Palace in Karaköy. Built in 1913, with a fascinatingly authentic architecture, the building provided a spacious venue for this delightful event. In 2010, the number of events that took place in a year and was organized by university communities started to decrease. At this point in time, thanks to the efforts and cooperation of a team of veteran RPG lovers, the whole lot of university science fiction and fantasy clubs that was still active in 2010 united to create a new community, which was never before seen in Turkey. The result of this collaboration is TAKT: Turkey Subculture Community. The main goal of the community was to gather those who were interested in anything subcultural, and organize different kinds of events. The first event by the community was named KONTAKT, which was a portmanteau of convention and TAKT. This first event took place in İstanbul Technical University's Maslak Campus, in November 26, 2011. Preparatory work for the event was labor-heavy and took a long time. After all the work was done by the team, Nintendo and CNBC-E (a Turkish television network) became sponsors. Next year KONTAKT 2 took place between June 30 and July 1 of 2012, in Yıldız Technical University Davutpaşa Campus. The following year, KONTAKT 3 took place between April 6 and April 7 in Yeditepe University. KONTAKT 4 took place between February 15 and February 16 of 2014 in Yıldız Technical University, and finally KONTAKT 5 took place between October 11 and October 12 of 2015, again in Yıldız Technical University. After the last event, no other KONTAKT convention was organized to this day.

Most important phenomenon of the era was "cosplay." Cosplay, or costume play, had its roots in Japan but in time it spread to the other parts of the world. After 2009, it started to get accepted by a substantial amount of people in Turkey. Cosplay is basically a performance art; those who participate wear costumes of different kinds of fictional characters and act like them. Even though culturally Anime and Manga were prominent at first, gaming and movies slowly gained more ground among the cosplay community. At this point, it should be noted that the most distinguishing detail of KONTAKT from other conventions was that it focused on a myriad of different kinds of topics, including cosplay. It was newly spreading in Turkey, and it became the highest point of the event. Those who attended KONTAKT saw a large number of people acting like their favorite characters, wearing costumes of varying details. The upper floor was completely devoted to RPG tables, and dozens of RPG games were experienced at the same time during the event. In addition, many companies opened up booths: promoting their brands and selling their products. Ceyda Doğan Karaş, project manager, editor, content manager, and cosplayer consultant, summarized the effects of these events on her life as:

> In my life, the world of FRP always blended with gaming and it got better and better with the friendships and experiences I have gained in the technology sector. If my pen has not been broken for the last 15 years, I owe it to FRP and the gaming world. I'm sure this will continue as well. (C. D. Karaş, personal communication, March, 25, 2019)

One of the major events of this era that had an impact on this subculture is a Satanism-related murder case on September 13, 1999, which quickly became one of the popular topics of Turkey. Following this incident, police departments raided many places they thought had connections with Satanism. Although FRP and Satanism were not associated in the public consciousness in 1999, FRP was also targeted in the following years because of misunderstandings. After an incident that took place in 2002, the father of a girl who committed suicide kept emphasizing that "FRP causes suicide" in his statements. Even *Lord of the Rings*, the novel by renowned linguist Professor J. R. R. Tolkien, came under fire. Many people believed the only reason for FRP getting a bad reputation and getting blamed was people who played these games tried to act like their characters even in the real life. Many FRP Café owners made statements about the subject. One of these reactions was the statement of Özgür Özol, one of the founders of Sihir Café, one of the best-known FRP Cafés of the time. Özol stated to the newspapers that[2]: "FRP is just another gaming type. It is similar to Cowboys and Indians games we have played when we were younger. Just like those games, people get together and took on roles in a world they imagine cooperatively. 4 or 5 people act inside a fantasy world on as long as they choose to. Having suicidal thoughts after playing this game is not that different if someone has them after watching a Hollywood movies."

With his statement, Özgür Özol emphasized that the FRP was just a game. In his article, "Do role-playing games promote crime, satanism and suicide among players as critics claim?", Kurt Lancaster also pointed to the fact that RPGs are no more dangerous than movies or novels, also concluding that RPGs provide a unique form of entertainment, that novels, comic books, sports, movies, television, or theater cannot replace or substitute for (Lancaster, 1994). It is important to note here that FRP players create different spheres of meaning between themselves, their fantasy personas, and their status as players of these games. They constantly play with their own identities and try out new ones, in a creative process of constructing and deconstructing of self (Waskul & Lust, 2004). Kaan Günay, who worked in Riot Games before, also provided a similar perspective with these researchers:

> When we look at the situation through a realistic perspective, FRP Cafés and similar places gave way to the existence to the 'job network' term that people aim to create nowadays knowingly, in a natural environment by providing a venue to people who had been a part of these similar cultures in their early years as kids/tweens/teens, and give them the chance to meet with other that had same kinds of experiences, and learn about cultures they had little to no knowledge of. A more cliché definition would be; 'The individuals who make up the game industry nowadays are the people you have played with in the past.' This creates a natural recognition. (K. Günay, personal communication, March, 29, 2019)

It should also be noted here that fantasy RPGs push the limits of classic game definitions. According to Juul (2003), they are not normal games because with the addition of a GM or DM, their rules are not fixed. Salen and Zimmerman (2003) argued that fantasy RPGs lack an important component of classic game

2 Lara satanist değildi. (2002, January 19). *Sabah Online*. Retrieved from arsiv.sabah.com.tr/2002/01/19/g02.html.

definitions: a quantifiable outcome. As a matter of fact, FRP can also be defined as a dice-playing game, in which people who experience the game were asked to act according to the race and class of the character they chose. When you look at its core, FRP experience is very much overlapping with the theater, but it was seen as an evil thing as Satanism events were going on and the beautifulness of the theatrical part was pushed aside. Eventually, many more people started playing FRP over the past years, and people noticed that FRP is just a "Game." Thanks to the introduction of more and more excellent fantastical literature and science fiction works, the support of cinema to this fantastical concept made both FRP gaming and the culture that is defined as a subculture more prominent.

Conclusion

RPGs have been a great influence in the gaming community since the 1970s. One of the most important reasons why it affects the entire gaming community is the fact that even in a period where tabletop box games are popular, they can be experienced with only pen and paper and are completely based on the role-playing logic. Nevertheless, the influence of the legendary books of *The Hobbit* and the *Lord of the Rings* series, written by well-known author J. R. R. Tolkien, cannot be denied. RPGs, which entered Turkey both as literature and games, have boomed in the 1990s as digital games.

Those who experience these games in Turkey have gathered in many different cafés like, Sihir, Saklıkent, and Kamer and in a way created a subculture. These are the places where the same culture is consumed and people talked in a language, which is so foreign for people who are unfamiliar with it, while it is a common tongue for people who have an interest in this topic. In these places, many novels are being read, and the information gathered while reading those novels are used in playing RPGs, which also helped the RPG community's birth and growth in Turkey since the late 1990s to mid-2000s. Also, many people have been talking about these issues through Internet and forums that have actively entered our lives in similar periods. In particular, FRPNET's RPGs have contributed significantly to its development after 2005. It managed to fill the place of the FRP Cafés, which spontaneously disappeared. Fahrettin Satgan, who worked in Peak Games and Crytek before, summarized his experiences as:

> "I don't know when people came up with 'Gamer' as a term. Although it is mostly used for people who play computer games, I see it as a way of life or something to base one's perception on and I define myself in this way as well. In this way, I think I know 'Gamers' well, and I enjoy working in this sector and I believe that I am successful. In a nutshell, the main factor in my decision to enter the game industry was not the places I've gone

to before, but the 'gamer' inside me that caused me to go to these places to begin with. On the other hand, the relationships I had in these places proved an undeniable advantage for me to find a place in the sector." (F. Satgan, personal communication, March, 22, 2019)

Nevertheless, it is still possible to see a lot of FRP tables in many university conventions in Turkey. Although the convention logic is an activity model from older times, it offers a structure that brings together people who have adopted a certain sense of entertainment. When it comes to the Geek and Nerd world, this becomes even more evident. San Diego: Comic-Con, one of the biggest conventions of the world, is one of the most important names that can be given as an example to these. This event that brings comics, games, sci-fi, and fantasy literature together is especially getting attention thanks to "cosplay." From this and the conventions that exist in FRP world being organized regularly in Turkey, become bigger than before since 2010. Thanks to the KONTAKT events, convention spirit has totally bloomed and has shown that crowds can be gathered under one roof in Turkey just like in others.

References

Apperley, T. H. (2006). Genre and game studies: Toward a critical approach to video game genres. *Simulation and Gaming*, *37*(1), 6–23.

Bowman, S. L. (2010). *The functions of role-playing games: How participants create community, solve problems and explore identity*. Jefferson, NC: McFarland.

Coe, D. F. (2017). Why people play table-top role-playing games: A grounded theory of becoming as motivation. *The Qualitative Report*, *22*(11), 2844–2863.

Daniau, S. (2016). The transformative potential of role-playing games: From play skills to human skills. *Simulation and Gaming*, *47*(4), 423–444.

Delmas, G., Champagnat, R., & Augeraud, M. (2009). *From tabletop RPG to interactive storytelling: Definition of a story manager for videogames*. In I. Iurgel, N. Zagalo, P. Petta, (Eds.), *ICIDS 2009*. LNCS, vol. 5915, (pp. 121—126). Heidelberg: Springer,

Dyson, S. B., Chang, Y., Chen, H., Hsiung, H., Tseng, C., & Chang, J. (2016). The effect of tabletop role-playing games on the creative potential and emotional creativity of Taiwanese college students. *Thinking Skills and Creativity*, *19*, 88–96.

Fine, G. A. (1983). *Shared fantasy: Role-playing games as social worlds*. Chicago: University of Chicago Press.

Juul, J. (2003). *Half Real. Video games between real rules and fictional worlds* (Doctoral dissertation). IT University of Copenhagen, Copenhagen, Denmark

Lancaster, K. (1994). Do role-playing games promote crime, satanism and suicide among players as critics claim?. *Journal of Popular Culture, 28*, 67–79.

Mäkelä, E., Koistinen, S., Siukola, M., & Turunen, S. (2005). The process model of role playing. In *Dissecting Larp, Proceedings of the 2005 Knutepunkt conference.*

Merilainen, M. (2013). The self-perceived effects of the role-playing hobby on personal development: A survey report. *International Journal of Role-Playing, 3*, 49–66.

Peinado, F., & Gervás, P. (2004). Transferring game mastering laws to interactive digital storytelling. *Technologies for Interactive Digital Storytelling and Entertainment Lecture Notes in Computer Science*, 48–54.

Salen, K., & Zimmerman, E. (2003). This is not a game: Play in cultural environments. In *DIGRA 2003 level up conference proceedings.*

Tychsen, A., Hithchens, M., Brolund, T., & Kavakli, M. (2005). The game master. In *Proceedings of the 2005 interactive entertainment conference.*

Tychsen A., Newman K., Brolund, T., & Hitchens, M. (2007). Cross-format analysis of the gaming experience in multi-player role playing games. In *Proceedings of the DIGRA 2007 conference,* Tokyo, Japan, pp. 49–57.

Waskul, D., & Lust, M. (2004). Role-playing and playing roles: The person, player, and persona in fantasy roleplaying. *Symbolic Interaction, 27*, 333–356.

Kaya Özkaracalar

Chapter 4 The Recent Horror Film Boom in the Cinema of Turkey

Introduction: Earliest Turkish Horror Movies

Until 2004, the number of theatrically released Turkish horror movies produced since the inception of Turkish cinema totaled less than half a dozen, and thus the horror genre was almost completely absent in the cinema of Turkey. Since 2004, however, we have seen a steady number of Turkish horror movies being produced and theatrically released. This trend, which initially manifested in the form of a handful of Turkish horror movies persistently reaching screens each year, dramatically accelerated in 2015 which saw 21 theatrically released Turkish horror movies. Hence, it can safely be said that horror has indeed become a staple of Turkish cinema, rising to the status of being the third most visible genre in the cinema of Turkey after comedies and romantic movies, although this third rank is admittedly a distant third.

The first Turkish horror movie appears to have been *Çığlık* (Scream; 1949). While the movie itself is lost, its theatrical poster and one-line plot summary published in reference books indicated it to have been a horror movie and its very recently resurfaced script has showed it to be a horror or thriller project with a plot about a conspiracy to drive a young woman mad to get her inheritance (Sekmeç 2018). The earliest Turkish horror movie available for viewing is *Drakula Istanbulda* (Dracula in Istanbul; 1953), an adaptation of an abridged and "nationalized" Turkish translation of Bram Stoker's *Dracula* which had changed the identities of the narrative's protagonists to Turkish nationals and the main setting to Turkey. After *Drakula Istanbulda*, there were not any other Turkish horror movies for almost two decades. *Ölüler Konuşmazki* (The Dead Don't Talk; 1970) was a very low-budget supernatural horror movie which went unnoticed even in the time of its release. *Şeytan* (The Devil; 1974), a Turkish remake of *The Exorcist* (1973), was a relatively high-profile effort in the sense of cast and crew involved, but nevertheless did not generate any extraordinary level of audience interest. Several Turkish movies in other genres such as medieval/mythical heroics and/or movies derived from comics occasionally featured horror motifs such as vampiric villains, and some Turkish exploitation movies were inspired from violent Italian giallo thrillers to some degree, but there were not any more straightforward horror movies in Turkish cinema after *Şeytan* for a long period of time. Turkish cinema's last flirtation with horror prior to the ongoing horror boom of the 2000s was the art-house favorite *Karanlık Sular* (Serpent's Tale, 1996), a vampire movie brimming with social allegories about crisis of the Turkish cultural identity[1].

Any discussion of the recent proliferation horror movies in Turkish cinema has to deal with the question of their scarcity in the past. This scarcity seems puzzling in the face of the fact that the Turkish cinema in its heyday had even produced dozens of Western movies, Western obviously being a genre with no domestic cultural roots and hence any alleged foreignness of the horror genre could not have been a factor in Turkish filmmakers' avoidance of it. Furthermore, imported horror movies had always been popular with Turkish audiences anyway; for example, the seminal Italian horror film *Suspiria* had played in Istanbul's largest cinema hall consecutively for three months. As I have argued elsewhere, "it is clear that the Turkish audiences were not culturally or psychologically allergic to horror cinema, but the Turkish filmmakers did not have enough confidence that they themselves could make commercially viable horror movies. The insufficient technical assets of the Turkish cinema industry in such areas as special effects, make-up and set design come to mind in this regard (see Scognamillo & Demirhan 1999: 69). [...] The lack of competent technical assets and know-how at the disposal of the Turkish commercial filmmakers might have understandably acted as a deterrent in indulging in a genre where they felt such logistics were necessary and they would not take risks until one 'chance event' or the other encouraged them and showed the way forward. And [...] the few experiments in horror filmmaking apparently did not turn out to be such 'chance events'. On the contrary, the reverse would occur decades later" (Özkaracalar, 2012, p. 250).

Furthermore, another issue which needs to be addressed in this regard is the absence in the Turkish cultural setting of certain motifs, such as vampires, werewolves, gothic castles, or serial killers, frequently utilized in conventional Western horror movies. It might have been indeed tempting to explain away the absence of a full-fledged Turkish horror cinema in the past with these absences. "Such essentialist lines of thought actually fall flat in the face of the facts that cowboys were in principle as alien to Turkish audiences as vampires or that the folk belief in vampire originated in Orthodox lands and was originally pretty much alien to, for instance, the Catholic and Protestant populations –until being

1 For a detailed discussion of these earlier Turkish horror movies made in this period, see Özkaracalar (2003) and also Özkaracalar (2012, p. 250-253).

appropriated by the popular culture there. Nevertheless, what has been shown as a recipe for the prospects of horror movie production in Turkey has been the option of utilizing the 'neglected' original horror motifs from the cultural heritage of Turkey itself (Evren undated [2005], p. 165–167). This option has not only been a conventional wisdom expressed by commentators, but has also been appropriated by most of the filmmakers involved" in the horror film boom of the 2000s which is largely driven by movies with Islamic motifs, jinns being the foremost of them (ibid.).

The Kickoff of the Turkish Horror Film Boom

The vibrant Turkish film industry had begun to feel the strains of an impending crisis in the 1970s due to a combination of various factors from the extension of television broadcasting and the parallel proliferation of television sets to an overall economic crisis in the Turkish economy in general; and the industry finally disintegrated to a large extent in the 1980s in the face of the home video boom (Öz & Özkaracalar, 2011). Nevertheless, a "new Turkish cinema" emerged from the mid-1990s onwards with production and box office returns of Turkish movies steadily increasing since then (Öz & Özkaracalar, 2017).

The first attempt for introducing horror into the repertoire of the flourishing new Turkish cinema came with a horror-comedy hybrid, *Okul* (The School, 2004) which drew 837,000 spectators, becoming the sixth most successful movie of 2004[2]. *Okul* had opened in January 2004 and the tail end of the same year saw the release of Turkey's first straight horror movie in many years: *Büyü* (Spell) which had been commissioned by Faruk Aksoy, one of the major Turkish producers, to veteran director Orhan Oğuz. A major fire broke during its premiere, threatening the lives of hundreds of people including several celebrities trapped in the theater; and live news coverage of the rescue operation during evening prime time added to the publicity of the movie. Despite involuntary bursts of laughter from audiences faced with incompetently written lines of dialogue and/or incompetent acting, and unanimous critical snubbing from reviewers, *Büyü* was nevertheless a box office success with 553,000 spectators.

Consequently, 2006 saw the unprecedented release of three new Turkish horror movies as well as one police thriller and one psychological thriller, both of which also tread firmly on horror territory. The first of this new batch to reach

---

2 For a detailed account of the development of *Okul* from a project of young author Doğu Yücel for one of his novels to be adapted into a film to its eventual production, marketing, and distribution, see Özkaracalar (2012), p. 253–254.

the screens was *D@bbe*, written, directed, and produced by a little-known young Turkish filmmaker educated in Japan, Hasan Karacadağ. It was picked up by the major distributor Özen Film which had also distributed *Okul* and *Büyü* and given an aggressive promotion campaign highlighted by extensive television spots. Like *Büyü*, it was also a commercial success with 539,000 spectators despite press reviews hitting on, above all, the performances of an amateurish cast.

Revolving around an apocalyptic prophesy mentioned in the *Quran* and giving it a contemporary spin about the internet, *D@bbe* also happened to be the emerging horror boom's first movie with pronounced Islamic motifs. (While *Büyü* had also utilized *Quran* verses about the sins of dabbling in magic in its marketing campaign as well as opening credits sequence, the plot of that movie itself had dealt more with what can be called pagan witchcraft and did not entail much Islamic motifs.) It was ominous that another one of the horror movies of 2006, *Araf* (Limbo), also featured Islamic motifs predominantly; even though *Araf* did not turn out to be a big box office attraction with 127,00 ticket sales, it may nevertheless have been a profitable exercise since its low production values clearly indicated it to have been a very cheap production in the first place. The demand and supply dynamic for new Turkish horror movies and the trend of Islamic horror movies leading and dominating this new Turkish horror boom was locked-in when a movie about jinn possession/harassment, *Musallat* (Pestering; 2007), directed by former television professional Alper Mestçi, attracted 301,000 spectators.

The dynamic for the production and theatrical release of Turkish horror movies and the trend of Islamic horror movies leading this boom would be given a big boost when the fifth entry in Karacadağ's *D@bbe* series, *D@bbe: Zehr-i Cin* (D@bbe: Poison of the Jinn; 2014), became a bigger than ever hit with 838,000 thousand ticket sales. Undoubtedly encouraged by this unprecedented success, producers and distributors in Turkey would take an even larger plunge into horror with the number of Turkish horror movies reaching screens more than doubling the next year, exceeding 20 and remaining around this level; since then, no single movie has yet come close to the box office success of *D@bbe: Zehr-i Cin* and the annual average returns have been erratic, as will be discussed in the last section.

Overview of the Films of the Current Turkish Horror Cinema

The abovementioned Karacadağ and Mestçi are the uncontested leading figures of the Turkish horror cinema. Of the 20 highest-grossing Turkish horror films (excluding the horror/comedy hybrid *Okul* and several horror parodies or "spoofs"), ten are by Mestçi and nine are by Karacadağ – and conversely, all the horror movies by these two filmmakers feature in this top 20 list. It should be added that the only film by a director other than Karacadağ or Mestçi in the list, *Şeytan-ı Racim* (The Accursed Satan; 2013) scripted by Murat Toktamışoğlu and directed by Arkın Aktaç, is ranked 17th and hence all the top 16 are by either Karacadağ or Mestçi.

Equally significantly, all but one of these 20 highest-grossing Turkish horror movies feature Islamic motifs, with the sole exception being Karacadağ's (as-of-date) last entry in the genre, the international coproduction *Magi* (2016) which pointedly turned out to be Karacadağ's least commercially successful movie even though making its way into the top 20 list, albeit at the 18th rank. Furthermore, when we look at the Turkish horror movies released in 2015, which was a pivotal year in the sense that the increase in the number of Turkish horror movies reaching screens accelerated dramatically by doubling from the previous year, we see that 17 of the 19 straight horror movies (that is, excluding a handful of horror/thriller hybrids) were Islamic oriented and that the two nonreligious efforts were among the least commercially successful Turkish horror movies of the year. Hence, whether we look at the most commercially successful ones over the whole period of the ongoing boom or if we look at all the movies in a given sample year, we see a clear domination of movies with Islamic motifs among Turkish horror movies in terms of both quantity and of box office success.

At first thought, it may be tempting to relate this domination to the rise of political Islam in Turkey in roughly the same period and see it as a consequent reflection in the cultural sphere of this hegemony. Nevertheless, while I concur that some degree of correlation is undeniable, a closer look at the movies in question will provide a more nuanced analysis rather than a reduction of the Turkish horror boom en masse to a reflection or consequence of an overall Islamist hegemony.

As noted above in the introductory section of this article, several staples of Western horror lore, such as vampires, werewolves, etc., are foreign to Turkish culture. Thus, it is natural for a Turkish filmmaker to utilize horrific figures from the cultural reservoir of Turkish people if/when s/he wants to make a horror movie with supernatural themes, and it goes without saying that the most predominant horrific figures from the cultural reservoir of the Turkish people are of Islamic character (even though some of them may have pre-Islamic roots in a cultural history perspective, but that is another issue which I will also touch upon later). It is more than understandable for a local filmmaker to use cultural motifs his target audience is familiar with from their culture. Consequently, using Islamic cultural motifs in a work of popular fiction produced with the aim of commercial mass sales does not necessarily mean having an Islamist agenda nor even necessarily riding on the bandwagon of rising political Islam. What is determining in this regard is not simply the mere presence of Islamic motifs, but in what kind of narrative contexts they are used.

When we look at the Turkish horror movies entailing Islamic motifs with this in mind, i.e., if they entail narratives and/or narrative strategies with not only Islamic but also Islamist orientation, we see that some of them do actually fit in with Islamist agendas in the sense that, for instance, their narratives involve denigration of non-religious characters, but these movies are not the majority of the lot, neither in the terms of quantity nor of box office success. On the other hand, one could argue that a handful of Turkish horror movies with Islamic motifs even entail veiled stabs at religious rhetoric or at religious positions; and a few of them carefully locate Islamic motifs within a more general cultural reservoir of the Middle East, including pre-Islamic and non-Islamic traditions. In between these two positions, that is, horror movies with an Islamist agenda and those with veiled critical positions on this issue, vast majority of Turkish horror movies with Islamic motifs are pretty much neutral and appear to utilize these motifs simply for the sake of providing supernatural horror narratives with motifs which are familiar to spectators in Turkey from their own sociocultural upbringing.

One example of a Turkish horror movie with an explicit Islamist agenda was *Ezan* (The Call to Prayer, 2015). This very low-budget effort, which can be labeled as "Z-grade" in terms of production values including an amateurish cast, tells the story of a young man who accidently runs over and kills a young girl while driving drunk and flees from the scene. A gypsy woman puts a curse on him. The movie does not portray his misdemeanor simply as a consequence of the hazards of alcohol consumption, but the implication is that he is a person who does not abide by Islamic prohibitions that designate alcohol consumption as a sin. Throughout the movie, several secondary characters note that he does not believe in God, his fiancé complaining that he does not even know how to pray. At the end of the movie, all is revealed to be a nightmare he had and the last scene shows him on his way to a mosque, heeding the call for prayer. These lofty messages did not save the movie from sinking to the bottom ranks of the box office with only 36,000 spectators.

Another movie which similarly portrayed a character with no religious beliefs in a negative light in 2015 was *Üç Harfliler 2: Hablis* (Those with Three Letters 2: Hablis) written and directed by Murat Toktamışoğlu, a prolific filmmaker in the new Turkish horror cinema[3]. He has scripted a total of six Islamic horror movies, directing half of them himself, all three in 2015. *Üç Harfliler 2: Hablis*,

3 Turkish for jinn is the three-letter word *cin* and hence the phrase "those with three letters" is a common reference to jinns in the Turkish context.

a routine jinn-possession movie, was the most commercially successful of his directorial efforts, selling 169,000 tickets and being the fourth highest grossing Turkish horror movie of the year. Dialogues between a religious and a non-believer character include lines such as "I don't believe in jinns," "But they are mentioned in the Book [Quran]," "I neither believe in that book nor in their existence," and "All the troubles which have fallen on us are because of you, because of your disbelief."

In 2018, Toktamışoğlu returned to horror cinema with *Kabir Azabı* (Suffering at the Grave) which he scripted only, leaving the directorial reins to his former collaborator, Arkın Aktaç. Since the market had been saturated by an abundance of jinn possession movies by 2018, Toktamışoğlu had perhaps wisely chosen to highlight another frightening motif from the Islamic cultural repertoire, the belief that the nonbelievers and the sinful (or their souls) would suffer agonizing pains in their graves even before the Judgment Day. The central character of the movie is a ruthless business attorney who causes suffering among poor people whose houses he forecloses, and he is in return apparently cursed by one of his victims. The plot of the movie recalls Sam Raimi's *Drag Me to Hell* (2009) which also told the story of a young and ambitious bank loan official cursed by an old woman whom she had evicted from her house. However, unlike *Drag Me to Hell*, the attorney in *Kabir Azabı* is not portrayed only as an embodiment of "savage capitalism," but also as a disbeliever in God. In one crucial scene, a poor woman about to be evicted asks him if he does not have any religious beliefs at all, with the implication that a believer would be merciful, and gets the blunt reply "No." Furthermore, the turning point of the narrative emerges when the attorney learns from a hodja that a curse would be lifted when the cursed seeks forgiveness and the curser grants it. However, the twist is that such a deal would work only if the cursed was a believer in God, albeit a sinner. Hence, the attorney is doomed no matter how he seeks redemption, and the movie ends with him shown suffering the dreaded pains in his grave. *Kabir Azabı* garnered 120,000 ticket sales, an above-average success for the declining fortunes of the Turkish horror cinema by 2018 as it became the third highest grossing Turkish horror film of the year, but nevertheless a near-flop when the facts that it was distributed by Warner Bros and provided with an ambitious promotion campaign are taken into account.

In brief, Turkish horror movies which denigrate nonbeliever characters are not infrequent in Turkish horror cinema, but they do not dominate nor lead the genre neither in terms of quantity nor in terms of box office success. They are not among the most commercially successful ones of the genre, their success varying from dismal to moderately successful. As noted above in the opening of this section, the cream of Turkish horror cinema, in terms of box office success, are those helmed by Karacadağ and Mestçi, two filmmakers whose names appear to have achieved a trademark value.

As noted above, Mestçi was the first Turkish director to make a movie about jinn possession. After *Musallat* and its in-name-only-sequel *Musallat 2* (2011), he helmed the loosely connected *Siccin* (Book of Sins) series of movies encompassing five titles so far, one each year from 2014 onwards till 2018 as well as taking over the *Üç Harfliler* series initiated earlier by the Toktamışoğlu-Aktaç duo. The box office performance of his horror movies has varied from 220,000 to 633,000, averaging 362,000. By his own account, he began his film director career with a horror movie because he had seen the commercial potential of the genre in the success of *Büyü* (interview with the author). Mestçi's horror movies, all featuring decent production values, indeed appear to be the work of a professional bent on providing commercially successful horror movies, and hence utilizing Islamic motifs simply because they are familiar to his target audience from their own upbringing rather than being accompanied with a political or ideological ulterior motive.

Karacadağ's utilization of Islamic motifs in his movies also stem from the same imperative while some of his later movies feature intriguing subtexts. Unlike Mestçi who has also made several comedy movies, Karacadağ's filmography consists solely of horror movies, not counting his unreleased, art-house-oriented obscure feature debut early in his youth. When he went to Japan to study film, he became familiar with Japanese horror movies and, in his own words, realized the creative potential of the genre (interview with the author). Thus, the box office success of *Büyü* was less of an inspiration but more of an opportunity for him to follow up on his fascination. Six of Karacadağ's nine theatrically released movies are sequels or in-name-only sequels to *D@bbe* which was actually inspired by, to the degree of being a Turkish remake of, the Japanese production *Kairo* (2001). As the series progressed, and as the jinn-possession theme showed the promise of being a reliable box office draw, Karacadağ began to downplay the apocalyptic element in the *D@bbe* movies and transformed it largely to a jinn-themed series. The box office performance of Karacadağ's movies has ranged between 227,000 and 838,000 in ticket sales, averaging 439,000[4].

4 These figures are for the movies' domestic releases in Turkey. At least three of Karacadağ's films have also been theatrically released in Germany and/or Austria, two European countries with sizable migrant Turkish populations. The same is also true for at least one of Mestçi's movies.

While Karacadağ's earlier contributions to the genre displayed heavy influences from foreign horror movies, the last three entries in his *D@bbe* series are rather unique in the Turkish horror cinema for several reasons and manifest the emergence of a persistent personal vision, coming close to or arguably even arriving at an auteur position. For starters, *D@bbe: Cin Çarpması* (D@bbe: Jinn Warp; 2013) entailed two protagonists, a female psychiatrist and a (male) hodja, contrasting her positivism with his metaphysics and eventually the position of the hodja prevailing, but their rivalry was presented as an amicable one between two collaborating compatriots (much like the relation between Scully and Mulder in the cult television series *X-Files*) rather than loading negative attributes to the skeptic character. Furthermore, the final surprise revelation at the conclusion of the movie regarding the identity and the motivation of the antagonist marked *D@bbe: Cin Çarpması* as a movie with a subtext on the antagonism between the rural and urban populations of Turkey, an antagonism presented here as being driven by envy and fueled by deprivation. This was the first instance in the new Turkish horror cinema where a horror movie with Islamic motifs had presented a narrative dealing with a socially relevant (and nonreligious) issue from Turkey's socio-cultural landscape. Karacadağ followed *D@bbe: Cin Çarpması* with the equally if not more radical *D@bbe: Zehr-i Cin* (D@bbe: Poison of the Jinn; 2014), which dealt directly with class antagonism, as it became apparent, once again, in the final revelation about the motivation of the conflicting parties of the narrative where conventional notions of protagonist and antagonist collapsed. This fifth entry in the *D@bbe* series was also striking for featuring a line which labeled "those infidels who never refrain from uttering prayers nor holding the Book [Quran] in their hands" as omens of apocalypse in an unexpected (in a movie with Islamic motifs) critique of the hypocrisy of showcasing a religious persona in public while secretly pursuing evil agendas. This was in marked contrast to the narratives of the above-discussed Islamist horror movies where profession of disbelief in God and consumption of alcohol and the like connoted being a bad person; here, on the other hand, outward displays of a pious behavior were being labeled as possible veils for true evil. Karacadağ continued in the same vein in *Dab6e* (2015) where the final revelation at the end concerned once again swept-under-the-carpet wrongs and a twist on the conventional "villain" position, and included a line stating that "it has become hard to distinguish the crooks from the pious." Last but not least, it should also be added that these later entries in the *D@bbe* series manifest a growing tendency of Karacadağ to extend the mythology of the supernatural content of his movies beyond the orthodox Sunni Islam theology into the pre-Islamic heritage of the Near East and, in the case of *Dab6e* which included a fleeting hint of vampirism, also into the non-Islamic heritage of the Balkans.

A Tentative Exploration of the Prospects of the Turkish Horror Cinema

As noted in the above sections, the number of theatrically released Turkish horror movies was less than half a dozen in the previous century. Thus, when at least one, sometimes as much as three, Turkish horror movie began to reach screens each year following *Okul* and *Büyü*, outnumbering the total output of the previous century in a span of a few years, this became a novelty for Turkish cinema. The annual output became 4 in 2013; 8 in 2014; and, finally, 21 in 2015, stabilizing around 21–22 between 2015 and 2018.

However, it should also be pointed out that the overall number of theatrically released Turkish movies have continued to increase while the number of Turkish horror movies have stabilized, so there is actually a tendency for a slowdown in Turkish horror cinema. To be more precise, the ratio of horror movies among all theatrically released Turkish movies have decreased from 15 % to 12 % between 2015 and 2018, even though the latest figure is still much higher than the 7 % of 2014.

When we look at the box office performance of these movies in the past five years (2014–2018) more closely, we see a tendency of diminishing returns, which incidentally was reversed in 2018: For three years, the annual total of spectators of Turkish horror movies steadily decreased from 1.9 million to 1.3 million, but bounced back to 1.6 million in 2018; and the share of horror movies in the annual gross of Turkish movies decreased from 5.5 % to 3.2 %, bouncing back to 3.6 % in 2018.

This decline can at least partially be attributed to the relatively poor box office performance of Karacadağ's latest effort in the genre, *Magi* (2016), a divergent product from his earlier output in the sense that it was an international coproduction helmed with an eye for foreign markets which in return failed domestically, and Karacadağ's subsequent absence in the scene since then. Currently, Mestçi remains the sole driving force in the Turkish horror cinema, the total ticket sales of his two horror movies in 2018 making up almost two thirds of the annual gross of Turkish horror movies in that year.

In sum, it can safely be said that the horror genre has made an inroad into Turkish cinema from which it was almost completely absent and carved out a niche for itself in the domestic market. In the past years, it seems to have reached its saturation point, and there are tentative signs of an impending comparative decline. Its success is largely dependent on the performance of one or two outstanding filmmakers, an observation which indicates a rather insecure future prospect in general.

The author would like to thank Prof. Özlem Öz for her help in compiling the statistical information regarding the box office figures.

References

Evren, B. (n.d.). *Türk sineması – turkish cinema*. 42nd Altın Portakal Film Festivali.

Öz, Ö., & Özkaracalar, K. (2011). What accounts for the resilience and vulnerability of clusters: The case of Istanbul's film Industry. *European Planning Studies, 19*(3), 361–378.

Öz, Ö., & Özkaracalar, K. (2017). The reemergence of İstanbul's film industry: A path dependence perspective. *New Perspectives on Turkey*, 56, 61–85.

Özkaracalar, K. (2003). Between appropriation and innovation: Turkish horror cinema. In S. J. Schneider (Ed.), *Fear without frontiers* (pp. 205–217). Surrey: FAB Press.

Özkaracalar, K. (2012). Horror films in Turkish cinema: To use or not to use local cultural motifs, that is not the question. In P. Allmer et al. (Eds.), *European nightmares: Horror cinema in Europe since 1945* (pp. 249–260). London & New York: Wallflower Press, Columbia University Press.

Scognamillo, G., & Demirhan, M. (1999). *Fantastik Türk sineması* [turkish cine-fantastique]. Istanbul: Kabalcı.

Sekmeç, A. C. (2018). Çığlık, bir kayıp film. *Modern Zamanlar*, 46, 24–30.

Tolga Hepdinçler, Tuna Tetik

Chapter 5 A Market on the Rise and "The Fall": The Distribution in the Turkish Film Industry

Introduction

Although, the distribution has been the overlooked process between production and exhibition, it is now regarded as one of the most anticipated domains of the critical film studies. Over than two decades, the relevance on the process has not been limited to the film studies: it expanded to a more complex and interdisciplinary research while advanced and broader system of networks are introduced. The rapid change of the audiovisual technologies in production and appearance of the new kind of channels in exhibition seem to introduce a new system of film distribution. The digitalization of industry is not only a technological aspect, it also frames a new kind of exchange of film as a commodity in the global market. The new kind of exchange introduced a few but complex dynamics. First, the emergence of digital recording and editing systems have relatively changed production costs and expenses. As seen in the example of Turkey, which is the subject of the chapter, it is quite clear that the transformation, also called the digital revolution, leads to a visible increase in the number of films produced. Second, while the number of the films is increasing, global flow of film as a commodity has gained speed via new channels of consumption. The introduction of digitalized exhibition channels such as SVOD (Subscription Video on Demand) and VMVPD (Virtual Multichannel Video Programming Distributors) platforms and the new media they have created have clearly changed consumption habits. And last but not the least, the new media in production, distribution, and consumption line introduced the new global market patterns. The integration of global actors to market and their domination to the market dynamics became clear in the last decade. The digital revolution is not only an aspect of the integration and so domination of global powers to the market, it also helped to establish the dynamics on which local markets were built. Furthermore, the establishment of the new market dynamics became effective in the formation of resistance against global film industries.

This chapter is focusing on film distribution in Turkey as a national cinema, which appears to be one of the remarkable cases regarding the number of films produced per year, the extensive number of admissions to the national and international productions, and the existence of global actors along with local agents since the early 1990s. The 2016 Annual Report of Turkish Film Industry Report by IKSV (Istanbul Foundation for Culture and Arts), one of the last comprehensive survey on the Turkish film industry, reflects a significant increase in Turkish film production, foreign language film screenings, and the relative rise in admission since the early 2000s. The report also figures consistent rise of admission and box office shares of Turkish films during this period. Only in 2016, 135 Turkish films holding 53 % of the admission shares of the market compared to 221 foreign language film admissions that give more than promising opportunities to local producers and distributors. Almost 60 million admissions to films, which is slightly higher than any other markets in Europe, make the market charming to international distributors just like Warner Bros and UIP. A basic comparison of the market parameters in the 2000s with the last decade of past millennia, when only a small group of international distributors and producers were on the market, reveals a relative rise of the distribution actors taking an active role in the industry.

Main arguments of the chapter consist a basic projection and a comparison of the changes of the Turkish film market in the 1990s when the major actors of distribution shaped contemporary industrial dynamics, development of the international conglomerates in the industry, the rise of local entrepreneurship, the role of alternative actors excluding mainstream film distributions, market shares of actors in the industry, and the effects on the content. Although all the market dynamics of the Turkish film industry reflects a rise and gross of the market, this chapter is questioning a projected fall of the market in terms of monopolization; loss of local ventures; inequality content segmentation of film on behalf of mainstream and blockbuster cinema; and the change in film-going culture with the advance of SVOD such as Netflix, Amazon Prime, Hulu, local SVOD like BluTV and AVOD like puhutv.

The Global Scene of Film Industry

Recent academic works on the local industries in relation with film distribution reveal a critical paradigm to the process previously defined with global dynamics. Respectable amount of articles on world cinemas questioning particularly political economy of the market and the influence of sociocultural scene to the process added to the academic debates. Although, film distribution is generally defined with the political economy of major industries such as Hollywood, a number of recent academic researches seem to frame a new paradigm of the film distribution in relation to national and/or independent cinemas and the unconventional genres such as queer cinema. A general review of academic literature on film distribution reveals at least three different aspects. The majority of works focus political economies, financial policies, and business-related issues of the global process (Harris, 2018; Vany, 2008; Drake, 2008; Parks, 2012; Ulin, 2013). Other than the researches focusing on the critical political economy of the process that deals with the concentration of ownership, capital, and labor; a vast body of works in this segmentation seem to focus on comparative research on the media economy, comprising the statistical information on box office, admission, profit, etc. A group of critical researchers define a process evaluated with the technological developments (Perren, 2013; Crisp, 2015; Lobato, 2012, 2007). Majority of the works in this segmentation seem to deal with emerging informal agents, the new ways of consumption while a new glossary related to the digitalization surfaced. The last critical aspect can be defined with the particular cases of national film industries and debates on local cultural and socio-economic effects on the distribution process that also frames the subject of this chapter (Papadimitriou, 2018; Himpele, 1996; Harris, 2018).

The film distribution is the process by which the films are allocated to exhibitors in order to be made available to view by the audiences (Kuhn & Westwell, 2012. It is mostly defined as a mediator process between production and exhibition which constitutes two major pillars of the film industry. This process includes negotiating with exhibitors and licensees, determining the number of prints to be ordered from the lab (or arranging for the digital exhibition of the picture), planning and implementing the advertising and promotional campaign, transporting the prints to the theaters for exhibiting (if prints are still used), and collecting film rentals or other revenue from the exploitation of the film in all markets and media (Cones, 2013, p. 129). According to Vany, "Once a film is produced, it is distributed to theaters who exhibit it for audiences. The distributor chooses a release pattern—the number and location of theaters in which the film is booked or licensed to play. Distributors also choose a date at which to release their films for exhibition, looking for high demand periods and seeking to avoid playing against films that are strong substitutes" (Vany, 2008, p. 12). A complex and more fragmented aspects of the film distribution process extends its definition that is not only limited with a basic linear process between production and exhibition. A complex system of network with the new technologies, marketing, campaign, and release strategies defined the film distribution process as the critical hub of the film industry:

> The job of a distributor or distribution company is to market a film and organize its delivery to, and release in, cinemas and ancillary markets, which include film rental, DVD or Blu-ray sales, pay-TV, pay-per-view, television broadcast, and digital streaming and download. A producer will license a film to a distributor for a specific length of

> time during which the distributor will conduct market research, develop and implement a marketing and advertising campaign, develop a release strategy, and organize the storing and shipping of prints. Once the film has been released, the distributor will also be involved in the accounting process, overseeing the collection of receipts from exhibitors and the securing of ancillary fees. Because the distribution process is expensive and risky, a distributor will take a large share of a film's revenue (Kuhn & Westwell, 2012, p. 566).

Although the word "risk" echoed a negative connotation, the distribution is the most profitable segment of the film industry. As Lobato mentioned, "Vast sums of money flow through distributors, and a large portion of these sums is retained in the form of fees, interest charges and profits. Given the distribution business is marked by high levels of ownership concentration and vertical integration, this is something to take seriously." The importance of the segment is not only limited with its profitability, it is also a determinant process dominated by the industry dynamics that shapes the audience reception, and an inscription of cultural difference via fragmentation of the audiences (Lobato, 2007).

The film distribution under the light of so-called revolution of digital technologies gained an ambiguous stance. As Lisa Perren states, "Intellectual property attorneys, acquisitions executives, festival programmers, television schedulers, web technicians, and marketing assistants all could be identified as part of the distribution business" (Perren, 2013, p. 166). Once also known as the middleman, distribution companies start to compete in a new form of assembly line while they are in the process to converge two pillars (distribution and exhibition) of the market. The competition of the market is not limited to its formal actors. Appearance of informal distribution modes is also related to how the cinema is defined with digitalization. The film as a commodity in distribution is transformed to a file can also be defined as a virtual file in circulation. The appearance of informal agents and ways of distribution such as P2P, torrent downloads, and authorized and unauthorized streaming services shaped the most complex boundaries of film distribution. Andrew defines the change of the process as "Digital technology enables information, software, text, pictures and, importantly, a film to be copied millions of times without loss of quality, downloaded without the knowledge of the copyright holder and transmitted around the world instantly over networks. Traditional models for film distribution are being overturned" (Sparrow, 2007, p.1). The appearance of informal actors affected the financial sustainability of the industry when an uncontrollable form of circulation is in question. Thus, the formal model connected to be established by major players was endangered by black-market or independent agents.

The complex organizational scheme of formal and informal agents is likely to be related to the financial power of the process. The traditional formal model of distribution has been constructed pragmatically on the financial dynamics of the market where primarily Hollywood studios operate as a part of transnational conglomerates. The model keeps off the distributor from financial risks with the arrangement of financing and distribution deals (Crisp, 2015). The deals shape a protective system of financing in favor of distribution companies ensured by the studios. Since the late 1970s, the conventional industrial model dominated by studios seems to have declined, and an industrial model depending on conglomeration where studios have relatively limited power established. The roots of a diverse process were established while the film industry was less globalized. According to Harris, "Theaters were the only first-view outlet, television was the only ancillary market, the home market was non-existent, and the international market was largely confined to festivals like Cannes. Distribution was straightforward" (2018, p. 246). Even though the market agents were primarily less fragmented, the new conglomeration model added a kind of diversity that is not localized with only film exhibition. The introduction of film-related merchandises, promotional organizations, and engagement with major film festivals define a complex model of distribution; global exhibition rights, TV broadcasts, and the recent digital screening process shaped an industrial model cannot be defined with the old school formal model. This change seems to trigger film distribution defined as the site of industrial and commercial intervention (Drake, 2008).

One of the other aspects of film distribution underlined by film scholars is the appearance of the independent distributors (Crisp, 2015; Parks, 2012). The output of independent productions in the 1990s made these films visible worldwide and increased the demand for a network that was not limited to festivals. According to Parks, "the digital Revolution democratized filmmaking and more films started to appear on the market than distributors could handle. Filmmakers were thrilled to exercise their artistic license making films on the new, inexpensive format that miniDV delivered. In the process, they flooded the market with independent films, and distributors couldn't keep up. Acquisition prices started to go down, because as the supply of independent films increased, distributor demand decreased" (2012, p. 1). This also effectively influenced local film industries where independent producers demanded exhibition opportunities other than festivals. The relative rise of the independent distribution companies in the small, national markets became essential for fulfilling the supply of local and independent producers.

Film Distribution in Turkey

The history of film distribution in Turkey is potentially similar to the small national market experiences. It constitutes models initially defined with the dominance of informal local agents that shape an integrated model of the producer, the distributor, and even the exhibitor; and later formal appearance of the international companies that dominate the distribution and implicitly the exhibition. Until the major global distributors appeared, the process seems to dominated by the small but powerful local distribution agents who were effective in the production process as the producers. Especially in the 1960s and 1970s when the Turkish film industry (also known as Yesilcam) gained a boom with popular Turkish films, an unconventional system was established to share a high amount of profit between producers and exhibitors due to the lack of a defined system of distribution. Hence, production and exhibition worked spontaneously and independently on either local or regional basis (Arslan, 2011, p. 77). The spontaneous model in question has two de facto paths for film distribution in regional basis. Primarily, in Istanbul, where it constitutes the largest market, a profit share model between producer and exhibitor has been established. The model operated informally between two agents of industry under the protection of profit-shared contracts that the theaters booked to the particular production companies. This system allowed the production companies to exhibit more films including potentially profitable films with low-profile productions. For the rural market, a commission system was established between producer and the individual distributors, which turned into regional enterprises in the 1970s. These models have also been effective for the exhibition of foreign language films. While Turkish films are rarely exported, a high amount of international films were exhibited in the Turkish theaters. Although, the importation of American movies since the 1920s and the other world cinemas such as Egyptian films during the 1950s define a diversity and global extension to the market, the distribution of international films shaped the unconventional modes of the market. Most of the imported films were distributed and exhibited independently through local distribution companies, until the 1990s.

The major shift in film distribution in Turkey appeared in the late 1980s after the decline of Yesilcam when the popular Turkish films lost their dominance in the market. Economical (financial crises of the late 1970s), political (the 1980 military coup), technological (the increase of the TV receivers and introduction of the home video), and cultural reasons (the decline of family spectatorship due to the erotic film wave of the late 1970s) speeded up this decline. The decline effectively caused a large-scale drop in the ticket sales and admissions. Although there has not been a significant decline in the number of films produced in the 1980s, the fall in the admission profits made most of the local film theaters to stop their operation due to the lack of audiences. According to Arslan, almost all the theaters in small towns closed, while the remaining survived by exhibiting erotic films (2011, p. 204).

In 1989, a formal shift was revealed in the film distribution of the Turkish film industry when major distribution companies started to operate in Turkey. Even though the appearance of the distribution companies were relatively late compared to other similar national markets, two major companies, UIP and Warner Bros, held the majority of market share in the 1990s. The legal regulations of 1989 that allow the international companies and entrepreneurs to operate in Turkish market seems to accelerate availability of distribution companies. Hence, two major international film distributors hold more than 70 % of the market share between 1993 and 1996 (Erus, 2007, p. 10). This process encouraged international industry agents to regulate formally the local distribution and exhibition models with the international market dynamics (Işığan, 1996). The most visible outcome of this new model appeared with the increase in the number of screens and the films exhibited. While the number of theaters with a single screen decreased, multiple-screened theaters started to operate. This led more films to be exhibited or the same film, mostly blockbusters, to be exhibited in multiple screens in the same theater. The other aspect of the shift was the displacement of regional entrepreneurs, loss of the limited financial power of local producers and distributors (Kalemci & Özen, 2011). Most dramatically, the number of Turkish films exhibited decreased while the theaters were occupied by mostly Hollywood productions. Meanwhile, only 12 Turkish films were distributed by three major companies under 10 % admission share between 1993 and 1996. In 1995, only two Turkish films were exhibited with 2 % admission share (Erkılıç, 2003, p. 254).

The recession of Turkish films in distribution unexpectedly ended in 1996, when a Turkish film *Eşkıya* (The Bandit, 1996) was distributed by WB and exhibited with a ticket sale over 2.5 million. This boom (aka Bandit Boom) triggered the revival of Turkish movies. The access of Turkish movies to the exhibition gained slow but consistent rise each year. The share of Turkish films in total box office rose to almost 20 % in 1996 ,when only five Turkish films distributed, the rise went over than 50 % at the end of the decade (Fig. 5.1).

At the second half of the 1990s, a few Turkish films achieved a great box office success. This stance moved into a total box office achievement of the Turkish film industry with a higher ticket sale success against the foreign films with more Turkish films distributed in the mid-2000s. Especially in 2004, the

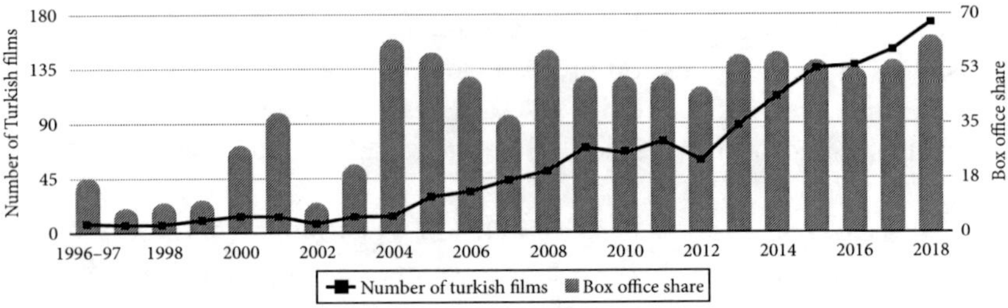

Fig. 5.1: Turkish films distributed/box office shares between 1996 and 2018. Data retrieved from Box Office Turkey

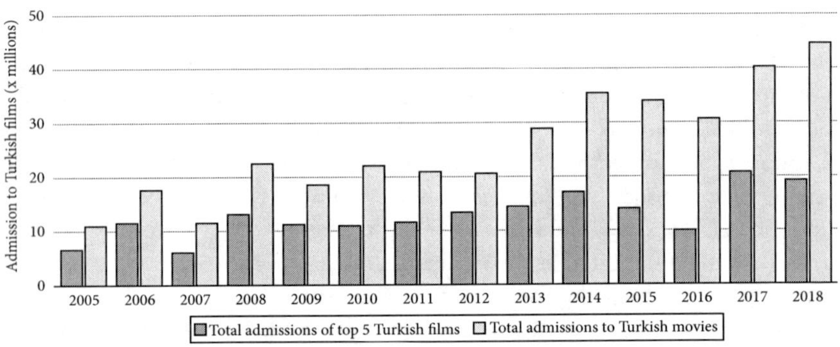

Fig. 5.2: Total admissions of top five Turkish films and total admissions to Turkish movies between 2005 and 2018. Data retrieved from Box Office Turkey

four Turkish blockbusters *G.O.R.A.* (2004), *Vizontele Tuuba* (2003), *Neredesin Firuze* (Where's Firuze, 2004), and *Hababam Sınıfı: Merhaba* (The Chaos Class Welcome, 2004) gained enormous success that raised the box office shares of Turkish films up to 50 % that has been a stationary rate for Turkish films until 2018. A numeral increase in Turkish films distributed is also evident between 2004 and 2018. Despite the box office success of Turkish films in the mid-1990s, the number of Turkish films that were distributed remained under ten films per year until 2004. From this year on, a radical increase in the number of distributed Turkish films was observed. The number of Turkish films that have been distributed since the second half of 2010 increased to more than 150 films per year. Increase in the number of Turkish films with the high box office rates shows a positive result towards the rise of the Turkish film industry.

However, the numerical increase of the Turkish films distributed is evident, and the shares of the box office remained constant compared to the total audience in the same period. This fundamentally affected box office share per film. While a small number of films show box office success, the box office of the remaining films is relatively limited, which is the invisible part of the box office distribution between 2005 and 2018. Especially in 2010, it is observed that the number of viewers of five films with the highest box office revenues reached half of the number of viewers of all Turkish films, despite the increase in the number of films (Fig. 5.2). In particular, it is observed that the productions of certain film genres have achieved commercial success, while the other productions constitute a view far from achieving the same commercial success.

Current Landscape of Turkish Film Distribution

By 2019, the two dominant processes for film distribution industry in Turkey could be observed. First, the radical transformation in the national-international market balance and second, the increase in the production and distribution of domestic films for certain film genres. The most critical development of the process is the contraction of the market against local distributors and the increase in the market share of international distribution companies. While the inevitable rise of Turkish films has improved in favor of Turkish production companies, it is observed that the same gain is not realized in the distribution and screening area. While national distribution companies represented half of the market in the 2000s, it was seen that the market share was radically below 10 % on average in the decade. Contrary to the increasing number of domestic production companies due to the number of domestic films released, it can be said that the local market in the distribution area is almost absent or steadily shrinking (Fig. 5.3). The fact that international distribution companies are also involved horizontally in the production and screening processes determines the popular preferences of the market. Despite the small but varied genre representations occurring in the second half of the 1990s, a trend towards homogenizing representation has emerged today on the axis of the same genre, comedy blockbuster and mainstream drama.

The first dimension of this process is the dominance of the market by international conglomerates. Although a positive outlook was observed in terms of the number of companies operating in the market in the first stage, it is observed that a large portion of these companies have very small shares in the market, whereas international companies have large shares within the market. As of early 2019, almost 40 distribution companies are in operation in

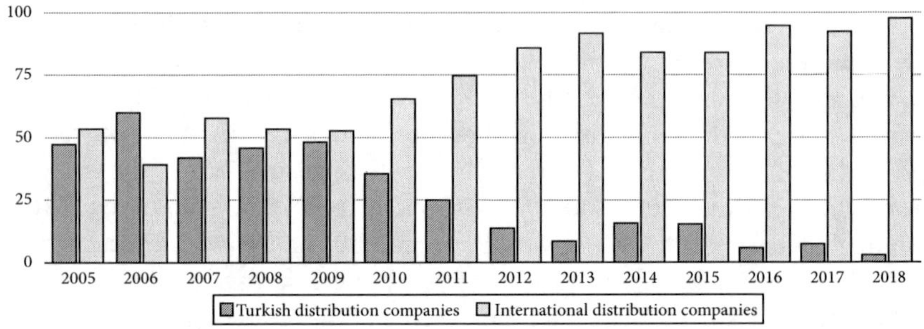

Fig. 5.3: Comparative market share between Turkish and international distributors. Data retrieved from Box Office Turkey

Turkey. This also reflects an extensive rise in the three-year period, compared to 16 distribution companies operating in 2016. But the negative aspect of the landscape appears with the dominance of the five major companies that hold a large amount of ticket share (95 %). The "magnificent five" as of the year 2018 are: CGV Mars (43 %), UIP (18 %), CJ Entertainment Turkey (10 %), Warner Bros (9 %), and TME Film (12 %). With the 2010s, major distributors such as UIP and Warner Bros keep their market share at almost the same level, while local distributors such as Özen Film, which has been active since 1941, have lost their market share. In this process, international distributors such as CGV Mars have taken the market share of major, national (Özen) or independent distribution companies. Another remarkable aspect of today's industrial landscape is the loss of market share of national distribution companies such as Pinama, Medyavizyon, and Tiglon[1] that relatively achieved high market shares through the 2010s.

The most notable development in the distribution market since the mid-2010s is that CGV Mars steadily increased its market share since 2015 and that CJ Entertainment entered the market effectively in 2018. Both companies work as the segments of a major company that operate internationally. In other words,

1 Tiglon, the local distributor of international production companies such as 20th Century Fox, has become another remarkable case of this period. While Tiglon's commercial success was mostly related to the international box office success of 20th Century Fox films and Turkish blockbusters, the company went bankrupt due to a financial crisis and most of its distribution operations transferred to TME Films in 2015.

Tab. 5.1: Market share of distribution companies between 1941 and 2018. Data retrieved from Box Office Turkey

Distribution Companies	Years Active	2010	2011	2012	2013	2014	2015	2016	2017	2018
Özen Film	1941–	12,06	15,64	1,23	0,38	0,31	0,21	0,10	0,11	0,31
Warner Bros.	1989–	17,80	20,88	16,91	17,38	19,33	11,11	17,47	17,02	9,67
UIP	1989–	29,26	33,15	32,11	45,48	31,16	28,42	28,91	26,48	18,50
CGV Mars	2014–	-	-	-	-	6,31	30,23	29,92	36,16	43,52
CJ Entertaiment Turkey	2018–	-	-	-	-	-	-	-	-	10,64
Medyavizyon	1990–	6,67	2,90	3,00	1,58	1,99	-	-	-	-
Tiglon (FiDA Film)	1999–2015	17,91	19,65	35,28	25,89	17,36	-	-	-	-
Pinama	1993–	12,79	5,30	8,78	6,54	7,13	11,12	2,68	5,37	0,36
TME Films	2014–	-	-	-	-	5,98	11,30	14,99	9,72	12,49
Minor Companies	–	3,51	2,48	2,69	2,75	10,43	7,61	5,93	5,14	4,51

CJ CGV Co. has two separate subcompanies providing services in Turkey. As of 2018, although these two companies were conducting their distribution operations under the same ownership, their entry into the local film distribution market was in different processes. Mars Entertainment Group was founded by Menderes Utku and Muzaffer Yıldırım in 2001 as a local distribution company. It served as not only a film distribution company but also spa and fitness centers. Mars distributed 184 movies between 2015 and 2017. CJ CGV Co. bought the film distribution and exhibition segment Mars Cinema of Mars Entertainment Group for 800 million[2] dollars in 2016. After that, the name of the company was changed to CGV Mars D. While CGV Mars holds 36.16 % of the market in 2017, the dominance increased to 43.52 % in 2018. CJ Entertainment Turkey entered the market as both distribution and production company in 2018.

As Tab. 5.1 shows, the market share of Turkish film distribution companies has been decreasing since 2010. Whereas international distributors such as CJ Entertainment Turkey, UIP, CGV Mars, and Warner Bros. dominate the market; a few Turkish distribution companies could keep working. Only five

2 Güney Koreli CJ CGV, Mars Cinema'yı 800 milyon dolara aldı (2011, April 4), *Hürriyet*. Retrieved from http://www.hurriyet.com.tr/ekonomi/guney-koreli-cj-cgv-mars-cinemayi-800-milyon-dolara-aldi-40081235.

international distribution companies held 95 % of the market share in 2018. In consequence of the monopoly in the Turkish film distribution market, alternative actors and local distribution companies are in danger of closing. Thus the audience is forced to watch selected movies distributed by selected international distributors in selected film theaters.

The Current Threat for Film Distributors in Turkey

In late 2018, a crisis between the major actors of the Turkish film industry triggered a long-going debate about the market shares. The so-called popcorn profit share crisis revealed an untold debate about market share inequality. This debate appeared when major producers of the market decided not to distribute their films with the high gross potential. The disagreement arises on the ticket sale shares distribution that Mars Entertainment Group holds the major percentage of the share with adding promotional profits such as popcorn and beverage sales. On the contrary, major Turkish production companies such as BKM (Beşiktaş Cultural Center), Çamaşırhane, and NuLook intimidated with the withdrawal or delay of their screenings with Mars distribution channels[3]. This crisis causes an agenda while three major producers are holding almost 80 % of the local blockbuster productions. The situation escalated when CGV Mars decided to evade this tread with a rigid declaration that focuses on finding new commercial faces to forthcoming Turkish blockbuster movies rather than reaching an agreement with major producers[4]. The debate ends up with a new law on cinema movies adopted by the General Assembly of the Turkish Grand National Assembly[5]. While the law became the first regulation since 2004 on Turkish cinema, it generally seems in a favor to Turkish film producers with a set of prohibition on the promotional operations. Although a consensus settled between both actors of the market, a twist appeared when BKM released its new movie *Organize İşler: Sazan Sarmalı* (Magic Carpet Ride 2; 2018) on one of the most popular SVOD platforms. The film released on Netflix while the movie was on screen

3 CEO of Movie Theater Chain Fire Amid Row with Producers (2019, February 19), *Hürriyet Daily News*, Retreived from http://www.hurriyetdailynews.com/ceo-of-movie-theater-chain-fired-amid-row-with-producers-141339.

4 Turkish Parliament to Discuss Movie Ticket Debate, (2019, January 9) *Daily Sabah*, Retreived from https://www.dailysabah.com/cinema/2019/01/09/turkish-parliament-to-discuss-movie-ticket-debate).

5 Law No. 7163 on the Amendment of the Law on Evaluation, Classification, and Supporting of Cinema Movies.

for two weeks at over one thousand movie theaters and with more than 3 million ticket sales. This triggered a new kind of debate that found its international precedent such as the premiere of Alfonso Cuaron's *Roma* (2018) on the same SVOD platform. Despite the negative echo of the popcorn crisis, the debate resulted in a new law that can be considered as one of the vital regulations on the Turkish film industry since some major global distributors such as UIP and Warner Bros. appeared in the early 1990s. That can also be considered a sort of oligopoly dominated by US major and a local distributor Özen Film.

Due to the popcorn crisis in Turkey, Turkish film producers changed the distribution company of their movies to CJ Entertainment from CGV Mars. Two major Turkish film production companies, BKM and Ay Yapım, began to work with CJ Entertainment. Therefore, CJ Entertainment Turkey became the leading distribution company by holding 34.5 % share of the market. BKM, NuLook, and Çamaşırhane are regarded as the leading producers on the market with the assistance of two main distribution companies: CGV Mars in 2018, CJ Entertainment in Turkey in 2019.

Until the crisis at the beginning of 2019, their relationship with distributors continued concordantly. Film theaters operated by leading distributors specifically released their movies. In one sense, the triangle of leaders (distributors, producers, and film theaters) of the market determines genres, actors, and stories.

Even though the number of cinema screens and Turkish movies in Turkey dramatically increase annually, this rise is beneficial for only Turkish mainstream comedy and drama films.

Thus, even award-winning art-house movies could not find enough places. In 2018, award-winning Turkish director Nuri Bilge Ceylan's *Ahlat Ağacı* (The Wild Pear Tree; 2018) was released only in 217 saloons in the first week in cinemas, although CGV Mars distributed it. In 2018, CGV Mars was the leading distribution company holding 43.52 % of the distribution market. The number of screens for *Ahlat Ağacı* is not as low as other Turkish art-house movies. The movie reached 246.766 admissions in 25 weeks. For instance, *Kelebekler* (Butterflies; 2018) was released in 77 saloons in the first week and reached 134.682 admissions, although the movie won the grand jury prize at the Sundance Film Festival. Whereas *Ahlat Ağacı* was distributed by CGV Mars, the distribution company (Chantier) of *Kelebekler* holds only 1.26 % of the distribution market in Turkey.

The current landscape of the film industry in Turkey mainly consists of Turkish comedy and drama movies that can gain the high number of screens due to their blockbuster potential. As Fig. 5.4 shows, several production companies and selected movies can take advantage of the rise despite the increase in the number of Turkish movies and production companies. Evaluation of the

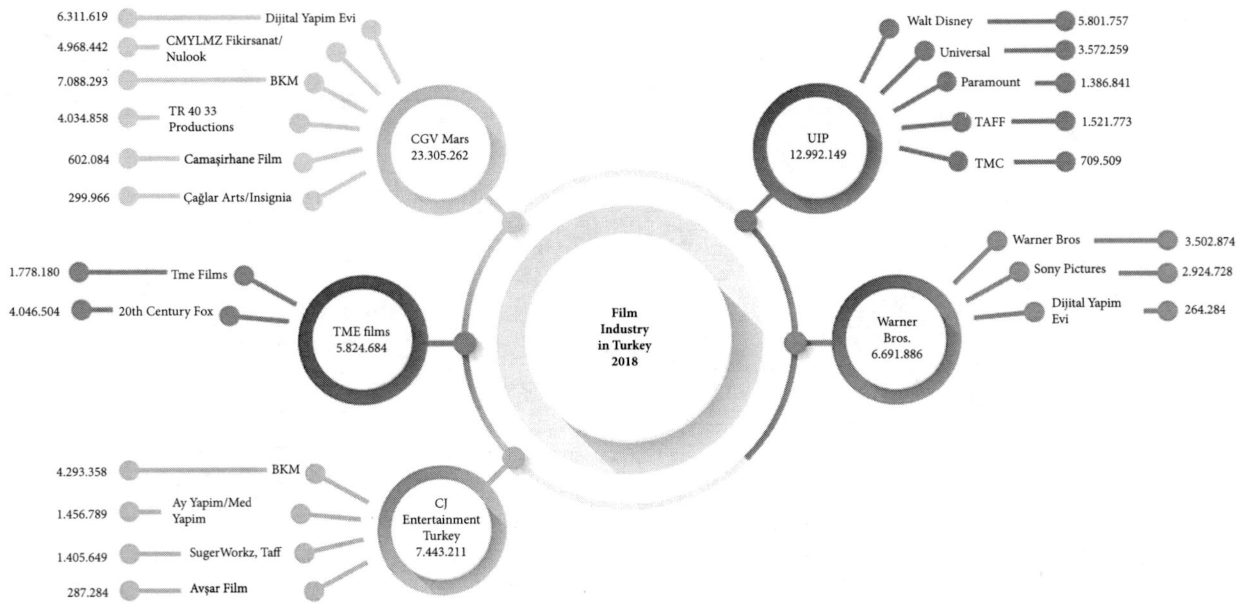

Fig. 5.4: Total admissions of blockbuster movies in selected genres of major production companies which were distributed by major distribution companies in Turkey, 2018

landscape according to Fig. 5.4 reveals that the dynamics of the market allows only specific companies, actors, and genres to rise to prominence. In this way, distribution companies and cinema theaters determine the blockbuster movies of the year in the Turkish film industry. Thus, the possibility of other platforms to release movies gets importance. Especially for the possible crisis mentioned above, digital platforms like Netflix Turkey can be considered as the threat of the current monopoly.

CGV Mars distributed *Ayla* (Ayla: The Daughter of War; 2017), *Arif v 216* (2018), and *Ailecek Şaşkınız* (What a Crush!, 2018) among its 94 movies in 2018. Three of them achieved over 15 million admissions in a single year. While Ayla is an action-war drama, the other two are goofy comedies. CGV Mars in 2018 had over 30 million admissions by distributing 94 movies including *Ayla*, *Arif v 216*, and *Ailecek Şaşkınız*. These three movies provide half of the box office revenue of CGV Mars in 2018. As Fig. 5.4 demonstrates, several movies of particular film production companies constitute the biggest blockbusters of the year. This situation is similar to the relationship between other major production companies and their distributors such as BKM, Ay Yapım and CJ Entertainment Turkey, UIP, and Disney. Thus, analyzing the current scene through the major blockbusters of the particular film production companies and their distributors is quite meaningful for revealing the standardization (what we call the fall) rather than examining all movies released in a year. Because of the previous box office achievements, these production companies have continued to make their movies in their relevant genres. After *Ayla* became the benchmark of its production companies, the producer goes on making drama movies that claim to be "based on a true story" with a high box office potential such as *Müslüm* (Muslum: Voice of Pain; 2018), *Türk İşi Dondurma* (Turkish Ice-Cream; 2019), and *Çiçero: İlyas Bazna* (2019). Whereas there is a prominent rise in the box office records; independent actors of the industry, movies in alternative film genres, and minor distribution companies have to face the facts of the fall. Distributors, film production companies, and specific genres benefit from the rise in the industry because independent companies don't have any other platforms to release their movies. However, a new threat begins to develop in the Turkish film industry.

Besides the strict competition between film distribution companies in Turkey and the crisis between the leaders in the market, Netflix Turkey launched its service in 2016. According to the data from Parrot Analytics, *Black Mirror* (2011–), *Stranger Things* (2016–), *Sense8* (2015), *Narcos* (2015–2017), and *La Casa del Papel* (Money Heist, 2017–) rank among the top 20 most in-demand digital original series in Turkey, 2018. Not surprisingly Netflix quickly becomes popular in

Turkey too. In 2018, the first Turkish Netflix Original Series *Hakan: Muhafız* (The Protector, 2018–) was aired.

Right along with the initiatives of Netflix in Turkey, there are two local VOD services in Turkey that are operated by two major Turkish media conglomerates. The first Turkish SVOD, BluTV, is launched in 2016. The audience has to pay monthly membership fee to get access to BluTV's catalogue. Its first original series, *Masum* (Innocent), was released in 2017. It drew attention with being the pioneer series in a Turkish SVOD. BluTV not only continues to produce local series but also gives popular Turkish series opportunities to continue in its platform. In this regard, BluTV transfers *Sıfır Bir: Bir Zamanlar Adana'da* (Zero One: Once Upon a Time in Adana; 2016–2019) from YouTube. *Behzat Ç.: Bir Ankara Polisiyesi* (Behzat Ç.: An Ankara Policeman; 2010–2013) will be continued in BluTV with the fourth season after six years when Star TV canceled it at the end of the third season.

puhutv is operated by Doğuş Group which is one of the major private sector conglomerates in Turkey. Its first quality series *Fi* (Phi; 2017–2018) is released in 2017. After several attempts to produce quality series such as *Dip* (2017) and *Şahsiyet* (Personality; 2018), puhutv serves as an AVOD that provides a wide range of catalogue including Turkish television series, popular movies, and television shows. Although Netflix Turkey, BluTV, and puhutv provide viewers to watch quality content whenever or wherever they want, they all still do not decide to produce own original Turkish feature-length movies. In this regard, releasing *Organize İşler: Sazan Sarmalı* on Netflix when the movie is still in theaters is a point to be noted, since the decision has a direct effect on film distribution and exhibition. It could be seen as a warning for film distribution companies to show that there are other platforms to release movies.

References

Arslan, S. (2011). *Cinema in Turkey: A new critical history*. New York: Oxford University Press.

Cones, J. (2013). *Dictionary of film finance and distribution: A guide to independent film Makers*. New York: Algora Publishing.

Crisp, V. (2015). *Film distribution in the digital age: Pirated and professionals*. New York: Palgrave Macmillan.

Drake, P. (2008). Distribution and marketing in contemporary Hollywood. In P. McDonald and J. Wasko (Eds.), *The contemporary Hollywood film industry* (pp. 62–82). New Jersey: Wiley-Blackwel.

Erkılıç, H. (2003). *Türk sinemasının ekonomik yapısı ve bu yapının sinemamıza etkileri*, (Doctoral dissertation). MSGSU Social Sciences Institute, Istanbul, Turkey.

Erus, Z. Ç. (2007). Film endüstrisi ve dağıtım: 1990 sonrası türk sinemasında dağıtım sektörü. *Selçuk İletişim*, *4*(4), 5–16.

Harris, L. C. (2018). Film distribution as policy: Current standards and alternatives. *International Journal of Cultural Policy*, *24*(2), 236–255.

Himpele, J. D. (1996). Film distribution as media: Mapping difference in the Bolivian cinemascape. *Visual Anthropology Review*, *12*(1), 47–66.

Işığan, A. (1996). *Türkiye'de film yapımcılığı*. (Master Thesis). Ankara University Social Sciences Intstitute, Ankara, Turkey.

Kalemci, R. A., & Özen, Ş. (2011). Türk sinemacılık sektöründe kurumsal değişim (1950–2006): Küreselleşmenin sosyal dışlama etkisi. *Amme İdaresi Dergisi*, *44*(1), 51–88.

Kuhn, A., & Westwell, G. (2012). *A dictionary of film studies*. S.I.: Oxford University Press.

Lobato, R. (2007). Subsinema: Theorizing marginal film distribution. *Limina*, *13*, 113–120.

Lobato, R. (2012). *Shadow economies of cinema: Mapping informal film distribution*. London: British Film Institute.

Papadimitriou, L. (2018). Film distribution in Greece: Formal and informal networks of circulation since the financial crisis. *Screen*, *59*(4), 484–505.

Parks, S. (2012). *Insider's guide to independent film distribution*. New York: Routledge

Perren, A. (2013). Rethinking distribution for the future of media industry studies. *Cinema Journal*, *52*(3), 165–171.

Sparrow, A. (2007). *Film and television distribution and the Internet*. Hempshire: Gower Publishing.

Ulin, J. (2013). *The business of media distribution: Monetizing film, TV, and video content*. New York: Focal Press.

Vany, A. D. (2008). *Hollywood economics: How extreme uncertainty shapes the film industry*. London: Routledge.

Funda Kaya

Chapter 6 The Flora of Film Festivals in Istanbul: From Mainstream to Counter-Festivals

Introduction

Currently, most cosmopolitan cities undertake different measures to construct their images on the global scale. Social and cultural events such as art exhibitions, galleries, museums, fairs, festivals, and sporting events boost economic activities at various levels and contribute to the cultural image and the cultural capital of cities on the local and global scale. These cultural events also set standards for aesthetic tastes and understandings of legitimate art across the country and the globe (Yardımcı, 2007, p. 3–5).

"Film festival" as a phenomenon is one of the substantial yet quite less discussed actors of the film industry. Film festivals are "dynamic networks" (Elsaesser, 2005) connected to other global festivals on the broader scale, "industry nodes" of film markets (Iordanova, 2015), and meeting points for audiences. On the one hand, film festivals support local and global projects and filmmakers during or after their production phases, but their decision criteria for the distribution of these few sources are neither devoid of subjective judgments nor of producing hierarchies. On the other hand, film festivals are also significant cultural events for the film critics, cinéphilia, and the public; while it should be kept in mind that the film selection criteria are not devoid of the globally set judgments of tastes for art films, or changing festival trends. Such tastes are shaped and reshaped during various periods; while some cinemas are trending in some periods, some are never ever recognized.[1] It is hard to strictly define the films exhibited in the prominent festivals as a genre in the conventional sense; like "art films" or "festival films," films that fit to festivals can be differentiated and clustered when juxtaposed to the blockbuster movies. In this chapter, both the concepts of "festival films" as well as a phenomenon of "film festivals" are discussed to locate how these analytical phrases are at work for the film festivals of Istanbul.

---

1 Iordanova (2002) explains how Eastern European (former-Yugoslavian) cinema has been reintegrated into cultural industries of new Europe during the 1990s through film festivals and pan-European funding bodies such as Eurimages. Romanian New Wave, Iranian cinema, and New Korean cinema might be thought as other examples of national cinemas that are fostered by international film festivals.

Istanbul, as the cosmopolitan center of Turkey with its huge economic and cultural activities, is the heart of production of film industry, but it might be argued that there is a relatively short number of film festivals in the city, parallel to the scarcities of film festivals across the country. This article aims to briefly cover the film festivals of Istanbul, their roles in supporting internal film production market, and their contribution to the cultural capital of the city. Some of the festivals of Istanbul are more audience oriented, they are theme-based or identity-based festivals that mainly privilege raising awareness of the public on certain concerns; some festivals are relatively independently funded and therefore free to showcase more political and oppositional content, so more stand like "counter-festivals" by their organization; while some are more industry oriented, take major European festivals as their role model, and are the very source for many independent art-house filmmakers for developing and exhibiting their projects. Together, they form the dynamic "film festival flora" of İstanbul for all of the members of the festival circuit: for film-lovers, filmmakers, film critics, volunteers, newsmakers, festival sponsors, festival theaters, jury committees, and the public.

In the following sections, first I will briefly discuss the concepts like "festival films," "art-films," and "independency of festivals" in order to locate how these conceptual frameworks are at work for the film festivals of Istanbul. I will also add commentaries from the semistructured interviews held with different participants of industry: a film critic in the managing board of SIYAD[2], an active independent film producer who has won awards from local and global scale festivals, and a festival volunteer working in a documentary festival for over ten years. These valuable contributions, provided by a cinephile, a producer, and an organizer, assist understanding the interconnected structure of film festivals in Istanbul and the local dynamics at work within this fluid festival flora. I will also add notes from a forum discussion recently held by current festival representatives of counter/alternative independent festivals of İstanbul[3]. Given the light of the existing literature on film festivals and the commentaries of the contributors, it might be concluded that current film festivals of İstanbul are not enough to

2 SIYAD: *Sinema Yazarları Derneği* (Film Critics Association) is an established nongovernmental organization composed of prominent actively writing film critics of Turkey. SIYAD is a member of FIPRESCI and annually organizes a prestigious award ceremony.

3 The International Labor Film Festival organized the forum discussion on May 5, 2019, as a part of their festival, and six participants representing six alternative film festivals discussed their experiences related to current festival processes. This two-hour roundtable discussion was recorded by their permission to be used in this article.

support the local demands of the industry at various levels. In addition, the relatively independent festivals need to share their know-hows and form their own network of information and solidarity for advancing or rather surviving their festivals. Lastly, film festivals significantly shape judgments of tastes, acknowledge new forms of aesthetics, help forming new waves, new cinemas, in short as Stringer puts: they have an "under-acknowledged role" in writing a film history of their own (2001, p. 134); and festivals of Istanbul are now writing their particular history. This article aims to understand a glimpse of their contribution to the Turkish film industry.

The Relationship of Festival Films and Film Festivals

Dina Iordanova underlines that film festival is a phenomenon that includes elements from three main lines of inquiry in film industry: production, distribution, and exhibition (2016, p. xii). Film festivals are not mainly sole arenas of exhibition but are critical nodes that create cycles of production financing, networking forums, and are distribution passages to the global exposure of films. Iordanova points that film festivals like Cannes, Berlinale, Venice, Toronto, and Busan are excessively industry oriented; and are critical industrial events all around the world with their pitching forums, film markets, funds, and prestigious awards (Iordanova, 2015, p. 7–8).

Similarly, Skadi Loist emphasizes that film festivals have always interacted with the film industry, providing a platform of networking and showcasing; but since the mid-2000s, festivals also have moved from more passive platforms of network to more active players as intermediaries in the industry. Today festivals get involved in various segments of training and funding of all stages of film production and distribution (2016, p. 59).

Dudley Andrew points to the fact that today, every film programmed by an A-list international festival becomes "de facto visible to spectators anywhere on the globe who seek out distinctive movies" (2010, p. vii). Nevertheless, not every film pleasures such privileges. Furthermore, festivals might be imagined as the arenas that embrace films that are labeled as "art-house," "independent," or "auteur" films, concepts none of which are fixed or consensual in film theory. Combination of these elements provide more challenging, critical, and open-ended filmic texts to audiences that might be labeled under an umbrella term: "festival films." Festival films cannot be thought as a genre in the conventional sense, but their deviances or distinctness can be pointed mostly with their unconventional aesthetic preferences or challenging filmic texts differing from more mainstream tendencies. It should also be kept in mind that such films are mostly exhibited, rewarded, funded, or acknowledged in particular contexts: in film festivals. Therefore, film festivals are also a form of distribution mechanism that have the power to create new trends and waves in cinema history, acknowledge auteur filmmakers on global and local scale, and direct the judgments of taste for cinema art.

It is like a vicious circle to ask the question whether festival films are mostly exhibited in festivals because they are financed or produced by their funds, through their markets; or because they are more art-house in the first place and therefore are rewarded and acknowledged by them. In either case, one might easily argue that there is an economy and network of film festivals that help the journey of more independent, art-house films on the global scale. The festivals of Istanbul also have their role in this power grid; they might highlight and introduce certain directors or films to the global market, or might increase their chances of distribution in the local market.

Thomas Elsaesser goes one step further by claiming that some films are now made for film festivals (2005, p. 87). In his influential work on festival networks of Europe, Elsaesser underlines that the festival circuit has become a key force and power grid in the film business, shaping various elements such as authorship, production, exhibition, cultural prestige, and recognition (p. 83). The cynical reference to the genre of "festival film" somehow ensures visibility and a window of attention for films that can neither rule the promotional budgets of Hollywood films nor sufficiently rely on the large internal markets to find their audiences and recoup their investments. Nonetheless, the concept of festival film also creates a relatively stable horizon of expectations to these films (p. 88–89). Paul Willemen also claims that festivals might seem to open up paths to global exposure and circulation, but in fact, they also produce a "bottleneck effect" so that noncommercial films remain outside formal circulation channels (as cited in Iordanova, 2015, p. 9).

The independent producer recognizes such a "bottleneck effect" in the Turkish film industry. She comments that sometimes the label "festival film" might damage the journey of an independent film in the Turkish distribution market. Films that are somehow outside the monopolistic distribution structure are labeled as either festival films or independent films, and audiences might position them as boring or serious automatically. These films have little chances of widespread distribution, therefore mathematically end up with low audience figures. She comments that festival film is like a "sticky concept" served like a template to label the films that are located outside the mainstream distribution mechanisms. Moreover, today film-going practices are technologically and habitually different from previous decades. She exemplifies by asking "how many people would see a film like Takva (Takva: A Man's Fear of God, 2006) today in the theaters?" a successful independent festival-tour film that has managed to sell over 350,000 tickets back in 2007 in Turkey[4]. She thinks that the film might not catch similar ticket sales today because of the new mainstream distribution conditions that systematically exclude the festival or art films in the mainstream market, or leave them with only few theater options for screening. For many films, film festivals might be the only exhibition option.

In the Turkish film industry, the financial awards of festivals might be the sole source of income for many independent filmmakers. The independent producer comments that these sources are very limited, and the film critic highlights that there are not much options for filmmakers in the current economical political system of filmmaking in Turkey other than these limited funds. Some national festivals like Adana, Ankara, Antalya, and Malatya are positioned as "fund festivals" in the minds of the producers. But it should also be kept in mind that most of these festivals require premiere screenings so that it requires a very delicate organization for producers on when to apply and which to eliminate. Furthermore, Antalya Film Festival, renown as the Cannes of Turkey, decided to cancel the national prizes, so that the monetary prize pool for national filmmakers had been drastically shrunk as of 2017. The independent producer comments that the festivals of İstanbul also have a mission to discover and highlight national films that produces a "push effect" on films in the international festival market. Unfortunately, most of the fund festivals mentioned above do not produce such an effect. The producer states:

> For instance the film Köksüz (Nobody's Home, Akçay, 2014) made its Turkey premiere in the International Istanbul Film Festival and glimmered there. Then the film had its international premiere in the Venice Film Festival. The festivals of İstanbul have such a mission, to highlight, discover and promote films in the international arena. If you don't privilege such a mission that it is a very big question mark on the success of your festival. This is a problem concerning all of the film festivals of Turkey. Other then Istanbul Film Festival, the only motivation behind applying other festivals is their monetary prizes. Istanbul Film Festival is still very prestigious. When you win the best film in Adana you receive greater amount of monetary prize but unfortunately, it has very minor impact on the international journey of your film (Independent film producer, March 2019, Personal Interview).

The film critic, who is also a cinephile and a regular festival attendant of the national film festivals, adds that some film producers have to privilege festival

4 https://boxofficeturkiye.com/film/takva-2006216. The film was watched by 349,530 spectators and made 2,490,836TL revenue.

funds because of the macroeconomical and political processes that shape the uneven distribution and promotional conditions in film industry. Özkaracalar comments that:

> It seems like such films are produced to get the awards and prizes in the festivals, and that option seems like an important dynamic in the minds of the filmmakers. I think that is totally understandable in the current macro-economical political contexts and processes. These films really have lower chances of hitting main theaters; they have relatively low promotion budgets compared to the mainstream films, and they face more problems during recovering their investments… all these serve to privilege the monetary prizes of film festivals in the minds of filmmakers. This is certainly a distorted order, but because of all such macro reasons we have such a distorted order (Kaya Özkaracalar, April 2019, Personal Interview).

Film Festivals of İstanbul

As de Valck proposes "film festivals come in many sizes and flavors" and different mechanisms and parameters might be operating within and through festivals in accordance with this differentiation (2016, p. 1–2). Likewise the globe, there are various international film festivals, thematic film days, film weeks, short film festivals, and documentary film festivals in Istanbul coming in many sizes and flavors. Some festivals provide only film screenings for a couple of days, while some provide significant finances to filmmakers to in a way support national production. In this chapter only the major and international film festivals of İstanbul are explicated. All of the film festivals make film screenings and invite international guests, but the more mainstream and major festivals, like International Istanbul Film Festival, also provide finances to filmmakers, organize prestigious prize ceremonies, and provide media coverage for both films and their events. These relatively mainstream festivals are chiefly sponsored by private corporations or supported by government funds[5]. As the festival event becomes international and bigger, many services like subtitling, press offices, industry and press screenings, facilitating networking opportunities, and providing social events require substantial funding and as a result the festivals become more dependent on a variety of stakeholders backing up the event financially (de Valck, 2016, p. 3). Therefore, in general, they might end up positioning themselves less controversial or taking less political risks in their film selections and screenings.

5 It should be kept in mind that their level of government contribution also varies drastically among the festivals.

There are also more audience-oriented film festivals in İstanbul, which thematically combine their film selections either to exhibit relatively art-house and independent films; or focusing on a certain genre like documentary (Documentarist); or to raise awareness in certain social identity–based issues, like women's festival (FilmMor), LGBT festival (KuirFest), human rights festival (Hangi İnsan Hakları Filmdays), and workers film festivals (International Labor Film Festival). These festivals are more independently funded; some are supported by certain social platforms, some find their funds from international consulates, and some are supported by Ministry of Culture on a very limited amount. These festivals are relatively more alternative festivals or rather can be called "counter-festivals," which take more political risks in their creation of film portfolio, they mostly produce their own screening spaces by themselves[6] and they are mostly self-funded and organized by volunteer efforts.

In the following section I will briefly introduce the film festivals of İstanbul, while also examining their distinct qualities, such as their relationship to funding (independent, government funded, private corporations, sponsors, etc.); their relationship to exhibition preferences (selection of films, screening theaters, etc.); and their financial and networking supports to national filmmaking industry (markets, awards, prizes, etc.) Broadly speaking, there are mainly two tendencies in film festivals of Istanbul: the ones that provide funds and networking opportunities to filmmakers, so that they support film industry in addition to film screenings; and the ones that select their films thematically to raise awareness on certain social issues. These two lines also locate the film festivals of Istanbul on a scale of more mainstream festivals to more alternative ones. There are also festivals neither politically engaged nor industry oriented, but providing only film days/weeks with special event occasions. In this article, those festivals are excluded.

Industry-Oriented Film Festivals of Istanbul

International Istanbul Film Festival (hereafter IIFF) was first presented as a film week in the summer of 1982 and evolved to an international film festival

6 Most of the independent festival organizers in the roundtable discussion stated that they had to either buy or fix technical equipment of screening theaters by themselves, or creating their own screening spaces by their own renovation efforts, they produced their screening spaces that were not film theaters before such as Ses Theater, Pera Museum, Salt Beyoğlu, Şişli Kültür Merkezi, etc.

throughout the years. In her book, Hülya Uçansu, an important figure who started up the festival and worked as the festival coordinator for 25 years, indicates that the festival was first initiated by the volunteer efforts of the Turkish Cinematheque (2012, p. 92–98), then in years it turned out to be the biggest and glamorous film event of Istanbul, inviting many international guests and screening films from A-list festivals of the world. The festival is accredited by FIAPF and acclaimed to be the internationally best-known film festival of Turkey (Akser, 2014, p. 141,150). IIFF is chiefly sponsored by various private corporations and organized by the Istanbul Foundation of Culture and Arts (IKSV) that is founded by one of the wealthiest families in Turkey, the Eczacıbaşı family.

Over the past years, the IIFF has exhibited more than 5,000 films, showcasing the cinema of over a hundred countries. The festival proposes its aim as "to encourage the development of cinema in Turkey, to help Turkish cinema attain international recognition and to promote films of quality in the Turkish market"[7]. In Turkey; Antalya, Adana, and Istanbul Film Festivals are the biggest and most popular film events and are highly directing the growth and popularity of the New Cinema (Özdüzen, 2016, p.102).

The festival has also contributed introduction of international institutions and organizations such as Eurimages to the Turkish market. In 2006, the festival decided to establish the "Meetings on the Bridge" program which is a coproduction market bringing producers, directors, scriptwriters, and representatives of institutions from Turkey and Europe together. Azize Tan, former festival director, indicates that it is a production platform for Turkish film projects to team up with possible international collaborators, and is not a market per se because the platform supports projects not only during distribution, but also during project development (Behlil, 2014, p. 159–160). Within the frame of the Meetings on the Bridge program, a Feature Film Project Development Workshop was initiated in 2008, and a Work in Progress Workshop in 2012. Furthermore, the festival provides a showcase for recent Turkish film productions, thus representing a rewarding medium. The festival draws a special interest to world classics, presenting retrospectives and curated sections. Having over 100,000 ticket sales in 2017, it is also considered the biggest film festival of Istanbul in terms of audience participation[8].

---

7 http://film.iksv.org/en/about-the-festival/history-2.

8 http://film.iksv.org/en/about-the-festival/history-2.

Numerous filmmakers, actors, and actresses visited the IIFF at its past editions[9] so the festival has relatively higher press coverage and is the most popular one among other Istanbul film events. Furthermore, the festival might be imagined to set standards for "legitimate art film" across the country. Tan underlines the fact that the cinephile audience that had been built up over the years as their greatest asset (Behlil, 2014, p. 160). Yardımcı (2007) points that symbolic communities are formed around similar forms of cultural consumption and correct ways of consuming that cultural product creates a "distinction" for those communities (p. 9). IIFF might be imagined as one of the most prestigious cultural products of Istanbul that also turns to be a symbolic capital for those owning IKSV's Tulip Cards, for cinephiles and film critics, and for local filmmakers who aim to win their prestigious awards.

The independent producer comments that IIFF is the top festival that contributes to the industry, because the festival guests significant international industry representatives and provides best opportunities for networking. Unfortunately, compared to the international festivals across the globe, IIFF is not as strong as them in terms of press coverage. The producer comments:

> It is very important for the filmmakers to have press coverage for their films and IIFF cannot create press coverage like Cannes or Berlinale even in the local level. The press coverage leverages the film's sales. International sales agents promote and distribute some films to their territories based on these criteria. Unfortunately IIFF does not have such a power to influence them as much as we would like to have. It has a certain amount of "pushing power" for the local market but there is a significant discrepancy compared to the international film festivals in terms of press coverage and leverage (Independent film producer, March 2019, Personal Interview).

---

9 Claudia Cardinale, Catherine Deneuve, Gérard Depardieu, Harvey Keitel, John Malkovich, Jeanne Moreau, Greta Scacchi, Sophia Loren, Patricia Arquette, Stephen Dorff, Barbara Sukowa, Jane Birkin, Ian McKellen, Bernardo Bertolucci, Chantal Akerman, François Ozon, Paul Schrader, Tsai Ming-liang, Park Chan-wook, Neil Jordan, Jane Campion, Alain Robbe-Grillet, Bertrand Tavernier, Carlos Saura, Nanni Moretti, Theo Angelopoulos, Paul Cox, Abbas Kiarostami, Jerry Schatzberg, Youssef Chahine, Emir Kusturica, Elia Kazan, Nikita Mikhalkov, Ken Russell, Roger Corman, István Szabó, Krzysztof Kieślowski, Nagisa Oshima, Ettore Scola, Michelangelo Antonioni, Peter Greenaway, Stephen Frears, Gus Van Sant, Alexander Sokurov, Jerzy Skolimowski, Marco Bellocchio, Klaus Maria Brandauer, Tony Gatlif, Todd Solondz, Elia Suleiman, Béla Tarr, Claire Denis, Claude Lanzmann, Leos Carax, Terence Davies, Ann Hui, Costa-Gavras, Peter Weir, Mike Figgis, Carlos Reygadas, Bille August, Marin Karmitz, Pawel Pawlikowski, Rolf De Heer, Lone Scherfig, Raoul Peck, Asghar Farhadi, and Volker Schlöndorff…http://film.iksv.org/en/about-the-festival/history-2.

Sponsors and private corporations mainly fund IIFF's festival budget. Tan underlines that IKSV foundation's nonprofit nature makes the festival a more independent one. The IIFF relies on ticket sales for 35 % of their budget (Behlil, 2014, p. 162). On the other hand, Yardımcı (2007) points to the facts that having private sponsors as the main source of budget creates an ambivalent position vis a vis the pressure to meet sponsors' needs. Because of the influence of corporate capital a pressure and a form of self-censorship might be felt in terms of selectivity and agenda setting. Yardımcı also questions the legitimacy of festival spaces as public spaces because of their relationship to funding. Any intervention in the sphere of culture is not without social implications, and this may easily turn to means to control the content of the art space since big companies may refrain risky undertakings (p. 11–12).

It would not be wrong to claim that IIFF is the main festival of Istanbul, and therefore, it also sets norms for how a festival should be. As Arslan (2014) puts it, IIFF is a "staple of the film culture in Turkey" (p. 138). It has an established brand image, and it is a well-organized, prestigious public film event. It has significant contribution to film industry by highlighting certain films, giving monetary prizes, and providing networking opportunities. The festival is also the most important film event for the audiences and the public; it sets norms for judgments of taste for legitimate art cinema while creating symbolic capital for loyal audiences. The IIFF is the closest festival to the Western standards. But the festival's relationship to funding might delimit its freedom at times of social and political crises.

Another industry-oriented film festival of İstanbul is International Boğaziçi Film Festival (BFF), which is organized by International Boğaziçi Cinema Foundation (UBSD) since 2013. The festival is relatively a new one, and compared to the other festivals of Istanbul, it receives a significant amount of funding support from the Ministry of Culture and Tourism. The festival aims at supporting national films, young talents, filmmakers and producers, and promoting the Cinema of Turkey both nationally and internationally. The festival is renowned as one of the "funding festivals" of Istanbul. BFF provides monetary prizes to the national films on best feature film, best directing, best actor, best actress, best screenplay, best cinematography, and best editing categories. The total amount of monetary prizes in the latest festival was 180.000TL, which is a very significant amount distributed among the festivals of Istanbul.

Unfortunately, compared to IIFF, the BFF does not create a vibe for audiences, nor is perceived as a big cinema event for film critics, cinephiles, or the general public. The festival screens prominent films of the year in a one-week period; and although they screen A-list festival films, the festival has not managed to create its audience yet. The independent producer underlines that selection of films is not enough on its own to be reputed as a prominent festival, since it is also very important to create a brand image for the festival in order to become a public film event. Based on her own experience of screening her own films in the BFF, the producer comments that:

> In BFF they also screen very good films like in IIFF. They both collect their showcases from A-list festivals like Cannes or Berlinale. In spite of the similarity of film selection, BFF cannot create its vibe as an event, the audience does not feel to state that 'I should not miss the Bogazici Film Festival, I have to be there.'.... as far as I've noticed only jury members are around in the Boğaziçi Film Festival, I mean there is not much opportunity to network there (Independent film producer, March 2019, Personal Interview).

Another international film festival of Istanbul is Rendezvous Istanbul International Film Festival, organized by Turkish Cinema and Audiovisual Culture Foundation since 1998. The festival is enlisted as one of the international film festivals of İstanbul by Municipality of Culture, but it cannot be claimed that it is a big film event for the city compared to the IIFF. The latest festival program includes nearly 20 films, and the latest screenings are held in only one location, French Institute Theater in Taksim. The festival is mainly organized as a cultural event and all the screenings are free of charge. Furthermore, the festival invites international guests and organizes events in addition to screenings, but they have relatively limited press coverage. The festival is organized by TURSAK (Turkish Cinema and Audiovisual Culture Foundation), an established foundation of Turkish film industry, and therefore provides a local network and meeting platform for the industry in the last instance.

As of 2016, the Rendezvous festival decided to focus on the cinema of a different country every year in order to improve cultural dialogue and economic cooperation between the focused country and Turkey. In the 2018 Rendezvous International Film Festival, France was the country in focus; and the issues connecting the two countries were discussed in the festival film screenings, panel discussions, workshops, and industry meetings. The festival also aims to promote Turkish cinema and cuisine together, and therefore organizes dinner organizations or workshops as a part of the festival.

To conclude, it would be insufficient to label the International Istanbul Film Festival as solely an industry-oriented festival, since the festival is not only one of the biggest "film event" of Istanbul but of Turkey. But when we isolate these festivals' direct contribution to the industry it might not be wrong to conclude that they are very limited on providing enough press coverage for films, on pushing international journey of films, or on supporting finances of the independent filmmakers. Furthermore, these relatively mainstream festivals mostly rely on government funds, private sponsors, and the A-list festival film screenings. Therefore, they take fewer risks while screening or supporting controversial contents and are in a way reproducing the global film culture of film festivals on the local scale.

Thematic Counter-Festivals of Istanbul

Today, the concept of "independency" in cinema not only concerns issues related to film production but also to film distribution. Festivals that act more independently from pressures of capital investors and government funding feel relatively free in their film selection criteria while facing much more problems concerning the limited number of available theater options for screenings and finances. The following film festivals of Istanbul are relatively "counter-festivals" that are mostly self-funded and voluntarily organized. These festivals produce their screening spaces on their own, select their films with critical thematic concerns, and include cinemas of the world not only outside the mainstream but also outside the main festival circuit. They in a way force the limits of the sayable and reshape the "distribution of the sensible" (Ranciere, 2004) in cinema art, while breaking the hierarchized and regularized structures of networks in film and festival industries.

International FilmMor (FilmPurple) Women's Film festival is a traveling film festival organized since 1998. The festival visits different cities of Turkey starting from İstanbul; and in 2018, the festival traveled to eight different cities of Turkey. According to the festival volunteer working in the organization committee, the number of cities visited changes according to demands because various organizations across the country invite FilmMor to their cities every year. İstanbul screenings are mostly held in the French Institute in Taksim, and occasionally more screening places are added like the small pocket theaters.

The festival's motto is "to make cinema, to contest, to produce, to dream and to act for women, together with women!" The festival envisions a life free of gender discrimination, sexism, and violence and aims to involve women in cinema, provide opportunities to express themselves via cinema and media, and make visible women's almost nonexistent representations and experiences via filmic medium. The festival organizes cinema workshops, courses and discussion panels, photography, video or design exhibitions, and conference-campaigns such as "Towards a Non-Sexist Media," "Building Gender Equality," or "Femicide is Preventable." The festival has not been financially supported by the Ministry of Culture for the past two years, and therefore takes financial support from various women's organizations. The FilmMor Festival starts at the week of 8th of March every year, and last year's focus director was Agnes Varda, whose major works had been screened for a month in many theaters.

Similarly, International Labor Film Festival is a traveling festival simultaneously organizing events across various cities of Turkey since 2006. The festival starts at 1st of May and continues for almost two weeks after. The festival screens both national and international films from various genres, such as short films, documentaries, animations, and long-feature films thematically bounded to be related to the problems that workers face through the globe. All of the screenings are free of charge, so the festival mostly relies on solidarity of volunteer labor, nonfinancial supports from municipalities, and sponsorships of labor unions.

The Labor FF coordinator indicates that their major problem is related to finding screening theaters. They rent places of municipalities for cultural activities, like Caddebostan or Baris Manco Culture Centers in Kadikoy; or they rent Pera and Yesilcam theaters and ask for major labor unions to provide the rent fees of these theaters. The festival does not have a major financial sponsor, nor delivers prizes. Since they do not sell tickets, they also do not pay royalty fees to films. The festival disregards monetary interactions as secondary, instead privileges networks and voluntary efforts in their whole organization. The film critic underlines that Labor FF might be thought as a counter-festival since the festival's film selection content and the way it is organized are alternative in the system.

Likewise, Documentarist: Istanbul Documentary Days is an independent documentary festival, which is celebrating its 12th year as of 2019. Alongside screenings of local and international documentaries, the festival also organizes workshops, lectures, presentations, and discussion sessions. The festival focuses on special topics or cinemas of regions and invites prominent honorary guests accordingly. In their program, there is a broad selection of documentaries presented from Turkey, as well as films under categories such as AnimaDocs, women, queer, and focus country documentaries selection.

Film screenings take place at Aynalı Geçit (Galatasaray), Chamber of Architects (Karaköy), French Institute (Taksim), and the Kadıköy Theatre (Kadıköy), while the side events will take place at other art centers. The festival coordinator indicates that they feel a state of "entrapment" in terms of finding theaters, resources, and finances and issues regarding censorship of films. The coordinator states:

> We always face problems of finding locations. Past five years we have only had one constant theater, the rest of them are either renovated or found from scratch. We

> transform our festival spaces ourselves, like Pera Museum or Salt Beyoğlu… Sometimes we do open air screenings. I must admit alternative places are always found, transformed when you really want (Necati Sönmez, May 2019).

The festival volunteer working for Documentarist indicates that they are an independent festival in Turkish situation since they do not rely on the main fund of Turkey, the Ministry of Culture and Tourism. Rather, they take funds from the consulates of different countries and therefore act more independently in the whole processes of the festival. For their film selection, Sönmez indicates that their mission is to dig out the films that mainstream festivals disregard.

> The task before us, I mean what is being more fruitful is, to find out the films that remain in the shadows of the world, remain outside mainstream festival exhibitions. We are very proud to introduce films and directors unknown to Turkish audience. I think this is our strength while competing with international mainstream festivals like ITFA-International Documentary Film Festival Amsterdam (Necati Sönmez, May 2019).

Concluding Remarks

İstanbul has the potential to articulate to the global capital and become a cosmopolitan global city (Yardımcı, 2005, p.45), but the film festivals of Istanbul seem to have significant problems. In Istanbul, there are two lines of film festivals: the ones that contribute more to national film production and those that focus more on audience participation. IIFF combines these both lines with its established brand image, ticket sales, and network opportunities for national filmmakers together with international producers. Istanbul Film festival has an established brand image in Western standards. Whereas Boğazici FF is more like the "fund festival" of İstanbul and is relatively under-established as a cultural event. Anyhow, these festivals provide significant contributions to national cinema industry with their monetary prizes, prestigious awards, press coverage, production workshops, and market networks. In the Turkish condition, because the Ministry of Culture funds are the sole source of production money for independent filmmakers who do not have certain amount of budget in advance, the festival awards and supports might be seen as very critical for their films' return of investment. Unfortunately, as the film critic underlines, these awards are like "vitamin tablets" that are very crucial yet insufficient to solve the major financial problems of the industry.

Furthermore, as the independent producer highlights, the film festival is more than prizes, awards, or film screenings. This phenomenon also includes dynamics related to networks, established relations, strong brand image, and diplomatic skills. Unfortunately, the festivals whose managing board and organizers change quickly have a very fickle structure and lack providing long-term relations to the industry. This also limits their pushing power to introduce national films to the global festival circuits.

In the film festival flora of Istanbul, major problems of counter-festivals are related to the limited number of exhibition options, finances, and political pressures on film selection. In order to overcome such matters, these more independently funded festivals of İstanbul produce their own screening spaces and rely on volunteer labor to decrease their costs. With this way, they are freer to screen controversial films and political content, reshaping the distribution of the sensible and limits to the sayable in film history. Unfortunately, these independent festivals are not industry-oriented and therefore relatively disconnected to the problems of independent filmmakers of Turkey.

Special thanks to Emine Yıldırım, Necati Sönmez, and Assoc. Prof. Kaya Özkaracalar for their insightful commentaries about film festivals of Istanbul.

References

Akser, M. (2014). Turkish film festivals: Political populism, rival programming and imploding activities. In D. Iordanova & S. Van de Peer (Eds.), *Film Festival Yearbook 6: Film Festivals and the Middle East* (pp. 141–155). St. Andrews: St Andrews Film Studies.

Andrew, D. (2010). Foreword. In R. Galt & K. Schoonover (Eds.), *Global Art Cinema: New Theories and Histories* (pp. v–xviii). New York: Oxford University Press.

Arslan, S. (2014). A glimpse at the history of film: Festivals and competitions in Turkey. In D. Iordanova & S. Van de Peer (Eds.), *Film Festival Yearbook 6: Film Festivals and the Middle East* (pp. 134–139). St. Andrews: St Andrews Film Studies.

Behlil, M. (2014). Meeting on the bridge: An Interview with Azize Tan, Director of the International Istanbul Film Festival. In D. Iordanova & S. Van de Peer (Eds.), *Film Festival Yearbook 6: Film Festivals and the Middle East* (pp. 157–165). St. Andrews: St Andrews Film Studies.

De Valck, M. (2016). Introduction: What is a film festival? How to study festivals and why you should. In M. de Valck, B. Krodel, and S. Loist (Eds.), *Film Festivals: History, Theory, Method, Practice* (pp. 1–13). New York: Routledge.

Elsaesser, T. (2005). *European Cinema: Face to Face with Hollywood.* Amsterdam: Amsterdam University Press.

Iordanova, D. (2002). Feature filmmaking within the new Europe: Moving funds and images across the East-West Divide. *Media Culture and Society Journal, 24*, 517–536.

Iordanova, D. (2015). The film festival as an industry node. *Media Industries Journal*, *1*(3), 7–11.

Iordanova, D. (2016). Foreword: The film festival and film culture's transnational essence. In M. de Valck, B. Krodel, & S. Loist (Eds.), *Film Festivals: History, Theory, Method, Practice* (pp. viii–xviii). New York: Routledge.

Loist, S. (2016). The film festival circuit. In M. de Valck, B. Krodel, & S. Loist (Eds.), *Film Festivals: History, Theory, Method, Practice* (pp.49–64). New York: Routledge.

Özdüzen Ateşman, Ö. (2016*). Film festivals and social movements intertwined*, (Doctoal Dissertation). Edge Hill University, Department of Media, Lancashire, United Kingdom.

Ranciere, J. (2004). *The Politics of Aesthetics: The Distribution of the Sensible*. G. Rockhill (Trans. and Ed.). New York, London: Continuum.

Stringer, J. (2001). Global cities and the international film festival economy. In M. Shiel & T. Fitzmaurice (Eds.), *Cinema and the City: Film and Urban Societies in a Global Context* (pp. 134–145). Oxford: Blackwell Publishers.

Uçansu, H. (2012). *Bir uzun mesafe festivalcisinin anıları: Sinema Günleri'nden İstanbul Film Festivali'ne*. İstanbul: Doğan Egmont Yayıncılık.

Yardımcı, S. (2005). *Kentsel değişim ve festivalizm: Küreselleşen İstanbul'da bienal*. İstanbul: İletişim Yayınları.

Yardımcı, S. (2007). *Festivalising Difference: Privatization of Culture and Symbolic Exclusion in İstanbul, EUI Working Papers*, European University Institute, Italy.

Nilay Ulusoy

Chapter 7 The Universe of Fashion Film in Turkey

Introduction

Millennium, which was filmed to promote Rıfat Özbek's collection at the winter-fall 1990 London Fashion Weekend by John Maybury, gave an idea about how the "latest fashion clothes" could be advertised to the MTV Generation prior to the fast fashion and global luxury age (Rees-Roberts, 2019, p. 6–7). With its choreography resembling Neneh Cherry's hit song *Buffalo Stance*'s video clip in 1988, models did catwalk with Özbek's designs for 20 minutes to music in front of a background that displayed fast-flowing kaleidoscopic colored designs. Although Rifat Özbek, who was born in Istanbul and became famous with his style in the 1980s and 1990s which was described by the British Fashion Council as "East meets West aesthetic," has steered towards home textile, he has been the messenger of a new change which influenced the advertisement industry as well.

"Wearable works of art," which is a creative and developing power in cultural production, or the mediation of clothes, has gone through changes with the developing social networking platforms. In the past 30 years or so, fashion weekends became international fashion shows which transformed into fashion weeks organized based on a specific calendar each year. Fashion films transcended being the backdrops of fashion shows and became the most basic pieces of each brand's season presentations. Fashion, which in commercial terms is an area in which advertising and branding are intertwined through cultural and artistic creativity, started existing in the digital world as well through a new narration form in which different areas and narrations became hybrid (Skjulstad, Morrison, 2016, p. 32). With the rise of Vimeo (2004) and YouTube (2005) and similar video-sharing platforms and the easy and fast sharing opportunity for low-budget short films and the speeding up of digital data transmission, online video communication caused fashion films or fashion clips to become a developing medium (Cope, Maloney, 2016, p. 117–121). Nathalie Khan (2012, p. 236) states that the fashion representation of fashion films developed by the Internet as an independent genre made fashion houses to get small production companies or famous film directors to shoot short fashion films starting with the 2010s. Besides the short video-sharing platforms mentioned above, fashion houses which established communication with the Gen-Z and Millennials generation on other social networks such as Facebook, Instagram, and Twitter, through innovative online content, left traditional campaigns behind and started presenting their new season clothes and accessories as a part of a greater story ("Top 10 Fashion Films of the Season", 2017).

According to Uhlirova, in a period in which the number of fashion shows decreased with the exception of fashion weeks, brands and designers began to allocate greater budgets to fashion films through fashion film festivals that started to be organized in numerous cities around the world other than the new media they use to reflect and promote their collections (2012, 151–152). In particular, starting with 2008, fashion writer Diane Pernet changed the name of her fashion film festival from "You Wear it Well," which she organized in 2006 for the first time, to "A Shaded View on Fashion Film" (ASVOFF) in 2008 with the boom experienced in the production of fashion films, and started organizing it at the Centre de Pompidou in Paris. After the efforts spent by Pernet, the popularity and commercial success of fashion films were proven with the fashion film festivals, which started to be organized in London, New York, Berlin, and San Diego (Cope, Maloney, 2016, p. 134).

After two small organizations held under the title Fashion Film Vol. 1–2 in parallel to Istanbul Fashion Week organized in Istanbul in 2012, there is a competition in which the best national and international film is selected each year as well, besides design works, art videos, and fashion documentary screenings within the scope of the Istanbul Fashion Film Festival, which started to be organized as an international festival starting from 2015 (fffistanbul, n.d.). In the festival, four films by Turkish directors in 2015–2018 were selected as the best Turkish fashion film each year. Fashion films comprises different types of films; it can be understood as short films inspired by the fashion universe with a strong focus on aesthetics; it can be apprehended as documentaries about fashion, art video recordings, comedy sketches, etc. It can have narrative or nonnarrative storylines, be inspirational or focused on self-derision, or have codes from film genres or video clips.

Fashion films as a critical tool help us to understand the fashion industry, what fashion represents, fashion culture, and fashion economy. It allows us to comment on fashion over animated pictures as tools which take fashion communication a step further beyond the definition of clothes (Rees-Roberts, 2018, p. 13). Therefore, certain aesthetic and cinematic preferences and characteristics of these four award-winning films shot for Turkish designers or Turkish brand and their common points and differences will be dealt with. Thus, it will be attempted to determine how fashion films, which are a fictional world in which film and clothes design concepts are formed, create the experience of fashion. In this manner, the answer to the question "What are the main functions and characteristics of Turkish fashion films?" determined as the main problem will be sought in the study. This article, which will attempt to identify how this hybrid and functional form, is reflected in the Turkish fashion world through the descriptive and qualitative study of the main features of the Turkish fashion films.

What Is a "Good Fashion Film"?

According to the founder of ASVOFF Diane Pernet, a "good" fashion film is firstly a film in which fashion is the leading actor. Fashion in nature affects people deeply in a short time but it is fleeting as well. Therefore, fashion films should carry these characteristics of fashion which create a sudden effect and are short. These short films which last from 30 seconds to 5 minutes are produced with the purpose of being shown in social media platforms and shared by people. In short, fashion films are completely commercial films which have specific objectives and criteria (Cope, Maloney, 2016, p. 134–135). From an aesthetic approach, fashion films are connected to what is currently identified as a "new media" genre. It is hybrid media where image and sound are used in order to intensify the sensorial experience, exploring synesthetic properties in film reception. According to Nathalie Khan (2012, p. 236–238), fashion films which transcend the forms of traditional fashion media and present "the latest fashion" with glittering representations are "digital animated images," which present a multisensory multimedia experience and inform the viewers about the creative process behind collections. Fashion films, which progressed, developed, and got popular with this "digital transformation," experienced by the fashion industry starting from the beginning of the 2000s, reflect and spread the spirit of the times through the clothes they present within a narration. With the permanent presence of digital cinema, fashion images can always remain new and belonging to the how and here. Thus, they are able to adapt to the sensitivities of the present time.

In the light of technological developments, the spreading of different content produced by the fashion world to the whole world in a simultaneous manner has allowed the current fashion system to create its own representation opportunities developing from the mass media system of the 19th and 20th centuries. The relationship between clothes and fiction in historical terms, or the mediation of wearable designs as fashion by animated pictures, goes back to the silent film period. The presentation of the clothes worn on the body, texture of the fabrics, their motions through the movement of the human body in a performative manner and by adding an experimental richness, the presentation of the concept and spirit of the wearable design is pragmatic work. It is a performance about brands and designers transmitting not only their clothes but also their universe through a story, about the social and cultural harmony of identity and taste. The viewers' understanding and desiring clothes in this manner is possible through "the fictionalizing of fashion." In brief, fiction makes fashion possible and makes it as something "experienced" transcending imagining (Wang & Juhlin, 2017, p. 2–3). In particular through online communities and sharing channels, the freedom for everyone to watch fashion shows from the front row has created the need to position the clothes, designs, designers, brand, and the viewers differently in fashion films. In the process of marketing in the new media area in which the differences between art and commerce, popular culture and public culture get blurred, the media sphere is more fragmented and consumer interest becomes more precious. Fashion films with the perception of branding as narrative prefer to tell a story rather than selling clothes (Khamis, Munt, 2010).

The production of fashion films is a part of the bargain between art and fashion. While fashion has the temporariness determined by popular culture, it contradicts with the timelessness and elitism of fine art. These two characteristics present us with a dilemma which defines the form of fashion films (Skjulstad & Morrison, p. 36). However, this dichotomy of fashion film dematerializes products and sets them apart from their physical characteristics; but paradoxically, fashion products can also become a real and subjective element with their own life and personality (Saloaga & Guerrero, p. 50). According to Nick Rees-Roberts (2018, p. 1–4) beginning with the 2000s, online image sharing culture in media platforms has carried fashion, which is a concept which unites commerce and culture to the popular branch of entertainment industry from an activity which appeals only to the fashion world. In short, fashion trends were born within a small group which had a sense of fashion and were carried to the streets. When Street fashion replaced fashion shows and created fiction films, biopics, television series, investigation reports, behind-the-scenes documentaries and other journalistic formats on fashion, and a fashion-literate online and offline public; fashion has its place in popular culture both as material object and digital image.

When fashion films appear as a hybrid form between short films, digital media products, and advertisement films; they were categorized within themselves as well. According to Mijovic (2013, p. 183), there are three types of fashion films: "nonnarrative" fashion films are those that are a sort of magazine editorials with movement; the "conventional narrative" type focused on fashion as an aspirational symbol; and the "organic narrative" type, where clothing is the center of the plot and the features and movements of the garments are essential. In nonnarrative and organic fashion films, there is narration and serialization as well. In some fashion films, while a good story grabs the interest of the viewers, the visual and auditory narration style of the story in another film allows the viewer to connect with the film and thus the brand, designer, and the clothes.

Cope and Maloney (2016, p. 122–127) deal with fashion films under three headings. Moving Look Book form which came to the fore in 2000–2005 was created for fashion brands to publish their collections with a soundtrack. These are in general moving catalogues in which they try to present the attitude of the collections of the commercially limited brands. Moving Editorial film aims at presenting clothes in a visually attractive manner with its printed fashion editorials in the same promotional scope. Creative film is the most eccentric type of fashion films, and they are the practice that most accurately present fashion films. Creative film, which has become the most important type in today's fashion world, is more artistically approached; is largely driven by narrative and storyline; or reflects a brand's ethos or mood through nuance or visual symbolism and representation. With all the suggested types of film previously mentioned, the context of the film's purpose is important to consider. How fashion film places creation and clothes in the narration of the film is an important Notion in terms of categorizing fashion film. According to this, while in "fashion as character" films viewers are a "commercial product"; in "fashion as action" films, fashion is narrated rather in a hidden manner within the story but it is there as a nuance. In "fashion as character" films, the products are framed by the designer or brand in the manner they are desired and a direct marketing is in question. In "fashion as action" films, the creative image is desired to be presented in a creative manner by the brand or designer through a more abstract narration rather than the products. Thus, viewers have a perception of the ethos of the brand.

Surely, all categorizations mentioned above always embody exceptional varieties as generalizations; however, the common point in all of them is to make the promotion of brands and collections memorable and crucially shareable. The aim is to identify what kind of a direction films follow by looking for answers to certain questions. While these answers are being sought to these questions, films are analyzed with a neo-formalist approach; and thus it will be attempted to identify how clothes are positioned within the narrations of films. These questions are:

Where was the film shot, and in what kind of an atmosphere and setting does it take place?
Who are the characters of the film?
What are the references or the inspirations of the film?
What is the purpose of the film or the ethos of the designs; how does this overlap with the film's atmosphere and narration?

A Short Look to the Best Turkish Fashion Film

As stated in the introduction part, the four films selected as the best Turkish Film[1] in the Istanbul International Film Festival successively are 2015 *Good Morning, Pallas Athena* by Emir Eralp for NOWNESS[2]; 2016 *Three Apostles* by Koray Birand for Zeynep Tosun; 2017 *The Universe* by Daghan Celayir for Que; and 2018 *Choke* by Omer Can Duman for Birelin. Firstly, the main common characteristics of these films at first glance seem to be that they were shot by Turkish directors for the collections of Turkish brands or designers. The only exception is Emir Eralp's film *Pallas Athena*. The three of the six pieces used in the film belong to a Turkish brand: Swimwear by Oye Swimwear, and the skirt and the blouse belong to Dice Kayek.

Emir Eralp, 2015's best film *Good Morning, Pallas Athena*'s director, has a background in the area of photography[3]. The film begins with the general plan shots in which moving clouds are seen, and then the camera shows a calm sea in which there is a small island. With the great depth of field given from the shore where the waves quietly crash, a male voiceover indicates the geographic location of the setting we see by saying, "Good morning clouds, good morning sun, good morning bright, blue, Aegean Sea" and makes it possible for the viewer to connect with the environment. Then, the voiceover[4] continues: "Good

---

1 While the best Turkish Films in the Istanbul International Film Festival were selected in 2015, 2016, and 2017 by *Elle* Turkey Magazine, which is one of the sponsors of the festival as "Elle's Choice," the film selected in 2018 was awarded as "The Best Turkish Film" (fffistanbul, n.d.).

2 Nowness is a video channel premiering the best in global arts and culture across Art and Design, Culture, Fashion and Beauty, Music, and Food and Travel (Nowness, n.d.).

3 Prior to the 1990s, in the periods in which attending fashion shows was a priority, the photographs of fashion shows were edited and shared in newspapers and magazines. Fashion films made it possible for designers to present the collection to the viewers with the curator point of view (Cope, Maloney, 118). Many fashion photographers have gone behind the camera to make music videos or to do shoots. The advent of the Internet changed things drastically. Nick Knight was the first to realize the web's potential; and in 2000, he launched showstudio.com, reinventing fashion images and the way people perceive them, giving life to a new genre, the fashion film (goodshortfilms.it, n.d.). Diane Pernet explains the reason why fashion photographers become leading directors of fashion films as being steered towards shooting films by the agencies they worked when she initiated ASVOFF (mortimerhouse.com, 2017).

4 Bordwell and Thompson (2008, p. 92) state that in films in which there is voice-over by a person who is not in the story, this noncharacter narrator adds objectivity and realism to the narration of the film.

morning, Pallas Athena[5]," and the scene reflects the sleeping young woman's face with a close-up shot whom we understand is the character Pallas Athena who gave the film its name; and identification begins with the protagonist. The film, which depicts the Greek goddess Pallas Athena all alone during the hot summer season and in nature in the Aegean Region, makes a reference with its name and the setting to Greek mythology. In the rest of the film, daily routine of Pallas Athena is visually presented to us with the accompaniment of the voiceover, which includes her waking up, brushing her hair, doing morning sports with gymnastics and swimming, having breakfast, resting while drawing, and preparing for war. In all of these stages, Pallas Athena wears different outfits which are references to Antique Greek costumes, and her whole body is shown with a wide shot within the setting Athena is in and as close-up. The film is black and white. In most black-and-white films, light costumes or brightly lit faces stand out while darker areas tend to recede. If there are several light shapes in the frame, audience will tend to look from one to the other. But if the background is light, black elements will become prominent (Bordwell, Thompson, 2008, 144). In the scenes in which Pallas Athena is wearing her dark-colored evening gown, her gymnastics shorts and blouse, and swimsuits, the background is set in light colors with the sky, bare forest, and thin tree branches; and in the scenes in which she wakes up with a bright sateen nightgown, the stone walls of the antique city are shown in darker colors. Particularly in the close-up scenes, we see that she touches the clothes. Borrowing from Laura Mark's study, Gary Needham refers to the "haptic" aesthetic of fashion films, where cinematic conventions like close-up and slow motion combine with diegetic and non-diegetic sound editing to deliver the impression of materiality (2013:108). In the closing scene of the film, Pallas Athena is wearing a one-shouldered and light-colored blouse and a dark-colored mini skirt which are Dice Kayek designs, which is a Turkish design brand. She has gladiator sandals on her feet. She puts on her helmet and girds herself with a sword (Fig. 7.1). While she walks towards the forest to find her enemies, the voiceover shouts: "Good luck, Pallas Athena." In the film in which various brands and collections of designers were presented, the clothes she wears in her depiction as the war goddess Athena who is also the goddess of strategy, intelligence, peace and the olive tree (Can, 1994, 48) display in a parallel narration with the garments which she wears while doing casual activities like sport,

5 Pallas Athena is the name Athena assumed after she killed her stepsister named Pallas and to remember her evil side. It also reflects the warrior side of the goddess. On the other hand, her name was given to the Athens city by the city people when she gave them the gift of olive tree (Can, 1994, p. 47).

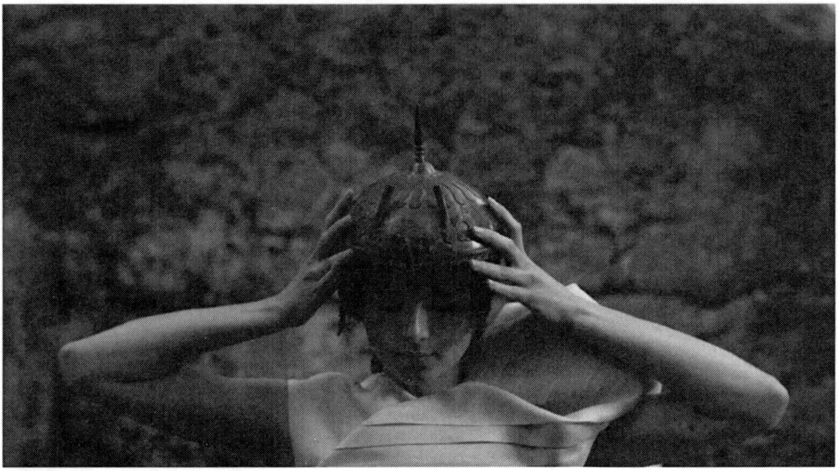

Fig. 7.1: Pallas Athena is wearing her helmet and she has Dice Kayek's one-shouldered blouse. Courtesy of Emir Eralp

swim, cook, paint. The light-colored sateen nightgown she wears while sleeping with a patterned skirt, the cotton shorts and t-shirt she wears while doing sports, the halter neck black mini dress she wears while painting and having a meal, and lastly the matching blouse and skirt, which brings her body to the fore to display the will and power in that graceful body, allow the viewers to witness that her character embodies all contrasting elements.

The best Turkish film of 2016 *Three Apostles*[6] by the fashion photographer Koray Birand for designer Zeynep Tosun's designs was shot in Kars which is located in the Far East of Turkey at the Armenia border. On the horse-drawn carriage that is shown through a bird's eye view through a drone shot, in the middle of a rocky field with mountains in the backdrop, there are three women[7] lying on pillows and fabrics with flower designs. In the scene where women are

6 Apostle means the first prominent Christian missionary to a region or group (https://www.merriam-webster.com/dictionary/apostle, n.d.).

7 Zeynep Tosun states in her Internet site that her designs reflect that women need to share their talents, desires, and stories with other women to support each other (https://zeyneptosun.com/, n.d.). It seems that the three disciples depicted as women wearing clothes which are different from each other but enliven and support each other and the environment they are in is in line with the ideas Zeynep Tosun has based her collections on.

shown from a high angle, the only other apparent thing is their naked legs; and the three of them are lying in the utero position. Thompson and Bordwell (2008, p. 190–191) state that the high-angle positions allow us to look down at the material within the frame. In this framed position, the main colors and sources of inspiration of the collection are presented to the viewers with the exception of the leading actor of the film. Montage sequences usually lack dialogue; they tend to come wrapped in music. In the background, Armand Amar's song *Home Part I*, whose rhythm is set by a woman's voice, starts playing. The three models are presented from time to time with long shots. In the long shot, figures are more prominent, but the background still dominates. The three main characters are shown again in the setting that is the source of inspiration for the collection; their appearance is one with the setting. Then, the camera introduces the characters to the viewers with a medium close-up shot. The first character is a Far Eastern young woman with beaded earrings looking at the camera, whose short black hair is prominent. The second model is a brunette who looks at the camera in the same manner. The third model who is a red-haired young woman is shown as embracing a peasant woman with her right arm. They are both looking at the camera with pride. The camera then presents their clothes with a medium shot slowly going up from their waist level with a tilt. The medium shot frames the human body from the waist up. Gesture and expression now become more visible. The medium close-up frames the body from the chest up. It emphasizes facial expression, the details of a gesture, or a significant object (2008, p. 183). The peasant woman is wearing a red patterned yemeni, and the red-haired young woman is wearing a red and flower-patterned dress. She has a bead necklace on her neck, and the two women are wearing a woolly shawl together. Although they do not look similar in appearance, they complete each other and the setting they are in. While the three characters are walking on a pebbled road with different dresses from the collection or riding the carriage pulled by horses which are ornamented with beads, they are shown in slow motion and with medium shots again The shaky camera provide a sense of dynamics, discomfort to the scene. On the other hand slow motion utilized in the same scene helps to tell the story of their visit while also communicating the feel of the travel on horse-drawn carriage.

Framing is mostly done to cut the foreheads of the models in the middle. The purpose is to direct the viewers' attention to the clothes. The models and thus the clothes are centered directly in the frame with a selected focus, where the background/setting is blurred; and the clothes which look bright and lively are brought to the fore for the viewers. More common than such near-perfect symmetry is a loose balancing of the shot's left and right regions. The simplest

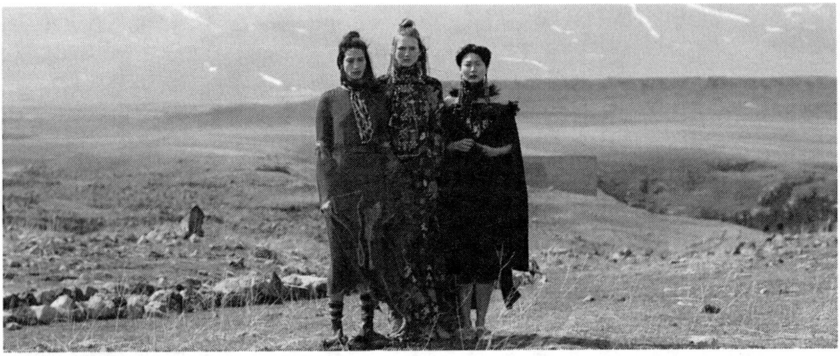

Fig. 7.2: Apostles with their garments with Central Asian patterns at the Kars plateau. Courtesy of Koray Birand

way to achieve compositional balance is to center the frame on the human body. Filmmakers often place a single figure at the center of the frame and minimize distracting elements at the sides. Many of earlier illustrations display this flexible balance. Other shots may counterweight two or more elements, encouraging audience's eye to move back and forth (2008, p. 143). On the last scene, the three apostles get further away on the carriage, while their colors slowly fade and they get blurred and lost within the background. Thus, while the three apostles sent by God are leaving Kars to go to another geography as the "missionaries of fashion" for the sake of duty, they mixed with nature in the highest plains of the Anatolian Peninsula (Fig. 7.2).

The best Turkish fashion film of 2017 by Dağhan Celayir was *The Universe* that was shot for the brand Que, which aims at appealing to a young consumer group with a high price segment and belongs to one of the oldest textile companies in Turkey, the Boyner group. In the opening scene, the camera follows a woman who is slowly walking towards the light in an empty scape which resembles a warehouse from the behind. The woman is wearing a light coat with a hood and high heeled shoes; the sound of the heels echo in the warehouse. The camera which does a close-up to the high heels whose sound we hear in the long shot brings the attention back to the footsteps. The camera does a 360-degree turn around the woman and we hear the ringing of a phone in the background while the camera is introducing the woman to us While the camera shows us the posters of the Que hanging on the walls, we climb the stairs and see the male character. Both are looking for each other in an abandoned building among

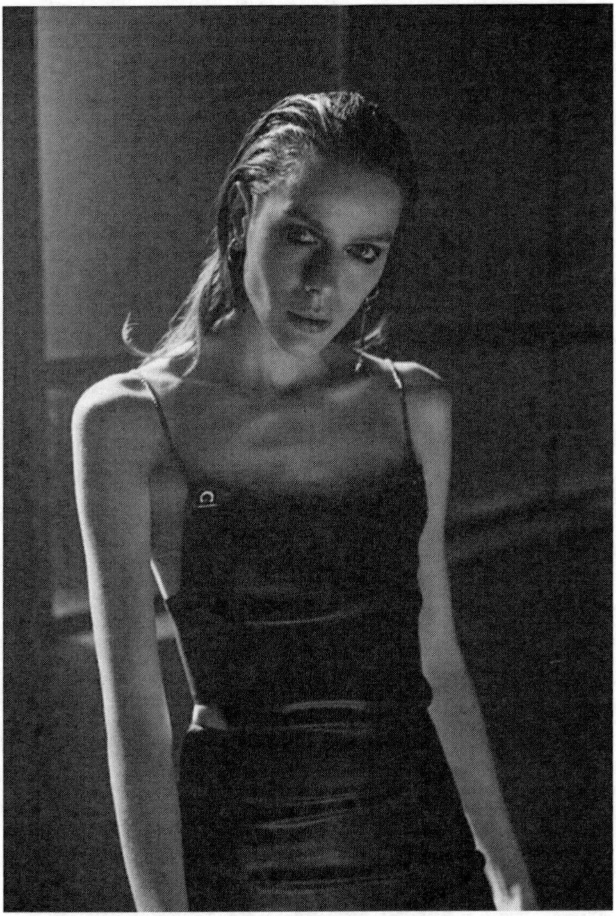

Fig. 7.3: *The Universe* (Dağhan Celayir, 2017), the couple who are looking for each with a film noir aesthetic in a desolate building within dummies who have similar outfits on, at an unknown time and setting. Courtesy of Dağhan Celayir

dummies who have similar clothes on. Dummies in general appear in films with a film noir aesthetic with detective and thriller stories with low-key lighting and a somber mood and indicate mystery and danger. Similarly, the color blue indicates the feeling of uncertainty (Thompson & Bordwell, 2008, p. 130–131) (Fig. 7.3). The male character turns on the record player and we start listening to what Alan Watts[8] has said on the universe as voice over. The female character who is listening to the text starting with the words "The real deep down you is the whole universe, you were a big bang" suddenly looks at the camera and comes eye to eye with the viewer.

As with other film techniques, sound guides the viewer's attention. Dialogue, as a transmitter of story information, is usually recorded and reproduced for maximum clarity. Important lines should not have to compete with music or background noise. Music is usually subordinate to dialogue, entering during pauses in conversation or effects. The task of music in film is to create a regular rhythm and to compress a series of actions into a shorter time frame (2008, 250). Then, the two characters pose for the camera in a photography studio prepared in the warehouse with various outfits accompanied with electronic music and follow the instructions of a female voiceover for the poses. The footage of the poses they give with the clothes, the earth, and the universe is presented through fast montaging. In the scenes, which are also presented through crosscutting editing (2008, p. 477) narrating events that took place in different settings, it is underlined that these simple but nonuniform clothes made up of Lycra fabric and leather with a combination of white, black, and silver colors are timeless and placeless designs that belong to the present time and the future and to any setting and environment. Although the gray color used in the clothes and the whole setting create an inhuman effect, the timelessness of the clothes is underlined again with Alan Watts' words on the immortality of the human soul (Fig. 7.4).

Ömer Can Duman's *Choke*, 2018's best Turkish film, with the motto "affordable luxury" (https://birelin.com.tr/en/birelinin-hikayesi-2/ https://birelin.com.tr/en/n.d.) for the Birelin brand makes use of two different color palettes which turn from blue to red. In the film, which begins with a camera movement moving away from a light blue–colored door, we see a deserted school building. The model who is wearing a white-collared blue dress, which resembles a primary school uniform, climbs the wooden stairs and takes out a sewing machine from her bag. Thus, the story consisting of three parts begins. In the first part titled "Hope," we see the female character who is sewing and wearing ruffled outfits made of flowing fabrics from black to white. She is desperately calling someone from an old telephone. In the second part titled "Joy," two women with the white-collared blue dress seen in the first part are playing among classroom

8 Alan Watts (1915–1973) was an English expert on comparative religion, a writer, and a philosopher. Watts, who introduced the Far Eastern religions to the Western culture and thus deeply influenced the Beat Generation, has preserved some of his work as voice recordings prior to his death.

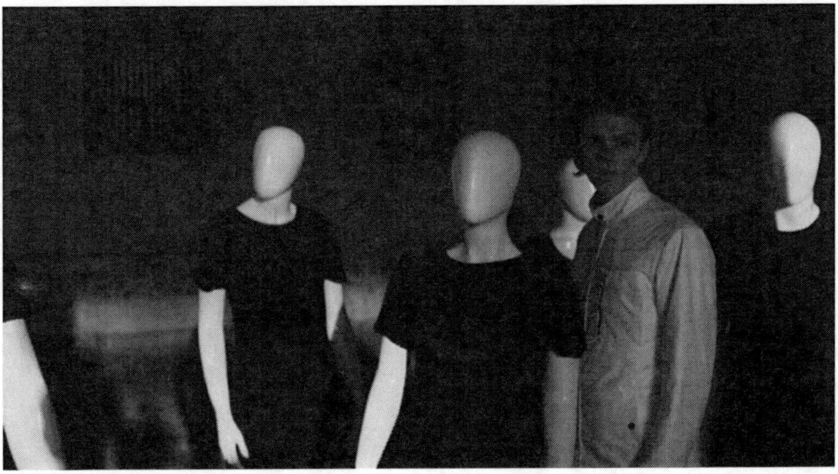

Fig. 7.4: *The Universe* (Dağhan Celayir, 2017). Courtesy of Dağhan Celayir

chairs. Then, we see them running in the garden with their white pantsuits with striped collars and cuffs which resemble sailor uniforms. According to Bordwell and Thompson (2008, p. 181–182), with point-of-view shots, we see the world as the hero imagines it to be, and they are very powerful. In the following scene, we hear the echo of children screams. Visual or auditory point of view offers a degree of subjectivity, mental subjectivity. In the third part titled "Passion," the female model with a blue, thin-strapped blouse and a white skirt having a meal on her own is shown in a relatively lighter setting compared to the rest of the film. She looks cheerful, and both the orange-colored drink in her large cocktail glass and the red rose petals she sprinkles on her meal add a warm color to the cool color palette of the film for the first time. When lightness values are equal, warm colors in the red-orange-yellow range tend to attract attention, while cool colors like purple and green are less prominent (Bordwell, Thompson, 2008, p. 144). In the narration that consists of three steps progressing from hope to cheerfulness, the story which begins with a cool color palette livens up when the red and orange colors appear as details, giving rise to emotional variety within the story. In addition, speed of motion in these three parts displays differences. While the Hope and Passion parts are presented with speed motion, the Joy part is presented with slow motion. In the film, montaging and real-time flow is changed on purpose, and real time is suspended. In particular, the hero's stress is reflected in the Hope and Passion parts with a fast plot. Its motion is shaped

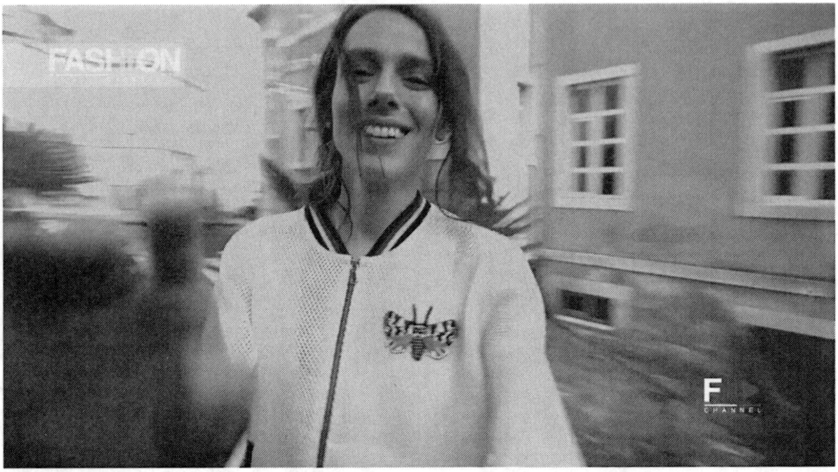

Fig. 7.5: *Choke* for Birelin (Ömer Can Duman, 2018). In the part titled "Joy," in which school memories of childhood and adolescence are remembered, the two characters follow one another with the point of view in slow motion. Courtesy of Ömer Can Duman

based on the location and the clothes worn and the emotion desired to be transmitted to the viewers. In the film, the speed of the scenes or the three parts in question are determined according to one of the character's wish to sew and speed. According to Khan (2012, p. 242–243), cutting is intrinsic to fashion, and the process of the outfit being shaped and created on the body also changes our perception of the body. The montaging of movement in the film and the arrangement of the timing within the frame allows the subject of the movement, the body in the fashion film, and the outfit which completes the body to be presented to the viewers in a new unity. It is required to present this object which creates the movement of unity of the outfit to be presented by underlining its superiority without removing it from its natural environment. The texture the flowing, creasing, and falling clothes in line with the bodies of the characters which move in both slow motion and speed motion scenes gains great importance in the film. Thus, as indicated in the website of the brand, the characters in the film are "experiencing the transition of emotions to achieve simplicity, its once again the Birelin woman; the interpreter of different multilayered emotions" and are able to reflect the moods reciprocally with the clothes they are wearing and the changes created with these moods (https://birelin.com.tr/en/ (Fig. 7.5).

Conclusion

> *"What makes a good fashion film is what makes any good film"*
>
> *Diane Pernet*

In filmic narration, costume can have specific functions in the total film. Costumes may be quite stylized, calling attention to their purely graphic qualities. By integrating with setting, costume may function to reinforce narrative and thematic patterns (Bordwell, Thompson, 2008, p. 123–124). In fashion films, clothes visualize the universe in which the design, production, and usage process of clothes have the leading role as performance related to the social and cultural harmony of identity and tastes besides supporting the story. The fashion film portrays a garment within style and performs the fiction (Wang, Juhlin, 2017, p. 3). Shorts films that promote fashion garments through audiovisual narrative set in place a universe that demands the viewer's investment in the fiction, bringing it to life through the literal embodiment of its elements.

In the case studies Marketa Uhlirova analyzes in her work on fashion films, a "synergy" forms between film effect and fashion effect, whereby sensorial persuasion and illusion address the viewer as both spectator and potential buyer (2013, p. 122). The phenomenological state thus achieved is analogous to the spectatorial pleasures associated with the cinema of attraction, based on the simultaneous experience of defamiliarization and the acquisition of new knowledge. Fashion film "extend[s] the properties of physical garments into new mental spaces where experimental effects of impressionistic and poetic cinema play a significant role – as do the qualities of sound and rhythm," she proposes (2013, p. 123).

Other than the narrative characteristics of the four films, their presentation of the clothes which they put at the center of the story are "organic fashion" films according to Mijovic in categorization and belong to the "fashion as action" category among the creative fashion films according to Cope and Maloney. In all four films, value transmission was realized with the help of the stories while the brands or the creative universe of the designers were being introduced. With the exception of the use of voiceover in *Pallas Athena* and *The Universe*, no dialogues were given in any of the films. In order to reflect the design universe, the use of music and sound effects in the films is noteworthy. In all the films, it has been underlined that fashion is a pragmatic work, it has both artistic and functional side.

Hence, four fashion films oscillate between narrative closure and the emphasizing of the pleasure of wearing, touching, or buying the garments displayed on screen. Indeed, movies promote the imaginative act of coming in contact with the material referents of the filmed objects as well as with the extended narrative universe that spectators see in the four movies. Another principle is that the four movies exemplify a genre of productions that exploit the style and persuasive power of costume in movement, along with the editing and narrative conventions of mainstream cinema, to redefine our understanding of commercial promotion and artistic practice.

References

Apostle. Retrieved from https://www.merriam-webster.com/dictionary/apostle. Retrieval date: 01.05.2019.

Bordwell, D., & Thompson, K. (2008), *Film art: An introduction*. Boston: McGraw Hill.

Can, Ş. (1994), *Klasik yunan mitolojisi*. Istanbul: Inkılap.

Cope, J., & Maloney, D. (2016), *Fashion promotion in practice*, London, New York: Fairchild Book, Bloomsbury.

Diane Pernet:Ffashion on film and the true meaning of style. (n.d.). Retrieved from https://www.mortimerhouse.com/notebook/article/diane-pernet/

ffistanbul, (n.d.), Retrieved from http://www.fashionfilmistanbul.com/. retrieval date: 01.02. 2019.

Khamis, S., & Munt, A. (2010). The three Cs of fashion media today: Convergence, creativity and control. *Scan Journal*, 8(2), 1–15

Khan, N. (2012). Cutting the fashion body: Why the fashion image is no longer still. *Fashion Theory*, *16*(2), 235–250.

Mijovic, N. (2013). Narrative form and the rhetoric of fashion in the promotional fashion film. *Film, Fashion and Consumption*, *2*(2), 175–186.

Needham, G. (2013). The digital fashion film. In S. Bruzzi & P. C. Gibson (Eds.), *Fashion Cultures Revisited: Theories, Explorations and Analysis* (pp. 103–111). London, New York: Routledge.

Nowness. (n.d.). Retrieved from https://www.nowness.com . retrieval date: 19.04, 2019.

Rees-Roberts, N. (2018). *Fashion film: Art and advertising in the digital age*.London, New York: Bloomsbury Visual Arts.

Skjulstad, S., & Morrison, A. (2016). Fashion film and genre ecology. *The Journal of Media Innovations*, *3*(2), 20–41.

The Rise Of The Fashion Short. (n.d.). Retrieved from http://www.goodshortfilms.it/en/articles/the-rise-of-the-fashion-short, retrieval date: 11.11. 2018.

Top 10 Fashion Films of the Season. (June 30, 2017). Retrieved from https://www.businessoffashion.com/articles/fashion-films/top-10-fashion-films-of-the-season-4, retrieval date: 01.02.2019.

Uhlirova, M. (2013). 100 years of the fashion film: Frameworks and histories. *Fashion Theory*, *17*(2), 137–157.

Wang, J., & Juhlin, O. (2017). "Fashion, fiction, function: mediating wearable design through fashion film", www.nordes.org, retrieval date: 12.11.2018.

https://www.alanwatts.org/, (n.d.), retrieval date: 01.04.2019.

http://www.emireralp.com/, (n.d.), retrieval date: 10.08. 2018.

https://zeyneptosun.com/, (n.d.), retrieval date: 01.04.2019.

https://birelin.com.tr/tr/, (n.d.), retrieval date: 01.04.2019.

Movies

Bilgiç, S., Bilgiç, N. (Producers). Celayir, D. (Director). (2017). The Universe QUE.

Bulut, E, (Producer). Eralp, E. (Director). (2015). Pallas Athena. NOWNESS.

Duman, O. C. (Director). (2018). Choke for Birelin.

Koçman, A. (Producer). Koray, B. (Director). (2016). Three Apostles. Zeynep Tosun.

Nazlı Eda Noyan

Chapter 8 Women of Animation in Turkey: animasyonunkadinlari.org

Why?

Animation is a tree with a big cool shade, plenty of fruits, and a swing. It is an idea written on a piece of paper, a character drawn, a muttered soundtrack, a sticker you paste on your notebook. Animation is ambitious and humble. Big-budget or independent, studio or student project. It is funding hunt, coproduction, a festival, an award, screening, a catalog, or a leaflet. Animation is accessible, viral. It is activism, awareness, possibilities, information, change, and reaction. Sometimes it is just a link. Animation is therapy, education, business, curiosity, enthusiasm, engagement, entertainment, experience, empathy, self-expression. Animation is aching neck, spun back, and red eyes. It is difficult, it is easy. It is magic and madness. It is without cultural, social, and technical boundaries. Animation is free, open-minded, versatile, consistent, precise, is dare, and patient. Animation possesses the ability to realize the radical ideas and dreams of those particularly excluded from creative systems of power. Animation is women.

I have started to pay attention to the proportion of women among jury members, decision-makers, award winners, and fund receivers years ago, when I was staring at a dozen of men standing side by side during a film festival's award ceremony in Istanbul, Turkey. In October 2016, ten best short animated films of the past decade in Turkey were selected by a jury of 17 filmmakers, critics, academicians, writers, and animators. Almost one third of the jury members were women. And among the ten films, five of them were of female directors, mine included. This was a promising change but not quite. Again two years ago, when I was asked to be the chair of an animation department, I knew animation was seen as a discipline usually known as the male zone like so many other fields in Turkey (or say in the world). Nevertheless, as an academic and animation director, it is fascinating to verify the growing visibility and the creative work that women are putting forward in animation – note that I am interpreting the term "animation" broadly to include things such as visual effects (VFX), character or concept design, and even script-writing and producing for animation. Nevertheless I could not help myself but wonder how many women are there in the history of animation in Turkey? What is the percentage of women in the commissions for film funds, film festival juries? What is the percentage of female creators, contributors, and crewmembers in the animated films? How many female directors are screening their work at international festivals? How many worked at animation studios, as academics, graduates from animation schools, etc.? Who are these women out there receiving funds for their animation films, being awarded, and commissioned? Who are these decision-maker women reframing animation, and how do they survive? What is the magic in their persistence?

> By looking back to see where we started, and by noting how far we've come, we stand upon a solid foundation to launch into how much further we need to go (womeninanimation.org).

In Turkey, we can say nearly half of the population is made up of women. So it would be truly legitimate to expect and hope for an equal existence of women in life. But it unfortunately is not the case. We cannot comprehend the economics of gender discrimination in the creative labor market without investigative reports. The use of gender-specific terms and labels inherited within the superficial coverage of important issues about women that lack analytical substance may do harm more than they do good. We can combat social, cultural, and economical narrow thinking by bringing to light the number of women reshaping success. Therefore the coverage should come with an analytical understanding of issues such as underrepresentation and gender inequality. But these reports hardly exist in Turkey and most parts of the world since the data is already gone or not even kept.

When young adults of today are growing up in a world in which women are poorly represented in the fields they aspire to join, we can raise visibility for the female figures who are otherwise being ignored by celebrating and honoring them. This may not be an educational revolution; nevertheless, confronting disparity by showing the other side of the coin can be a powerful thing. Fortunately, there are global organizations trying to keep track of the answers to these questions. Founded in 1995, WIA (Women in Animation) describe their mission as follows: "Animation now reaches audiences of diverse age, gender, ethnicity, and culture. As its growth continues, so does the need to ensure that animation content represents the world as it should be – a world where women are equally represented, both behind the scenes and on the screen, to move culture forward." According to WIA, more than 60 % of animation and art school students are women, but the drop off rate as they move into industry is staggering, with only 20–40 % of professional roles and creative jobs held by women. Clearly one of the major barriers is the transition from education to career in a "a boy's club." Animation director Niki Lindroth von Bahr puts this in a wider context: "It is of course a matter of the total male domination in all powerful positions, that's been going on forever" (Brewer, 2018). WIA aims to make the ratio of women holding up decision-making positions or creative roles (such as creator, director, art director, lead writer as WIA puts forward) to that of men 50/50 by 2025. According to facts and figures in the industry presented at EWA, European Women's Audiovisual Network's Focus on Women Composers meeting at Berlinale 2019, the most male-dominant areas within gender of key creative roles in all movies in US cinemas during 2017 are music composers and cinematographers. They are followed by directors, writers, editors, and producers. Females dominate production designers, casting directors, and costume designers. In the animation world, technical roles such as generalists, compositors, and 3D and VFX artists are hugely male dominated. Executive producer Kitty Turley affirms that women are present in production roles, yet not directorial roles nor technical roles, explaining that in a typical animation studio, "men are the creative leads and women are the jobbing crew animators or producers" (Brewer, 2018).

Within the animation world in Turkey, a similar demographic exists. Anima İstanbul, one of the oldest and biggest animation production studios still active today, has 5 animator women and 13 animator men. And the proportion of women to men as directors, supervisors, coordinators, technical directors, generalists, modelers, and previs artists is 16 women to 30 men (Ünal, 2017). In Graph 2000, an animation company producing Kral Şahir TV series as well as two feature animation films, out of 13 technical crew working for the TV series, one is a woman; but for the voice cast there are four women and eight men (Varol Yaşaroğlu, personal interview, 2019). In ISF Production Company, for "Rafadan Tayfa" TV series and feature film, there were 13 women crew members. And now there are five women working in animation department and two women for other positions (İsmail Fidan, personal interview, 2019). If we look into the information about universities' animation departments gathered from Council of Higher Education search engine and the universities' own official websites, the first animation department founded in Turkey, Eskişehir Anadolu University, with 166 students almost ⅓ and amongst 360 graduates slightly above 100 are female. In Dumlupınar University, Cartoon and Animation Department, Kütahya, Turkey, the percentage of female students in overall number of students between the years 2009 and 2017 is 43.6 %. Out of 28 academics with Ph.D degrees working at animation departments in Turkey, ten of them are female[1] (2018). On March

1 Their numbers and their area of specialization: Başkent Üniversitesi (1), sculpture; İstanbul Aydın Üniversitesi (1), graphic design and graphic education; İstanbul Kültür

16th, 2019, Animation Without Borders University and Industry Colloquium took place at Bahçeşehir University Cartoon and Animation Department. Representatives from five universities' animation departments, 14 representatives from animation and technology companies or TV channels, and one governmental institution in Turkey joined the meeting. Among these representatives who were discussing the problems, solutions, possibilities, and dreams regarding animation; there were 17 men and 10 women. Some of the problems put forward during the colloquium were the awareness about animation as a profession; the lack of middle-term and long-term governmental policies to promote, sustain, and develop the animation sector; the lack of human resource and financial support; and the insufficient awareness about and application of copyrights[2]. Among other discussed topics, one topic that was not really underlined or elaborated on was gender equality and inclusiveness: The number of female students studying in the animation departments is quite high, but the rates in the industry are falling. The proportion of women to men in universities' academic staff, students, and minor and major animation studios dictate that women holding different positions in animation are hardly equally represented. They represent one third of the whole.

Üniversitesi (3), graphic design, communication design, industrial design, and architecture; İstanbul Maltepe Üniversitesi (2), art education, painting, art history, and film and TV; Eskişehir Anadolu Üniversitesi (2), graphic design, film and TV, and animation; İzmir Yaşar Üniversitesi (1), ceramics and glass; Dumlupınar Üniversitesi (none); and İzmir Dokuz Eylül Üniversitesi (none).

2 The sector is quickly consuming its employees and is constantly looking for young and cheap labor. There is a lot of talent migration to abroad. Therefore, there are no experienced people in the sector, and there are no projects to compete with international quality. There were also solutions discussed: With little steps, there are internationally acclaimed and branded cartoon characters and animations such as Kral Şakir by Varol Yaşaroğlu. These success stories need to be known. Good implementation of the RTÜK law, which states 20 % of animation content on national TV channels should be locally produced, would be a very accurate move for the development of the animation industry in Turkey. The number of young and child population is very high. Therefore, with the new platforms such as Apple TV +, Amazon, Youtube Kids, Netflix, the need for animations with safe internet content is very high. Animation-related sectors such as game are growing rapidly. The Ministry of Industry and Technology's Design Center initiative will positively affect the communication between animation studios and universities and the employment of university graduates. There are educational projects for different disadvantaged groups. If supported, they will benefit both to educated workforce and to create awareness about the profession.

Is this because of some rules and behaviors that promote sexism or what can we pinpoint from the numbers? At the end of the modern era, equality became an ideal phenomenon for almost all human societies. How can there be a system regulated among the aristocrats and the people, between men and women, between parents and children without a clear hierarchy? Property has been a prerequisite of long-term inequality (Harari, p. 21 Lessons for the 21st Century, p. 81). Lack of economical power and cultural expectations seem to be the source of gender inequalities and some of the obstacles that working women are facing. The division of occupations into women's jobs and men's jobs through cultural codes has negative consequences[3]. In Turkey, there is a lack of women's policy. Although, a law on part-time work to attract women to employment is adopted, what has been done is not holistic policies. Turkey is creatively very dynamic, full of inspiration and stories. And yet, issues such as women's presence in creative industry are hard to neglect. But such issues may not be only Turkey's problem: according to Gender Equality Report 2018 by The Swedish Film Institute (with an in-depth knowledge on how the funding is distributed in the film industry), all men and women alike can make high-quality film with a great diversity of stories, low-budget and high-budget films alike. Nevertheless, we find fewer women both behind and in front of the camera when film's budget is getting higher, even though there is no statistics suggesting that films made by women will be of lower quality. Outside the industrial context, "independent" animation is where we see women the most. As it may sometimes be reliant on external arts funding or an educational context in which to start, still it can be achieved relatively inexpensively, dependent upon the style and approach of the film; and once the location, materials, and time have been secured to make the film, it is possible for women to have full control over the production process (Wells, 1998, p.199). Animation director and Bafta winner Nina Gantz says she saw an equal balance at school, and even on the indie film circuit, but when it came to the commercial world it became more male dominated (Qtd. in Brewer, 2018). So, the market appears to have greater faith in the commercial potential of men even though there is no firm evidence to support this. Gender Equality

3 The percentage of men who say that men are more entitled than women to work in an environment of unemployment is 42 % and of women are 25 %. Forty percent of men think that men are better managers than women, while women rate 26 %. About 57 % of men say that women who are overly tied to their jobs have problems; 60 % of males think that children are affected negatively by the mother's work. Fifty percent of women think that children of working mothers will be responsible ("Woman has no name in business life", Bloomberg Businessweek, 45).

Report 2018 also states that although, women live longer on average and go to the cinema just as much as men, there are very few films portraying older women (Serner, 2018).

During Berlinale 2019, EWA facilitated a series of workshops for the women of cinema industry. One of them was a "private and professional life balance" workshop[4], a title that can hardly be found for a male version. In this workshop, some of the topics that were discussed included, what do women in cinema industry prioritize in their lives? "Presenteeism" seems to be the most problematic demand of the industry – especially hard on women with children, single moms, and women with old family members. The other issues are as follows: the guilt women are facing, trying to do far too much, to please everyone, the need to set limits, learning to ask, to speak up, to negotiate with one's self first and later with others, the need for more flexible working hours, day care, equal rights, equal pay, sustainable economy, and the need to evaluate money and time. All seem to be global issues and needs of women.

> We want women from all backgrounds of the industry and at every stage in their career to fulfill their potential and realize their dreams (www.animatedwomenuk.com).

With brief exceptions dating back to the 1960s and especially from 1990s till today, in an accelerating rate animation in Turkey has been an outlet for women telling stories. But where are they in the history of animation? Some of the information regarding animation history may be inaccurate, not for lack of research, but for lack of solid resources. Many women in the early days were not mentioned at all or used male versions of their names. As a result, the stories of these artists shimmer dimly through stories from industry older timers and the occasional mention in film credits; and in the end, we are surprised by the quantity and stories of these women[5] (Tupper, 2014). In 1991, Nanette Salomon makes

---

4 The other workshop titles included "networking in festivals and markets," "self-promotion in the industry," and "chasing the money."

5 Tupper summarizes some of these names with their great achievements and interesting stories (2014): Helena Smith Dayton, 1879–1960, is regarded as the American pioneer of stop-motion puppet and clay animation. Lotte Reiniger was the first female animator and animated feature director. Edith Vernick, American, Fleischer Studios animator and in-betweener in the 1920s–1930s; Hermína Týrlová, 1900–1993, Czech stop-motion animator practicing 1920s–1980s. Lillian Friedman, working for Fleischer Studios, was the first female studio animator with a screen credit in 1933. Out of the 11 titles Friedman worked on, she was only credited for six. In 1934, LaVerne Harding became the second woman in animation history to receive an onscreen credit. In 1980 Harding won a Winsor McCay Lifetime Achievement Award, one of the highest honors

the following claim in one of the most influential texts of feminist art history, "Art Historical Canon: The Sins of Omission": "In our own historical moment, women have fought for and regained the privilege and the responsibility of having a say in the ways culture gets produced and disseminated. Feminists have opened places within canonical discourse to allow for the inclusion of women as artists and women as critics. But at this juncture, inclusion alone is not enough. Feminist practice has produced several strategies for dealing with the academic field of art history and its canon. Primary among these is the archeological excavation of women as creators. We need creative and sustainable strategies to put in doubt the so-called 'normal' selections, to open new paths for different readings to be possible, to have fresh perspectives those emphasize the construction of subjectivities, to contribute in developing new suggestions of visual reading, it is the time to fight with sins of omission." Animated Women UK[6], launched in 2013, is a good example of fresh perspectives. It supports a network of women who can help each other achieve success at every stage of the animation or VFX

---

an animator can achieve. Out of 161 Winsor McCay awards she is one of only nine women to receive the honor. The first woman Walt hired for the story department was Bianca Majolie, whose first project was *Pinocchio*. When the Hollywood Citizen News got word that Disney had hired their first female artist they did an expose on her, but never mentioned her name. Sylvia Moberly-Holland was the second woman hired by Disney's story department. Retta Scott was the very first woman to animate for Walt Disney Animation Studios and received screen credit as an animator. Mary Blair started out as a Disney concept artist in 1940; Blair's unique style and mastery of color gave Disney films such as *The Three Caballeros*, *Cinderella*, *Alice in Wonderland* and *Peter Pan* their iconic look. Blair designed literally the entire visual world in "It's A Small World." Posthumously, in 1991, Blair was given the Disney Legend Award, and in 1996, given the Winsor McCay Award. Eunice Macaulay became the first female animator to win her own Academy Award for her film *Special Delivery* in 1978. As one of the first female Japanese animators, Kazuko Nakamura is considered by many to be the mother of modern anime. Hailed as the second female Japanese animator, Reiko Okuyama was hired as an in-betweener and in 1959 was promoted to second key animator. When she became a mother, it was expected that she would step down to become a homemaker, her bosses got pretty pushy about it, right down to threatening her husband's job too. So, she left…and came back with the industry unions backing her up. With their help, Okuyama won the right for Japanese women to balance work and family without sacrificing their careers. Women's existence in animation had also been a matter of age, ethnic and racial background in the world. Brenda Banks' career took off in the mid-1970s; she became the first black female animator.

6 It is inspired by an event hosted in 2011 by Women in Film and TV and the London International Animation Festival.

pipeline by networking, mentoring, showcasing, recruitment, and education with the aim to see results such as: better female characters on screen and an increase in women-led startups and in women winning awards in technical areas.

When we look at the written history of animation, so far, in Turkey, what do we see? We see men. Animation history in Turkey grows from the same root of Turkish Cinema: Shadow play going back to the 13th century. Caricaturistic, sarcastic, and episodic inclination towards total performance seemingly links shadow play Karagöz with modern animation. However, these obvious links have not been fully explored in the following years, particularly after the disappearance of shadow play as an entertainment form in the early 20th century (Ürkmez, p. 87). Canan Balan mentions although there have been some strong female characters within the narrative of shadow play, there were no female shadow play masters (personal interview, 2017). The other art form that resembles animation as an attempt to represent images in motion is the art of miniature just like the miniatures of Nakkaş Osman's Surnama-i Hümayun (1582) depicting a parade in the circumcision ceremony (Hünerli, p. 30). Very interesting to see within the history of miniatures when they were extremely popular, there were no women miniature artists mentioned, but today there are so many female miniature masters at work. During the 1930s, after being exposed to some animated films by Disney and others, it was mainly caricaturists who first expressed interest and laid the foundations of modern animation in Turkey. Cemal Nadir Güler, the creator of the famous caricature character Amca Bey, started a film starring him but was never able to finish it. Unfortunately, there is hardly any actual films or visual materials left from our animation history's early stages and the important pioneers. They are either lost or perished for some reason just like *Fertek Rakı*, first animated commercial film (1932, producers unknown) or Eflatun Nuri Erkoç's *Dolmuş ve Şoförü* (The Minivan and Its Driver, 1942) a film of 37 frames or a 3-minute long artistic animation *Zeybek Oyunu* (The Zeybek Dance, 1947) created by Vedat Ar and his Filmar studios team and 15 students at Fine Arts University. The first full-length animation film *Evvel Zaman İçinde: Nasreddin Hoca, Keloğlan, Gülderen Sultan* (Once Upon A Time: Nasreddin Hoca, Keloğlan, Gülderen Sultan, 1951–1960) directed by Yüksel Ünsal based on protagonists from humorous stories related in traditional Turkish Fables (female artist Aysel Kolak Ünsal and Güzide Sağıroğlu Atasev worked in this production). This film got lost in Metro-Goldwyn-Mayer Studios, USA, for technical processing and development after many years of work of a big team of people. This disappointment caused a recess in animation-making for a long time. This film is an important example showing us the fascination and habit of using traditional stories in animation and the first female character as one of the protagonists. Technical conditions were still not in place in the 1960s, such as development of films, but the advertising sector with studios dedicated to animation began to develop in Turkey. Some used the money they earned from advertising to produce short animated films such as *Koca Yusuf* (1966) and *Bu Şehri İstanbul* (1968). In order to be different from the Disney style or European approach, as a personal quest a national sense of aesthetic drove Yalçın Çetin to take inspiration from and make use of the line structure of Karagöz. *Cici Can* in 1962 became the first to combine animation and live footage (Ürkmez, p. 91). As an important cultural and social landmark related to animation history in Turkey was the foundation of Sinematek Society in 1965, soon to reach 10,000 members. The New Cinema magazine of Sinematek, Bosphorus University Cinema Club, and Hisar Short Film competition in 1967 were all productive environments and forces for animation and cinema. How many women filmmakers were involved? Unknown. Turkey's very first documentary to use animation was the short film *Direklerarası* made by the team of Oğuz Aral, Feruh Doğan, Tekin Aral, and Eflatun Nuri in 1968. Other landmarks were the first experiment in stop motion Mehmet Celal Ülken's *Kibritler ve Böcü* (Matchsticks and Maggots, 1967), Tonguç Yaşar's *Amentü Gemisi Nasıl Yürüdü* (How the Ship of Creed Sailed, 1969) with co-writer and art historian Sezer Tansuğ, the first animation to pass the preselection of Annecy Animation Film Festival; and Tan Oral's awarded then later censored short animation film *Sansür* (Cencor, 1970, 16mm – 7 min.). In the 1970s we see commissioned animation work on traditional folk tales and traditional stories by animators like Derviş Pasin and Ateş Benice. In 1973 TRT state TV began broadcasting nationwide. State-ruled media also meant censorship and politicization of animation. In the 1980s, technical revolution took place as a result of Turkey's change in the financial structure and increased import trade. Advertising and media industries developed further. With technical development came the spread and democratization of animation. Nevertheless there also was a change in the social and cultural spectrum in Turkey; the rise of right wing and Islamic politics also have shaped the commissioned films. In the 1990s, major change consists of the impact of US companies entering Turkish market with local branches and the unfair competition between foreign and local films. The year 1990 also is a landmark for our animation history as Anadolu University began to offer the first academic degree in animation; and later the graduates and the academic staff shaped the animation world in Turkey. Founded in 1995, Anima Istanbul later joined by Sinefekt and 1000Volt followed as VFX and postproduction companies. In

2008, Turkey's first children's television channel, TRT Çocuk, began broadcasting; and many commissioned projects rooted in folklore, traditional stories, and historical characters again began to flourish.

According to Tunç and Lent, women animators began appearing in Turkish animation in the 1960s, echoing the fact that female students were 35 years later accepted to art schools[7]. They were working with traditional techniques closely with a male mentor and later with a male partner. Aysel Konak Ünsal worked as the background artist with her animation director husband Yüksel Ünsal for the production of *Evvel Zaman İçinde* in 1950s. Ayla Seyhan is the first known animator woman who worked closely and under the mentorship of Vedat Ar in the 1960s and 1970s at Filmar producing stop motion and puppet animations. Very sadly, Ayla Seyhan is ill and unable to give interviews; and her films cannot be located. In 1972, Meral Simer with her husband Tonguç Yaşar and Sezer Tansuğ made *How Spring Ended* (Fig. 8.1). In 1978, Meral Erez won the first prize at the Balkan Film Festival with her short animation *Il Gatto*; later she worked with her husband Cemal Erez in France and Turkey. From 1980s till today, there is a spread of computer technology and university education devoted to animation. Also, because of the publications for children like Doğan Kardeş and Milliyet Çocuk Magazines; and exposure to cartoons and animations from different countries such as France, Japan, USA, Belgium, and Italy and existence of TRT as the main buyer of animated series and the support of Ministry of Culture and Tourism for animation, we see a boom in the numbers of women getting involved in animation as scriptwriters, producers, directors, animators, VFX artists, character designers, concept artists, illustrators, voice actors, and educators in Turkey. There are very limited written or visual material and documentation about women of animation in Turkey. As we need representation of women in every discipline and role models for especially technology-related areas, building a venue to share these women's stories seemed extremely important.

7 Sanayi-i Nefise Mektebi was the first fine arts school of the Ottoman Empire founded in 1882 in Istanbul. İnas Sanayi-i Nefise Mektebi meaning "Fine Arts School for Women" was established in 1917 with the proposal and initiative of painter Mihri Hanım in order to give art education to women. A total 27 Muslim and 6 Christian female students enrolled in the first year.

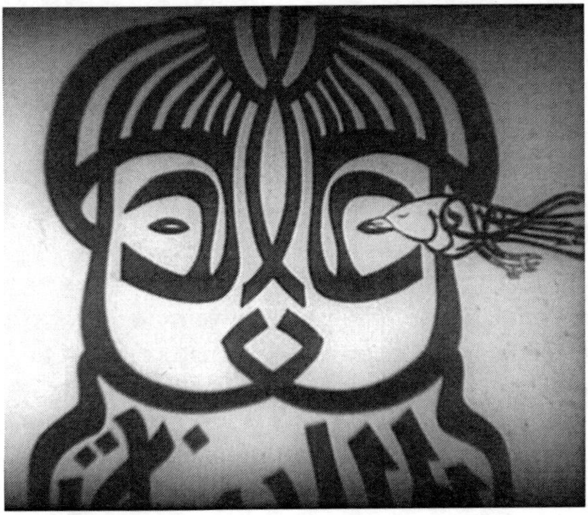

Fig. 8.1: How Spring Ended (Meral Simer, Tonguç Yaşar, Sezer Tansuğ, 1972)

What?

Women in Animation's Legacy and Archives Program is a great example for a venue with the mission of honoring and preserving the predecessors by oral histories (producing video/audio/photographic oral histories of animation community), profiles from the past and present (short articles about historical and current members that appear online), and a digital archive of films and visual material and a database (online resource for all information about women in animation). "Women of animation" in Turkey, too, is a historical research into unwritten stories of these women through interviews with pioneers such as producer and animation department founder Seher Karabol; director of animated short film *How Spring Ended*, Meral Simer; cartoonist Piyale Madra whose work has been made into animation with her getting involved in the process; character designer and feature film codirector (with İsmet Kurtuluş) Nermin Er; animation producer Yonca Ertürk; feature film *Kötü Kedi Şerafettin*'s codirector (with Mehmet Kurtuluş) and commercial film director Ayşe Ünal; feature film *The Sandman and the Lost Sand of Dreams* director Sinem Sakaoğlu; V/FX artists Akça Elmas and Tijen Pal; animator Lamia Karaali; animation producers and scriptwriters Ayşe Şule Bilgiç and Arzu Demirel; TV producer Sevilay Bozdemir; animation studio director Yeşim Aktaş; a bit younger generation of animators Özgül Gürbüz; animation director and contemporary artist Özlem Sulak; animation scriptwriter Nefise Abalı; directors and animators Akile Nazlı

Kaya, Fulya Tokaoğlu, Işık Dikmen, Nurbanu Asena, Melis Balcı, and Ege Okal; and many more. A total of 55 women including female animators, VFX artists, writers, producers, educators, directors, illustrators[8], editors, character designers, and voice actors were interviewed over the course of 2.5 years to be presented on animasyonunkadinlari.org. This list was put together by going through the written history, festival catalogues and websites, film credits, universities, various animations, film and TV networks, associations and societies, as well as friendly suggestions. The interviews explore these women's role in commercial and independent animation in Turkey. Fifty-five women talked about their academic and professional background, what animation meant to them, what they seek in their production process and in team members, what they value the most in their work, their inspirations, the issues they face to access the industry/practice, thoughts on animation industry and education in Turkey, and the future of animation. And these women talked about how – if ever – they were influenced by their gender or if their womanhood has influenced their work. Is there anything that makes these women's animations any different than that of men's?

> At no point do I wish to be in conflict with any man or masculine thought. It doesn't enter my consciousness. Art is anonymous. It's not competitive with men. It's a complementary contribution. (interview with Barbara Hepworth, sculptor)

Wording can be very tricky. Saying something politically correct is more important than saying it in a politically correct manner[9]. Though, using gender as a filter through which we analyze creativity is limiting. Not wanting to be included in lists such as "animator women" is a perfectly legitimate response for an individual to take. An animation artist whose work has nothing to do with her gender should probably not be labeled. Nevertheless, the counterpoint to this idea is the fact that women animators are animators, but they are not just animators, they are more than that. In a world charged with differences such as gender, the question of how your gender influences who you are and what you do are vital

8 "Women of the line" section is opened due to the suggestions from some illustrator women themselves.

9 There are articles like "Why Aren't 'Women Street Artists' Just 'Street Artists'?" and "How Not To Write About Women Artists" both of which take the terminology issue as its center. Critics often argue that the term "women artist/ designer/ filmmaker/ etc." or its sister phrase "female artist/ designer/ filmmaker/ etc." does more harm than it does good. The act of grouping women into one happy contingent or into "revised" versions of art history may seem reductive – as Guerrilla Girls very creatively and sarcastically underlined as one of the items within their list of "the advantages of being a woman artist."

questions. Identity carries a big load of history with it as well. An individual may prefer_not to focus on gender or race in her work, but this does not mean that issues of gender are not at play. When I first started the research and got in touch with these women, putting a working title to my research and naming my area of interest was challenging. Because, academically and professionally putting the word "female" or "woman" forward when we try to describe someone or someone's work seems problematic or even odd. Meral Erez, one of the pioneers of animated short film in Turkey said, "I reject to be included in any kind of categorization. I am an artist" (2017). Just like Georgia O'Keeffe who said, "Men put me down as the best woman painter… I think I'm one of the best painters."

In his book *Understanding Animation*, Paul Wells discusses the notion of a "feminine aesthetic" by stating that women's animation is less censored in its concerns, working in forms that move beyond hyperrealism, and seek to be more subjective. According to him, women animators more readily seek to express themselves in ways that trust and exploit the ontological equivalence of imagery. The creation of animated dream-states mixes easily with subjective interpretations of fairytale or poetry, which in turn sits comfortably with the use of the document, tendency, or the overt use of abstract symbolism. This enables women animators to address topics many male animators could not deal with. All these films demonstrate a feminine aesthetic, which could not have been achieved in live action filmmaking (1998, p. 199).

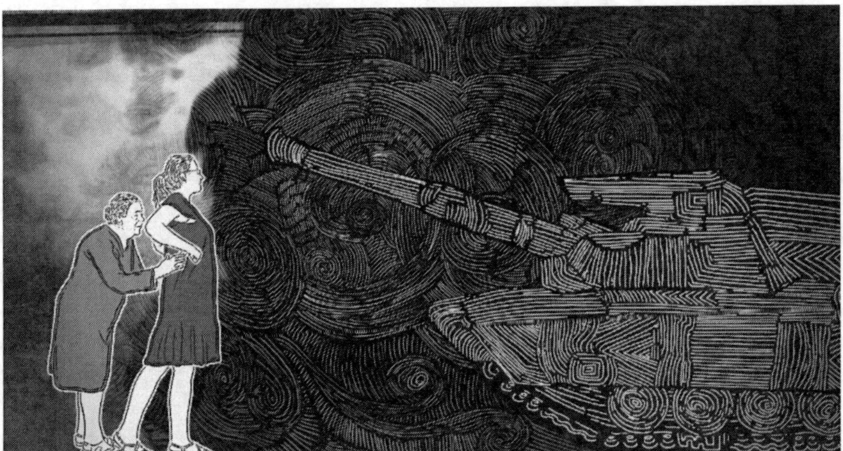

Fig. 8.2: Cup of Turkish Coffee (Nazlı Eda Noyan, Dağhan Celayir, 2013)

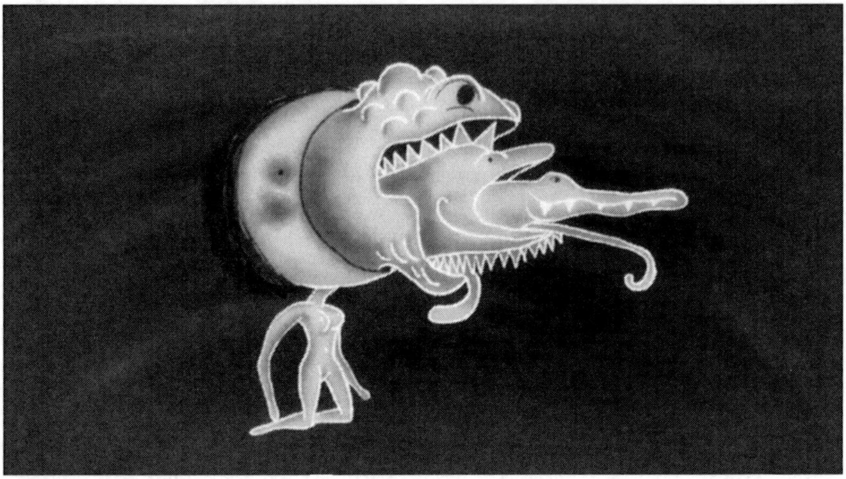

Fig. 8.3: Girl, Slipped Inside (Işık Dikmen, 2012)

Any film made by woman or a story about a woman does not necessarily make it a feminine or gendered story. What makes a narrative not masculine, but of woman? Ursula K. Le Guin's *The Carrier Bag Theory of Fiction* (1986) shows us the non-masculine and almost rebellious ways of narration. A narration that does not necessarily involve a linear progress. A narration that wanders around the possibilities available to all, a narration that is independent. No wonder, there are more women in "independent" animation arena then they exist in commercial animation (Tab. 8.1). According to Wells, essentially, animation, more than any other form of film-making, offers the opportunity to operate in a safe space and create auteurist cinema outside the constraints of patriarchal norms, both with regards to the means of production and the modes of representation (1998, p.199). You may name it as a resistance to the male representations of women such as "Boopism" (Wells & Cabarga. 1988, p 53–81; Hendershot, 1993; Smoodin. 1993: 30–9) or personal, social, and political agendas concerning men. Fundamentally women's animation creates the context in which the personal becomes inevitably political, because it is opposed to male-dominated commercial arena as well as self-evidently orthodox animation through its more radical, experimental, and irreverent nature. Wells argues the feminine aesthetic has become more recognizable, and more self-conscious, since the 1970s, when it informed the overt politicization of female artworks per se (1998, p.200). From the 1970s till today, in

Tab. 8.1: Commercial feature animations in Turkey with the highest number of audience: Retrieved from https://boxofficeturkiye.com, 13.10.2019

Name of the Film	Year, Production Studio	(Total Weeks) Total Audience	Gross (TL)	Director	Women Involved as Director, Producer, Scriptwriter or Creator
Allah'ın Sadık Kulu: Barla	2011, Ser Film	(25 Weeks) 2.227.113	15.669.213,75 TL	Esin Orhan	Director Esin Orhan
Rafadan Tayfa Dehliz Macerası	2018, ISF Film Production	(24 Weeks) 1.799.280	20.437.614,52 TL	İsmail Fidan	
Kral Şakir Korsanlar Diyarı	2019, BKM	(1 Week) 659.571	11.163.295,00	Haluk Can Dizdaroğlu	
Kötü Kedi Şerafettin	2016, Kare Kare Film	(7 Weeks) 359.176	4.565.215,00 TL	Ayşe Ünal, Mehmet Kurtuluş	Director Ayşe Ünal
Köstebekgiller: Perili Orman	2015, Arzum Film, Siyah Martı	(14 Weeks) 409.407	4.335.884,00 TL	Mustafa Kotan	Producer, Arzu Oduncu İmamoğlu
Kral Şakir Oyun Zamanı	2018, BKM, CJ Entertainment Turkey	(15 Weeks) 346.964	4.125.583,16 TL	Berk Tokay, H. Can Dizdaroğlu,	
Fırıldak Ailesi	2017, BKM	(7 Weeks) 314.939	3.807.760,40 TL	H. Can Dizdaroğlu, Berk Tokay	
Köstebekgiller 2: Gölge'nin Tılsımı	2015, Arzum Film	(9 Weeks) 218.438	2.368.691,00 TL	Kudret Sabancı	Producer, Arzu Oduncu İmamoğlu
Pepee: Birlik Zamanı	2016, Düşyeri	(12 Weeks) 151.249	1.769.502,22 TL	Hüseyin Emre Konyalı	Producer, Scriptwriter, Ayşe Şule Bilgiç

an accelerating rate animation in Turkey has been an outlet for women telling stories. According to Wells, women's animation recognizes the shift from the representation of woman as object, to the representation of woman as subject. The feminine aesthetic seeks to reveal a woman's relationship to her own body; her interaction with men and other women; her perception of her private and public role; her social and political identity within the domestic and professional space as determined by law; and also, the relationship between female sexuality, desire, and creativity (Wells, 200, 1998). (Piyale Madra *Ademler ve Havvalar*, Nazlı Eda Noyan *A Cup of Turkish Coffee*" (Fig. 8.2), Deniz Öcal *Vitality*, İdil Ar Uçaner *The Garden*, Özgül Gürbüz *Playing House*, Fulya Tokaoğlu *Aunty* (2013), and Işık Dikmen *Girl, Slipped Inside* (2012) (Fig. 8.3). The feminine aesthetic mistrusts language, perceiving it as the agent of masculine expression, preferring to express itself in predominantly visual terms, using a variety of forms, and reclaiming and revising various traditions (Wells, 199, 1998). In order to construct a feminine aesthetic, it is necessary to abandon conservative forms and create radical texts, which may demand greater participation from viewing audience. As Wells points out, Lotte Reiniger's silhouette animation, based on Chinese shadow theater, exhibits a feminist tendency, depicting emotional states through lyrical movements of figures, emotional gestures, the lightness of touch, and the subtlety of expression – a profound departure from the (male) agendas of the evolving cartoon. She said, "Disney films are technically perfect; too perfect" (Pilling, 1992, p. 15), hinting at the impersonality of industrialized, masculine cel-animation, and secure of her own femininity as an expressive tool in the creation of her own work (201, 1998). As can be seen in Nurbanu Asena's *Invisible Walls* (2017), Özlem Sulak's *Emek* (2017), Akile Nazlı Kaya's *Nazlı in Zlin* (2006), Melis Balcı and Ege Okal's *Merkür* (2015), women of, animation in Turkey are not interested in folkloric or traditional stories, historical characters, or heroes but rather Zen philosophies, spiritual questions, individual-personal stories, and actual issues related to politics and everyday life with female characters. It may be observed that, although the subject matter and style of the films vary, there is a growing number of animator women from the younger generation working with hybrid genres such as animated documentary to express rough topics related to women's lives or human rights issues in Turkey. They have started out with traditional subject matters and techniques like that of man's. They are exploring and experimenting with different techniques. There is one category or group we can fit these women in, because they are all diverse. Men of animation have cartoon, cinema, engineering, and animation background; whereas for women of animation, graphic design seems to be the main academic foundation for most followed by cinema or animation background; but we do see a sculptor or even a dancer. One-third of these women have studied or worked abroad. Their films are screened at festivals, art shows, and online. Their audience is diverse. Unfortunately in Turkey, there are hardly any funds and sponsors to support animation other than that of the Ministry of Culture and Tourism, which indeed is very controlling and limiting. So the majority of the films are independent, self-sponsored, or coproduced excluding TV productions. In animation for children, there are lots of female producers like Sevilay Bozdemir and female creator-driven TV animation series like *Pepee* by Ayşe Şule Bilgiç or female leads like Niloya created by Arzu Demirel. *Köstebekgiller* was a popular TV series for TRT Kids before becoming one of the high grossing feature film with animated characters. The production studio owner is Arzu Oduncu and the scriptwriters is Arzu Yurtseven. Women are more likely to find place in children's media. Is it because their stories and characters are different from those of male's in terms of pedagogy or child caring? "We, as a society, have historically pushed girls and boys towards different preferences. As women move from education to career or stepping up the ladder of career, women's more feminine qualities like nurturing, willingness to please, and patience are praised just like their ability to facilitate and enable the creative voice and vision of men. It's a restrictive pattern that upholds the status quo." (Brewer, 2018). Mary Ellen Bute dispelled myths concerning women and the use of technology and enjoyed the control and rejection of functionalism in creating personal works as well as perceiving her work as art and the expression of feeling, fully estranging herself from cartoon humor (Wells, 1998, p.201). On a parallel subject, studio manager Natalie Busuttil believes the wide gender divide in 3D animation is particularly due to its subject matter. "I think there is an idea as to what being a successful 3D artist involves, which errs towards sci-fi, fantasy and action films. For some women this is great, but it's not everyone's cup of tea. I think we can do more to shatter this perception. Animation is a varied and multifaceted world – you don't have to work on photorealistic alien horrors or the latest superhero action movie to be a 3D artist" (Brewer, 2018). Self-doubt is the patriarchy's most insidious weapon. Although this may not be the sole reason there are many women directors in the animation world codirecting with male partners, especially in the commercial animation world. In Turkey, this has been almost a norm at the beginning, though this tradition may be observed to be diminishing towards recent years. Ayla Seyhan and Vedat Ar, Meral Erez and Cemal Erez, Meral Simer and Tonguç Yaşar, Ayşe Ünal and Mehmet Kurtuluş, Nazlı Eda Noyan and Dağhan Celayir, and Akile Nazlı Kaya and Tomaş Doruşka have been creative partners in major amount of movies.

What Does It Mean to Be a Woman of Animation, and What Are the Ups and Downs?

Name, title, and date of interview	Year of birth	Answer
Betül Gaye Dinç illustrator, writer 30.09.2018	**1994**	I love telling women stories because I grew up with them. In all the stories I hear, no matter your social class, ethnicity, belief, sexual orientation, or world view, you face many problems even in your daily life because you are a woman. After all, unfortunately, we are still in a country where Anıt Sayaç (an online monument simultaneously counting the number of women murdered in Turkey, anitsayac.com) operates. Nevertheless, as a positive aspect, I met very valuable people and institutions because I advocated for women's rights rather than being a woman. Istanbul Women's Museum is one of them. On the other hand, the negative effects of stereotyped women's drawings and the sexist language used in the cartoons and magazines I have seen in previous years have definitely had a negative effect. That's why I didn't like to read many superhero comics and caricatures.
Rümeysa Önal animator 23.09.2019	**1992**	Since throughout history, women have been hampered in education and work due to their gender, they live in almost every part of social life defending themselves and their abilities. We have a strong empathy caused by this pressure and this is a "must" for storytellers. I do not think that there is an obstacle that cannot be overcome by women whose development is not prevented.
Hatiye Garip illustrator 28.08.2018	**1992**	I usually like stories and illustrators that include adventurous female characters. So far, when I think about the editors and art directors I've ever worked with in Turkey and other countries, they are mostly women. I want to be able to cooperate with men more. On the other hand, I cannot help questioning the meaninglessness of evaluating gender by splitting it into two.

Name, title, and date of interview	Year of birth	Answer
Melis Balcı and Ege Okal director, animator 13.04.2017	**1990**	Ege: We are obviously living in a world dominated by men. There are few female directors, all the big studios run by men. Melis: This is not an issue specific to the animation field. Every woman who tries to exist with the qualifications and the work forces attributed to men experience the same problems.
Elif Yemenici illustrator, writer 23.07.2018	**1989**	After school, the number of women actively producing something in art is decreasing considerably, but I think this is generally connected with everyone's own choice. Going under the influence of social roles or resisting it is included in these choices. For example, considering the notion of motherhood, I have not experienced it, but I assume that such a situation could undermine the production process.
Nurbanu Asena director, animator, illustrator 08.03.2017	**1988**	Now, I think I like female artists more in visual works. Actually, I think most of the sector are men, but since there are women artists around me, I didn't feel the inequality of women and men in this industry.
Begüm Günceler voice actor 20.03.2019	**1986**	Animations have male characters as well as female characters. Maybe the positive side for me is that there's always a princess coming out from Disney.
Nefise Abalı scriptwriter, educator 10.12.2016	**1985**	Animation industry in Turkey is predominantly a male world. Some of these men have a high ego… So I know that there are times when I couldn't cope with this kind of men and retreat to my shell. When I first entered the world of animation, I tried to learn everything from storyboard to render. The most obvious thing I've experienced is that the director can intervene in my script easily and not inform me about it. Nevertheless, he does not intervene without consulting the male artists who conduct other processes. Of course, the disadvantage is that my material is the script. And you know, everybody (thinks they) can read and write.

(*continued on next page*)

Name, title, and date of interview	Year of birth	Answer
Işık Dikmen director, animator, educator 27.03.2014	**1985**	I can't say I'm disadvantageous or more advantageous because I'm a woman. But while I'm making a film, I examine myself and share what I understand from myself. Since I'm a woman, of course I'm examining this too! I tried to understand and share my menstrual pains while I was making "Girl, Slipped Inside."
Fulya Tokaoğlu director, animator, educator 31.03.2017	**1984**	As a woman, I did not experience any obvious obstacle due to my gender, but sometimes, out of the blue, I witnessed those who say that women cannot do this job.
Serin İnan scriptwriter, director, producer 01.10.2018	**1982**	In fact, when I was first interested in animation, they asked me why I wanted to sit in a room and animate like "bang one's head against a brick wall". I always thought they wouldn't ask this if I was a man. Animation is a serious infrastructure and requires a lot of discipline. They probably wanted to scare us because they thought we couldn't keep up with this.
Sibel Bozkurt cartoonist, writer 22.07.2018	**1982**	When I write and draw what I have in mind on paper, I think there is no negative or positive side of being a woman. But in business environment, you need to make more effort than a man. It's a pity that while we are creating we're also in competition with people with strong connections.
Can Deniz Şahin, producer 16.01.2019	**1980**	Since I'm in the production department, I can say that the only negative thing about my gender is to make my own voice heard in the men's world. There is a communication model that progresses regardless of hierarchy: Even the opinion of someone who is inexperienced or not knowledgeable about your subject matter may sometimes seem more important than yours. As an individual, not as a woman, if I know that the decision made is wrong, and even if I see it and know it's a removable error, I condone it. I respond to the eyes that turn to me when the error is noticed by rolling my eyes. Those who work with me know, it has been a very effective method.

Name, title, and date of interview	Year of birth	Answer
		The main plus about being a woman is that I can organize many tasks at the same time, without overlapping each other. We, the women are able to design projects in a way that does not cause conflict, we are much more organized and able to produce constructive solutions in crisis.
Ece Burgaz, cartoonist 19.08.2018	**1980**	Even though we have a role model like Oğuz Aral that gives importance to women cartoonist, we still have friends in the world of cartoon who think "women can not be cartoonists." My master Doğan Pehlevan took me seriously and didn't spare me his support, and as I struggled, he taught me everything he knew… If I had showed my work to a sexist cartoonist, I would have probably dealt with many annoying problems. The most striking struggler for the existence of women in the world of cartoon is Tuncay Akgün, who manages Leman, L-Manyak and Ms. Yanı. He opened the doors of the magazine like a school for cartoonists without differentiating men and women. With the efforts of him and Ramize Erer, women cartoonists find a place for themselves, and newcomers are trained. In Bayan Yanı magazine, of course, I have an effort to represent the world from the point of women and to determine the common situations we all experience. Harassment, discrimination, social pressure, psychological violence, I have experienced all of these things, like most women. What happened to me and because of the country's agenda inevitably reflected in my cartoons. I think we as a society still live in a very primitive period. I don't like to deal with these issues in my work, but sometimes I can't help it.
Akile Nazli Kaya animator, director 05.05.2017	**1980**	Occasionally I have encountered prejudices such as "she is a woman, she knows less or cannot manage." I once received a comment about my work that was "too good to be expected from a woman"?!

(*continued on next page*)

Name, title, and date of interview	Year of birth	Answer
Özgül Gürbüz character designer, director, educator 05.04.17	**1980**	Unfortunately, today women can be exposed to all kinds of negativity. When necessary, reactions should be reacted in such cases, but I think that this should not incite us as victims of psychology, but rather motivate them to achieve better things. "Being a woman" can't make me advantageous or disadvantageous at work. But my "thoughts about being a woman" or the value that I give myself, regardless of my gender can do that.
Özlem Sulak videograph, director 10.04.2017	**1979**	Directing is one of the professions where we see women at least. Even though we're used to seeing women as actors in front of the camera. But happily it changes over time. If you are a woman in creative professions, your job is difficult. Especially if you're a mother. Since infrastructures such as kindergartens and caregivers are not in creative professions, it is very difficult to catch up with my children with time constraints.
İdil Ar Uçaner director, illustrator 21.03.2019	**1979**	I have an interesting story about it: I don't want to give a company name, but let's call it my first internship. I was incredibly excited over there, and I thought I finally found what I wanted to do. I spent 9 months internship there and someday my boss called me. I was so excited I was wondering if I'd finally get a job offer. He told me that already there are not many women in the industry, so the environment is not suitable for me, and maybe I should evaluate my potential in the customer relations department'. I remember feeling the boiling water pouring down my head. This was very depressing for a while, but then' on the contrary, I was stubbornly hanging on to what I loved. So I thanked him for his contributions. Apart from that, it was not an easy experience for me to be the head of the team as a female director in the companies I worked for. As in everywhere, I have come across to men with barriers such as not being able to get directives from women director.

Name, title, and date of interview	Year of birth	Answer
		But somehow, everything went the way it should be and sat on the track. As long as I focus on my work, this is no longer a problem. The benefit of being a female director is perhaps attracting attention. Because we're very few in Turkey and I believe it is very valuable. Apart from that, of course, my female instincts come into play when I make movies and these feelings help me to be dragged into a whole new place. After all, everyone's process and way of creation is completely different, and it doesn't seem right to me to divide it clearly into men and women …
Zeynep Akçay animator, director, academician 10.04.2017	**1978**	Last year, however, I had the opportunity to talk to two women in senior positions at Disney and Sony, and they talked about how much male dominance the industry still has. It's still not easy for a woman to be a director or producer in a big-budget movie.
Deniz Öcal animator, director, educator 15.03.2017	**1978**	The support of female animators to each other can be priceless. Sisterhood comes into play. As women, our sensitivity and passion are higher. Creativity is parallel to being a mother, creating a film is actually giving birth to a child. It's inherent in women.
Tijen Pal VFX, educator 29.03.2017	**1976**	Separating something as a man or a woman is nothing more than a social impact. Being a woman in Turkey in the field of animation is being in the situation of a minority. In the years that I started working, many of my animator friends chose illustration, graphic design, or other areas for their existence. I found that the only reason for that is the struggle to survive socially. Working conditions are severe and there is a sexist system. Repeated, long and demanding working hours of up to 16–18 hours each day. In the following years after having a child, it became impossible for me and I chose not to use the capacity fully and opted for projects according to my own organization. But, I have to admit that I have always felt that I am privileged. Because I believe that women are more resistant than men.

(*continued on next page*)

Name, title, and date of interview	Year of birth	Answer
		We were a few people for many years, but I'm looking forward to the future with optimism thanks to the rise of female production and postproduction professionals in the last 10 years.
Aylin Zoe Tinel editor, educator 16.05.2017	**1975**	It turned out to be a con. I wasn't very aware. I was also surprised when people tried to explain it to me later. As the industry is predominantly male dominated, it doesn't suit their book to see woman other than in the art, costume and organization areas. So they're not used to seeing women in creative fields. Of course, this is not for everyone. Anyone who doesn't have self-esteem issues wants women especially in their creative team. Intuition, sensitivity and patience are important elements for an editor, and a woman is inherently advantageous in the possibility of having these elements.
Nazlı Eda Noyan director, creator, academician 02.04.2017	**1974**	I grew up listening to female stories in a matriarchal family. One day, I realized that the stories I heard outside my house were men's stories told to men by men. I wondered why. Now I see that the main reason is inequality of opportunity. The imposed rules, structure, process and support are not for women. A vicious circle that you often fall into to express yourself is the word "female" that we put in front of a profession as in the use of "female director." However, it is precisely for this reason that the femininity of those who succeed in defending their profession despite a thousand difficulties and unequal conditions due to their gender should be emphasized.
Aysun Topar voice actor 23.03.2019	**1984**	It was an advantage. My voice is suitable to speak in the age range of 8 to 40 years, I can voice over a boy in child voices, but you cannot get the sound of girls from boys. So, I can say that being a woman is an advantage especially in the variety of animation jobs.

Name, title, and date of interview	Year of birth	Answer
Arzu Oduncu İmamoğlu producer, founder 19.04.2017	**1974**	I don't think there is any negative aspect of being a woman in the animation field. As a woman, it is obvious that the struggle for existence in trade and business life is a general problem, so we cannot reduce it to animation only. On the contrary, I think that the woman's vision has an enormous advantage because of her emotional and detailed perspective and her ability to think more artistically and creatively. I saw that the management of my team was similar to the instinct of motherhood with the logic of an authority established in rights and justice established with love. We were able to do our business jointly with great synergy. Our communication was sincere and creative in order to interpret the script and reflect it to lines and movements. I think being a female manager is one of the factors that increase the motivation of the team and increase the sense of ownership. If your job is art, especially being a woman, working with women means you are leading one-zero to success.
Sinem Sakaoğlu director, writer, animator 02.01.2017	**1974**	I am a director who uses animation technique frequently and particularly. From time to time, I take my share as a director of female-male inequality in the sector. Especially in Europe, the advertising world is still a very male world. Luckily, I have been able to work together with a small group of people for whom gender discrimination has never worked. Otherwise, the advertising world cannot be tolerated. In my feature film adventure, I survived a few incidents until I formed the group I worked with.
Ayça Sığırcı creator, scriptwriter 15.10.2018	**1972**	I did not experience the pros or cons of being a woman. Maybe there were pros. I would say I am patient and constructive, but these features are also present in men.

(*continued on next page*)

Name, title, and date of interview	Year of birth	Answer
Yeşim Aktaş director, creator, producer 25.04.2017	**1971**	Seeing gender bender characters changed my vision as a child.
Yonca Ertürk producer, educator 17.03.2017	**1970**	We are trying to turn the difficulties of facing questions like "do women understand this business" to our advantage by saying "there are women who do this job."
Lamia Karaali VFX, cartoonist, educator 07.04.2017	**1970**	The advantage of being a woman is perhaps using intuition, compassionate approach to work and colleagues, being more flexible and creative. When I was working, I sometimes pushed my body's strength limits, and I realized later that it was a side effect of working with a community that was almost exclusively male.
Akça Elmas VFX 13.04.2017	**1969**	Since I've never lived this life as a man, I don't think I can find out what makes me a woman. I cannot fully distinguish whether some of my traits, which are advantages or disadvantages, stem from being a woman or my personality traits. If I make a guess, it has had an advantage, especially since I first started, there weren't many women in the field of visual effects, and it wasn't perceived as a profession for women, so people were surprised, and I felt like I achieved something difficult. So, I may have been prouder of myself. Although it wasn't quite right, I think this feeling has had positive effects. The disadvantage is that I was below my capacity. I've read a research study, when men prepare their CVs, if they only have done 30 % of something; they put it down as something they know well. Women do not put it down unless they think they know at least 80 % of it. In terms of presenting yourself to the outside world, as well as in terms of competition and the ambition of promotion, perhaps I would have gone further and approached my capacity more.

Name, title, and date of interview	Year of birth	Answer
Eda Oral cartoonist 29.09.2018	**1966**	When I started to draw in the girls' section in *Gırgır* magazine as a woman cartoonist, it seemed strange to me, why there was a different section. I guess it's because there are fewer girls.
Meral Simer animator, director 29.03.2017	**1948**	There for sure have been the pros as well as the cons, to the extent that it is in every field.
Meral Erez yönetmen, senarist, animatör, eğitimci 12.03.2017	**1947**	In my opinion, I don't really see a distinction between men and women in the field of art. If it is "art," it is not appropriate for me to look for gender here. There shouldn't be the naming of a "female artist," as there is no such thing as a "male artist."

Then

"Animation is Don Quixote business"

İdil Belli

Will everything be better in 5 years? Even though technological advancements and the effect of social media made animation more accessible to a wider group of people and there is an increase in the number of visibility and representation of women in the animation world with the efforts of WIA or the CEO change in Pixar after John Lesseter left his seat to a man and a woman after the sexual assault allegations, old man's club continues. Natalie Busuttil says that while a few years ago, you may have only seen one or two women in an animation studio of 40 artists, she is observing "a sharp increase" in that ratio. "Especially in character design, concept art and 2D animation, women are sometimes outnumbering men in many schools I've visited, and that's being reflected in the work coming out of those schools, where sexuality and gender are subjects that are being explored more frequently than I've seen before" (Qtd. in Brewer, 2018). There has been huge changes over the last few years, with the industry becoming more aware of the issue and taking action. This means more films by women directors being included in festivals, more female jury members, and a few star women are being acknowledged, "leading the way for other young talents." More inclusive solutions promoting gender equality are getting produced. Initiatives, resources, or festivals like WIA, Animated Women, Punanimation Directory of Women, Trans and Non-Binary Animation and Motion Graphics Artists, Leeds Animation Workshop, The Animation Workshop, Women Who Draw, Free the Bid, Femmes d'Anim, French Women Animators Database, Bayan Yanı Comics Magazine, Directed by Women, Women in Film and Television International, Tricky Women Film Festival, London Feminist Film Festival, Annecy Film Festival, Film Mor and Flying Broom Women Film Festivals in Turkey, İstanbul Women's Museum, etc., are putting a spotlight on the subject. Although some animation company executives make statements about "the expectations of society from them are different," "women can not stand the late working hours, so they can hardly succeed." But what is success? Men have defined "success" for centuries. Anna Ginsburg echoes that "role models are a key factor representing women in the industry. They showed me you don't have to be cruel to be a successful person." In order to be successful, what kind of human investment are we talking about? Research shows that the most individual features needed for the future are listed as follows: sense-making, social intelligence, innovative and adaptive thinking, intercultural competence, computational thinking, new media literacy, interdisciplinary work, design mentality, cognitive understanding management, and virtual collaboration. We are entering a period where our human characteristics that make us who we are will be very useful for us (Kadılar, 2019, p. 8–9).

The number of audience interested in female stories will get higher. Different voices, expression, and creativity is demanded. In 2002, during an interview in the Cannes Film Festival, Salma Hayek, the producer and leading actress of *Frida*, talked about her long-time dream of telling women stories, particularly addressing Latin women. In describing her efforts, she shared the most important outcome of her own: "If you want to tell stories of women or minorities in the sector dominated by men, you must prove that you are actually making money by making the films." Hayek said in order to persuade men she has used the strategy of backing up her idea with the use of data proving that women are very important consumers and a necessary community for economic power. And she succeeded. A new wave of women in animation and a wider change are on the horizon. "Society is confronting subtle but equally destructive forms of misogyny and intersectionality too. We make a concerted effort to work with female talent, supporting them to develop their unique voice and bolster their egos" (Brewer, 2018). Women have been a significant part of children-related media in the animation world for many years. It is somewhat empowering to see the fairly recent discussions about childcare during animation-related conferences, festivals, and markets. Just like the one in the Society for Animation Studies email group. We must support women who are giving animation a new voice and beauty by acknowledging their efforts and achievements. Women in animation should keep continuing their quest for different media, venues, languages, and methods in order to tell their stories, and make it economically, artistically, technologically, and culturally sustainable. Areas such as music, sound design, editing, and VFX will be occupied by more women. So there are lots of things to be done for the women in animation. What I know for certain is that we need more professionally organized women and the documentation and representation of their work. Today, women are at the heart of industrial and economical existence as well as a social and cultural resistance. There is hope.

References

Akçay, Z. (2017). *The most watched turkish animated feature: A dead born propaganda Film*. Retrieved from https://blog.animationstudies.org/?p=1958.

Brewer, J. (2018). *Why is there a lack of women in animation, and what can we do about it?*. Retrieved from https://www.itsnicethat.com/features/why-is-there-a-lack-of-women-in-animation-internationalwomens day-080318.

Evren, B. & Yıldırım M. (2014). Türk Sinemasında İlk Uzun Metrajlı Canlandırma Film: Evvel Zaman İçinde, Adana Büyükşehir Belediyesi Kültür Yayınları.

Kadılar, R. (March, 2019). What do we need in times of this incredible change?. *Bloomberg Businessweek*, 8–9.

Le Guin, U. K. (1986). *The carrier bag theory of fiction*. S.I.: Ignota Books.

Lent, J. A., & Tunç A. (1999). In a man's world: Turkish women animators. *Animation World Magazine*, *3*(11).

Harari, Y. N. (2019). *21 Lessons for the 21st century*. New York: Spiegel & Grau.

Hünerli, S. (2002). Development of animation in Turkey. *Selçuk İletişim Dergisi*, *2*, 30–34,

Noyan, N. E., Erez, M., & Erez, C. (June, 2007). Son karenin hikayesi röportaj. *Altyazı*, 52–53.

Serner, A. (2018). Walking the talk. In *Gender equality report 2018*. The Swedish Film Institute.

Tupper, C. (2014). A history of women in animation: Mothers of a medium, Rertrieved from https://www.themarysue.com/history-women-in-animation/

Ürkmez, B. (2017). Turkish animation: A contemporary reflection of the Karagöz Shadow play. In S. V. de Peer (Ed.), *Animation in the Middle East: Practice and aesthetics from Baghdad to Casablanca*(pp. 84–106). London: I.B. Tauris.

Wells, P. (1998). *Understanding animation*. London: Routledge.

Yarman, E. S. (2018). Kibele. Tasarım Üzerine Skeptik Saltolar Kadınlar Nerede. Retrieved from https://manifold.press/kadinlar-nerede

Ömer Vatanartiran

Chapter 9 Dubbing as a Creative Industry in Turkey

Introduction

Ferdi Tayfur, a Turkish engineering student in Berlin, takes a break from his studies in 1924 and works as a mariner on ships in different countries across Europe. Several adventures later, he decides to return to Istanbul and ends up acting in movies in 1931. Around the same time, the İpekçi Brothers, after entering the film industry as foreign movie importers, decide to produce their own movies. They also believe that foreign-language movies (in English, German, or French) could be shown in Turkish. So, they transform an old bakery located in Nişantaşı, one of Istanbul's modern neighborhoods, into a studio where they can record voice-overs. They hire Nazım Hikmet, the famous poet who also acts, writes screenplays, and acts at the same time as voice-director of the dubbing session. Instead of working with the celebrities of the Istanbul city theater, Nazım convinces Ferdi to be the voice of foreign actors in dubbed movies. A leading newspaper, *Cumhuriyet*, announces the premier of the *King Kong* movie, emphasizing its Turkish voice-over. İpek Studio's vision and initiative is very well received.

Thus and so, the dubbing industry in Turkey took its very first steps in the 1930s. Ferdi Tayfur became one of the pioneers of this field, supporting new artists and directors and enjoying his notoriety as one of the most recognized voices in the country. However, he did not consider himself to be an employee in the creative industry. For him, like many other artists who somehow ended up in the industry, it was merely an artistic passion he pursued after his working hours at a foreign company. He would need several more years to be able to work as an independent and self-standing artist. Fortunately, his apprentices and successors enjoyed being in-demand artists, working in well-established studios with better conditions and inheriting a know-how of the profession. Important developments follow in the 1960s and in the 1970s: TRT, the Turkish state radio and television, is established and Turkish cinema sees its golden age. In the 1990s, private television channels emerge. As of the 2000s, thematic channels on digital TV platforms emerge. And nowadays, global and local digital movie channels are more and more widespread in Turkey. Still, voice-over artists in our day, including the writer of this chapter, do not define themselves as workers of a "creative industry."

This chapter aims to create awareness among the professionals and entrepreneurs of this vast sector as well as policymakers, by highlighting the dynamics that shape it. To do this, it will describe the dubbing sector – one of the most important branches of the Turkish creative industry. Secondly, the actors of the field and the economic value they create will be portrayed. Furthermore, the way in which the educational system contributes to the development of the sector will be analyzed. Moreover, the challenges and problems in this rapidly changing global environment will be discussed with final recommendations for a more healthy industry.

The Rise of Creative Industries

After the salutation of economically fruitful and artistically talented professionals by the British New Labour government in 1997 (de Peuter, 2011 & Henry 2007), specific lines of business have gained importance not only for certain neoliberal policies of governments (Howkins, 2001; Hartley, 2005), but also for researchers forming a brand new academic field under the title "creative industries." Any literature review in this domain touches upon the definition of the DCMS – Department for Digital Culture, Media and Sports of United Kingdom – underlining that "creative industries represent a set of interlocking, knowledge-intensive industry sectors focusing on the creation and exploitation of intellectual property" (Henry, 2007). This comprises industries like advertising, performing arts, video games, fashion, music, publishing, TV and radio, visual arts, industrial design, and architecture where creative cultural aspects are combined with a broad economic spectrum in highly dynamic environments (Caves, 2000; Braun, 2007). Although there are different models using different categorizations defined by various institutions such as DCMS, UNESCO, the European Commission, and Americans for the Arts (Arslan, 2017); they all stress the multidimensional and interrelated characteristics of the professions which form each category. For example, a music production is not created by an artistic talent alone, but sound engineers, marketing people, promotion agencies, and art directors are all involved in the process. Caves (2000) names it "creative input" and "humdrum input"; while the former refers to artists who "create out of inner necessity," the latter undertakes paperwork, strategies, and commitments. In other words, the artist creates the content and the businessperson delivers it. Similarly, Throsby (2010) explains creative industries by using the marriage of art and commerce. While human creativity in any cultural industry forms the "core of the concentric circle, the periphery circle contains commercial activities." Thus, cultural aspects referring to "individual creativity and talent" and economic aspects indicating "intellectual property and economic growth" (Hemels & Goto, 2017) are in close cooperation in the definition and existence of this sector. In any case, it is a business model which is based on creativity, technology, education, and international mobility.

Taylor (2007) counts flexible working environments and styles, low-cost communication technologies, and the chance of specialization as indispensable features of creative industries. As one of the first academic figures who raised concern for this domain, Florida (2002) highlighted "creative class employees," influential people with high education and income levels who prosper in certain environments and parts of the world. According to him, the combination of "technology, talent and tolerance" lead to a better performing economy. Leadbeater (1999) supports this idea by drawing attention to the role of microenterprises encouraged by an economy where know-how circulates freely and equally. Thanks to positivist data which confirm the optimism of gurus like Florida, Leadbeater, and Howkins; international commercial organizations and governments have been following promotive policies to keep industry growth rates high (Higgs, 2008 & Lazzeretti, 2008).

While creative industries are glorified in terms of their flexible schedules, project-oriented collaborations, contract labor, transitive career paths, and innovative ways of working by this optimist discourse; they are criticized for the very same reasons from a political economy perspective. Writers like Gill and Pratt (2008), Cunningham (2011), Neilson and Rossiter (2008), and Peuter (2011) drew attention to the fine line between artist independence and precarity. The romantic depiction of the artist who creates art for art's sake in full autonomy is challenged by these approaches (Flew, 2011). To illustrate, Fuchs (2012) argues that playful working spaces are merely new forms of exploitation of human labor. From insecure noncontractual positions to irregular work in discontinuous projects, together with high levels of stress among employees due to long working hours (Hesmondhalgh & Baker, 2011); this perspective mainly criticizes neoliberal government policies. In other words, working without contracts, lack of routine, and flexible dress codes are the Achilles heel of a creative employee; they both empower and put them at risk. So, the myth of the bohemian artist paves the way for easy exploitation of labor (Ross, 2000).

Dubbing as a Creative Industry

The dubbing profession touches on all the discussions briefly explained above. First of all, it is a highly dynamic sector where different occupations interrelate. Many different employees cowork so that a voice-over session can come to life. Business developers get into contact with foreign movie producers, their law departments prepare agreements, and customer agents execute the communication between the studio and the production company abroad. Then, translators prepare the text, and directors read this text and develop an artistic perspective together with linguistic and semantic solutions. The next stage is that sound engineers execute the technical recording devices and sound quality, musical directors conduct the orchestra, and cast agencies find the most matching voice-over artists for a better price. Communication directors get into contact with celebrities if they follow a "star system" strategy – as Bilton (1999) uses the term – to minimize the uncertainty of the success, an assistant helps the director during the session to follow the lines and check the whole text, and finally the voice actor performs in front of the microphone. After the recordings, sound engineers finish mixing and mastering, then representatives of the foreign company evaluate the performance and issue payment. A similar cycle applies to commercials and advertisements but different actors like scriptwriters, client agents, the client himself/ herself, and the art director of the campaign movie are present during the vocal recordings to guide the artist. Here, while the creative input is generated by the writers, translators, sound engineers, art directors, and voice-over artists; accountants, customer agents, business developers, and legal experts take care of the humdrum input, in Caves' (2000) description. In another perspective, the former embodies the core circle of the concentric circle, while the second group of work forges the periphery circle in Throsby's (2010) words. Indeed, it is the concentric circle model which ranks "dubbing" with this specific name. However, the majority of the models include dubbing under the title of television, broadcasting, audial media production, content creating studios, etc., as WIPO, UNCTAD, NESTA, NOIE, KERN, and DCMS do. This indicates how hybrid the sector is, as Cunningham (2002) also underlines in order to explain the nature of creative industries; the economic value created is a result of the interaction of different particles of a whole.

Secondly, technology is essential for any creative economy, as Florida (2002) puts it, including for the dubbing sector. From movie theaters to digital platforms like Netflix, many different communication channels offer new spaces for creative employees. First the arrival of television, then cable TV, followed by digital TV platforms and Internet channels have all expanded the scope of the business. Not only that, digital technology has changed the way recording, mixing, mastering, and (Işıkhan, 2016) content sharing are carried out; a faster production with higher quality than analogue infrastructure made possible. From microphones to headsets, monitors and mixers to talkback controllers, control rooms to sound insulation materials; a wide array of innovations are presented. Easily adaptable home studios have also led to the facility of remote recording for freelance artists and business opportunities for small enterprises. There are even online voice cast agencies who bring together artists and brands. In brief, dubbing is becoming more and more convenient for converged operations of "creative individuals, production, sales and consumers" (Weckerle Gerig & Söndermann 2008) to add value to the economy.

Dubbing in Turkey

Undoubtedly, the dubbing industry in Turkey has been impacted by all the technological progress as well. The launch of the state television in 1964 was a milestone for the industry, and it rapidly became a brand new sphere for dubbing artists in addition to cinema movies. In 1972, the first foreign series and TV commercials were broadcast. This resulted in the establishment of dubbing departments where strict language and pronunciation rules applied. Until the launch of TRT 2 in 1986, TRT served as the one and only TV platform in the country. In 1990, the first private TV channel Star 1 entered the industry and many others followed. This proliferation in the broadcasting sector, leading to the production and broadcasting of more TV programs and commercials, brought many new opportunities for dubbing industry employees. In addition to new recording and dubbing departments established at the new TV channels, independent studios and voice cast agencies entered the scene to address the needs of outsourced content. Telemarketing programs and 0 900 numbers, video games, VCDs and DVDs enlarged the scope of service, as well. The emergence of digital TV platforms like Digiturk or D-Smart has offered another huge opportunity for the sector. Unlike cable TV, which broadcasts original content without a voice-over, digital television platforms opened new thematic channels, with Pay TV and pay per view options where many more in-house; outsourced, or imported content meet viewers. Finally, online platforms like Netflix, BluTV, or puhutv have boosted the sector offering considerable content to be dubbed.

The Scope Expands

Mass media is not the only area where dubbing employees serve, but there are many other clients from the service industry illustrating the interrelated character of the sector. Especially, after the development of customer relations, the practices like IVR, telebanking, e-learning, online instructions, and smartphone applications contributed to the growth of the industry. Similarly, closed-circuit videos specially produced for company events, advertorials, presentations, and public announcements are significant service areas. Statistics correspond with the growing scope explained with technological progress above. Dubbing sector is represented under the title of "motion picture, video and television program production services, sound recording and music publishing; programming and broadcasting services" on TÜİK researches, the Turkish Statistical Institute. According to their statistics, the turnover rate of the whole sector between 2009 and 2017 grew 275 %. Moreover, the number of employees in the industry increased from 7,902 to 10,728. Finally, the growth rate of the production value has been 263 % in 8 years.

An interview with the head of Imaj Productions, one of the leading and oldest companies in the Turkish dubbing sector, confirms the view that the industry has been growing due to new media, global collaborations, and technological facilities. Other than conventional works such as movies, documentaries, and commercial recordings, and long-time collaborations with international giants like Disney, UIP, Warner Bros, National Geographic, Discovery Channel, and Paramount Pictures; there are more and more service areas such as international implementation agencies. For example, Imaj works with three companies based in the United Kingdom – Zebra, Hogarth, and TagLondon, who produce advertorial content for an international audience. The company receives films, then finds matching voices, records the voice-over not only in Turkish but also in a wide spectrum of languages, completes the mixing and mastering, and then sends the final version to the company to be released in different regions. In addition, Turkish brands operating globally, such as Beko, produce commercials and work with Imaj for their international audience. Imaj offers a voice cast service not only in Turkish but also in 70+ other languages, including artists living abroad. In this case, any artist living in London records at a home studio for Imaj, sends it online, and Imaj makes the mix and mastering and shares the product with the customer. This reminds Florida's (2002) technology and talent elements of his 3T model. In other words, it is an organization model that could be hard to imagine in conventional economies; justifying Bilton's (2007) idea that new economy is based on flexible organization models where self-motivated, autonomous, and qualified employees collaborate. There are more than 40 independent dubbing studios in Istanbul not including in-house studios at ad agencies and TV channels such as TBWA, Medina Turgul DDB, NTV, Digiturk, and TRT. Thirty-seven of these are located on the European side of Istanbul. More specifically, they are clustered mostly around Beyoğlu, Şişli, and Beşiktaş. Kadıköy appears to be a rising area for studios. This settlement confirms Florida's tolerance of the 3T model, "the relation between job efficiency, creativity and urban atmosphere"

(Öztürk & Çıracı, 2015); indeed, employees of this creative class work in tolerant, encouraging, free, and artistically and culturally inspiring neighborhoods.

Trained Creative Labor: Functions and Dysfunctions

Another important indicator displaying the growth of the sector is the increasing number of schools whose graduates enter to the industry as sound engineers, dubbing directors, and voice-over artists. For example, universities like 9 Eylül, Bilgi, Istanbul Technical, and Süleyman Demirel used to offer a music education for performers, composers, or instrument players only but since the 2000s, they have also been offering courses, creating special research centers, or independent departments dedicated to musical technologies (Arıcı & Birdal 2017). In other words, self-educated sound engineers trained in the sector have given place to academically formed professionals. Similarly, in addition to augmenting a number of conservatoires, there are more and more schools and courses for voice-over artists specialized in articulation, pronunciation, grammar, and elocution training. Multiple student clubs, elective courses in universities, private schools, or continuous education centers welcome students keen on making a career as a voice artist.

Though there is a trend toward providing academically trained creative labor for the market, employers or mediator agents still do not necessarily seek a degree as a criteria for hiring or representing voice-over artists. In spite of the fact that schools raise the level of artistic quality and reinforce their attitude, they may be limiting as well and a diploma does not guarantee getting the attention of "gatekeepers" in the marketplace (Caves, 2000, p. 22). Furthermore, the increase in the number of schools and studios has triggered a dysfunction for voice-over artists. A similar case to the one put forward by Ursell (2000) happens here in Turkey: There are so many graduates in the media sector that they consent to lower wages. This aspect coincides with critical perspectives of writers like Gill, Pratt, Cunningham, Neilson, Rossiter, de Peuter, Hesmondhalgh, and Baker. Despite the numbers shared above verifying a profitable, productive, and growing industry in close relationship with global partners; the conditions of creative employees do not correlate with overall statistics. In 1986, artists working for the TRT went on strike because of the discontentment related to wages. It resulted in favor of these artists. However, several attempts in the 2000s have remained inconclusive. First of all, their decision for the strike was a response to lower income due to the increasing number of studios hiring inexperienced artists willing to be paid at any wage. They wanted to form a union not only to consolidate the artists against employers but also against new artists who reduce the average prices. Nevertheless, the industry's quick reflex to hire new talent and the lack of governmental policies invalidated the movement. Only in 2011, voice artists could found a union representing a wide spectrum of acting. Since then, they have called studios several times together to negotiate on minimum wages. The process entitled "Social Dialogue" concluded with an agreement among the union and 17 different studios on minimum wages for Netflix productions. Specifically, all content lasting more than 20 minutes, whether it be a documentary or a movie, will be executed on a minimum tariff. At the moment, the union strives at maximum membership of voice artists. In the meantime, it makes efforts to convince the employer studios to work according to certain principles such as minimum wage, employment standards, and social security. However, their attempts have not reached to the point of applying sanctions on companies, artists, and cast agencies. This aspect of the industry overlaps with De Peuter's (2011, p. 421) emphasis on "decomposition or the undermining of workers" as a consequence of destandardized work conditions and lack of a union to fight against it.

Creative industries are mainly based on transient, nonpersistent projects; employers are left alone without protective corporate contracts (Raunig, 2009) and so are the dubbing artists. Indeed, voice artists in Turkey generally work without commitment, in full autonomy and flexibility, but they face an uncertain environment alone. One year they are offered plentiful job opportunities, the next, they desperately wait for work offers with less bargaining power. Moreover, as Christopherson (2008) argues, project-oriented business processes based on multiskilled freelance labor empower personal networks rather than the unions who have less control over a dispersed workforce. Hardt and Negri's (2009) proposal for a basic income provided by governments for irregular and unsecured employees of different industries could be considered for dubbing sector as well. There are many freelance voice artists, dubbing directors, and sound engineers who struggle in this fluctuating environment, and who become more and more dispensable because of the continuous entry of labor from numerous schools. Considering their contribution to the added value in economics and worsening conditions, they deserve "policy attention" (Potts & Cunningham, 2010) to counteract the high-pressure factors surrounding them.

Conclusion

In conclusion, since its infancy in the 1930s, the dubbing sector quickly adapted itself to technological changes and the global environment in Turkey. It became a respected domain of cultural production, not only due to producers' and engineers' passion for new technologies and devices, but also artists' strong performances on the microphone. Thus, it has been a significant branch of creative industries in Turkey which stands at close touch with industries like advertising, film, broadcasting, video game production, education, and entertainment. A growing number of artists, directors, tonmeisters, sound engineers, and briefly creative employers cowork with professionals from marketing, finance, communications, etc., in international environments. Every dubbing session creates an economic value which statistics show has been growing aggregately, especially since 2011. Though new digital technologies presented a threat to the studios and cast agencies in terms of the proliferation of home production, online cast agencies and cheaper freelance artists; they have kept their high-quality policies technically and artistically; therefore, they did not suffer from a shift toward freelance online services. However, creative employees working in irregular, unsecured, and discontinuous conditions in a highly competitive environment suffer from the lack of government policies encouraging employing agencies, studios, and novice labor according to the union's standards and ethical codes. Certainly, more research would serve to increase awareness among policymakers, entrepreneurs, and employees around the growing precarity in the industry. Especially, a deeper look at voice artists' working conditions, their dilemmas between the sense of autonomy and insecurity, and their perception of the industry they serve would contribute to the development of effective arguments for creative industries in Turkey. A research questioning whether being freelance is indispensable as an artist or just a consolation in an uncertain working habitus without protective legal measures would inform a future legal framework. In short, the dubbing sector is worth taking a closer look at, for a better, more comprehensive understanding of creative industries in Turkey.

References

Arslan, G. (2017(. Yaratıcı endüstrilerin yükselişi: geçmiş, bugün ve gelecek, *Anadolu Üniversitesi Sosyal Bilimler Dergisi, 17*(4), 109–122.

Braun, E., & Lavanga, M. (2007). *An international comparative quick scan of national policies for creative industries*. Rotterdam: Euricur for the Miinistry of Education, Culture and Science of the Netherlands.

Bilton, C. (1999). *The new adhocracy: Strategy, risk and the small creative firm*. A Working Paper of the Centre for the Study of Cultural Policy. Warwick.

Bilton, C. (2007). *Management and creativity: From creative industries to creative management*. Malden, MA: Blackwell.

Caves, R. E. (2000). *Creative industries: Contracts between art and commerce.* Cambridge: Harvard University.

Christopherson, S. (2008). *Beyond the self-expressive creative worker. Theory, Culture & Society, 25*(7–8), 73–95.

Cunningham, S. (2002). From cultural to creative industries: Theory, Industry and policy implications. *Media International Australia Incorporating Culture and Policy, 102*(1), 54–65.

Cunningham, S. (2011). Developments in measuring the creative workforce. *Cultural Trends, 20*(1), 25–40.

Flew, T. (2011). The creative industries: Culture and policy. London: Sage.

Florida, R. (2002). *The rise of the creative class: And how its transforming work, leisure, community and everyday life.* New York, NY: Basic Books.

Fuchs, C. (2012). Dallas smythe today – the audience commodity, the digital labour debate, marxist political economy and critical theory: Triple C: Communication, Capitalism & Critique. *Open Access Journal for a Global Sustainable Information Society, 10*(2), 692–740.

Gill, R., & Pratt, A. (2008). In the social factory? Theory. *Culture & Society, 25*(7–8), 1–30.

Hardt, M., & Negri, A. (2009). *Commonwealth.* Cambridge, MA: Belknap Press of Harvard University Press.

Hartley, J. (2005). *Creative industries.* Malden, MA: Blackwell.

Hemels, S., & Goto, K. (2017). *Tax incentives for the creative industries.* Singapore: Springer.

Henry, C. (2007). *Entrepreneurship in the creative industries an international perspective.* Cheltenham: Elgar.

Hesmondhalgh, D., & Baker, S. (2011). *Creative labour: Media work in three cultural industries.* London: Routledge.

Higgs, P., Cunningham, S., & Bakhshi, H. (2008). *Beyond the creative industries: Mapping the creative economy in the United Kingdom.* London: NESTA.

Howkins, J. (2001). *The creative economy.* London: Penguin Books.

Işıkhan, C. (2016). Ses teknolojisi kapsamında 90'lar sonrası Türkiye'de yayıncılık sektörü ve yayıncılıkta mikrofon tercihi üzerine bir araştırma. *Uluslararası Sosyal Araştırmalar Dergisi, 44*(9),1458–1465.

Lazzeretti, L., Boix, R., & Capone, F. (2008). Do creative industries cluster? Mapping creative local production systems in Italy and Spain. *Industry & Innovation, 15*(5), 549–567.

Leadbeater, C. (1999). *Living on thin air: The new economy.* London: Penguin.

Neilson, B., & Rossiter, N. (2008). Precarity as a political concept or fordism as exception. *Theory, Culture & Society*, *25*(7–8), 51–72.

Öztürk, F., & Çıracı, H. (2015). Cultural/Creative industries in Istanbul: Beyoğlu case. *ITU A-Z*, 1(12), 67–82.

Peuter, G. D. (2011). Creative economy and labor precarity. *Journal of Communication Inquiry*, *35*(4), 417–425.

Potts, J., & Cunningham, S. (2010). Four models of the creative industries. *Revue D'Economie Politique*, 1(12), 163–180.

Raunig, G. (2009). *Creative industries as mass deception from Critique of creativity: Precarity, subjectivity and resistance in the creative industries.* London: Mayfly.

Ross, A. (2000). The mental labour problem. *Social Text*, *63*, *18*(2), 1–31.

Taylor, C. (2007). *Creative industries: Developing relationships between higher education, enterprise and innovation in the creative industries.* Cheltenham: Edward Elgar.

Throsby, C. D. (2010). *The economics of cultural policy*. Cambridge: Cambridge University Press.

Ursell, G. (2000). Television production: Issues of exploitation, commodification and subjectivity in UK television labour markets. *Media, Culture & Society*, *22*(6), 805–825.

Weckerle, C., Gerig, M., & Söndermann, M. (2008). *Creative industries Switzerland: Facts, models, culture*. Basel: Birkhäuser.

Burak Tamer, Barkın Engin

Chapter 10 Turkish Independent Music Industry in the Last Decade

Background

The sociocultural and the socioeconomic role of the musicians have been transformed remarkably throughout the ages and music's aesthetic progress has always been in a mutual relationship with technology. Yet the most dramatic shift regarding the creation and reception of the music has been enabled by the invention of sound recording in the late 19th century. Once an art only experienced via live performances, recording technology and its mass-produced domestic formats have rapidly created the music industry with a vast financial potential and inevitable cultural impact. As the pace of evolution in music industry increases, the ways audiences experience music have dramatically transformed over the past decade. The demystification of the sound studio by the introduction of consumer-level audio interfaces has made it possible for artists to produce their music independently. The widespread use of social media and the introduction of streaming services for music playback have made it possible for artists to release their works without the aid of a record label.

Starting from the Attalian (1985) view of considering the economy of music as premonitory to the macroeconomic conditions, the same tendency is clearly evident in the last decade in Turkey. There has been a rise in the number of independent, often collective, musical networks, based on the new production and distribution methods made possible by digital technologies. We continue to encounter Turkish emerging artists who do not release their works in any physical format yet get paid by streaming services' royalties. Some of these artists even manage to strike the attention of international record labels and sign contracts for their following works. This rebalancing of the creative music industry has also supported the growth of Turkish independent labels as well as education programs on music and sound technologies, new studio and producer initiations.

How well do these new sets of economic, technological, and logistic balances function in translating the independent musicians' creative output to produce music media that actually is able to meet with the related audience? With regard to this analysis, what could be certain aspects that would make the creative music industry prosper? This research will present a survey on the current status of the Turkish independent music industry, taking into consideration the effects of technological advancements during the last decade.

Introduction

The evolution of music industry

It is worth setting up a background on how music is consumed today prior to focusing on the Turkish independent music scene, since there is a continuous evolution regarding listening habits shaped by the technological, socioeconomic, and cultural contexts. Streaming via digital services such as Spotify, Apple Music, Tidal, YouTube, etc., has become the most popular format for music consumption today (IFPI 2017). This technological advancement has allowed users to reach a vast archive without having to own the actual music media in physical format, even without having to spare space for the content on their hard drives whether it is a computer or a mobile device. This seemingly limitless access to an extensive repertoire of music anywhere/anytime where there is Internet connection available should definitely be considered an upgrade for listening experience.

This feature of streamed music renders recorded music media more accessible than any time in the history of record industries; yet there is a significant amount of musical information lost due to data compression (Mpeg Layer III, Apple Audio Codec, and Ogg Vorbis are some of these codecs employed by digital streaming services) applied by the streaming services to reduce file size. Therefore, it should be noted that despite this easy access, music listeners are experiencing a degraded version of the actual music production. The loss of resolution, often accompanied by the hyper-compression applied during audio production presents a tendency to repurpose music playback into a background mood-setting procedure rather than a listening experience with rich, detailed spectral and dynamic qualities.

The rebirth of vinyl in a digital age may be considered as a reaction to this dilemma. Loudness Normalization applied by the digital streaming services since 2017 supports a listening experience with more dynamic contrast (Katz, 2015); yet productions that exceed the proposed loudness unit value are still encountered today.

Streamed music introduces the concept of data-driven personalized listening experience. Digital services collect user data to develop "Taste Profiles." The dynamic data generated by the user interaction is constantly processed along with user's nonmusical information to build a profile (Nowak & Wheelan, 2016).

The algorithm then is able to recommend new music to the user, develop personalized playlists, and display advertisements.

As well as tailoring listening habits, the digitalization of music has had its effects on the musicians' creative processes and music production. The introduction of a variety of affordable audio interfaces that comprises microphone and instrument inputs along with analog-digital converters has claimed recording and audio production available to amateur musician and producers. Music production became more portable than ever before. The democratization of the production process complements the digital music distribution companies via which it is possible for the independent musicians to bypass the record labels and release their works online. However, without a considerable budget for promotion or the aid of a record label's PR services, the independent musicians' releases cannot meet their related audience in full potential. The streaming services' data gathering algorithms are criticized for having a biased or limited scope, therefore not contributing to diversity of musical expression/genres and supporting independent music releases (Lena, 2018). The revenues generated by streaming are shared by the digital streaming services, performance rights organizations, record labels, and finally musicians as stated in their contract with the label. Spotify pays approximately $0.007 per stream which is the lowest rate among digital streaming services (RIAA 2017). The lack of transparency in revenue distribution has become a debate topic even among popular musicians who protest against unfair royalty payments (Byun, 2016).

The evolution of independent music

Aesthetic and economic independence of musicians has been a dynamic and multifaceted subject, providing valuable information regarding the socioeconomic and sociocultural changes as a result of the cultural, economic, political, and technological developments in a particular era. Haydn and Beethoven are often considered as the earliest examples of composers in the history of Western music, who had assumed control on their compositional output and were not financially dependent on institutions and patrons (Tschmuck, 2012). After the invention and evolution of audio recording, music continues to be an experiential good; and now the same performance, immortalized in the recording, can be experienced repetitively by the listener.

Releasing records has become a new tool for the artists to reach bigger audiences. Records did not only allow musicians to gain capital from the sales but also promoted their live performances. On the other hand, producing, distributing, and marketing a record was a highly costly financial act; therefore the quick formation of an oligopoly industry structure was inevitable (Byun, 2016). Major record labels often followed a populist approach in terms of musical genre representation in order to ensure further market expansion. Consequently, this aesthetic limitation with certain culturally oppressive overtones paved the way for independent labels in the early 20th century in order to focus on genres from diverse cultural backgrounds. Independent music production continues to be an essential part of music industry towards the end of 2010s (Tschmuck, 2012). In the 21st century, the concept of independent music entails control on artistic and financial matters for recording/performing musicians. Therefore, in this chapter, independent music is used as an umbrella term representing musicians from different aesthetic disciplines, instead of representing a specific musical genre.

An artist, who wants to avoid artistic or financial compromise, has essentially three options for releasing records in the last decade: signing with an independent label, forming their own label, or self-releasing music using a digital distribution company. Considering the amount royalty payments musicians make from streaming playbacks, live performances provide the most sufficient financial means. Attending a concert is still considered an authentic experience; the audience encounters performance of the musicians without the limitations of the recording media and digital distribution channels.

Independent labels frequently focus on a specific genre, on a compositional methodology, or on a contextual idea and often assumed to have less restrictive approach towards artists'/producers' creative intentions. For the last 30+ years, independent labels such as Ada Müzik, Kalan Müzik, Fono Müzik, Baykuş Müzik, and A.K. Müzik in Turkey still specialize on specific genres from diverse backgrounds. What they share in common is a less mainstream-focused policy throughout their discography. Still, all of the labels mentioned above have relatively complex corporate structures, and thus they form a middle ground between major labels such as DMC, Sony, and Avrupa Müzik (they have the most percentage in the market shares as of 2014) and small/boutique labels (Lena, 2018). The 2000s and 2010s saw an exponential increase in the number of boutique labels either run by a single person or belonging to bands/collectives/organizations. These labels will be discussed in detail in the following sections.

According to Wintel's Worldwide Independent Market Report 2018, independent labels had a growth of 11.3 % globally in 2017, which is more than the overall growth of the majors by 10.2 %. On a global scale, independent labels had a market share of 39.9 %. In 2017, it was 37.5 %. Independent labels use the distribution channels of major labels in many cases, yet the increasing importance of digital downloading and streaming renders this dependency unnecessary.

Again, Wintel indicates that the 46 % increase in the revenues for independent labels is generated by streaming only.

Müyap's Turkish Music Industry 2018 Report shows a steady decrease of the revenues generated by the sale of the physical formats. Sole exception is the case with the LPs, which expanded its share dramatically over the years. Digital sales have the biggest share in the overall Turkish market. Streaming made a big leap back in 2015 and has a steady percentage since. The market shares of major and independent labels are not specified. There is no statistical study carried out regarding the number of independent labels, their annual releases, and sales/streaming revenue. This chapter will focus on a selected collection of independent labels to evaluate the economic and cultural aspects.

The Independent Music Scene of Turkey, 2008–2018

This section investigates the deviation from the conventional hierarchy of record industry in Turkey in the last decade. The emergence of independent artists creating works by employing new production methodologies enabled by digital recording and education programs for sound engineering and sonic arts helped to develop a vibrant independent scene. Digital distribution suggests a relatively easier global market reach for musicians by eliminating the cost and the logistics of physical formats. The leading independent labels and artists' current status is evaluated in conjunction with the available distribution channels, authors' right societies, and PR resources; and thus presents insight into factors that shape the economic sustainability of the independent music scene and diversity of cultural expression.

Music production

Digital evolution has transformed the music industry in various levels ranging from the production stage to consumer end. It is no longer a requirement to use a professional studio facility to record, mix, and master albums. Independent artists prefer to work in cost-effective and stress-free environments and bypass the pressure of having to complete performances/compositions within the reserved time of a professional studio. As this approach leaves more room for creative experiments, "producing at home" has become one of the popular choices, where the musician uses an audio interface coupled with a computer running a digital audio workstation (DAW) that features recording, editing, overdubbing, and processing functions (Byun, 2016). There is a substantial amount of commercial software available such as digital instruments, real-time sound processing applications, and DAW. Some of these present periodic subscription models to the consumer so that the musicians can pay to have access to the software during phases of production and do not have to purchase a perpetual license.

From a technical standpoint, the highest resolution PCM (pulse code modulation) digital audio captured in a professional recording studio is obtainable with portable devices. The other factors of the signal chain that shape sonic quality include microphones, pre-amplifiers, and analog to digital converters. A professional digital recording studio is able to present a rich selection of each stage as well as a controlled acoustic environment to perform in, but independent musicians prefer employing "in the box" software solutions where they can creatively compensate for the shortcomings of the home studio, hence the differences in sonic quality become less significant and objective.

Repositioning of the musician–production relationship has commenced small-scale commercial studios run by independent producers. Record labels no longer fund album productions. Musicians are expected to cover their production expenses, which were once considered startup investments by the record companies to establish agreement for a contract (Byun 2016). Independent labels cover the publication, distribution, and promotion costs of the albums; the degree of economic involvement in each step depends on the scope of the project. Though not thoroughly documented, independent music releases in Turkey constitutes only a small fraction of the actual market dominated by the mainstream labels (Lena, 2018). Therefore, online distribution, digital releases, and promotion via social media are favored among independent labels.

The emergence of independent labels and studios coincide with the foundation of graduate and undergraduate education programs on sound technologies. Istanbul Technical University Center for Advanced Studies in Music (MIAM) has been a milestone in this regard. The program offers graduate and doctoral level studies on Sound Engineering and Design and Sonic Arts. The program also houses the biggest music library in Turkey (Miam, 2019). Istanbul Technical University Music Technologies, Bilgi University Music, and Yıldız Technical University Audio Design Departments are undergraduate programs that comprise music production courses. Bahçeşehir University Sound Technologies graduate program was founded in 2013. The program focuses its education directly on music production and supports emerging fields such as music information retrieval, digital instrument and audio processing applications design, studies on musical acoustics, and postproduction techniques. SAE Institute's entrance to Turkey in 2010 lasted for six years; the international creative media institute terminated its campus in Istanbul in 2016.

The transformation of traditional label

Traditional major labels often operate under similar corporate structures. They have been responsible for finding new artists, investing the production costs (later to be recouped from the profit), distributing the recordings to larger markets, and promoting them in order to attract more attention for the product. They have been also frequently criticized for their exhaustive bureaucracy and creative control, and have been accused of financial exploitation of the artists, legally bound to "less than fair" contracts (Albini, 2003). Similar corporate hierarchy and financial targets can be observed in more complex independent labels. Smaller establishments have typically provided an alternative path for musicians since the initiation of the music industry. In terms of logistics and market share, major companies have continued to dominate the market, although occasional setbacks caused by economic crisis or administrative faults had been encountered during the 20th century (Tschmuck, 2012). One of the latest challenges for the major labels was the emergence of digital file–sharing platforms in the late 1990s. The very first example regarding the violation of the copyrights using digital technology was the notorious Napster case (Nowak & Wheelan, 2016). Despite all the legal battles against piracy, physical sales steadily decreased throughout the 2000s in a global scale; and this situation triggered a paradigm shift once again for the music industry. Turkish music industry was no exception (Müyap, 2018). More established labels have had to adapt to the inevitable evolution of legal downloading and subscription services in the last decade, while some of the independent ones have halted production such as Doublemoon/Pozitif or have started to produce records infrequently such as Elec-trip. At the same time, online distribution single-handedly helped the labels with microeconomic resources to exist on a modest level.

During the last 10 years, there have been several options for musicians in Turkey to release their records besides the conventional methods. The relatively less complicated strategy is releasing your music without a label. Open/free platforms such as YouTube, Bandcamp, and SoundCloud are among the most favorite services; and legal download and subscription services have permitted direct access to musicians representing themselves. According to the Pro-Music website, the following platforms are considered as legal in Turkey: iTunes (download), Spotify (stream), Apple Music (stream), Deezer (stream), YouTube (stream), Izlesene (stream), Muud (download and stream), and Fizy (download and stream). Izlesene, Muud, and Fizy can be only accessed via labels; therefore musicians without contractual obligations cannot be presented on those local online organizations. International download and subscription platforms (including the ones which have not been mentioned by Pro-Music, such as Tidal, Amazon, Google, etc.) can be accessed via digital distribution companies as will be discussed in the next chapter in detail (Pro Music, 2017).

Another option for the independent musicians is to form their own record label. Newly established independent acts such as Lin Records, Lu Records, and Domuz Records have been founded by recording artists, who initially released their own material. Later on, they have become a roof for other musicians as well. Collectives such as M4NM or institutional labels such as Bilgi Music can be considered as variations of a similar independent agenda. There are also other small/boutique labels, which specialize on various genres actively in the last decade. Often associated with less conventional styles of music; Audioban, Shalgam, Tantana Records, Müzik Hayvanı, Tektosag, Dunganga, Personal Space Records, Hammer Müzik, and Partapart are among the active labels of Turkey in the 2010s.

With the direct control on her/his financial means, an established independent artist might choose to stay independent. Often artists who have succeeded to gain a larger following over time have either been approached by the bigger independents/majors in Turkey or signed with international labels in order to expand their operations outside of local borders. There are a growing number of Turkish artists releasing albums and performing worldwide. A selected list of artists and bands will be mentioned as case studies later in order to give a better sense of the potential the local scene contains.

Online distribution and streaming in Turkey's independent music scene

The digitalization of music on both production and consumption ends has enabled distribution without any physical media and logistic costs. Visiting a record store and going through shelves to browse artists and genres is no longer a requirement to experience new music. Untethered from physical media, the digital music sets off ripples that continue to reorganize the way we encounter music in social and economic contexts (Nowak & Wheelan, 2016).

Orchard, Believe, CD Baby, Distrokid, Tunecore, Ditto Music, AWAL (Artists without a Label), and LANDR are some of the favored online distribution services among independent musicians. Orchard (owned by Sony) in particular is active in Turkey due the company's agreement with the publishers' rights organization MÜYAP (MÜYAP, 2008). These services remove the need for a middleman and deliver the clients' music to a collection of online download and streaming services such as Spotify, Apple Music, iTunes, Tidal, etc. Digital distributors feature a number of additional services for publishing royalty collection including YouTube monetization. Employment of YouTube's Content ID technology allows digital distributors to place claim on any video that contains the artist's original music. CD Baby offers sync licensing program; opting in this program allows the distributor to license the artist's original music for movies, advertisements, TV shows, video games, and YouTube to generate revenues of neighboring rights (CD Baby, 2019).

LANDR and Mondotunes represent a further step in the evolution of digital music distribution by offering audio mastering services, which allows the independent musicians to submit their works directly after the mixing stage, thus eliminating the need for conventional mastering. Although this would not be a preferred choice for established artists since signing in to such service will restrict the control of the musician over the last phase of music production, it presents a basic standard to independent musicians who have no access to professional digital audio mastering services within the specified price range. LANDR features a mastering service that uses AI and machine learning to replicate mastering processes applied for digital codecs, and therefore removes the involvement of a mastering engineer altogether (LANDR, 2019). Mondotunes offers conventional mastering services via employment of an in-house mastering engineer (Mondotunes 2019).

Having set this background, examining selected independent artists' online data as case studies will help us build a framework of Turkish independent music scene's structure.

Canozan is an independent musician living in Istanbul. He studies at Bahçeşehir University Sound Technologies program, produces his music, and releases works via CD Baby and Distrokid. Following his debut album in 2015, he released a single in collaboration with Deniz Tekin, another singer/songwriter who is signed to Avrupa Müzik in 2017. After this release Canozan's followers on Spotify started to increase significantly and he gained recognition. Canozan kept interest of followers alive by releasing 17 singles and two albums in two years and therefore maintained his position in the recommendation algorithm of Spotify, gaining the chance to reach a wider audience. Under no contract with any record label, Canozan managed to collect royalties through digital distribution services while still keeping 100 % rights and ownership of his works. He recently opted in the nonexclusive synch-licensing program of CD Baby and works with ILS Vision, the largest multichannel YouTube network company in Turkey for copyrights management and content monetization on YouTube (ILS Vision, 2016).

According to MÜ-YAP's report on Turkish Music Industry in 2018, 58 % of Turkish audience favor digital streaming and download services for music consumption. Physical media sales are on the decline except for vinyl LPs, which have been in ascension since 2013. According to a recent survey carried out by the research company Zenna, 82 % people in Turkey use YouTube as the main digital platform to listen to music, and it is followed by Spotify with 26 % and Fizy with 24 % (Zenna, 2018).

Currently Canozan has nearly 400,000 monthly listeners on Spotify; his top tree tracks have established over six million streams. Digital distributors provide analytics to artists; it is possible to monitor reports of sales and payment history, display stream values with graphs and other statistical data. According to Canozan's analytic reports, he has an approximate average of 20,000 streams per day and two million streams per month (Özçelik, 2019). Collecting revenues has enabled him to sustain as an independent artist. Though Avrupa Müzik's effect on his initiation cannot be underestimated, we can consider Canozan a representative of an independent musician who is able to benefit from the business model formed by digital distribution channels and streaming services.

MESAM and MSG are Turkish trade organizations that provide authors' rights protection while MÜYORBİR focuses on performance rights. These trade organizations collect and deliver revenues generated by digital sales; however, musicians lose a considerable amount of income due to deductions of tax, trade organizations, and record label commissions. The contact between the record label and musician sets the rules for label's share but the commission applied by the Turkish trade organizations are not clearly indicated (MSG, 2015). Transparency of digital revenues distribution has not been achieved when compared to the accessible and flexible services of the global digital distributors. Fizy comes as the third most popular streaming service in Turkey and does not display stream number statistics of artists; this action coincides with the attitude of Turkish publishers and trade organizations that want to keep their revenue distribution analytics private.

Quoting Byun's reference on Bowie theory, live performances are the only unique situation left, and concert touring will become a significant source of sustainability for musicians. Recent Turkish independent scene provides examples such as Gaye Su Akyol and She Past Away in correspondence with this concept. Gaye Su Akyol manages digital releases via Turkish independent label Dunganga Records and physical copies via an international label titled Glitter Beat. Her 2019 spring/summer tour dates feature 40 concerts in Europe and Turkey. She Past Away's (Metropolis Records) 2019 tour dates feature 40 global concerts including one in Istanbul, Turkey. The success of both independent artists as touring musicians does not translate efficiently to Spotify statistics when compared to the previous example of Canozan who is supported by remediated listening habits. Akyol has 140,000 and She Past Away has 54,000 monthly listeners on Spotify; both artists' popular tracks approximate five million streams. This difference could be a factor of audience's preference of conventional music consumption methods since concert touring provides potential for growth on all platforms.

The employment of Bandcamp should be taken into consideration, especially when dealing with the experimental musical releases of the Turkish independent scene. Bandcamp's "name your price" system stands out among other streaming services. The site is a combination of stream and download methods and therefore does not offer subscription. The user is able to stream albums without paying and can pay the amount specified by the authors in order to download a copy. The audio files can be in high resolution, which is an advantage over other digital platforms.

Bandcamp employs an online payment system titled PayPal to manage transaction, which was banned by the Turkish Government in 2016 due to tax conflicts (PayPal 2016). PayPal had to cease all its activity in Turkey; therefore, independent musicians were no longer able to claim their revenues.

Experimental independent releases find less audience, chance for promotion and recognition, and thus get less streams and periodic listeners on Spotify. Artists such as Kim Ki O and İpek Görgün are signed to international labels, yet their statistics display that they cannot sustain with digital royalty payments. Prominent bands such as Baba Zula, Nekropsi, Replikas, and Ayyuka who had their career highlights during the period prior to the shift in listening habits to streaming have not displayed corresponding success via digital services. This may be due to the dedicated audience's tendency to consume music via physical media, yet it is also a proof that these musicians have been unable to interact with the younger generations.

The Effects of Digital Media Revolution

One of the fundamental requirements for the independent musicians to sustain their career is to be able to make sure that their creations would reach potential audiences. Often there would be no available budget for hiring professional public relations agencies to develop a suitable strategy. Therefore, musicians themselves have to determine their own methodology for publicity and promotion. Although there are many benefits in terms of distribution, digital platforms have caused a highly competitive industry regarding the amount of supply available in the market. According to the statistics, approximately 1000 new tracks are uploaded to each digital platform on a daily basis (A Journal of Musical Things, 2018).

Traditional media outlets such as music magazines have gone down in numbers in Turkey throughout the last decade regardless of the musical genre they focus on. *Blue Jean*, one of longest lasting mainstream magazines, shut down its doors after almost 30 years of activity in 2016. The local version of the international *Rolling Stone* magazine ceased production earlier in 2009 after only three years of activity, while *Roll*, an autonomous initiative, also published their last issue in 2009 after 13 years (Lena 2018). *Bant*, a magazine that started publication in 2004, changed its name to *Bant Magazine* in 2011 and became a dominantly online media. The only surviving example of printed media is *Andante*, a classical music magazine that has been in print since 2002. In addition to *Bant Mag*, several online magazines and blogs are active in terms of music journalism with broader aesthetic perspectives. Hafif Müzik, Bir Baba Indie, Back to the Sound, Redbull Türkiye, Avaz Avaz, and In the Void can be listed as the leading examples. Majority of the music radios and TV stations predominantly allocate their broadcast time to mainstream music, thus it is not likely for an emerging artist to make an appearance on these channels.

Consequently, social media has become the sole way to reach people for the majority of the artists. Each medium requires a slightly different approach in order to get in touch with the listeners. In general YouTube and Instagram seem to be the most preferred ones in Turkey. Let's look at some numbers of followers of some established independent artists in order to have a clear picture of social media potentiality. Ezhel, a recent hip-hop artist, who has self-released his debut record in 2017, achieved a huge commercial success. He has 1,200,000 followers on Instagram, 539,000 subscriptions on his YouTube channel, 210,000 followers on Twitter, and 108,00 likes on his Facebook page. Another example from the hip-hop scene, which seems to be on a popularity rise in Turkey, is Ben Fero. Again, as an independent artist, he has 477,000 followers on Instagram, 252,000 subscriptions on YouTube, and 48,000 followers on Twitter. Considering the absence of mass media support, these numbers not only represent the scale of their achievements but are also a proof on how they can be in direct touch with their audience.

Another popular genre in Turkey in the last decade can be categorized under singer songwriter category. Majority of the established artists who belong in this genre either have started as independent artists or have signed to the major labels for their upcoming releases. Deniz Tekin has started to share her compositions on her YouTube and SoundCloud pages in 2014 and after attracting serious attention, her debut album *Kozakuluçka* has been released by Avrupa Müzik (Gülbaba 2019). She has 33,000 subscriptions on YouTube and 106,000 followers on Instagram. Another new generation singer/songwriter Nilipek has self-released her debut album *Sabah*, and her second album *Döngü* has been released by an independent label Lin Records. She has 47,000 subscriptions on her YouTube channel, 27,000 followers on Instagram, 10,000 likes on her Facebook page, and 7,000 followers on Twitter.

Streaming platforms also offer new possibilities for the artists to be recognized. Besides the algorithms they employ to offer users new artists based on their musical preferences, playlists generated by the companies or by the users themselves have also been instrumental for the new musical discoveries. Similar to the idea of mix tapes from the cassette era, digital playlists might either comprise of a specific genre/concept or may consist of personal musical choices of a specific user (Purcell & Randall, 2016). Although YouTube is not an audio-only platform, video playlists can be arranged. For the audio-only streaming applications, playlists are a crucial part of the digital experience.

Another way for the artists to receive attention has been to contribute to the soundtracks of TV series or feature films. Especially local TV series has become increasingly popular in Turkey and the number of productions is constantly increasing. Besides the original soundtracks composed especially for the shows, producers have started to license songs by lesser-known artists, which might create a significant demand for the artist and the song. One of the most popular examples is the highly rated TV series called *Çukur* produced by Ay Yapım. For each episode, several songs from an already existing repertoire, often from diverse range of artists, are used. Ceylan Ertem's rendition of "Zalım", a folk song by Aşık Mahsuni Şerif, had been used in the eighth episode of the show in 2017; and afterwards it received approximately 8 million streams in Spotify, 89 million streams in the official YouTube channel of the label Arda Yapım, and 11 million in the official YouTube channel of Çukur, making the song the most popular song she has contributed. Even older songs from relatively less popular experimental artists could get attention, as it is the case with the band Replikas. The song "Yaş Elli" from their second album *Dadaruhi* which was released back in 2002 by Ada Müzik became a minor hit after being used in the first and second seasons of *Çukur* three times, receiving again several million streams.

Apart from the cultural shifts caused by the digital age, live performances are still the most validated way for musicians to promote their work and receive a considerable income. Although there have been exceptions such as Canozan, royalties coming from the digital platforms have been not enough for the majority of the independent artists to financially survive; thus live performances have gained more significance over time. There has been an increase in the number of the live performance venues since the late 1990s in Turkey, which enable musicians to perform their own compositions. In the past, musicians had to perform cover songs in the clubs due to financial concerns of the owners. As of 2018, the most active venues with various capacities in Istanbul, cultural capital of Turkey, are Babylon, IKSV Salon, Zorlu PSM, Borusan Müzik Evi, Volkswagen Arena, Peyote, Karga, Nayah, Mecra, Arka Oda, Bant Mag Bina, and Dunia.

Besides the local venues and festivals, several artists and bands have been touring outside of national borders. Baba Zula, She Past Away, Gaye Su Akyol, Ah Kosmos, Konstrukt, Jakuzi, and Kim Ki O are among the well-known acts to tour around the globe. All of the artists mentioned above also have record deals with international labels. Baba Zula and Gaye Su Akyol are working with Glitter Beat from Germany. She Past away recently signed with Metropolis Records from America for their upcoming third album. Ah Kosmos worked with Denovali Records from Germany for her 2015 album *Bastards* and recently released her latest effort *Beautiful Swamp* from Compost records based in Germany as well. Jakuzi is signed by the City Slang records again from Germany, and Kim Ki O has been working with the French label Lentonia. Konstrukt released their collaboration albums with Keiji Haino from Karlrecords from Berlin. İpek Görgün is working with Touch from England. Another important release has come from Sub Rosa based in Brussels in 2016. "An Anthology of Turkish Experimental Music 1961–2014" contains a selection of artists working in the experimental and electro-acoustic music scene. There are many more examples indicating that independent artists from Turkey are drawing increasingly global attention over time.

Conclusion

Since its inception, music industry has been in constant evolution. Digital era accelerates the pace of change in the industry, and the local scene in Turkey has been affected by the similar global trends. Democratization of the music production and distribution process enabled by digital technology has led to a rise in the number of independent artists and labels. This could be regarded as a revolution for Turkish independent music scene since musicians who would have no access to production, distribution, and promotion channels can now represent themselves in the global music market. Social media has eliminated the need for mainstream media channels. However, the ease of digital music publication has introduced new parameters to the industry. The quantity of the releases is at their peak value in the history of recorded music, which makes competition fiercer than ever. Considering the audience's point of view in this ever expanding repertoire, it is constantly getting harder to browse, connect, and incorporate artists/genres to their musical selections. Physical media is no longer a primary source of music consumption in Turkey. The factors that determine the commercial success of musical releases are either driven by the major labels or trending genres in Turkey. Cultural diversity in musical expression does not receive enough support to prosper within borders. Meanwhile, artists outside of mainstream are the ones to achieve international success.

Considering the analysis and evaluations presented in this chapter, it is possible to say that the Turkish younger generations' preferences coincide with the digital means of music consumption, which will continue to evolve. Independent musicians' employment of international distribution services may be directed to national resources with the adaptation of national trade organizations. Clarification of digital revenue distribution has to be achieved in order to contribute to a healthy music industry. On the other hand, the amount of artist and music introduced into the market almost on a daily basis might overload the industry as well, creating a vast number of semiprofessional acts. Turkish trade organizations apply quotas when processing digital revenues to overcome this problem, yet musicians that remain under the specified range are not able receive financial restitution for their works. Nevertheless, concerts seem to continue to preserve its function as the main financial source for the artists.

References

A Journal of Musical Things. (2018). *You'll be stunned at how many songs are added to streaming music services every day*. Retrieved from http://ajournalofmusicalthings.com/youll-be-stunned-at-how-many-songs-are-added-to-streaming-music-services-every-day-i-was

Albini, S. (2003). *The problem with music*. Retrieved from https://archive.org/stream/TheProblemWithMusic/TheProblemWithMusicBySteveAlbini_djvu.txt

Attali, J. (1985). *Noise: The political economy of music*, Minneapolis: University of Minnesota Press.

Byun, C. H. C. (2016). *The economics of the popular music*. Basingstoke: Palgrave MacMillan.

CD Baby. (2019). *License your music*. Retrieved from. https://cdbaby.com/license-your-music.aspx

Digital Age. (2018). *Türk insanının müzik dinleme alışkanlıkları ve dijital müziğin yükselişi*. Retrieved from https://digitalage.com.tr/turk-insaninin-muzik-dinleme-aliskanliklari-ve-dijital-muzigin-yukselisi

Gülbaba Music and Artist Management. (2019). *Deniz Tekin*. Retrieved from https://www.gulbabamusic.com/deniz-tekin

IFPI. (2017). *Global music report 2017*. Retrieved March 10, 2019, from. https://www.ifpi.org/news/IFPI-GLOBAL-MUSIC-REPORT-2017.

ILS Vision. (2016). *About us*. Retrieved from http://www.ilsvision.com.tr

Katz, B. (Ed.). (2015). *Recommendation for loudness of audio streaming and network file Playback*. New York: Audio Engineering Society Technical Council.

LANDR. (2019). *Online audio mastering*. Retrieved from. https://www.landr.com/en/online-audio-mastering

Lena, F. (2018). *Türkiye'nin müzik endüstrisinde çeşitlilik*. İstanbul: Kreksa Kültür Yayınları.

Miam. (2019). *Miam history*. Retrieved from http://www.miam.itu.edu.tr/en/history

Mondotunes. (2019). *Mondotunes Mastering*. Retrieved from. https://www.mondotunes.com/mastering

MSG. (2015). *Sıkça sorulan sorular*. Retrieved from https://www.msg.org.tr/s-s-s

Müyap. (2008). *Online music in Turkey*. Retrieved from http://en.mu-yap.org/news-category/news

Müyap. (2018). *Türkiye müzik endüstrisi 2018*. Retrieved from http://tr.mu-yap.org/wp-content/uploads/2018/06/TÜRKİYE-MÜZİK-ENDÜSTRİSİ-2018.pdf

Nowak, R., & Wheelan, A. (Eds.). (2016). *Networked music cultures: Contemporary approaches*. Emerging Issues. Bristol: Springer.

Özçelik, Can Ozan. Personal interview, March 15, 2019.

PayPal. (2016). *Türkiye'deki müşterilerimiz için önemli bilgilendirme*. Retrieved from https://www.paypal.com/tr/home

Pro Music. (2017). *Legal music services*. Retrieved from https://www.pro-music.org/legal-music-services-europe.php

Purcell, R., & Randall, R. (Eds.). (2016). *21st century perspectives on music, technology, and culture: Listening spaces*. Basingstoke: Palgrave MacMillan.

RIAA. (2017). *Mid-year 2017 news and notes*. Retrieved from https://www.riaa.com/wp-content/uploads/2017/09/RIAA-Mid-Year-2017-News-and-Notes2.pdf

Tschmuck, P. (2012). *Creativity and innovation in the music industry*. Bristol: Springer.

Wintel. (2018). *Worldwide independent music report 2018*. Retrieved from http://winformusic.org/files/WINTEL%202018/WINTEL%202018.pdf

Ali Çağıl Ömerbaş

Chapter 11 Hip-Hop Culture in Turkey

Introduction

The second half of 2010s witnessed a rapid expansion in the Hip-Hop culture in Turkey. From the beginning, this culture has been appreciated and represented by the masses. MCs (Master of Ceremony) rap about significant issues, such as gentrification and effects of global policies, with extremely clever and obviously well-educated verses, which (I thought) were non-existent in Turkish rap. There are music producers that make us see the equivalents of masters like J Dilla or DJ Premier in Turkey is no longer a distant dream. In this chapter, I will try to present some milestones from the Hip-Hop culture in Turkey. I will mainly focus on rap music, as it is the most recognized element of this culture.

It is important to clarify what Hip-Hop means, as in many contemporary discussions, it is frequently used to describe music: rap. However, this term defines a culture, which also contains rap music. One of the most prominent MC and Hip-Hop advocates, KRS-One states that "Rap is something you do / Hip-Hop is something you live" in his song "9 Elements" (2003). Although he lists nine elements that form the culture, four of these elements are commonly used: DJing (Disk Jockeying), B-Boying (Break dancing), MCing, and Graffiti (Chang, 2006, p.xi). This chapter will present a summary of the development of Hip-Hop Culture in Turkey, from the earliest B-Boys in Germany to the contemporary commercial success and widespread acceptance of this culture, mainly focusing on rap music.

Origins in the Diaspora

The initiation of Turkish speakers to Hip-Hop did not happen in Turkey; the culture was first embraced by the second-generation Turkish immigrants in Germany during the early 1980s. Then, West Berlin hosted some clubs frequented by the American soldiers who were stationed there. Turkish immigrants befriended these soldiers and started to learn about Hip-Hop for the first time. American media was also presenting some rap songs as well, films such as *Wild Style* (1982) and *Beat Street* (1984) were being appreciated by promising Hip-Hop aficionados, as well as the related articles published in *Bravo* Magazine (Diessel, 2001, p.167). Although there were native rappers before the immigrants, rap in Turkish attracted particular attention as a manifestation of failure in integration of the guest workers into society (Cheeseman, 1998, p.193), as the racist attacks in the early 1990s and the rise of Turkish street gangs in response clearly illustrated (Soysal, 2004, p.68).

The early 1990s witnessed some racist attacks against Turkish immigrants, resulting with mortalities (Mölln in 1992, Solingen in 1993). Subjected to such acts of violence, the Turkish youth embraced Hip-Hop Culture as a perfect instrument to announce their presence in a foreign and arguably hostile country (Solomon, 2009, p.308). As Hip-Hop was also invented and applied by the oppressed minority in United States, it was more than suitable for the people who suffer similar conditions in Europe. The laid back and emotional black musical culture was also seen as something opposing the German way of life, according to Turkish musicians of the time (Ickstadt, 1999, p.574).

Turkish young men living especially in Berlin first started to rap in English language, as they have been exposed to American songs mainly. However, they have found ways to integrate their mother tongue to this culture. The Turkish culture was first introduced into Hip-Hop by The Islamic Force. Boe-B, the founder of the group, (Bülent İpek) was producing beats using Turkish musical motifs since 1986 and rapping over those beats in English, but their first album, *Mesaj* (The Message, 1997) was released in Turkish. Although "oriental rap" is frequently associated with the famous band Cartel (Çınar, 1999; Diessel, 2001), it was the My Melody/Istanbul single (1st Class Records) from 1991 by Boe-B and DJ Derezon – also a member of Islamic Force – that made the term widely accepted in the Hip-Hop scene (Altunay, 2017).

Alongside Cartel project, which reached number one in charts during the mid-1990s, Levent Soysal describes İslamic Force as the apex of Turkish rap (2004, p. 71), forming their narratives on issues such as expat, plurality, equality, and human rights. All the struggles of these young expats – in Germany and in Turkey – are expressed in their music, what they have been living through and how they are willing to choose music as an instrument of resistance instead of violence. They do not suggest a violent nationalistic solution for the continuing discrimination in Germany and Turkey, but rather express the disappointment of the band members and seek a universalist point of view, in accordance with the teachings of Afrika Bambaataa, one of the pioneers of Hip-Hop culture whom Boe-B idolizes (Soysal 2004, p. 76). After witnessing Cartel's success, İslamic Force also sought a place in the Turkish market. The shifted attention after the separation of the Cartel project in the Turkish market and untimely death of Boe-B in 1999 prevented the band from getting their deserved recognition in Turkey (Soysal 2004, p. 77–78). Remaining band members Derezon and Killa Hakan (Hakan Durmuş) are still pursuing their music careers; especially Durmuş is still enjoying his lasting fame in both Germany and Turkey.

As I have mentioned, Islamic Force was active since the mid-1980s, using English lyrics in their songs, until *Mesaj* was released in 1997. However, the greatest success of Turkish rap predates this release with two years. Although there were successful efforts to compile a rap album in Turkish, such as DJ Mahmut, Volkan T, Murat G, and Kmr's collaborative effort *Looptown presents Turkish Hiphop* (1994), it was the Cartel (1995) project that really attracted attentions in Germany and Turkey in 1995. The project was initiated by producers Ünal Yüksel, Ozan Sinan, and Yüksel Mutlu in their studio, Ypsilon Music in 1994 (Kaya 2001, p. 200; Soysal 200, p.72). These three entrepreneurs combined already active Hip-Hop aficionados/practisers from various parts of Germany: Erci-E (Ercüment Ergün) from Berlin, Karakan [Blackblood] from Nuremberg, and Da Crime Posse from Kiel. Karakan consisted of two members: Kabus Kerim (Kerim Yüzer) and Alper Ağa, who was a part of an earlier project called King Size Terror, who published the first song that includes a verse in Turkish in "Bir Yabancının Hayatı" [Life of a Foreigner, 1991]. Da Crime Posse had two Turkish members, M.Ali and InceEfe. The remaining members were Olcay/Ole from Germany and Babalu, who was Cuban. These seven musicians are responsible for the greatest moment of glory in Turkish Hip-Hop, replacing Michael Jackson in Germany and Sezen Aksu and Tarkan in Turkey on the top of the music charts (Cheeseman 1998, p. .201).

Cartel has chosen a different public image from İslamic Force. On his book *Sicher in Kreuzberg* (2001), which presents an elaborate account on development of Turkish rap in Germany, Ayhan Kaya categorizes Islamic Force as universalist political rap (p. 188), whereas he claims that Cartel's songs are examples of cultural nationalist rap (p. 182). Throughout the album, motifs of Turkishness and nationalism are repeated countless times, as in the song called "Türksün" [You are a Turk]:

telefon edip arkadaşlara bir	Call your friends, let them know
haber ver	Tonight we're gathering to show this
bu gece toplanıp göstereceğiz, bu	country is ours
ülke bizim ya	Whoever sees us on street fears a lot
bizi sokakta görenlerin korkuları çok	Still it is no match for the fears of the
bizden ölenlerin korkularına	deceased on our side
mukayese yok	We did not started this game but we
bu oyunu biz başlatmadık ama biz	gonna end it
bitireceğiz	We'll make the ones doing evil to the
suçsuza kötülük yapanlara kan	innocent eat blood
yedireceğiz	That day seventy young Turks are ready
o gün yetmiş türk genç hazır sokakta	on the street
beş dakika sürmedi polis	Under five minutes the squad car has
arabası yolda	departed
hakiki katillere değil, bize geldiler	Not for the real killers but for us
coplarla, sopalarla bizi dövdüler	Beating us with batons and sticks
nasıl çalışsak, nasıl yapsak, nasıl	How should we work, how, how shall
yaşasak?	we live
yabancıyız bunu onlar unutmayacak	We are the foreigners, they ain't
sen türksün	gonna forget
(almanyalı)	You are a Turk
bunu anla, bunu unutmamalı	(from Germany)
	Understand this, never forget

These lyrics by Erci-E suggests (or threatens) the excessive use of violence against discriminative circumstances, stressing the unification under Turkishness. Their style and the content of their songs were similar with the gangsta rappers in the United States. This subgenre is characterized with its emphasis on the gangster lifestyle, i.e. emphasis on violent lives of people especially living in ghettos and the riches this lifestyle could bring. There were also some active Turkish gangs in those years, but Soysal states that the gangster appearance was mainly for posing, and those people were petty criminals at most (2004, p. 68).

Nationalism used by Cartel was strictly based on conditions in Germany in the mid-1990s. The problem is that the actual nationalists back home did not see this clearly and interpreted the band's songs all too literally, using Cartel's discourse to support their anti-Kurdish arguments. The lines of a project resisting fascism in a country were being used in the name of fascism in another one, which is defined by a paradox by Alev Çınar (1999). When the band members landed for their 1995 tour in Turkey, they were welcomed by the Graywolves –members of the far-right political party – at the airport. This situation was not too enthusiastically met by some of the band members. Da Crime Posse was a leftist formation with non-Turkish members, and did not appreciate being called Turkish boys (Cheeseman 1998, p. 202–3). Erci-E was not happy with the association as well. In an interview he confesses that, having grown up in Germany, they have really limited ideas on what was going on in Turkey (2011).

Apart from political discussions, Cartel was extremely well received in Turkey and initiated the rap branch of the Hip-Hop culture in Turkey. Ozan Sinan relates this success with the band's media coverage in Europe and a little with Turkish people's inferiority complex in their relation with the West: Cartel created the assumption that Turkish musicians have beaten the westerners in their own game and made Turkish culture recognized by Europeans (Diessel 2001, p. 176). Turkish graffiti artist Turbo (Tunç Dindaş) believes the boredom caused by the popular Turkish music at that time was another reason for the band's success, in addition to risen nationalistic feelings of the people then (2011). Despite their success, association with political parties and some monetary problems led the separation of the original band after the Turkey tour (Cheeseman 199, p. 202). Although some existing members and some new ones tried to vitalize the project again with some collaborations with popular artists (e.g. with Maffay in 1998) and a brand new album in 2011, Cartel did not enjoy its previous glory days in Turkey. On the other hand, the fuse they ignited was showing its effects in motherland.

The Culture in the Mainland

Cartel received a significant success in the Turkish market, selling 180,000 copies (Çınar 2000). Turbo states that the majority was introduced to rap with Cartel and the former examples are underground in Turkey (2011). He also tells he first noticed Hip-Hop around 1982, through breakdancing (Jöntürk 2003, p.187). The first legitimately distributed Turkish rap album is Hedef 12's [Target 12] *Tam İsabet* [Bulls Eye,1996] in 1996. The band was from Bursa and consisted of three members: Maho.B (Mahmut Akın), Heel-M (Murat Akın), and Tex (Tarkan Yaşar). Lyrics focused on problems and dangers of urbanization, growing up, and generation conflicts and environment. Also, a couple of songs were about money and women.

Some other albums were also published in the second half of the 1990s, but the most significant album of these early years of Hip-Hop was compiled by Turbo in 1999, and it was called "Yeraltı Operasyonu" [Underground Operation]

(Kod Müzik). It is important to note that artists were mainly responsible for the distribution of their albums in those years, mainly by selling CDs themselves in concerts or parties. So when an album was released by a record company, this was considered a significant event (Solomon 2005, p.9). Turbo was already working relentlessly for spreading the Hip-Hop culture; he was a graffiti artist since 1986 and he was preparing Hip-Hop pages for an extremely popular teen magazine, *Blue Jean*. He was also a member of a rap project called Statik, which also featured on the compilation.

Yeraltı Operasyonu included songs about drug abuse, problems of urban life and the dangers it presents, environmental problems, and artists' statements about their experiences. Compared to the former examples, the message and tone of the compilation is harsher. This compilation presented songs from MCs who have released demo recordings at the time, and most of them are regarded as Hip-Hop legends today. Silahsız Kuvvet [Unarmed Force] (Yunus Özyavuz), who will later change his stage name to Sagopa Kajmer, has contributed with four songs and a collaboration. Nefret [Hate] –the collaboration of Ceza [Punishment] (Bilgin Özçalkan) and Dr. Fuchs (Tarık Gamert) – presented four, and Yener Çevik was involved with two songs.

Turkish Old School

In 1999, a Turkish MC living and working in Germany, Fuat Ergin visited Turkey to participate in a Hip-Hop party and saw the potential of this culture in Istanbul (TRT). Although recently he stated that he regrets meeting some people there (Abatay, 2019a), his visit resulted with his moving to Istanbul couple of years later. Alongside him, the listed MCs above constitute the "old school" rappers of Turkey. However, for Turkish musicians, being old school does not signify a distinct musical style (the term is used to define the Hip-Hop music until 1984 in the United States), but being a veteran rapper. When Fuat Ergin came for the party and then for the concerts, he was bringing copies of his self-published albums. His first album, *Hassickdir?* [Fukoff?] (1999 Kokpit Records) became a sudden hit among the not so crowded Hip-Hop heads and, as Turbo describes, brought himself an incredible fan base, showing the aficionados of this culture how underground should be (Dindaş 2011).

After their contribution to Yeraltı Operasyonu, Ceza and Dr. Fuchs have published two more albums as Nefret. Turbo considers this band as one of the milestones within the Turkish Hip-Hop culture (Dindaş 2011). Their first album titled *Meclis-i Âlâ –İstanbul* [High Council-Istanbul] (2000 Hipnetic Records) sold about 20,000 copies as of 2002 (Solomon 2005:11) and the other album *Anahtar*

[Key] (Hipnetic Records), which was released in the next year, rapidly sold over 22,000, also securing some media coverage (pp. 12). Despite such selling figures and the media coverage, Solomon appreciates the band's ability to remain underground, which is tied to the band's productiveness and their constant criticism of superficiality of the mainstream culture. Nefret also declares its position as the truth telling mechanism in the middle of all this fake and mediated existences.

As of 2002, Ceza continued his solo career with Med Cezir [Flux and Reflux] (Hammer Music). Halil Haluk Ataklı, the owner Hammer Music, describes the solo career of the MC as the beginning of popularity of rap in Turkey. His popularity increased throughout his career and encouraged many MCs to participate in the Hip-Hop scene, which resulted in many new releases (2011). Thomas Solomon describes Ceza as the first rap star in Turkey and holds him partially responsible for Hip Hop culture securing a place within the Turkish popular culture (2009, p. 308).

Although the producer of Med Cezir was Sagopa Kajmer who also collaborated with Ceza frequently throughout early the 2000s, a personal beef sent the rappers in different directions dissing each other in new releases. Sagopa Kajmer started addressing seemingly conservative Hip-Hop enthusiasts more and more throughout his career. He was sharing images with known conservative figures from Turkey. Also Islamic motifs in his music became increasingly attention-grabbing, as the lyrics of his independent 2012 release *40* demonstrates: "And First you need to be a human/To be a human, first you should become a subject [of Islam]/Becoming a vessel requires heart/Dogs also have heart /You need to become Abraham, Adam, Yunus [Emre], Mohammad!" Recently he has stated he was an atheist (Milliyet, 2018), but we are yet to see how this declaration will affect his music and his relations with his fans.

Among the old school MCs, Yener Çevik from İzmir represents a particularly interesting position. He is among the oldest MCs in Turkey and among the very few that are still active from the Cartel era. He wrote and self-distributed his first single, "Liseli Genç" [High School Youngster], in 1995. The song spoke of the dangers, such as drug abuse, surrounding the young people. Along with Liseli Genç, another song by him *Töre* (traditional code), which discussed the heavy burden of traditional codes on people, has appeared on Yeraltı Operasyonu. Different from the previously discussed Turkish MCs, Çevik actually comes from the ghetto listening arabesque music, which he still enjoys most other than rap. Martin Stokes defines this genre as an urban music for urban listeners, defining an ever-corrupting city that constantly exploits the poor and invites its listeners to express their anger to their fate (Stokes 199, p.1). It also expresses the reaction of periphery's reaction to the forced Westernization attempts of a central reform (p. 99). All these issues can be traced in

Çevik's lyrics: "loaded would say one plus one equals three/ men wearing tights are marginal, etc." Lines from *Baba Yorgun* [Daddy's Tired, 2016] imply the alienation from the members of the upper class, who are radically different from the artist. "I have written you a poem, the poet has single cane and a broken tooth/All these lines are labelled "from the ghetto" since my childhood/I dunno bro, when has it started, when it ended" lyrics of *Donar* [Freezes] clearly expresses such alienation. This alienation as well as lots of other motifs in Çevik's songs are shared with the arabesque music. In addition to that, he prefers singing over beats that contain arabesque forms and samples. Because of these properties, Çevik is considered as the first arabesque rapper in Turkey (Flow Radyo 2019).

Commercialization and Subgenres of Rap in Turkey

Arabesque rap was founded partly in Germany but definitely moulded into a solid rapping genre by Yener Çevik. There are still many successful MCs expressing their desires and frustrations employing this genre. Among the contemporary rappers, Gazapizm [Indignationism] (Anıl Acar), who was born in Elazığ but raised also in İzmir (the -izm part of his stage name refers to this locality), is probably the most prominent example. Also being the founder Argo İzmir, one of the most well-known Hip-Hop crews, Gazapizm released two albums with extreme streaming numbers on Internet: *Yeraltı Edebiyatı* [Underground Literature] in 2014 and *Bir Gün Her Şey* [One Day Everything] in 2016; both were released by the company Argo Müzik. His frequent topics are the unforgiving street life, people's suffering in contemporary urban environments, and injustice. His attitude is elegantly put into words especially in his 2016 song, "Yok" [Absent, 2016]:

Kadın ve uyuşturucu ticareti, ovuşturur rezaleti Soruşturup nezaketi bulmayacağın bir yer burası Ghettolar ve sosyeteyi birbirine bağlayan bir çukur sanki Çok da nadir boş gezen Junkielerin arasından sıyrılıp ben ilerlerken Türkü bardan tekme tokat kovulur bi' müzisyen Bi' ağlayıp, bi' gülümser Soğutur bu şehirden bu manzara ki	Women and drug trafficking rubs the disgrace Even by asking you will not find kindness here As if it is a pit connecting the ghettos and high society Wanderer is a rarity As I make my way through junkies A musician gets kicked out of the folk bar with fists Cries a bit, smiles a bit This scene disinclines even from the city

Gazapizm's fame truly outreached people even from outside of Hip-Hop aficionados when one of his songs, "Heyecanı Yok" (No Exaltation, 2017) was used in an extremely popular TV series called *Çukur* (The Pit, 2017). The song's success was competent with the series' and brought MC a Golden Butterfly award in the "song of the year" category, distributed by the popular newspaper *Hürriyet*. The MC also closed a unique deal considering the Turkish Hip-Hop culture and counterpartyed for production of a new sneaker series made by a Turkish brand, Kinetix, in 2018. There have been instances of rappers acting in commercials, like Ceza did for candy and soft drink labels, but dedicating a product to an MC happened for the first time with Gazapizm. He donated the money from this deal to an NGO working with homeless children.

Besides Gazapizm, Ezhel [Unwary] (Sercan İpekçioğlu) has won the "best musical breakthrough" category Golden Butterfly Awards in 2018. Despite the name the award suggests, he has been performing since the late 2000s with the title "Freestyle King," which he won in a rap battle in 2011. The rapper became a nationwide phenomenon with his debut album, *Müptezhel* [Chronic, 2017] in 2017 (KOAL). As of March 2019, the artist has more than 1,200,000 followers on Spotify and his monthly streaming is over 1,500,000. These figures are extremely significant as they exceed the numbers expected from Turkish rap. The success becomes more apparent when we consider one of the inventors of "old school" in Turkey Ceza, whom many Hip-Hop aficionados call "the maestro," has nearly half of Ezhel's figures on Spotify. Even the phenomenal mainstream pop music artists like Sezen Aksu (about 1 million) and Tarkan (about 1400000) fall behind these figures when monthly listeners are considered. His songs mainly deal with modern urban life of Ankara and his stance against the social injustice. Chronic marijuana smoking motif is also existent in many of his songs, like he states in the hook part of "Geceler" (Nights): Lights appear brighter under the influence of weed/Smokes get inhaled/Stars and sounds become my guide in darkness/ Moon is more beautiful than the sun. This particular song caused Ezhel a lot of trouble during 2018. A concerned citizen has filed a lawsuit against the rapper, claiming that he is endorsing and encouraging drug abuse (Aydın 2018). After serving nearly a month in prison, he was acquitted (Uzun, 2018).

Ezhel is not the only rapper who has faced lawsuit regarding the drug references. Khontkar (Onur Dinç), a successful İzmir rapper, has faced similar charges around the same time with Ezhel, spending two months in prison, until acquitted. Recently an Eskişehir rapper, Ceg (Volkan Ayvazoğlu) and Server Uraz from İstanbul, who had released the album, were found guilty of the same charges; and they are waiting for the court to uphold the decision (Abatay 2019b). This wave of suing MCs has seemingly accomplished nothing though.

Rappers like Khonktar, Ceg, or more contemporary examples such as Ben Fero (Ferhat Yılmaz) are representing a way more upbeat school in rap. Their music describes a way of life full of rap-related success, parties, homies, women, drugs, videogames, and exercise. They almost instantly obtain high streaming numbers. Ben Fero, for example, released his first album in late February in 2019 and in less than a month he reached more than 1 million monthly listeners on Spotify.

Another school also frequented by Turkish musicians is native tongues. Alan Light describes this rap subgenre as: "The sound was varied, funny, and gentle, and the "Afrocentric" emphasis of the rhymes was warm, ecologically and socially concerned, and not too preachy. … This was rap that was nonthreatening, politically correct, and didn't have the tainted feel of a crossover ploy" (2004:143). MCs like Aga B from Ankara or Kamufle from İstanbul express their opinions and frustrations in a mellow way in their music and voice their feelings in an ironical way. Aga B, for example, complains about the current state of Hip-Hop in his 2016 song *La N'olur* [Please Yo] (Voo Doo Records) and begs the ones who are responsible to hate him and leave him alone so that he and Voo Doo crew can focus on what they are doing. There is another group of musicians who rap about similar concerns, but using less statements and expressing their opinions through stories. Rappers and producers like Da Poet, Kayra (Onur İnal), Farazi (Burak Demir), and their project 90 BPM with Savai and Sorgu constitute good examples of this school.

Some MCs prefer to express their concerns on similar issues in a more militant manner. Saian and K"st are two of the representatives of political rap. Both in their solo careers and their collaboration Otonom Piyade's [Autonomous Private] (2017) albums and EPs (extended play), they aggressively criticize the ongoing situation as a result of ruling class's decisions, like in "Kokoroz" [Minger]: "Death cheerers, flag barers/Ones bragging about 500 years ago/ Ones only react only when they hurt/Phallocrats, patriarchs/And bugs, gather around/I picked flowers from graves of under-sixteen-year-olds for you." Here the call is made to the caricaturized conservative right-wing voters reminding the death of teens as a result of bad policies or armed state forces' interventions.

Gangsta rap narrates the violent lifestyles of people usually living in underprivileged parts of the cities. These narrations often include affiliations with street gangs and suggest violent solutions for the encountered problems. Gangsta rappers may visually support their attitudes with gang-related outfits, tattoos, and gestures. Selo (Selahattin Ergün) and his band Alaturka Mavzer [Turkish Style Mauser], İstanbul Trip and their collaboration Kadıköy Acil [Kadikoy Emergency] could be listed as among gansta rappers. Rather than narrating the problems in ghetto, these MCs present statements about their strength and their crew, underlining the possible problems their enemies could face when they come.

Hip-Hop culture was first introduced to Turkey almost 20 years later, through the pioneers among the diaspora in Germany. Although it had a slow start in its first years, with the efforts of Turbo and the widespread success of his compilation, this culture was kickstarted. Especially Ceza's success has encouraged many aspiring musicians to contribute to this culture. Today there are many musicians who can make a living with their music. Although there are more tasks at hand to develop this culture in Turkey, the progress so far is promising. A future, which can provide similar opportunities of the global mainstream artists to the Turkish Hip Hop aficionados, does not look so distant today.

References

Abatay, B. (2019a). *Rap müziğin sevilen ismi Fuat: Söylemek istediğim her şeyi söyledim*. Retrieved from https://www.birgun.net/haber-detay/rap-muzigin-sevilen-ismi-fuat-soylemek-istedigim-her-seyi-soyledim.html

Abatay, B. (2019b). *Ünlü rapçiler Server Uraz ve Ceg'e hapis cezası*. Retrieved from https://www.birgun.net/haber-detay/unlu-rapciler-server-uraz-ve-cege-hapis-cezasi.html

Altunay, M. (2017). *Islamic: Force-my melody/Istanbul*. Retrieved ftom https://djmahmut.wordpress.com/2017/05/26/islamic-force-my-melodyistanbul/

Aydın, Ç. (2018). *Son dakika… Fenomen rapçi Ezhel tutuklandı*. Retrieved from http://www.hurriyet.com.tr/gundem/son-dakika-fenomen-rapci-ezhel-tutuklandi-40847455

Chang, J. (2006). *Can't stop won't stop: A history of the hip-hop generation*. New York: St. Martin's Press.

Cheeseman, T. (1998). Polyglot politics. Hip hop in Germany. *Debatte: Journal of Contemporary Central and Eastern Europe*, *6*(2), 191–214.

Cinar, A. (1999). Cartel: Travels of German-Turkish rap music. *Middle East Report*, *211*, 43–44.

Diessel, C. (2001). Bridging east and west on the" Orient Express": Oriental hip-hop in the Turkish diaspora of Berlin. *Journal of Popular Music Studies*, *13*(2), 165–187.

Dindaş, T. (2011). *Tunç 'Turbo Abi' Dindaş Hiphoplife Röportaj*. Retrieved from https://hiphoplife.com.tr/roportaj/134-tunc-turbo-abi-dindas-hiphoplife-roportaj.html Retrival date: 16.08.2019

Ickstadt, H. (1999). Appropriating difference: Turkish-German rap. *Amerikastudien/American Studies*, *44*(4), 571–578.

Jöntürk. (2003). *Bir gençlik çığlığı hiphop kültürü*. İstanbul: Akyüz Yayın Gurubu.

Kaya, A. (2001). *Sicher in Kreuzberg. Constructing diasporas: Turkish hip-hop youth in Berlin*. Bilefeld: Transcript Verlag.

Light, A. (2004). About a salary or reality?-Rap's eecurrent conflict. In M. A. Neal & M. Froman (Eds.), *That's the joint!* (pp. 137–145). London: Routledge.

Milliyet. (2018). *Sagopa Kajmer 'dini inancım yok' dedi!* Retrieved from http://www.milliyet.com.tr/sagopa-kajmer-dini-inancim-yok--magazin-2677827/. Retrieval date 16.06.2019.

Solomon, T. (2005). Living underground is tough': Authenticity and locality in the hip-hop community in Istanbul, Turkey. *Popular Music*, *24*(1), 1–20.

Solomon, T. (2009). Berlin–Frankfurt–Istanbul: Turkish hip-hop in motion. *European Journal of Cultural Studies*, *12*(3), 305–327.

Soysal, L. (2004). Rap, hiphop, Kreuzberg: Scripts of/for migrant youth culture in the WorldCity Berlin. *New German Critique*, *92*, 62–81.

Uzun, Ü. (2018). *Ezhel cezaevinden çıktı*. Retrieved from https://www.sabah.com.tr/yasam/2018/06/20/ezhel-cezaevinden-cikti

Discography

Aga, B. (2016). La N'olur. Voo Doo Records.

Cartel. (1995). Cartel. Mercury Records.

Çevik, Y. (2016). Sokak Dili ve Edebiyatı. ILS Music.

Ceza. (2002). Med Cezir. Hammer Music.

Fuat. (1999) Hassickdir?. Kokpit Records.

Gazapizm. (2014). Yeraltı Edebiyatı. Argo Müzik.

Gazapizm. (2016). Bir Gün Her Şey. Argo Müzik.

Gazapizm. (2017). Heyecanı Yok. Argo Müzik.

Hedef 12. (1996). Tam İsabet. Ada Müzik

Islamic Force. (1991). Melody/Istanbul. 1st Class Records.

Islamic Force. (1997). Mesaj. De De Records.

Kajmer, S. (2012). 40. Independent release.

King Size Terror. (1991). Bir Yabancının Hayatı. Arvis Records.

KRS-One. (2003). 9 Elements. Koch Records.

Mahmut, D. J., et al. (1994). Looptown presents Turkish Hiphop. Looptown.

Nefret. (2000). Meclis-i Âlâ –İstanbul. Hipnetic Records.
Nefret. (2001). Anahtar. Hipnetic Records.
Piyade, O. (2017). Hal ve Gidiş Sıfır. Independent release.
Turbo et al. (1999). Yeraltı Operasyonu. Kod Müzik.

Filmography

Beat Street. (1984). Orion Pictures.
Çukur. (2017). Ay Yapım.
Söyleyeceklerimiz Var. (2011). TRT Türk.
Wild Style. (1982). Rhino Entertainment.

Idil Karademirlidağ Suher, Çisil Sohodol, and Nilüfer Geysi

Chapter 12 An Overall Picture of Creativity in Turkish Public Relations Industry

Introduction

With a rapid change in technology, global competition in communication sector including fields such as public relations and advertising has gained momentum. Creativity, in this competitive environment, is essential to stay in the game beyond providing an advantage (Cook, 1998; Kabanoff and Rossiter, 1994). Public relations (PR) as a part of creative industry (DCMS, 2016) and as a practice of "managing the communication between an organization and its publics" (Grunig and Hunt, 1984, p. 6) should approach creativity closely.

Creativity is relevant for various areas in the organizational study (Ford and Gioia, 2000); when it comes to PR programs or campaigns, most public relations consultancies adopt creativity as a core value (Parker, Wayne and Kent, 2015). Mack (2016) argues for PR agencies that they "must follow in the footsteps of da Vinci and become 'creative engineers' to keep pace with our diversifying industry." The creative PR industry has boosted in the last decade and the creativity gap between PR agencies and other agency types is smaller than ever (Bruell, 2015).

In addition to the practical value which creativity has, it has a theoretical interest (e.g., Estanyol and Roca, 2015; Wilcox and Cameron, 2012; Willis and Estanyol, 2018) in PR. Although it is a deep and multilayer subject, research on creativity in PR is unsatisfactory. The existing studies mostly focus on individual, social, or organizational creativity based on psychological scales (e.g., Amabile, 1996; Ford, 1996) rather than creative execution. Therefore, there is a need of portrayal of creativity as a whole. This study contributes to an emerging area in the industry by examining the entire situation of creativity in Turkish PR industry.

This chapter is designed as follows. Firstly, creativity is explained to define the scope of the concept; then it is explored how creativity is used in the field of PR. The methodology part presents detailed information about the research process. In the findings part, results of the research are presented. Discussion and conclusions include key subjects around creativity in PR.

Defining Creativity

Creativity is a complex concept that has been defined by many scholars in many different fields such as psychology, sociology, and communication. The complexity derives from both broadness and abstractness of the concept. "Creativity defies a precise definition because it is largely unseen, nonverbal, and unconscious" (Torrance, 1998, p. 43).

Definitions of creativity differ based on the perception of concept as a process or product. As a process, creativity "is the forming of associative elements into new combinations which either meet requirements or are in some way useful" (Mednick, 1962, p. 220). Halpern (2003, p. 193) states that creativity is "defined solely by its end product." According to scholars who accept creativity as product achievements such as solution to a problem, a performance in tests, contests, etc., are mentioned as 'creative' (Barron and Harrington, 1981). The following definition introduces creativity both as a process and product. "Creativity means a person's capacity to produce new or original ideas, insights, restructuring, inventions, or artistic objects, which are accepted by experts as being of scientific, aesthetic, social, or technological value" (Vernon, 1989).

Creativity, in general, is associated with originality and appropriateness (Acar et al., 2017; Andreasen, 2005; Runco and Charles, 1993; Runco and Illies 2005). 'Original' corresponds to 'different,' 'unexpected,' and 'novel' in the creative research literature (Altesch, 1996; Caroff and Besançon, 2008). Appropriateness refers to the fit between the creative work and the audience (Kilgour and Koslow, 2009; White, Shen and Smith, 2002). A creative work should be meaningful and useful for those who will be subject to the creative idea (Diedrich et al., 2015; James et al., 1999). When considered from this point of view, creativity differs according to the context it is used in, because creativity in arts does not always necessitate usefulness while in advertising it is essential (El-Murad and West, 2004).

Creativity is usually presented as something magical or elusive; however, it is not different than utilizing old ideas through new methods or new combinations. "These days, no one can be called 'creative' who decides to 'reinvent the wheel', nor can one earn that ascription for writing the lines 'To be, or not to be'. Creative ideas are novel, surprising, unexpected—sometimes even shocking" (Simonton, 2001).

Despite lack of consensus, discussed definitions and understandings of creativity contribute to clarification of the concept in terms of the field in question, PR.

Creativity for PR Practices

How creativity is understood in PR is important for the context in which professionals perform. PR practitioners work in different areas such as internal communication, media relations, event management, corporate social responsibility, crisis management, marketing public relations, digital media, lobbying, issues management, and political communication. All these activities aim to create a benefit like raising awareness, changing attitudes or behaviors (Smith, 2013). Creativity is a necessary component in this process for "publicity, company promotions, fund-raising, and political elections" (Sitzman, 2001, p. 16).

A PR campaign is developed on four steps including research, planning, implementation, and evaluation (Hendrix et al., 2012). Smith (2013) argues that especially in the implementation step, where tactics of a campaign are put into practice, creativity attracts the attention. Moriarty (1997) remarks that the most important thing behind a creative PR campaign is a big idea. According to Moriarty, a creative campaign idea can solve communication problems. There are also other views that position creativity in different components. "The real value lies in achieving creativity within an organization's key messages, objectives and strategy" (Parker, Wayne and Kent, 2005, p. 9).

Creativity in PR as "the ability each of us has to create something new by bringing together two or more different elements in a new context, in order to provide added value to a task" (Green, 2010, p. 7) is related with results recognized by third parties. Green presents arguments to emphasize role of stakeholders for the creative process. "Creativity is a process that results in novelty, which is accepted as useful, tenable or satisfying by a significant group of others at some point in time" (2010, p. 6). "Significant group of others" means people who have the power to influence the organization.

Since creativity is not a concept agreed upon in terms of its content and extent, evaluating creativity is a significant issue. "The very essence of the creative is its novelty, and we have no standard by which to judge it" (Rogers, 195, p.351). Moriarty (1997) suggests that risk, relevance, impact, and originality make a big idea creative. It is argued that, for public relations practices, originality is only the first criterion that necessitates accomplishment (Smith, 2013). The changing role of creative directors that Salzman (2016) emphasizes indicates the significance of effectiveness:

> The role of creative genius is becoming less central in the communications universe. It used to be about a creative god or maybe a team of creative gods whose powers of divination and innovation were almost mystical. Now creativity is as sexy as ever, but it's rooted in science: intelligence, data and, yes, also the unique seductive ways that data can be harnessed.

Different institutions granting award in fields related to PR have different categories and evaluation criteria. There are several distinguished creativity awards in PR worldwide. The Golden Awards Excellence (GWA) is one of these which is granted by IPRA (International Public Relations Association) in 37 categories related to different fields of PR. Creativity is considered in 12 of them. There are also other awards valued among the industry such as PR Week Awards that has a special category for "best use of creativity." Cannes Lions, International Festival of Creativity, as an outstanding celebration of creativity, has PR as a category for 10 years. Evaluation criteria of the award are weighted as 20 % idea, 30 % strategy, 20 % execution, and 30 % impact and results (PR Lions).

In Turkey, awarding creativity does not have a long tradition. The oldest award in the field of communication sector is Crystal Apple Festival that has been granted since 1989 (Crystal Apple). Felis Awards is one of a few celebrations of PR creativity which defines its aim "to highlight the role of effective creativity in advertising and marketing industries" (Felis Odulleri). Communication Consultancies Association of Turkey (IDA) has category of "creative content development" and "frame breaking project" (Prida Odulleri). Turkish Association of Public Relations (TUHID) considers creativity as one of its criteria of Golden Compass Public Relations Awards (Altın Pusula Halkla İliskiler Odulleri). Golden Compass is the most prestigious and rooted award of PR in Turkey.

Methodology

This study adopts a qualitative approach based on survey in order to frame the creativity in Turkish PR industry by analyzing the views and perceptions of PR practitioners on the issue. For this aim, following research questions are established:

RQ1: How do PR practitioners view quality, priority, and level of creativity in the Turkish PR industry?
RQ2: How do PR practitioners describe and define creativity in PR?
RQ3: What are the influences that affect creativity and barriers that prevent PR practitioners from being more creative?
RQ4: How do management of PR agencies approach the creativity issue, and what are their practices for better creative work?
RQ5: How do clients approach the creativity issue, and what are their expectations from agencies?

Purposive sampling strategy is used within the scope of this study to recruit PR practitioners working in diverse PR agencies. Purposive sampling is "appropriate to select a sample on the basis of knowledge of a population, its elements, and the purpose of the study" (Babbie, 2013: 204). The questionnaire was sent to 310 PR practitioners working in PR agencies. A total 170 of them (55 %)

answered the questions; 35 of the total 170 participants stated that they have master's degree, 120 participants have undergraduate degree, and 15 of them have associate degree. Looking at the areas where the participants graduated, 55 of the them received PR education. Forty-four of the participants graduated from a field of communication other than PR. Looking at the proportion of participants who did not receive communication training, 38 of the participants graduated from the field of economic and administrative sciences and 33 of them from a field of social sciences other than these. As the participants examined the positions they worked, it was seen that the largest group consisted of account executives (n: 75). In addition, 20 participants work as media relations experts, 18 participants as strategists, 17 participants as managers, 15 participants as digital project managers, 14 participants as copywriters, and finally 11 of them as creative directors.

This study is based on Holmes Creativity in PR Report 2017 (The Holmes Report, 2017). The Holmes Group that was established in 2000 has the mission of reporting and analyzing trends and issues on PR. Creativity is one of these issues. The report was launched in 2012, and it has been published five times till today. In the report, the measurement instrument was not provided; therefore, questions and answers were taken into consideration to establish the questionnaire form. It was established in Turkish and pilot study was conducted.

A total of 30 questions were asked; three of them are demographic questions. All questions are multiple choice; some of them are available to check all that apply. In some specific questions, respondents were asked to evaluate the changes in last five years. In the original research, the improvement over the 12 months was asked. However, this is the first study in Turkey, so improvements over the five years were evaluated in the questions.

The data is collected through printed survey booklets between April 2019 and May 2019. The questionnaire forms were sent out to the agencies in person. SPSS 20 is used to analyze the data.

Findings

Findings of the research are categorized according to the research questions and each title presents relevant findings.

PR Practitioners' View of Quality, Priority, and Level of Creativity in Turkish PR Industry (RQ1)

In this section, findings of questions that aim to depict quality, priority, and level of creativity in the Turkish PR industry are provided. Firstly, the participants

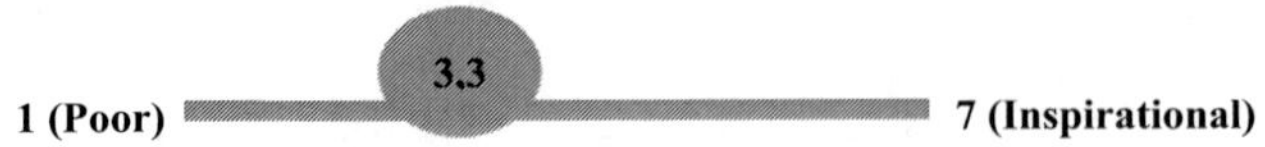

Fig. 12.1: Mean score of quality of creativity

Tab. 12.1: Improvement in the quality of creativity in PR campaigns in the last five years

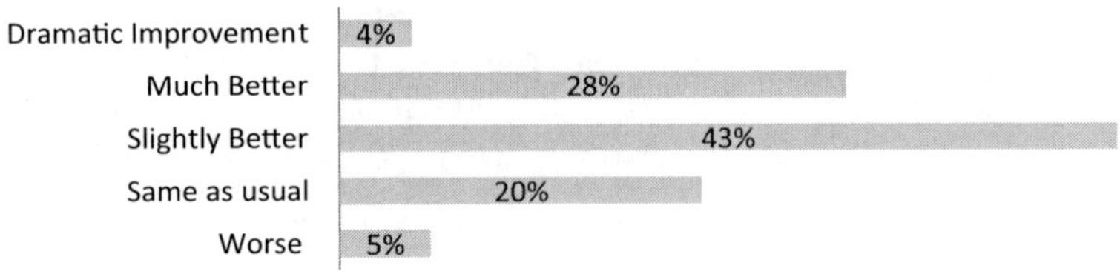

were asked to respond to a Likert-type question: "How would you describe the quality of creativity in the PR industry in Turkey?"

The quality of creativity is evaluated below the average with mean score of 3.3 (see Fig. 12.1). However, when the participants were asked to evaluate the improvement in the quality of creativity in PR campaigns over the past five years, 75 % think that the quality of the creativity is at least slightly better (see Tab. 12.1). It demonstrates that the industry is developing itself on the creativity issue.

It is also asked "How high a priority is creativity for your current business?" Findings demonstrate that creativity has low priority (57 %) in the industry. There are 28 % who think that it is at average level. Four percent of PR professionals think that creativity has no priority at all and 11 % of them think that creativity is prioritized at a high level in the industry (Tab. 12.2).

Respondents were asked to rank the creative quality of the agency types that serve in the communication sector (1 is the lowest rank and 7 is the highest rank). PR practitioners think that the most creative agencies are digital agencies; advertising agencies are ranked at the second place. PR agencies are at the third place with 3.9 mean score (see Tab. 12.3). On the next question that asks to describe the level of creativity at their own agency, they think that it is not very different than the creativity in PR industry (M:4,1) (see Fig. 12.2).

As it is seen in the findings of questions related to RQ1, creativity is not prioritized in Turkish PR industry. When results are compared to the results of the original study conducted in 2015, 2016, and 2017; it is obvious that it has much more priority at global level (63.8 % of respondents in 2015, 85 % of respondents in 2016, and 83 % of respondents in 2017 think that creativity has 'high or

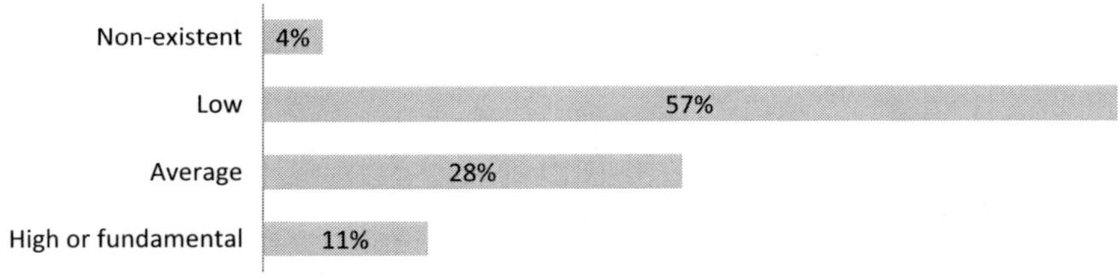

Tab. 12.2: The priority of creativity in the PR industry

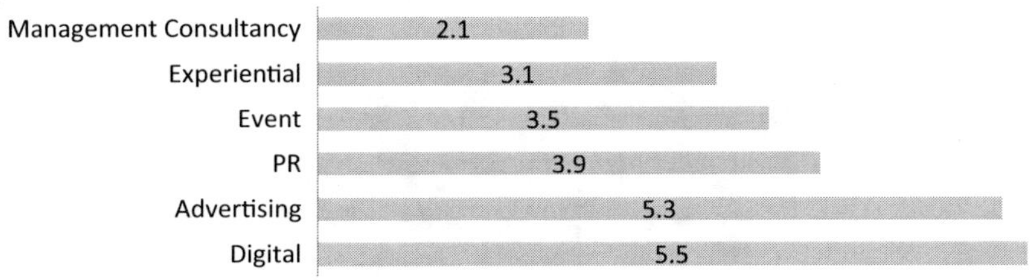

Tab. 12.3: Ranking of agency types in terms of creativity

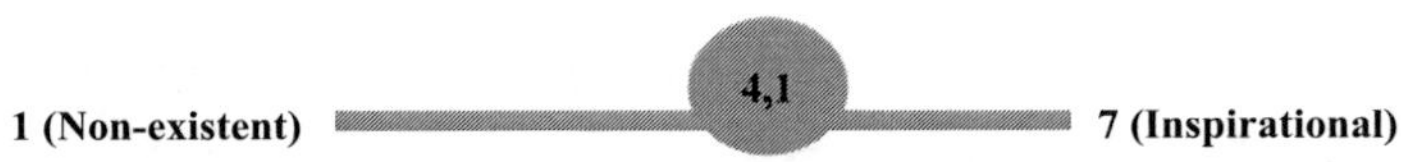

Fig. 12.2: Level of creativity at respondents' own PR agency

fundamental' priority in the industry). Similar to the results about priority, the quality of creativity in the global scale has been evaluated as higher than the Turkish PR industry.

Another dimension measured by this research question is the creative quality level of PR agencies among other agency types and agencies in which the participants work. Although they consider creative quality level of their own agencies as higher than the industry, the results are close to each other (M: 3,9 for PR agencies, M: 4,1 for their own agency).

Describing and Defining Creativity in PR (RQ2)

There are three questions in this section that describe and define creativity in the PR industry.

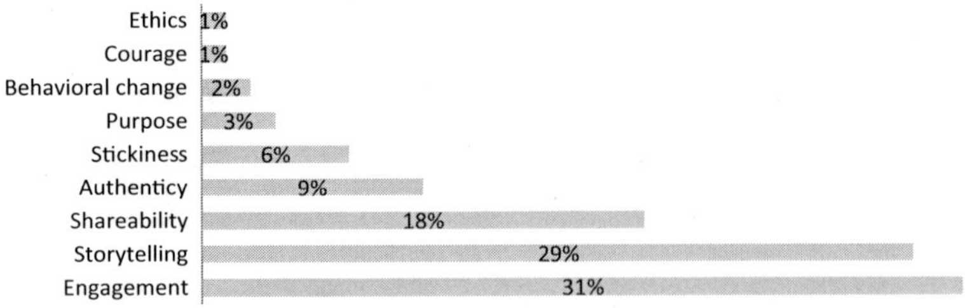

Tab. 12.4: Factors that drive creative a big idea in PR work

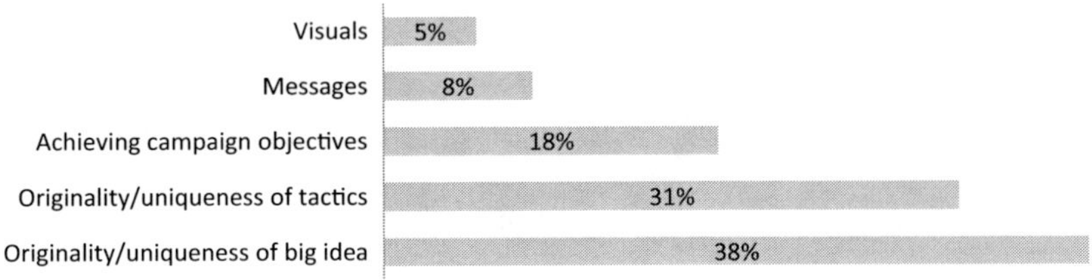

Tab. 12.5: Criteria of a creative PR campaign

The first question asking drivers of creativity of a big idea in PR work demonstrated that majority of PR practitioners (31 %) accept 'engagement' as the most important factor, while 29 % of them think 'storytelling' as significant. Ethics (1 %), courage (1 %), behavioral change (2 %), and purpose (3 %) are the least significant factors in terms of this issue (Tab. 12.4).

In addition to the factors affecting creativity of a big idea, the most important criteria to evaluate whole PR campaign as creative were also asked. Results indicate that originality and uniqueness of big idea (38 %) and tactics (31 %) are the most important ones. Achieving campaign objectives (18 %) has lower importance than others. While 8 % pointed out significance of messages, only 5 % considered visuals as important (Tab. 12.5).

Another question focused on creative techniques which participants use. In the questionnaire form, there were 18 different techniques listed such as 'random words' and 'artistic expression.' However, only four of the techniques were rated. Among the prominent techniques, 'brain storming' has the highest rate with 90 % (Tab. 12.6).

According to findings, creativity in PR works is defined and described with uniqueness and originality. The results show that creating an original or unique big idea which corresponds to planning stage of PR process and implementing

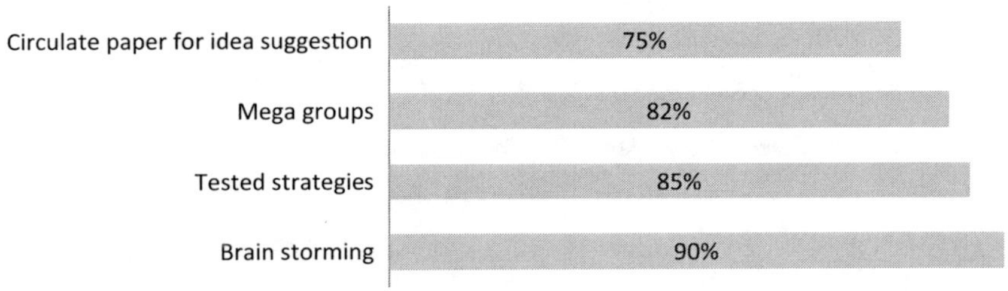

Tab. 12.6: Preference of creative techniques

them as tactics make a PR campaign creative. One of the prominent findings about RQ2 is that the majority does not consider achieving campaign objectives and creating behavioral change as important for PR creativity.

Brainstorming technique is the most popular one among participants to generate a creative idea. Mega groups technique is also significant according to the results (82 %). Therefore, it can be claimed that group synergy is important for creativity. Although originality and uniqueness define the PR creativity, 'tested strategies' is the second popular creative technique which is reconsidering what worked before and why it worked. It indicates the importance of experiences for creativity.

Influences That Affect Creativity and Barriers That Prevent PR Practitioners from Being More Creative (RQ3)

The third research question figured out factors that affect or prevent creativity. Findings of four questions are provided in this section.

When the most important reason for not becoming the leading agency in terms of creativity among other agency types is asked, PR practitioners think that client structure is the first reason (52 %). Budget is an obstacle for 20 % of them. Factors related to agencies' strategic capabilities (18 %) and understanding (20 %) are also prominent. There are only 2 % who think PR agencies are already leading in creativity (Tab. 12.7).

The question about trends that are influential on creative works was multiple choice, and the participants were able to choose more than one option. Real-time marketing is the most influential trend (68 %) affecting Turkish PR practitioners. Visual-/image-led communication, cocreation, mobile, celebrities/influencers, and product placement are also popular with more than 50 % score (Tab. 12.8).

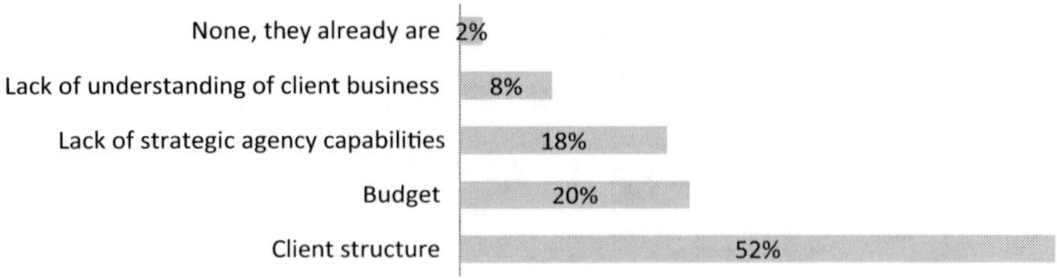

Tab. 12.7: Barriers to PR agencies becoming the lead creative agency

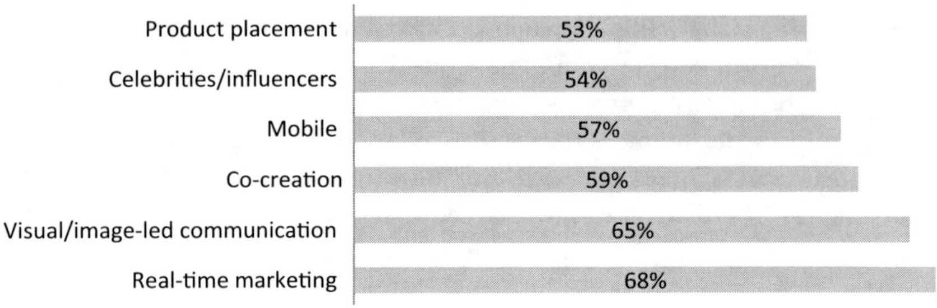

Tab. 12.8: Trends that are influential on creative works

The barriers that prevent PR agencies from being more creative were also asked in the study. This question was convenient to choose more than one answer. Participants claimed that client/agency feedback or risk aversion is the most important barrier for agencies (85 %). According to results, there are different opinions on creative quality which prevents creative works (76 %). Except own risk aversion of the agency and lack of time, all barriers are about clients and understanding between agency and clients (Tab. 12.9).

According to the results of the question of "What would improve your own or your company's creative capabilities?" 72 % of participants thought that educating clients is the most important factor. Ability to take more risks (70 %), clearer client briefs (66 %), and more budget (66 %) are also prominent factors (Tab. 12.10).

Results from this section indicated that problems related to clients are the most important reasons that stop PR practitioners or PR works from being more creative.

The results about factors that are thought as important to improve creative capabilities are in line with results of barriers of creativity. Since, clients and

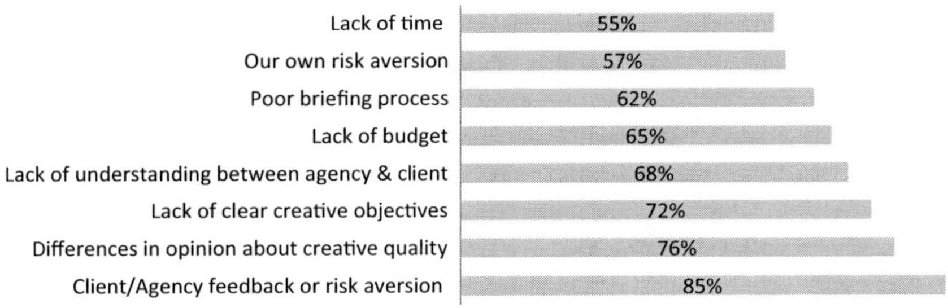

Tab. 12.9: Barriers that stop PR agencies from being creative

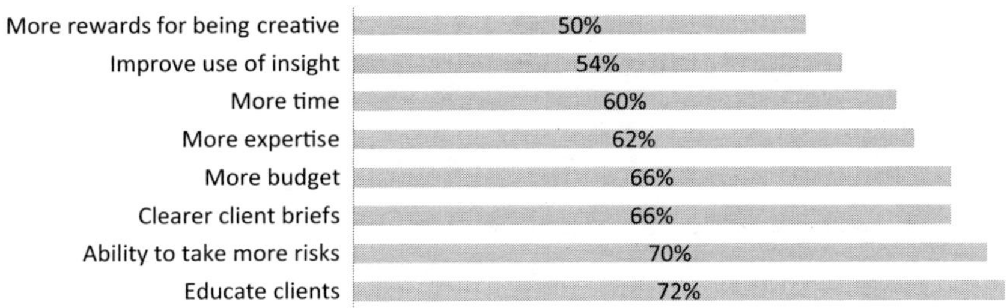

Tab. 12.10: Factors that help to improve creative capabilities

briefs seem as key actors preventing agencies from being creative, it is thought that educating clients and clearer client briefs can improve creative capabilities.

When it comes to influences on creativity, it can be seen that real-time marketing and visual-/image-led communication are major trends of today's PR. It is also significant that virtual/augmented reality and internet of things are not popular among Turkish practitioners as much as the global scale.

Approach of Management of PR Agencies to the Creativity and Their Practices for Better Creative Work (RQ4)

The mentality of managers of PR agencies is crucial on this issue since they shape the structure in the industry. Findings of eight related questions are provided in this section.

The participants were asked "How high a priority is evaluation of your creative ideas?" with a Likert-type question. The mean score is below the average (M:3) (Fig. 12.3).

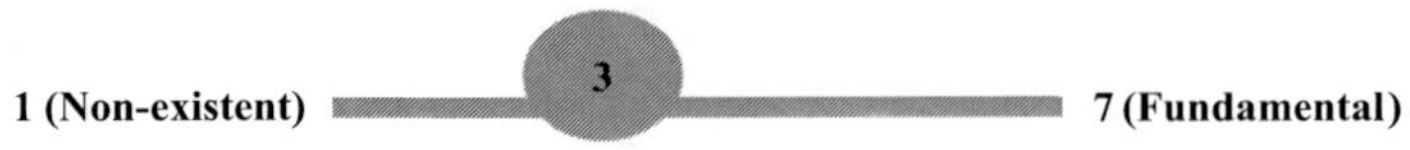

Fig. 12.3: Mean score of priority of evaluating creative ideas

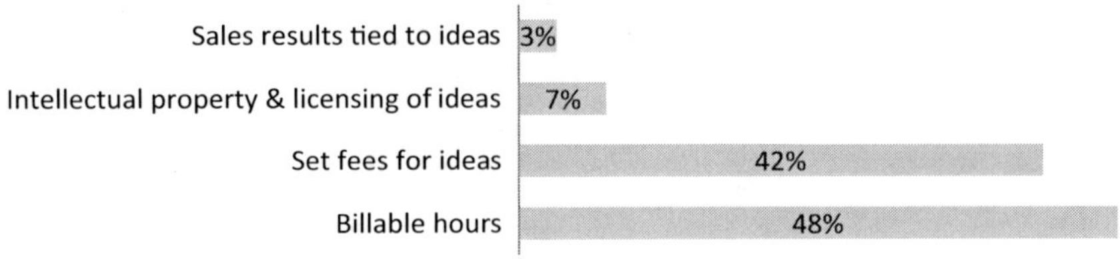

Tab. 12.11: Preference of being paid in terms of developing ideas

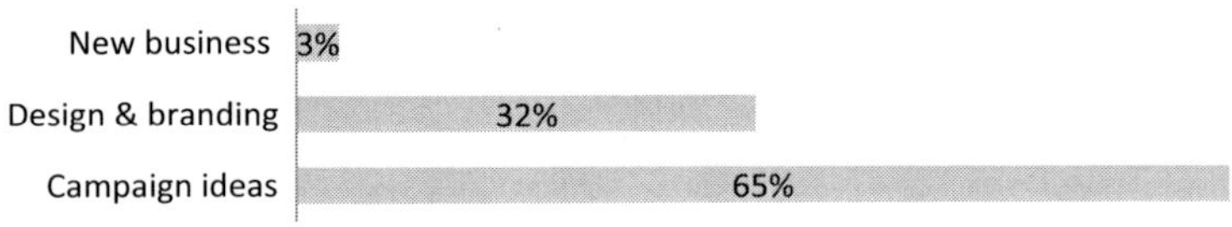

Tab. 12.12: Creative director's role and key duties in PR agencies

Respondents were asked to learn about their preference of being paid in terms of developing ideas. A total of 48 % of the participants prefer to be paid according to billable hours and 42 % prefer set fees for ideas. Intellectual property and licensing of ideas (7 %) and sales results tied to ideas (3 %) are not preferred much among the PR practitioners (Tab. 12.11).

A question about creative director's role and key duties in PR agencies was asked to the participants. The majority (65 %) accepted creative director's main role as being responsible for campaign ideas. There are also 32 % of PR practitioners thinking that creative director's key duty must be design and branding. Only 3 % of them associate creative directorship with new business (Tab. 12.12).

It was asked whether the agencies in which participants work have a creative director or not. While 21 % of the participants work with a creative director, 30 % of them consider about hiring a creative director and 45 % of them would like to have but they cannot afford it. Only 4 % of participants consider duties of a creative director as everyone's job (Tab. 12.13).

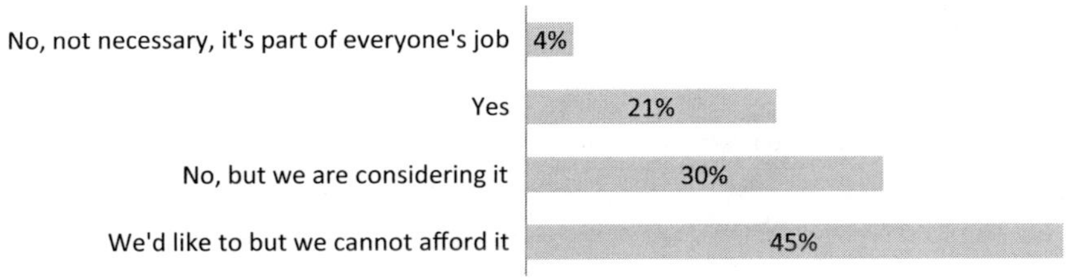

Tab. 12.13: Availability of creative director

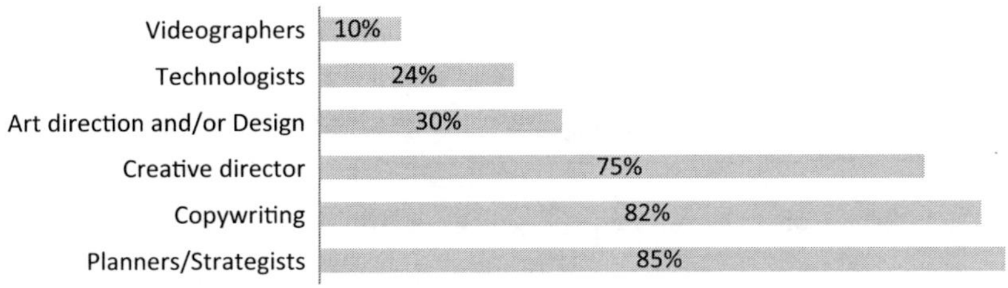

Tab. 12.14: Types of creative talent that the agency needs

According to the findings of the question about creative talent that the agency needs, the most needed creative talent in Turkish PR agencies is planners or strategists (85 %). Copywriters (82 %) and creative directors (75 %) are also necessary. Art directors, technologists, and videographers have lower importance in terms of creativity for agencies (Tab. 12.14).

When participants were asked "What stops creative talents joining your agency?", the top choice is that they prefer to work at another agency (52 %). Thirty-five percent of participants find salaries higher elsewhere. It is seen that the problem about trying to hire them is low (10 %). There is almost no one who said his or her culture is not receptive (%3) (Tab. 12.15).

The last two questions within this section is about human resources practices of agencies on encouraging creativity and creative behavior. More than half of participants (55 %) stated that their agencies do not have any incentives system. The most popular incentive is promotion opportunities (25 %) and internal awards follows it (20 %). Fifteen percent of the participants state that demonstrating creativity is encouraged by financial awards in agencies. They were also asked "How good are your company's HR practices – remuneration, appraisals, rewards, training – when it comes to supporting creativity?" The mean score of

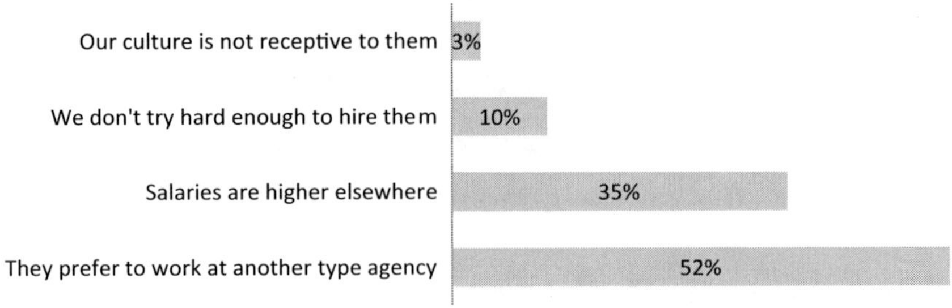

Tab. 12.15: Factors that stop creative talent joining the agency

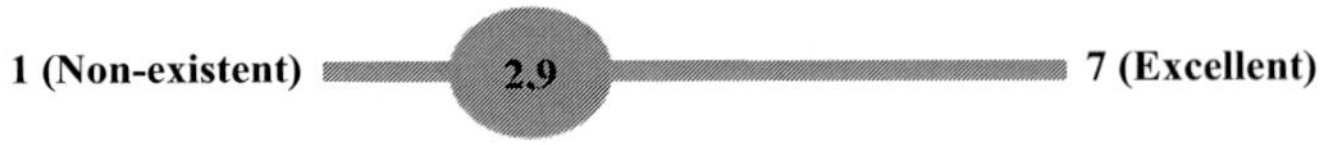

Fig. 12.4: Mean score of performance of agencies at HR practices

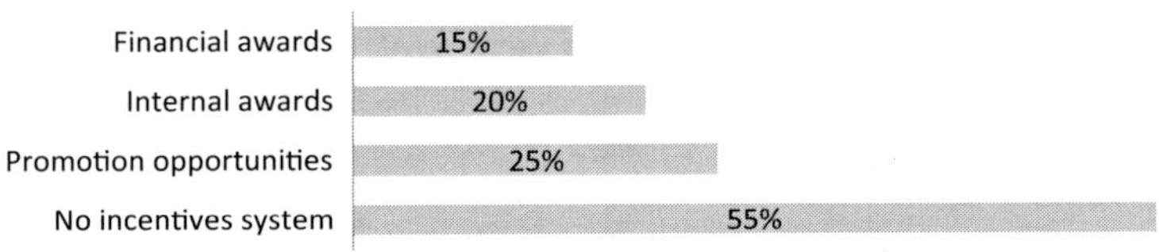

Tab. 12.16: Ways of encouraging creativity and creative behavior

the answers is below the average (M: 2,9) which is in line with the previous question (Fig. 12.4, Tab. 12.16).

The approach of management of PR agencies towards creativity can be interpreted based on their priority to evaluate creative ideas in works of the agency. Mean score (M:3) of this question shows that effectiveness of creative ideas is not essential for agencies. This result supports results of the question about criteria of creativity which shows that achieving campaign objectives has 18 % priority.

Moreover, although it is thought that creative talents work in different agency types than PR agencies, most of PR agencies do not have incentives system to encourage creativity. Creative directorship is considered as important by PR practitioners (96 % of the participants have or have the intention to hire a creative director), and developing campaign ideas is seen as their most important duty.

Clients' Approach to the Creativity Issue and Their Expectations from Agencies (RQ5)

The last section looks into approach of clients towards creativity and also investigates their expectations from agencies.

In line with the aim of the section, participants were asked "How would you describe the receptiveness of clients to creative ideas?". It is noticed that PR practitioners see their clients' receptiveness to creative ideas below the average (M: 3,2) (Fig. 12.5).

Respondents were also asked that "Compared with 5 years ago, are clients more or less likely to approach their PR agency for big creative ideas?" The results show that clients apply to PR agencies for creative ideas above the average (M: 5,4) (Fig. 12.6).

The last question of this section sought an answer to the question of "How important is creativity when clients decide whether to hire you or your agency?" As it is seen in Fig. 12.7, PR practitioners' response is above the average.

As findings indicate, PR agencies' view about creativity and expectations of clients is consistent with results about quality and priority of creativity in the Turkish PR industry. They think that clients' receptiveness to creative ideas is not totally inspirational and is not very important to decide to hire the agency or not. On the other hand, there is a dramatic change in demands of clients about big creative ideas in the past five years. Similarly, creative quality in PR is below the average (M:3,3) and 75 % of the participants state that the quality is getting better.

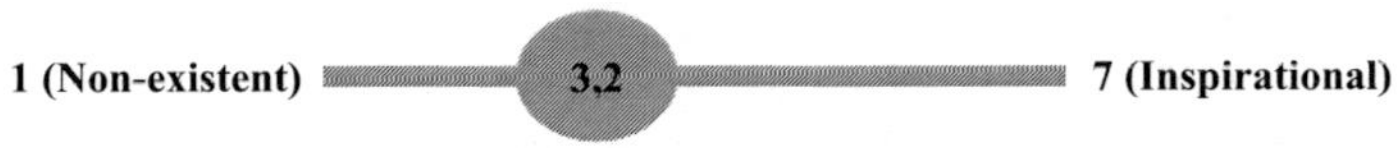

Fig. 12.5: Mean score of receptiveness of clients to creative ideas

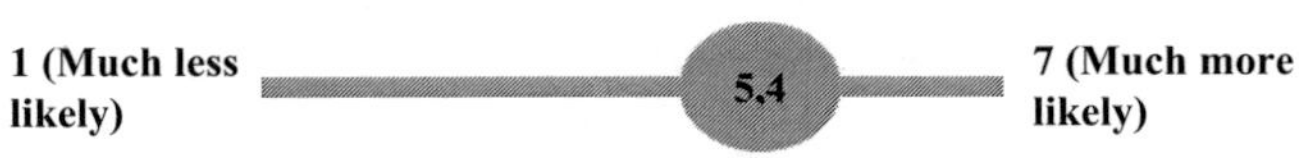

Fig. 12.6: Mean score of clients' approach to their PR agency for big creative ideas

Fig. 12.7: Mean score of importance of creativity to hire the agency

Discussion and Conlusion

The results of this study indicate that quality of creativity in PR works is not perceived as impressive among Turkish public relations professionals. Similarly, creativity is not a priority for them. On the other hand, findings show that there is an improvement in the quality compared to 5 years ago. One of the major reasons of quality and priority levels of creativity is related with its position in the industry both in global and national scales. In comparison to advertising, PR has a shorter history with creativity. Porter Novelli President Julie Winske states "The [creative] industry has been very comfortable talking in an unabashed way about amazing creativity, and that may be new to the broader PR industry" (cited in Bruell, 2011). PR category in Cannes Lions International Festival of Creativity is a good example to reveal the status of PR in creative industries. As mentioned before, PR is accepted as a category for 10 years in the festival; however, it must be taken into consideration that the festival has been organized since 1954.

A key characteristic of a successful, creative PR campaign is asserted as originality or uniqueness of big idea or tactics. There are several studies claiming that creativity in PR is associated with originality (e.g., Daymon, 2000; Estanyol and Roca, 2005; Sitzman, 1980). Originality is essential for creativity; however, it is not adequate by itself. This is because original ideas may be noneffective or useless (Runco and Jaeger, 2012). In PR, it is essential for a creative idea to be realistic and applicable (Daymon, 2000).

According to PR practitioners, the most important reasons for not being more creative are related to clients; clients are not acknowledged as risk takers and determined. They believe that better briefs and client educations can improve the creativity. This study confirms Estanyol and Roca's (2015) study which indicates that clients should take more risks for more creativity. Likewise, El-Murad and West's (2003) study asserts that managers and clients are likely to less risks and reject the creative idea. Moreover, it argues that taking more risks will lead to increased levels of creativity in the industry. Apart from that, basically, creativity at participants' own agency is evaluated as higher than average of the industry.

The way public relations agencies manage the structure about creativity determines the extent to which creativity is encouraged or prevented. According to the results, creativity is not motivated by the management despite the perceived quality of creativity. Since creativity has a positive relationship with encouragement and motivation (Hennessey, 2010), agency managers should be more considerate on the issue. This study also highlights the significance of planners, strategists, and copywriters in terms of creative work. Importance of these positions arise from creative process. Creative process has four main steps: in the "problem or task presentation" step, the problem is tried to be understood; in the preparation stage, information about the problem or task is gathered; idea generation step consists of searching memory and environment; idea validation step includes last version of the creative work (Amabile, 2018, p. 94). Especially the second and third steps necessitate a supporting team including planners or strategists. Another important point about agency structure is that key duty of creative director is seen as developing campaign ideas. The role assigned to creative director take the blurred line further, which is between PR, advertising, and marketing.

Another significant outcome of the study is about evaluation of creativity. Although several scholars and practitioners in the communication field link creativity with achieving campaign objectives and effectiveness, Turkish PR professionals dissent with them. In a study of Parker, Wayne, and Kent (2005, p. 18), creative ideas are associated with "practicality, performance, effectiveness and success rate." Similarly, in PR Lions Awards, it is stated to the attendees that the work is "judged on the creative implementation of your chosen PR technique in order to earn attention and achieve desired campaign outcomes" (canneslions.com). Runco (2007) discusses 'effective replies to changes' in terms of creativity. In advertising industry, which can be a benchmark for PR industry, there are numerous studies that link creative messages with effectiveness such as purchase intention (Heiser, Sierra, and Torres, 2008; Kover, Goldberg, and James, 1995;), ad recall (Higie and Sewall 1991), attitudes toward the brand (Mehta, 2000), and likeability (Leather, McKechnie, and Amirkhanian 1994).

Results demonstrating 'engagement' and 'storytelling' as the most important factors that make a big idea creative conform with the nature of PR. The engagement concept has involved in the field of PR in 1990s (Johnston, 2014). Since that time concept of engagement has picked up, "... building culture and cultivating engagement became one of the central tasks of public relations" (Jelen-Sanchez, 2017, p. 934). Engagement is "a core concept for a public relations philosophy grounded in notions of mutually beneficial relationships [...], which takes into account the multiple assumptions, values, beliefs and visions that publics [...] may hold" (Motion, Haar and Leitch, 2012, p. 54). Today's dominant PR view which requires relationship building (Gruning and White, 1992; Ledingham, 2003) sees one of the core functions of PR as storytelling (Heath, 2006). "One reason that perspectives become widely believed is because they are embedded into stories that are told over and over through interpersonal conversation and mass media. Much of the discourse used by public relations relies on narrative-the story" (Heath, 1992, p. 57). The competition in the communication industry and the rise of social media compel professionals to listen and respond stakeholders. Success of campaigns are not only measured by metrics such as number of likes, clicks, or page views. Concepts such as interaction, relationship, engagement, and participation are new significant metrics (Fisher, 2009).

The most influential trend on PR that the study points out, real-time marketing, has been on the front burner for the last decade. "Real time marketing is the practice of creating content inspired by a current topic, trend or event" (Kerns, 2014, p. 15). Today, speed and agility matter rather than media buying power or scale of the work (Scott, 2011). Creative people in the PR agencies have a key role in this practice; this is because creativity is important to develop content in real time (Lotte et al., 2018). It requires the ability to think the right thing at the right time and put it into practice at the right place. Besides creative execution, success of a real-time work depends on both paid and earned media as well as the story it tells (Crenshaw, 2013).

Although a minor part of respondents think that visuals are the most important part of a creative PR campaign, visual-/image-led communication is a popular trend affecting them. Visual communication is accepted as more clear than verbal messages (Bulmer and Oliver, 2006); it helps to engage with audience faster with more emotion (Julian, 2018) and it supports learning and understanding (Levie and Lentz, 1982). Visual contents are at the core of PR and other marketing communications (Comms Lab, 2017) in the age where Instagram has 1 billion monthly active users (Smith, 2019) and YouTube is the second most popular website in the world (Alexa, 2019). If companies want to understand and build relationship with the audience, they need to speak their language which means the visual language that is creative and engaging (Comms Lab, 2017).

After all, this study, drawing a picture of creativity in the Turkish PR industry, shows that creativity is an emerging area and it will be more important than ever. In order to improve the quality of creativity, the PR industry with its all components – PR agencies and clients – should change their point of view. They should give priority to creativity and evaluation of creativity. PR industry knows and talks about creativity; however, several inadequacies prevent the creative revolution.

References

Acar, S., Burnett, C., & Cabra, J. F. (2017). Ingredients of creativity: Originality and more. *Creativity Research Journal*, *29*(2), 133–144.

Alexa. (2019). *The top 500 sites on the web*. Retrieved from https://www.alexa.com/topsites.

Altın Pusula Halkla İliskiler Odulleri. (n.d.). Retrieval date May 20, 2019. Retrieved from http://www.altinpusula.org/altin-pusula-halkla-iliskiler-odulleri.html.

Altsech, M. B. (1996). *The assessment of creativity in advertising and the effectiveness of creative advertisements*. Unpublished doctoral dissertation, Pennsylvania State University.

Amabile, T. M. (1996). *Creativity in context*. New York: West-view Press.

Amabile, T. M. (2018). *Creativity in context: Update to the social psychology of creativity*. Routledge.

Andreasen, N. C. (2005). *The creating brain*. New York: Dana Press.

Babbie, E. R. (2013). *The basics of social research*. Cengage learning.

Barron, F., & Harrington, D. M. (1981). Creativity, intelligence, and personality. *Annual Review of Psychology*, *32*(1), 439–476.

Bruell, A. (2011). *In PR category, PR shops come up short while ad agencies stand tall-creative agencies prevail in best use of social media and best PR-driven campaigns*. Retrieved from http://adage.com/article/special-report-cannes-2011/cannes-pr- shops-short-ad-agencies-stand-tall/228428/.

Bruell, A. (2015). *Like a girl. Wins PR grand prix*. Retrieved from https://adage.com/article/special-report-cannes-lions/a-girl-wins-pr-grand-prix-pr-agency-s-role-unclear/299169

Bulmer, S., & Buchanan-Oliver, M. (2006). Visual rhetoric and global advertising imagery. *Journal of Marketing Communications*, *12*(1), 49–61.

Caroff, X., & Besançon, M. (2008). Variability of creativity judgments. *Learning and Individual Differences*, *18*(4), 367–371.

Comms Lab. (2017). *The power of visual communication: Showing your story to land the message*. Retrieved June 20, 2019 from https://www.pwc.com.au/the-difference/the-power-of-visual-communication-apr17.pdf

Cook, P. (1998). The creativity advantage-is your organization the leader of the pack? *Industrial and Commercial Training*, *30*(5), 179–184.

Crenshaw, D. (2013). *PR should own real-time marketing*. Retrived June 11, 2019 from https://crenshawcomm.com/pr-should-own-real-time-marketing/.

Crystal Apple. (n.d.). Retrieval date June 11, 2019. Retrieved from http://2017.kristalelmafestivali.com/icerik/festival/About.asp.

Daymon, C. (2001). Cultivating creativity in public relations consultancies: The management and organisation of creative work. *Journal of Communication Management*, *5*(1), 17–30.

DCMS. (2016). *Creative industries: Focus on employment*. Retrieved from https://assets.publishing.service.gov.uk/government/uploads/system/uploads/attachment_data/file/534305/Focus_on_Employment_revised_040716.pdf

Diedrich, J., Benedek, M., Jauk, E., & Neubauer, A. C. (2015). Are creative ideas novel and useful? *Psychology of Aesthetics, Creativity and the Arts*, *9*, 35–40.

El-Murad, J., & West, D. C. (2003). Risk and creativity in advertising. *Journal of Marketing Management*, *19*(5–6), 657–673.

El-Murad, J., & West, D. C. (2004). The definition and measurement of creativity: What do we know? *Journal of Advertising Research*, *44*(2), 188–201.

Estanyol, E., & Roca, D. (2015). Creativity in PR consultancies: Perception and management. *Public Relations Review*, *41*(5), 589–597.

Felis Odulleri. (n.d.). Retrieval date May 20, 2019. Retrieved from https://felisodulleri.com.

Fisher, T. (2009). ROI in social media: A look at the argument. *Journal of Database Marketing and Customer Strategy Management*, *16*(3), 189–195.

Ford, C. M. (1996). A theory of individual creativity in multiple social domains. *Academy of Management Review*, *21*, 1112–1134.

Ford, C. M., & Gioia, D. A. (2000). Factors influencing creativity in the domain of managerial decision making. *Journal of Management*, *26*(4), 705–732.

Green, A. (2010). *Creativity in public relations*. London: Kogan Page Publishers.

Grunig, J. E., & Hunt, T. T. (1984). *Managing public relations*. Forth Worth: Holt, Rinehart and Winston.

Halpern, D. (2003). Thinking critically about creative thinking. In M. A. Runco (Ed.), *Critical creative process* (pp. 189–208). Cresskill, NJ: Hampton Press.

Heath, R. L. (1992). Critical perspectives on public relations. In E. L. Toth & R. L. Heath (Eds.), *Rhetorical and critical approaches to public relations* (pp. 37–61). Thousand Oaks, CA: Sage.

Heath, R. L. (2006). Onword into more fog: Thoughts on public relations' research directions. *Journal of Public Relations Research*, *18*(2), 93–114.

Heiser, R., Sierra, J., & Torres, I. (2008). Creativity via cartoon spokespeople in print ads: Capitalizing on the distinctiveness effect. *Journal of Advertising Research*, *37*(4), 75–84.

Hendrix, J. A., Hayes, D. C., & Kumar, P. D. (2012). *Public relations cases*. Boston: Wadsworth Cengage Learning.

Hennessey, B. A. (2010). The creativity-motivation connection. In J.C. Kaufman & R.L. Sternberg (Eds.), *The Cambridge handbook of creativity* (pp. 342–365). Cambridge: Cambridge University Press.

Higie, R. A., & Sewall, M. A. (1991). Using recall and brand preference to evaluate advertising effectiveness. *Journal of Advertising Research, 31*(April/May), 56–63.

James, K., Clark, K., & Cropanzano, R. (1999). Positive and negative creativity in groups, institutions, and organizations: A model and theoretical extension. *Creativity Research Journal, 12*(3), 211–226.

Jelen Sanchez, A. (2017). Engagement in public relations discipline: Themes, theoretical perspectives and methodological approaches. *Public Relations Review, 43*(5), 934–944.

Johnston, K. A. (2014). Public relations and engagement: Theoretical imperatives of a multidimensional concept. *Journal of Public Relations Research*, 26(5), 381–383.

Kabanoff, B., & Rossiter, J. R. (1994). Recent developments in applied creativity. In C. L. Cooperand & I. T. Robertson (Eds.), *International review of industrial and organizational psychology* (Vol. 9, pp. 283–324). New York: Wiley.

Kerns, C. (2014). *Trendology: Building an advantage through data-driven real-time marketing*. New York: Palgrave Macmillan.

Kilgour, M., & Koslow, S. (2009). Why and how do creative thinking techniques work?: Trading off originality and appropriateness to make more creative advertising. *Journal of the Academy of Marketing Science, 37*(3), 298–309.

Kover, A. J., Goldberg, S. M., & James, W. L. (1995). Creativity vs. effectiveness? An integrating classification for advertising. *Journal of Advertising Research, 35*(6), 29–39.

Leather, P., McKechnie, S., & Amirkhanian, M. (1994). The importance of likeability as a measure of television advertising effectiveness. *International Journal of Advertising, 13*(3), 256–281.

Levie, W. H., & Lentz, R. (1982). Effects of text illustrations: A review of research. *Educational Communication and Technology Journal, 30*(4), 195–232.

Lotte M. W., Mazerant, K., Kamphuis, A.-L., & van der Veen, G. (2018). Let's Get Real (Time)! The potential of real-time marketing to catalyze the sharing of brand messages. *International Journal of Advertising, 37*(5), 828–848.

Mack, A. (2016). *PR is not enough: We must all become polymaths to thrive.* Retrieved June 15, 2019 from http://www.prweek.com/article/1401088/pr-not-enough-become-polymaths-thrive

Mehta, A. (2000). Advertising attitudes and advertising effectiveness. *Journal of Advertising Research*, *40*(3), 67–72.

Moriarty, S. E. (1997). The big idea: Creativity in public relations. In C. L. Caywood (Ed.), *The handbook of strategic public relations and integrated communications* (pp. 554–563). Boston, MA: McGraw Hill.

Parker, Wayne and Kent. (2005). The management of creativity in the public relations process. Retrieved May 25, 2019 from https://printreranduri.eu/wp-content/uploads/creativitatea-in-relatii-publice.pdf.

Prida Odülleri. (n.d.). Retrieval date May 20, 2019. Retrieved from http://www.pridaodulleri.org/kategoriler.html.

PR Lions. (n.d.). Retrieval date May 20, 2019. Retrieved from https://www.canneslions.com/enter/awards/reach/pr-lions.

Rogers, C. R. (1995). *On becoming a person: A therapist's view of psychotherapy*. Boston: Houghton Mifflin.

Runco, M. A., & Charles, R. E. (1993). Judgments of originality and appropriateness as predictors of creativity. *Personality and individual differences*, *15*(5), 537–546.

Runco, M. A., Illies, J. J., & Eisenman, R. (2005). Creativity, originality, and appropriateness: What do explicit instructions tell us about their relationships?. *The Journal of Creative Behavior*, *39*(2), 137–148.

Runco, M. A., & Jaeger, G. J. (2012). The standard definition of creativity. *Creativity Research Journal*, *24*(1), 92–96.

Salzman, M. (2016). Why nothing matters more in PR than creativity. Retrieved June 12, 2019 from https://www.dandad.org/en/d-ad-pr-creativity-features-opinions/

Scott, D. M. (2011). *Real-time marketing and PR: How to instantly engage your market, connect with customers, and create products that grow your business now*. Hoboken, NJ: John Wiley and Sons.

Simonton, D. K. (2001). Creativity. In C. R. Snyder & S. J. Lopez (Eds.), *Handbook of positive psychology*. Oxford: Oxford University Press.

Sitzman, M. (1980). Creativity and public relations. *The Public Relations Quarterly*, *25*(4), 16–17.

Smith, K. (2019). 49 incredible Instagram statistics. Retrieved June 18 from https://www.brandwatch.com/blog/instagram-stats/

Smith, R. D. (2013). *Strategic planning for public relations*. New York: Routledge.

The Holmes Report, Ogilvy and Now-Go-Create. (2017). Creativity in PR: A global study. Retrieved June 5, 2019 from: https://www.holmesreport.com/ranking-and-data/creativity-in-pr

Torrance, E. P. (1988). The nature of creativity as manifest in its testing. In R. J. Sternberg (Ed.), *The nature of creativity* (pp. 43–75). New York, NY: Cambridge University Press.

Vernon, P. E. (1989). The nature-nurture problem in creativity. In *Handbook of creativity* (pp. 93–110). Boston, MA: Springer.

White, A., Shen, F., & Smith, B. L. (2002). Judging advertising creativity using the creative product semantic scale. *The Journal of Creative Behavior*, *36*(4), 241–253.

Wilcox, D. L., & Cameron, G. T. (2012). *Public relations: Strategies and tactics*. Boston, MA: Allyn and Bacon.

Willis, P., & Estanyol, E. (2018). Collaborative creativity, leadership and public relations: Identifying and addressing research limitations. In S. Bowman (Ed.), *Public relations and the power of creativity: Strategic opportunities, innovation and critical challenges* (pp. 135–148). Bingley: Emerald Publishing Limited.

Burcu Eker Akgöz, Elif Engin

Chapter 13 Understanding Hallmark Events: Case of Şeb-i Arus

Events are as old as human communication and part of our collective lives. It enables people to come together, to have a quality time and to reach a satisfaction. The emergence of the concept of leisure time and the desire of people to spend their leisure time with entertainment and celebrations have led events to be more planned. Today, events are more culturally centered than ever before. Culturally, socially and economically contributions of the events were noticed by both corporations, governments and non-governmental organizations. Since the events played an important role in human communication, these institutions gave importance to event management. Governments are making activities as part of strategies for economic development, nation image and destination tourism, while corporations benefit from events within the framework of image development, reputation and marketing strategies. Events earlier used to be a part of the hospitality, tourism, leisure and recreation industries or as a support service to businesses. Now, with changing and challenging business life, the events industry has emerged on its own and a knowledge has been created in this field. However, the events spread from a restricted area such as festivals and concerts to wide industries like sports, trade fairs, brands, etc. Nowadays, events are involvements where billion dollars are invested to gather large masses and bring people from different geographic regions together and make them live different experiences. Because of these experiences they create, they help participants to form memories in terms of emotions, thoughts and experiences of the participants.

Event management has become so important in the world that the number of large-scale events has increased. Events that reach large participants include many important areas such as culture, place of event, community integration and participation. Especially mega, major and hallmark events are the ones that have important contributions in a wide spectrum. Hallmark events, defined by Getz (2012, p. 51) as iconic events, play an important role in conveying cultural heritage to the masses in terms of their contribution to the community and the place where the event is held. Cultural events are seen today as an important part of the creative industries. The symbolic and economic impact of the term "culture" leads to new strategies of representation. Cultural events usually focus on artistic and community elements expressed through its content. Cultural events such as hallmark events both improve the quality of life of the city, help create the image of the city's tourist destination and, most importantly, provide economic development. The more important economic development is, the more important is the regional development. As Getz points out, hallmark events are so related to local people and destination that it is not possible to think separately from the culture. Cultural structure, values, symbols and meanings expressed by local people are very important in hallmark events compared to other events (Getz, 2012, p. 51).

Culturally important and largest hallmark event in Turkey is Şeb-i Arus which is held in the city of Konya. Şeb-i Arus means Wedding Night in Turkish. It is the night when the great leader of mysticism and Sufism, philosopher, scientist and poet Mawlana Jalaluddin Rumi died. Mawlana Jalaluddin Rumi calls this night the 'Night of the Wedding' that he thinks of as the night of convergence to his beloved God. Rumi's death anniversaries were held in the weeks corresponding to 17 December and called as Convergency Anniversary International Commemoration Ceremonies, also known as Şeb-i Arus by public. (https://www.mawlana.com/seb-i-arus/) Seb-i Arus is an event that transmits the cultural and religious values and symbols of society to the masses. This significant event that contributes the location both economically and destination tourism includes many events of various sizes.

In this chapter, Seb-i Arus, which is an important event as a hallmark event, will be analyzed. While analyzing the event, the features of Hallmark events and the contributions of the cultural heritage to the city of Konya and the local people will be taken into account.

Events Communication

Events are as old as human communication and part of our collective lives. It enables people to come together, to have a quality time and to reach a satisfaction. For these reasons, events are very important both socially, culturally and economically. The traditions, rituals and celebrations that have come from the past to the present day form the basis of events in today's modern sense.

Event is called the activity which is organized by the departments such as public relations, corporate communication, marketing and human resources that provide to contact with internal or external stakeholders and create the content according to the desired messages. Nowadays, all these plans have been transformed into an industry where large number of employees have been involved, have economic benefits and need to be managed by professionals.

According to Cambridge Dictionary, event means anything that happens, especially something, important or unusual (www.dictionary.cambridge.org). Throughout history, it has been an activity that enables people to come together and socialize. Berridge (2007, p. 5) states that the earliest definitions come from Donald Getz and J.J. Goldblatt in the early 1990s who specify an event as 'unique', 'one-off', 'special', and 'beyond everyday experience'. Hence, they are immediately separating events from other routine activities such as work. Goldblatt (1990) describes the event as,

> A special event recognizes an unique moment in time with ceremony and ritual to satisfy specific needs', and Getz (1991), defines as 'is an opportunity for leisure, social or cultural experience outside the normal range of choices or beyond everyday experience. '

By the time, the definition and content of the event has changed, the concept became visible in various fields and industries. Beech, Kaiser and Kaspar use the word 'event' generically. They include a number of terms which are commonly used. These are: carnival, conference, convention, exhibition, expo, fair, festival, fete (small-scale of event), messe (trade fair) and show. They also made the classification of events such as sports events, cultural events, business events (including conferences and trade fairs) and other events. (2014, p. 3–4)

Special events are set apart from the normal activities of daily life, and its purpose is to celebrate, enlighten, entertain or challenge the experience of a group of people. They are rising from non-routine occasions that have leisure, cultural, personal or organizational objectives. Getz (2007:27) states, 'to the customer or guest, a special event is an opportunity for a leisure, social or cultural experience outside the normal range of choices or beyond everyday experience.'

Therefore, categorization of special events are as follows:

- Leisure Events: Leisure, sport, recreation.
- Personal Events: Weddings, birthdays, anniversaries.
- Organizational Events: Commercial, political, charitable, sales.
- Cultural Events: Ceremonial, sacred, heritage, art, folklore (Shone and Parry, 2010, p. 4–5)

While events can be categorized such as these, sometimes it is difficult to distinguish one event from another. For example, a festival can be considered both as cultural and organizational event. At the same time, defined categories are useful as a starting point. They guide the event planners on how to organize and improve the event. With this road maps, it is aimed to reach the goals of events. On the other hand, special events differ in terms of majority, size, complexity, internationalization, size and the number of participants.

When defining special events, its key characteristics are mentioned as 'non-routine' and 'unique'. The characteristics of events can be grouped together as: uniqueness, perishability, labor-intensiveness, fixed timescales, intangibility, personal interaction, ambience, and ritual or ceremony (Shone and Parry, 2010, p. 15–18).

- **Uniqueness:** Uniqueness does not mean that the same kind of event will not happen many times, but the environment, participants, audience or other variables make the event unique. Thus, each one will be different.
- **Perishability:** If the event is considered as unique and hugely changed, its repetition does not happen exactly the same way. There can be a reasonable level of standardization for each activity. They will be dissimilar in terms of being different and time dependent.
- **Intangibility:** When you join an event, you will experience the activities and you will remember it, but there are a few tangible things remaining for it. So, some giveaways and gifts are efforts to make the experience of the event more tangible; a memory to show friends and family such as a program, postcards, named chocolates, etc.
- **Ritual and ceremony:** Looking at historical times, ritual and ceremony often played an important role in events. In practice, modern ceremonial activities are redevised versions of ancient traditions, but the ritual of doing it still keep going.
- **Ambience and service:** Ambience is one of the most important outcome of all the characteristics of events. While an event with the right ambiance can be a perfect one, an event with the wrong ambience can be a big failure. Some events may need some help to keep it going well such as music and games, decorations, food and drink, etc.
- **Personal contact and interaction:** People involved in the events are often the part of the process. For example, in sports people are not only watching, but they also have a share in creating the atmosphere; they interact with the participants and the staff, and they are all a part of the whole experience.
- **Labor-intensiveness:** When the event is more unique and more complex, it is more likely to be labor-intensive, in terms of both operation and organization. In these types of services, it requires high levels of staffing and communication between the organizer, client and the event manager to make the event a success.
- **Fixed timescale:** Even though, the timescale can be very short, for example, the opening ceremony for a new road, the planning phase can take about three years. For planning special events, timing must be kept in mind for events to

be successful and striking. It is better to break up into sections rather than taking place at once, without a break.

Special events are events that go beyond the routine in everyday life and are activities to stimulate everyday life. Nevertheless, the society in which we live is constantly changing and evolving. As a result of developing technology and social needs of people, the expectations for events have changed or even increased. All events are based on service and socialization of humanity. With the help of classifications and characteristics, these events guide us to understand the nature of events and how to design them.

When creating special events, the event designer and event participant have different expectations from this activity. Their common point is to provide a 'unique moment' and 'memorable experience'. With this experience, events are kept in mind, remembered and this experience is shared with others.

O'Sullivan and Spangler (1998, p. 5) expressed in their book that event experiences include the following:

- participation and involvement in the consumption;
- the state of being physically, mentally, socially spiritually or emotionally engaged;
- a change in knowledge, skill, memory or emotion;
- the conscious perception of having intentionally encountered, gone to or lived through an activity or event; and
- an effort directed at addressing a psychological or internal need (Getz, 2007, p. 176).

Everyone participating in the event has different expectations. While some of them want to have a good time and socialize, the others participate in events to get knowledge, see different cultures and for psychological needs. Although the experience changes from person to person, it will be remembered as the moment shared by at the end of the event. Briefly, experiences in the events can be described as reality, observation, satisfaction, living through, etc. Therefore, experiences are individualized. While memorable and emotional experiences are important in terms of the effectiveness, the venue of the event also plays an important role in that experience. Venues are places that convert intangibility to reality, create events and an opportunity to experience.

An appropriate venue is of primary significance to the overall success or failure of the event and should complement the theme of the event, e.g. alongside the Pyramids to communicate an Egyptian theme, e.g. for the Aida Concert 2000 (Yeoman et al., 2015, p. 20). Thus, one of the most important part of the events is searching for the venues that are suitable /right place for event participation. Venues make the events, special and unforgettable for their target audience. Venues' atmosphere plays a crucial role in event management.

The decision of venue in the event is a process that should be evaluated by two sides. While organizers try to ensure audiences not to have unfavorable times inside and outside the event area, event participants want to experience unique moments and add a new experience to their lives. Therefore, the importance of venue selection is very important in order to achieve the purpose of the event. The common purpose of all events is to enable people to come together and spend time together. So, events have to be managed well each time, and the events have to be different from each other in terms of creative aspects.

There are several factors for choosing potential venues or sites. These are:

- **Availability:** Date(s) and duration, including move-in and move-out requirements and acceptable service levels.
- **Location:** Accessibility by air and ground transportation, proximity to other attractions and the surrounding environment.
- **Rates:** Rental fees, costs for site development, food and beverage prices and surcharges.
- **Attendance:** Occupancy capacity, anticipated behaviors, arrival and departure modes and ancillary activities before, during and after the event.
- **Function type:** Educational, spectator, ceremonial, social, political, etc.
- **Event elements:** Room dimensions, spatial requirements, activities, access logistics, storage, and administrative functions.
- **Style or personality**: Conservative, adventurous, youthful, mature, rustic, luxurious, unique, traditional, theme-specific, etc. (Silvers, 2004, p. 66)

Events identify with the venue (place) where they occur. During and after the event venues leave memories that are remembered together with that place in people's mind. And also, every event carries the cultural characteristics of the community in which it occurs. As events are repeated whether they become traditional, or international, they consequently become a whole with the place and culture eventually.

> Culture varies geographically, so the influence of place and culture on events are reinforcing. In turn, events influence the places and cultures in which they occur, especially when mega-events are imposed on a culture that has not experienced such investment and media attention, and also when new events spread across the globe. Some events achieve 'iconic' status so they can occur anywhere and still be successful, but they still

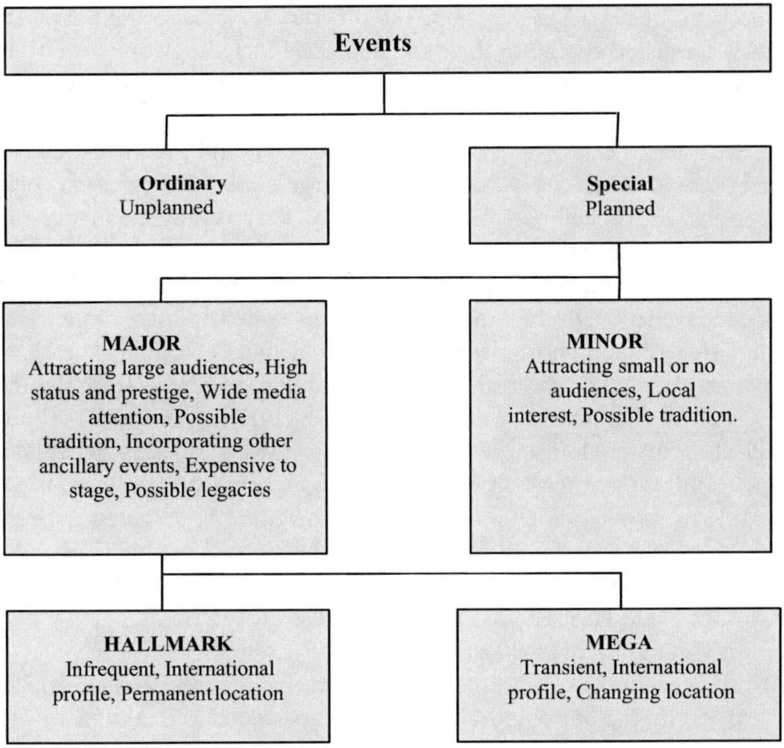

Tab. 13.1: A definition for events (adapted from Jago & Shaw, 1998). (Masterman, 2009, p. 13)

> require specific venues and leave some kind of tangible legacy in terms of urban renewal, tourism and transport infrastructure, social and environmental change. (Getz, 2007, p. 20–21)

Whether it is a small-scale or a large-scale event, event planners need to have these specialties for creating a successful event. In the event industry, besides these features, they also need to have good communication skills, forward-thinking and ability to keep up with rapid changes.

Hallmark Events

Besides the leisure, personal, organizational and cultural events, events can be categorized as such:

Events can be classified or grouped in different ways. Jago and Shaw (1998) suggest a model according to their size and scale including explanation of the relationship between the various types of event. The model is initially divided into two parts according to whether the events are planned (special) or not (ordinary). Secondly, special events are classified as major and minor events. Lastly, major events are separated as hallmark and mega events. They make a connection between major, hallmark and mega-events. They also define major, minor, hallmark and mega events as special events.

Major events are capable of economic benefits, attracting significant visitor numbers and media coverage according to their scale and media interest such as The Open Championship, staged at different links golf courses each year, Silverstone has the British Formula One Grand Prix and The Isle of Man hosts the TT Races. Mega events are large events which reflect in the global media and affect entire economies. Some of them are FIFAWorld Cup, IAAF World Championships, Olympic Games and Paralympic Games (Bowdin et al, 2006, p. 16–18). In minor events, financial issues that were highlighted during the session is an evidence for the key role of volunteers. Absorbing the cultural experience was enhanced by leisure activities including walks through Hyde Park, Buckingham Palace and visits in popular streets of the shopping precinct, Piccadilly Circus (Lagos et al., 2019, p. 148).

Hallmark events are one of the major events that are frequently defined and searched in the literature and are especially associated with the place of the event. These events are important in terms of being on an international scale, identifying with the location and making significant contributions to tourism. The academicians, who have done very important research on event and event management, state that hallmark events provide a wide awareness and attract attention to the place where the event will be held.

Bowdin et al. suggest that 'hallmark events' refer to those events that become so identified with the spirit of a town, city or region that they become synonymous with the name of the place, and earn extensive recognition and awareness (2006, p. 17).

Hallmark events are not only a tourist attraction, but also create an image and identity for host communities. The success of the event increases the power of the image of host communities. Hallmark events are also symbols of quality and authenticity because of the features they contain. In addition to being a creative event, they also have cultural implications. For Getz, hallmark events represent a specific category characterized by an authentic link to a specific area or culture. They are associated with the image of the community or of the host destination.

For Jago and Shaw as well as for Getz, the events that have made their mark like hallmark events are identified by mutual dependence on the host destinations that evolve into institutionalization (Tara-Lunga, 2012, p. 772).

The literature has addressed hallmark events in terms of definition, function and form (Getz et al., 2012:48). They are known for their goal-oriented development and management in touristic destinations, and their status is defined as: longevity; quality of the brand image; the significance; and value. Although classifications vary, they are generally classified as having different characteristics. Unlike mega or big events, hallmark events are rarely recognized by scale of the audience and media interest (Getz et al., 2012, p. 48).

There are many definitions in the literature of hallmark events. The following definitions are the most common ones.

For Getz: (Getz, 2007, p. 24)

> Hallmark Events are those that possesses such significance, in terms of tradition, attractiveness, quality or publicity, that the event provides the host venue, community or destination with a competitive advantage. Over time, the event and destination images become inextricably linked. Hallmark Events are, by definition, permanent 'institutions' in their communities or societies.

According to Hall: (Hall, 1989, p. 263)

> "Hallmark tourist events are major fairs, expositions, cultural and sporting events of international status which are held on either a regular or a one-off basis. A primary function of the hallmark event is to provide the host community with an opportunity to secure high prominence in the tourism market place."

Richie defines Hallmark events as: (Ritchie,1984, p.2)

> major one time or recurring events of limited duration, developed primarily to enhance the awareness, appeal and profitability of a tourist destination in the short and/or long term. Such events rely for their success on uniqueness, status, or timely significance to create interest and attract attention."

To put forth the common features of these important definitions, they all mention about the importance of the destination and the destination as an important market place for tourism. However, it is an important tourist attraction as a cultural event so that it contains local motifs. Graham Devlin Associates (2001) and Marques (2011) state that cultural events can improve the quality of life in a city, provide more creative activities, increase the number of visitors, create new partnerships, educational opportunities, lead to economic and social benefits, improve the image of the city as a tourist destination and help to achieve civic objectives (Ferreira et al.,2015, p. 95).

It is acknowledged that the functional characteristics of hallmark events increase their importance as tourism products in the places where they host, and are allowed to make significant tangible contributions to the tourism of the event. An important feature of Hallmark events is their close relationship with host destination (Todd, Leask & Ensor, 2017, p. 496). Host destination and hallmark events are often co-branded, and they must stay according to the spatial community environment (Hall, 1989, p. 266).

Hallmark events are sustainable and beneficial for their community. Reflecting these tangible features, Hall defines hallmark events as 'image builders of modern tourism' (Hall, 1992, p. 1). Therefore, its permanence is placed within destinations to the extent that it becomes the symbolic elements of the image and brand of destination (Getz, 2008, p. 411). Hallmark events with cultural characteristics should also involve the local community in the whole organization. It is expected that the local people will stand for events and participate voluntarily in the smooth implementation of the organization. Otherwise, the event will not achieve a total success. Therefore, local participation is very significant. Moscardo (2007) has argued that even if an event attracts substantial numbers of tourists and generates revenue but does not create community involvement, it is unlikely to have much of an effect on regional development. It means that without the local involvement the event remains 'disconnected' to the locality. The importance of the events needs to be based on both economic and sociocultural values (Pasanen et al, 2009:113).

Events have also become a tool for regional development because of their economic benefits. This can be another factor that will enable local community to involve event. The local economy will develop with a hallmark event that will attract the attention of the wider masses. Especially in small areas where income sources are limited, the events will cause the economy to revive and the local people to be strengthened. According to Allen et Al. (2002), developing existing cultural events and event tourism is very attractive, especially for small- and medium-sized places (Pasanen et al, 2009, p. 113).

Cultural events can improve the quality of life in a city, provide more creative activities, increase the number of visitors, create new partnerships, educational opportunities, lead to economic and social benefits, improve the image of the city as a tourist destination and help to achieve civic objectives (Graham Devlin Associates, 2001; Marques, 2011 cited in (Ferreira et al, 2015, p. 95). The more important economic development is, the more important is the regional development. Apart from the economic perception of regional development, social and cultural developments are also crucial for event and destination. While hallmark events are so related to local people and destination, it is not possible to think about culture separately.

Festivals and events are becoming increasingly important for the region and the tourism industry, particularly in the regional areas where current sources of income are more limited than in metropolitan areas. They are important in more than one perspective. Events and festivals are considered to be of social and cultural importance for the towns and regions that host themselves as well as economic. Most of the events are important tourist places, some of them even in low season. Events can also help create a positive image for the region and provide a competitive marketing advantage in similar places (Allen et al., 2002 cited in Pasanen et al., 2009:113).

Cultural structure, values, symbols and the meaning expressed by local people are more important in hallmark events than other events. Getz et al. state that hallmark events are iconic by their nature. The basic meaning of iconic is something with a symbol or symbolic value. Referring to the news rather than the planned events, Levy (2007) described the iconic events as the winners of the legendary status in the cultural arena. When applied to hallmark events, this means that the media should always attract the attention of the media and they should enter the popular realm (Getz et al., 2012, p. 1).

> Holt (2004) discussed iconic brands in the context of cultural icons; that is, people, places or things that convey symbolic meanings, gain mythical standing, reflect cultural values and identity aspirations. The culture industries, according to Holt, want to create and profit from cultural icons, and this certainly includes planned events. By referring to Holt's ideas, we argue that iconic/hallmark events must embody valued traditions (which convey cultural meanings and the identity of the host community), and gain "mythical standing" through longevity, media attention and positive reputation." (Getz et al., 2012, p. 51)

For hallmark events, Getz et al. state that three principles are articulated, the first being a foundation for the second, and the third being optional: (Getz et al., 2012, p. 52)

1. Hallmark event refers to the function of events in achieving a set of goals that benefit tourism and the host community, namely: attracting tourists; creating and enhancing a positive image that is co-branded with the destination/ community; and delivering multiple benefits to residents.
2. Over time, the hallmark event as a tourist attraction also becomes an institution and its permanence is taken for granted. Its traditions generate a stronger sense of community and place identity. The event and city images become inextricably linked.

3. Hallmark events can also exist within the context of social worlds and for special-interest groups as iconic tourist attractions that facilitate communities and identity building.

Hallmark events differ from other events in terms of highlighting both cultural values and destination. Hallmark events are significant for destination tourism and are also economic source for the place where the event is held and for the community. One of the most important hallmark events in Turkey is Şeb-i Arus. This event is an international one, and it has significant contribution to the city of Konya and its people. This hallmark event is the one that spread the cultural heritage to the world.

The International Commemoration of the 745th Anniversary of Mawlana-Rumi's Reunion as a Hallmark Event

City of Konya as a cultural heritage

Konya has existed until today as one of the most important ancient cities of the world. It is understood that the settled city life started in the prehistoric age, and Çatalhöyük, which is close to the city center, is known as the oldest and most developed Neolithic settlement center. Çumra Çatalhöyük is recognized as the center where the food culture started for the first time in the world, where agriculture was done, the fire was used, the settled life was taken and the common defense against wild animal attacks was made. Similarly, in the Alâaddin Hill, neolithic traces similar to Çatalhöyük are encountered. Konya has been home to important civilizations throughout the ages as a settlement from the Neolithic to the present. Thus, the city had many works of art created by different production and production techniques of different societies. At the time of the use of hieroglyphic writing before the Egyptians in Konya (3500 BC.), the first house of architecture and the remains of the first sacred building were found. The earliest Christian settlements and the oldest churches in Anatolia during the Christian era are also found in this region. Konya, which is the capital of the Seljuk State, extending from the Chinese border to the Byzantine territory is an important accommodation and trade center on the Silk Road. It is also an important city where hundreds of Islamic civilization works, many Islamic scholars and Sufis have been raised and settled. In this city there are the tombs of important historical figures, sultans and viziers who ruled the Anatolian Seljuk State, and spiritual conquerors such as Mevlâna. Although it is an important settlement center in every period of history, Konya has gained its true identity and wealth, thanks to the Seljuk Sultans. The famous scholars, philosophers, poets, Sufis, teachers and other artists of this period were gathered here in the years of 1096–1277 when Konya was the capital city of the Anatolian Seljuks, and they became the cultural center of the city with their works. This period which can be called 'The Golden Age of Konya' continued until the mid-13th century. Especially Mawlana has enlightened humanity with his ideas and philosophy, and he left some works such as Mesnevî and Dîvân-ı Kebîr. As a result, many madrasas, mosques, libraries, tombs, fountains, castles, inns, baths, bazaars, bazaars, bridges and palaces were built throughout the city[1].

In the Ottoman period, scientific, cultural and artistic movements continued in Konya and the city continued to be the center where famous scholars, poets, historians and philosophers gathered. In this period, many mosques, fountains and madrasas were built from the architectural point of view. Konya is a rapidly growing and developing city in the Republican period, and today it is an open-air museum with artifacts from the Seljuks, Karamanogullari and Ottomans. Konya, one of the oldest settlements in the history of humanity in the world, carries the traces of many civilizations within the long historical period[2].

Mawlana Jalaluddin Rumi

Mawlana Muhammad Jalaluddin -i Belh-i Rumi is the representative of humanism, the great thinker of the east, the great leader of mysticism and Sufism, philosopher, scientist and poet. The real name of Mawlana is Jalaluddin Muhammed. He is also known as Hüdavendigar. Later on in his life, he became famous all over the world with the nickname "Mawlana" which means master. Because he spent a large part of his life in Anatolia, known as the Rum land, he was called also 'Rumi'. At the same time, the name 'Mawlana' refers for love and ecstatic flight into the infinite. (Kızbaz, 2008, s. 14)

Rumi was born in Wakhsh (Tajikistan) under the administration of Balkh in September 30, 1207 to a family of learned theologians. Mawlana Jalaluddin's father, Bahauddin Veled, was a great scholar and a respected figure. He was a respected clergyman who knew well the customs and traditions of Islam from a special family lineage, who internalized fiqh and hadith sciences. The reasons why his father left Belh were the contradictions with Harzemşah about philosophical knowledge on Islam, his greater acceptance by society and political

1 *Tarihçe.*(n.d.).Retrieved from https://konyakultur.gov.tr/index.php?route=pages/pages&page_id=1.

2 T*arihçe.*(n.d.).Retrieved from https://konyakultur.gov.tr/index.php?route=pages/pages&page_id=1.

inbalance in Belh. Escaping the Mongol invasion and destruction, Mawlana and his family traveled extensively in the Muslim lands, performed pilgrimage to Mecca and finally settled in Konya, Anatolia, then part of Seljuk Empire. When his father Bahaduddin Valad passed away, Mawlana succeeded his father in 1231 as professor in religious sciences. Mawlana, then 24 years old, was an already accomplished scholar in religious and positive sciences. Mawlana is the author of six volume didactic epic work, the `Mathnawi', called as the 'Koran in Persian' by Jami, and discourses, `Fihi ma Fihi', written to introduce his disciples into metaphysics. If there is any general idea underlying Mawlana's poetry, it is the absolute love of God. His influence on thought, literature and all forms of aesthetic expression in the world of Islam cannot be overrated. Mawlana Jalaluddin Rumi died on December 17, 1273. Men of five faiths followed his bier. That night was named Şeb-i Arus (Night of Union). Ever since, the Mawlawi dervishes have kept that date as a festival[3].

History of Şeb-i Arus

Şeb-i Arus means 'Wedding Night in Turkish' ('Şeb' in Persian: night, 'Arus' in Arabic: weddings). It is the night that Mawlana Jalaluddin Rumi died. Mawlana Jalaluddin Rumi calls this night the 'Night of the Wedding' which he thinks of as the night of convergence to his beloved God. Rumi's death anniversaries were held in the weeks corresponding to 17 December and called as Convergency Anniversary International Commemoration Ceremonies also known as Şeb-i Arus by the public.

The Mawlawi Sama Ceremony is a mystical ceremony that contains religious elements and themes, and thus has detailed rules and qualifications. This ceremony, which is special to Mawlawi, was carried out in a disciplined manner starting from the time of Sultan Veled and Ulu Arif Çelebi while he was working without a certain rule at the time of Mawlana Jalaluddin Rumi (d. 17 December 1273). These rules have been developed until the time of Pir Adil Çelebi and have come to the present day by taking its final form. The way of preserving the culture and especially the Semâ ceremony, which has become an important part of the Turkish history and culture emerged in the 13th century and which has become an important part of the Turkish history and culture in the course of time, is to be conveyed and introduced to the next generations without destroying the technical and internal perfection and originality of this tradition. The Mawlawi Sama Ceremony, which was announced as a Masterpiece

3 *Life of Rumi*. (n.d.). Retrieved from http://www.khamush.com/life.html.

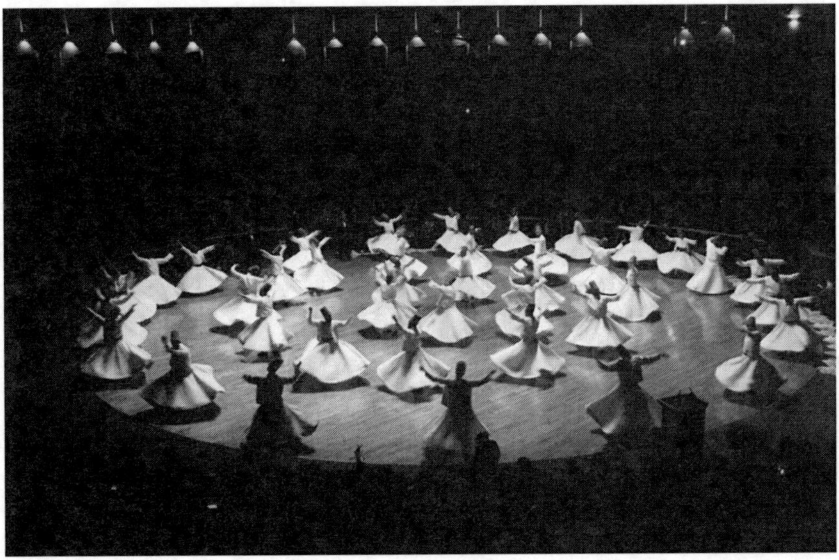

Fig. 13.1: Sama Ceremony. (2018). Daily Sabah. Retrieved from https://www.dailysabah.com/religion/2018/12/03/seb-i-arus-ceremony-to-gather-people-in-konya-for-745th-time-this-week

in 2005 within the scope of the UNESCO Masterpieces of Oral and Intangible Cultural Heritage of Humanity, was introduced to the whole world in 2008 by registering UNESCO on the Representative List of the Intangible Cultural Heritage of Humanity in our country[4].

Today, Mevleviye can be found in many Turkish societies around the world, but the most active and famous centers of the event are located in Konya and Istanbul. Mevleviye, which is gradually spread throughout the Ottoman Empire, is an ascetic Sufi order founded in 1273 in Konya. Mevleviye is famous for their whirling dances. They begin to turn around on their left feet in short twists, using the right foot to drive their bodies rotate with the left foot at the same time. And it is also recommended fast for several hours before whirling. During the ceremony, whirlers' eyes are open but unfocused, so in this way images become flowing and blurry, and their body is intended to be supple. A specific musical repertoire is played in the dance ceremonies or Sama, which is

4 Unesco miras listesinde Konya (n.d.). Retrieved from https://konyakultur.gov.tr/index.php?route=pages/pages&page_id=28

called 'ayin' (rituel). Dancers were trained in mevlevi-houses (mevlevihane) for 1,001 days. They have also studied about codes of behavior, beliefs by practicing prayer, religious music, ethics, poetry and dance. They returned to their families and jobs after the end of the training, but they still stayed as a member of the order. All mevlevihanes were closed in 1925, in consequence of secularization policies. In the 1950s, performances were allowed by Turkish government again, and restrictions were eased in the 1990s. As a result, many Sama ceremonies are no longer in their traditional contexts. They are simplified to meet commercial requirements and shortened, but they still perform for tourists[5].

Şeb-i Arus 2018

Information on Şeb-i Arus 2018 ceremonies is obtained from the Republic of Turkey Governorship of Konya Provincial Directorate of Culture and Tourism. In addition to conducting telephone interviews with the Directorate, detailed information and visuals were obtained via email.

The Commemoration Ceremony of Mawlana's International Reunion Anniversary (Şeb-i Arus) first started in 1937 in the city of Konya with activities such as tomb visits, conferences and concerts. The Commemoration Ceremony of Mawlana's International Reunion Anniversary (Şeb-i Arus) was held for the 81st time this year. The commemoration activities of Mawlana in the 745th anniversary of reunion were prepared with the title 'Time of Peace' (Selam Vakti) this year. Sufism was accepted by Mawlana; in essence, it is based on universal principles which are a gift of Islam to humanity. These principles accept all humanity as a manifestation and sign of the title of the Creator's creation. According to this acceptance, every human being deserves the Peace (Selam), in other words, the glory of this and beyond. This emphasis on eternal happiness depends on the person living with the creator, to himself, to other people, or even to other beings, that is, to peace. In this year's commemoration ceremonies and all of the events carried out, the concept of 'Peace', which holds an important and priority place in the sufist views of Mawlana, has been tried to be shown in all dimensions. The title 'Time of Peace' can be found in the concise expression of Mawlana which is 'the waves of peace roll in the sea and wash away the hatred in hearts'. Whatever belief and language, Selam means peace, harmony, harmony,

5 Mevlevi Sema ceremony. (n.d.). Retrieved from https://ich.unesco.org/en/RL/mevlevi-sama-ceremony-00100.

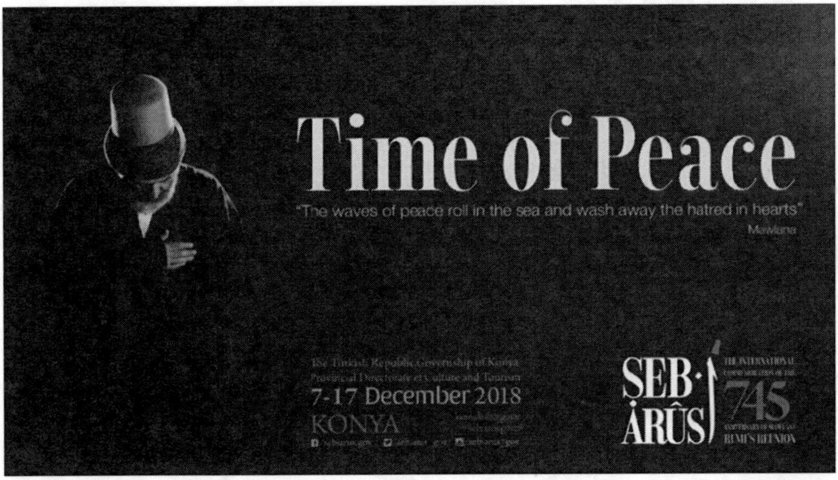

Fig. 13.2: Time of peace. (2018). Republic of Turkey Governorship of Konya Provincial Directorate of Culture and Tourism.

love, compassion, peace, respect and goodness, good wishes, altruism, empathy; refers to every trait that makes human beings human[6].

The ceremony is organized under the auspices of the Presidency, in cooperation with the Ministry of Culture and Tourism, Konya Governorship, Republic of Turkey Governorship of Konya Provincial Directorate of Culture and Tourism. Non-governmental organizations, the chambers of industry and various committees also work for ceremony. A total of 3766 programs were held in the stage and halls of the 81st anniversary of the commemoration ceremonies of Mawlana. Commemoration events were held within the scope of the first day opening program; as in the ancient tradition, Shams al-Tabriz's Tomb was visited and after that 'Time of Peace' march was held. The march started from the front of 'Governer's Office'; the musicians in front of the marching delegation came to the front of the tomb with greetings and hymns in accordance with the Nevbe Ceremony. After the Nevbe Ceremony, delegation went to the Tomb of Mawlana and the opening program was started with Gülbank, Aşr-ı Şerif and Pray.

They called another important event as "Front Tomb Meetings". They set up a big tent in front of the Mawlana Tomb. Thereafter the first day march, 'Tomb

---

6 *Selam Vakti*. (2018). Retrieved from https://konyakultur.gov.tr/images/uploads/files/745-Toren-Program-Kitapcigi.pdf

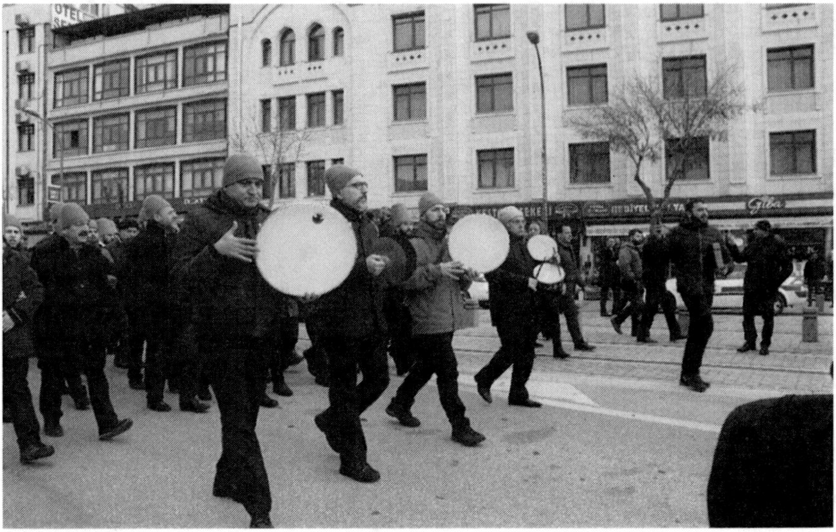

Fig. 13.3: March of time of peace. (2018). Republic of Turkey Governorship of Konya Provincial Directorate of Culture and Tourism.

Meetings' were opened, and the participants were served with 'Tekke rice' by the Konya Metropolitan Municipality. The Tent was set up for visitors where they can spend time after the Mawlana Tomb visit. In a short time, this event got the most positive response from the visitors. The Tent was open between the hours of 10 am and 11 pm. For kids, various events including shadow play, theater and Mawlana's advice were performed in the Tent. The posters prepared in accordance with Mawlana's belief were distributed. Musicians and ensembles from and outside Konya performed music concerts. Two different chat sessions were made by well-known names and opinion leaders of Turkey and Konya with visitors. These sessions got great attention by the participants. The theme of this sessions were the motto of 'Time of Peace'.

Throughout 11 days, many different events are organized. The content of these events are as follows: 15 Sama (Mukabele-i Şerif), 15 Masnavi lessons, 40 Front Tomb Meeting, 14 exhibitions, 3 panels, 15 conferences, 2 award ceremonies, 1 presentation, 1 signature day, 1 Nevbe ceremony, 17 Turkish Sufi music concert, 15 Masnavi talks, 47 workshops, 1 Symposium, 22 Music of Tekke, 23 talks, 1 opera, 21 stands/art quarry mevleviye and 3215 theaters. Other institutions that support the event are Konya Metropolitan Municipality, Selcuk University,

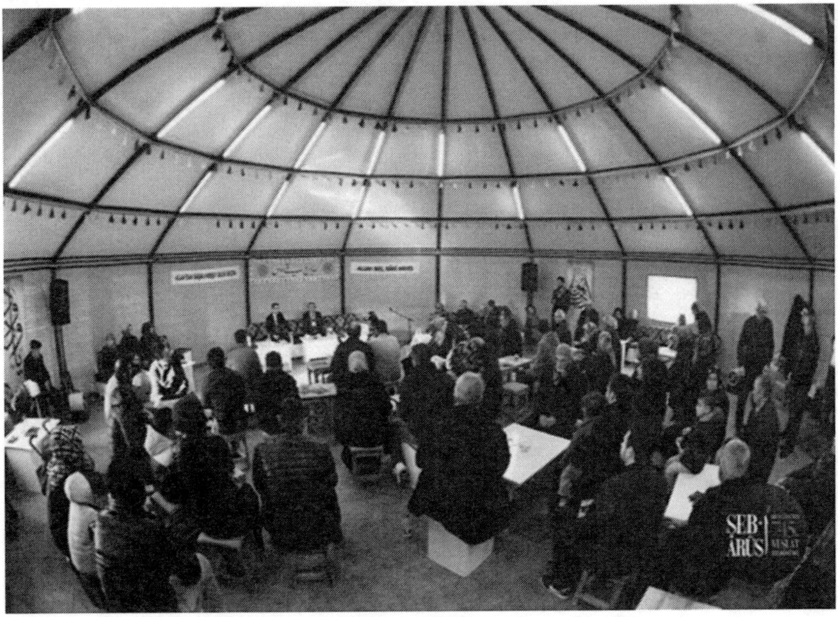

Fig. 13.4: A moment from the chat sessions. (2018). Republic of Turkey Governorship of Konya Provincial Directorate of Culture and Tourism

Necmettin Erbakan Unıversity, KTO Karatay University, International Mawlana Foundation and Research Center for Irfan Civilization. In addition, a 45-second public service announcement was prepared for Mawlana Ceremonies, and it was translated to English and Persian. PSA was broadcasted on TV channels of TRT, CNN, Habertürk, NTV, Net TV, Kanal 7, ATV, Kanal 24 KonTV and Kanal 42 TV channels. In addition, Ministry of Culture Turkeyhome, Metropolitan Municipality, universities, hotels, tour companies and internet sites published it on video sites.

Conclusion

The Commemoration Ceremony of Mawlana's International Reunion Anniversary (Şeb-i Arus) first started in 1937 in the city of Konya with events such as tomb visits, conferences and concerts. In 2018, 81 of the commemoration ceremonies were held with modern forms of event. This event, also known as Şeb-i Arus, is an international event of Konya, which is an important city with

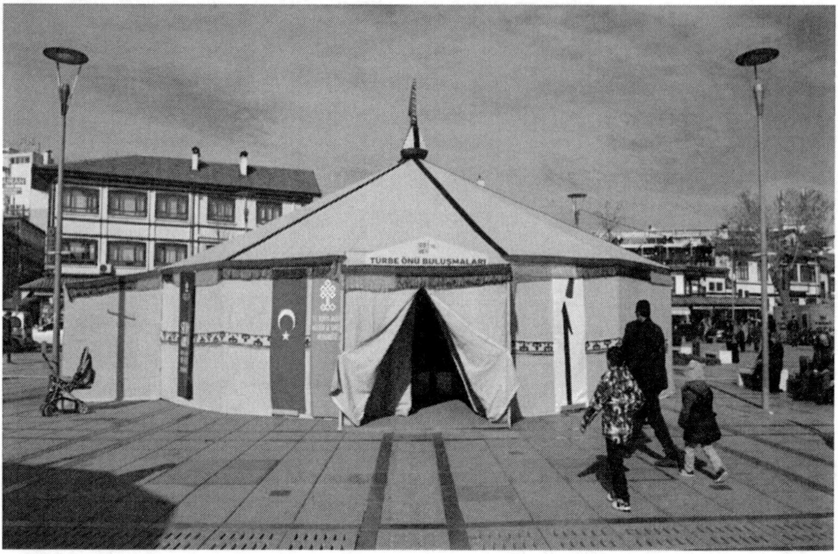

Fig. 13.5: Front tomb meeting. (2018). Republic of Turkey Governorship of Konya Provincial Directorate of Culture and Tourism

its cultural heritage in terms of history. Another important feature of this event is to create a touristic city image for the city of Konya and to be able to integrate with the city. Şeb-i Arus event includes many events of various sizes. Şeb-i Arus which means 'Wedding Night' is the night of Mawlana's union with his beloved God. According to Mawlana, death is the return to the original just because its source is a divine ore; it is return to God. Therefore, Mawlana's Reunion with God, which is December 17, is the closing day of the event. On December 17, after the afternoon pray, the prayers rise to the sky for Mawlana. The biggest event, which is considered as the gala night of Şeb-i Arus, is performed on December 17 with the whirling dervishes.

Through Şeb-i Arus, a large number of visitors reached with many different events. Shortly after the event, the Head of Republic of Turkey Governorship of Konya Provincial Directorate of Culture and Tourism, Mr. Abdüsettar Yarar, shared the number for the participation at the Evaluation Meeting of Şeb-i Arus. 200.000 of local and foreign audiences participated in the events for 10 days. Also, 13 ambassadors have attended the events. During the week of December 7–17, 11 events were performed on the weekdays and 4 Mevlevi Ayin-i Şerifs were performed on weekends. Except for the December 17, there were 38.222

visitors in the Mawlana Cultural Center. The Ayin-i Serif (December 17) was followed by 9,500 audiences. 3.766 programs were carried out within the scope of events. 3000 people participated March of Time of Peace and to Nevbe Ceremony on December 7. On December 17, 27000 visitors attended the Prayer Ceremony in the presence of Mawlana. 600 students from primary schools participated in the events for children in front of the Tomb Meetings, and 30000 people attended in the conversations at the tents with Sufi music concerts and mysticism. A total of 850 Iranians participated in the concert of Şehram Nazıri in the Selçuklu Convention Center. 17000 people watched the Artworks of Mevlevihane, and 20000 people visited exhibitions at the Mawlana Cultural Center. Tickets were sold through 672 agents for Şeb-i Arus events. According to the ticket sales on the internet, the Mawlana Cultural Center and the Konya Metropolitan Municipality Sports and Congress Center Ahmet Özhan concert and the Mevlevi Memorandum were followed by 47722 people. That is to say, events were carried out with 99 % occupancy[7].

The results of social media studies conducted by Necmettin Erbakan University Akademedya department are as follows: A page opened on Facebook with the name of Şeb-i Arus had direct access to 3,325,291 people. It had received 68,295 comments, public service announcements and other videos about ceremonies were viewed 738,417 times. 227 posts were shared on the Instagram page, the number of posts reached 13,571 and the number of postings was 444,557. 993 Tweets were shared from Twitter, and the page was visited by 5,600 people. It has been viewed 152,400 times in total, and tweets received 7,250 interactions. Social media pages of Akademedya were visited mostly by users in Istanbul, and then they were followed by İstanbul, Konya, Ankara, İzmir and Bursa. There were entries to this pages from the countries such as Turkey, Egypt, Algeria, Azerbaijan and Germany. Due to the prohibition of social media in Iran, entries from Iran have not been determined. The survey of Akademedya on December 7–17 was conducted in the field by a total of 2070 people, of which 1500 were domestic and 570 were foreigners. According to this survey; the highest admiration has come to Türbeönü Encounters Tent., second one was the 'Ask Me' mobile consulting service and third one was Mevlevihane Presentations. According to the same survey, Ahmet Özhan's repertoire and performance this year was highly appreciated.

7 *Şebi, Arus Şenliklerini 2000 Kişi İzledi.* (n.d.). Retrieved from https://www.trthaber.com/haber/kultur-sanat/seb-i-arus-torenlerini-200-bin-kisi-izledi-399010.html.

When we look at history, Konya, Mawlana and Şeb-i Arus events are a cultural value that is integrated with each other. With the fundamental doctrine of Mawlana which is 'come no matter who you are' and in the line of his philosophy that brings people together, the main themes of events were formed. Every year the changing theme and different events form the basis of creativity. In the event categorization of Jago and Shaw by 1998, they defined the hallmark event with the attributes of infrequent, international profile and permanent location. According to this, hallmark events are rare and unique in terms of not being held frequently. They emphasize the importance of exhibiting international profile and to be done in a permanent and specific place. Şeb-i Arus is a unique and infrequent special event because it is the specific day range to be held once a year and that it is the time of the year for Mawlana's reunion with his beloved God. The visitors, ambassadors and media members from many different countries are in Konya during the event, and public service announcement and printed materials are translated into different languages. This points out that this event has international profile. This unique and international event is held in the city of Konya every year because this city is the one where Mawlana lived in and died.

Şeb-i Arus, which is a hallmark event in terms of both its size and its being a tourism attraction, is also strengthened with the participation of local people. On December 8–18, 15 conferences were organized by the universities, public institutions, foundations and associations in Konya. It is important for local communities to contribute to the event. The occupancy rate of the hotels in Konya is 100 % during the 11 days of the events. During this period, the economic contribution of the event to the tradesmen reaches 30–40 %. The highest level of participation is the opening march and closing night. For Şeb-i Arus, an important event for tourism agencies, tickets were sold by 672 agents this year. Getz (2012) also says that hallmark events as iconic events play an important role in delivering cultural heritage to masses and contributing to the local community. Hallmark events both improve the quality of life of the city, help create the image of the city's tourist destination and, most importantly, provide economic development. The more important economic development is, the more important is the regional development.

The commemoration ceremony of Mawlana also serves to the recognition of Sufi music and Sufi culture as well as the recognition and adoption of Sufism. It has a very important mission as a cultural event. Therefore, Şeb-i Arus is an important hallmark event that put the city's cultural heritage forward. Mawlana is a world famous poet, father, scholar, theologian and Sufi mystic, who is integrated with the city of Konya, and, therefore, Konya is also often called as City of

Mawlana. It is not possible that the events carried out in the memory of such an iconic person are not iconic and lack cultural heritage.

In addition to being a touristic city with a cultural heritage, Konya is also a university city. In Konya there is Selçuk University that is one of the most important universities in Turkey. The contribution of university students studying in the city also increases due to this hallmark event. During the event, university students were employed in the information bureaus, which were created for the participants to obtain information. Another important feature of Hallmark events is that it can turn the place of the event into a tourist attraction. Konya is an important tourist city except for the month of December. Sama shows are held every Saturday throughout the year. The most visited places are the Mawlana Tomb and the Mawlana Museum.

According to Getz, there are three principles of hallmark events. The first being a foundation for the second, and the third being optional (Getz et al., 2012, s. 52). First, the function of the Hallmark event is to benefit tourism and the host community, so attracting tourists, creating a positive image and providing multiple benefits to the residents. In this respect, when we evaluate Şeb-i Arus events as a hallmark event, it is an event that attracts tourists to the city, creates a positive image and contributes economically to the local people. For example, during Şeb-i Arus, guests coming from Iran attracted great interest for Music Concert of Şehram Nazıri İrfanî which was held at Selçuklu Convention Center. Therefore, this event will be continued in the coming years. The second principle is based on the realization of the first one. The hallmark event that becomes a tourist attraction with time becomes an institution and its permanence is accepted. It creates sense of community with a stronger tradition and place identity. Şeb-i Arus has taken an institutional structure due to its long-standing feature, increasing number of participants and its international reputation. Konya Culture and Tourism Directorate officially registered the Şeb-i Arus Mawlana's Reunion Anniversary of the International Commemoration Ceremony to "TURKPATENT". The application of Konya Culture and Tourism Directorate, which applies for brand and logo, has been accepted by Turkish Patent and Trademark Agency (TÜRKPATENT). Sama ceremonies were also included in UNESCO's list of intangible cultural heritage in 2008. Şeb-i Arus events have reached such an integrity with the city that it is also called as city of Mawlana. The third principle is optional. Hallmark events can also exist within the context of social worlds and for special-interest groups as iconic tourist attractions that facilitate communities and identity building. Particularly the communities formed by the people reading and studying on the teachings of Mawlana and the communities formed within the framework of the principles of Sufism constitute the context of social world.

Considering all these aspects, this hallmark event attracts the attention of the masses – both local and international – with its special structure and it is a unique event in terms of creating a social doctrine and community.

References

Allen, J., O'Toole, W., McDonnel, I., & Harris, R. (2002). *Festival and special event management*. Milton: Wiley.

Beech, J., Kaiser, S., & Kaspar, R. (2014). *The business of events management*. Harlow: Pearson Higher Education.

Berridge, G. (2007). *Events design and experience*. London: Routledge.

Bowdin, G., Allen, J., Harris, R., McDonnell, I., & O'Toole, W. (2006). *Events management*. Oxford :Butterworth-Heinemann.

Cambridge dictionaries online. (2011). Retrieved from www.dictionary.cambridge.org

Daily Sabah. (2019, February 3). Retrieved from https://www.dailysabah.com/religion/2018/12/03/seb-i-arus-ceremony-to-gather-people-in-konya-for-745th-time-this-week

Ferreira, M. R., & Sarmento, J. (2015). Internal stakeholders perspectives in a cultural event: The case of Noc Noc, Guimarães-Portugal. *Ekonomski Vjesnik: Review of Contemporary Entrepreneurship, Business, and Economic Issues*, *28*(S), 93–107.

Getz, D. (1991). *Festivals, special events, and tourism*. New York: Van Nostrand Reinhold.

Getz, D. (2005a). *Festivals, special events, and tourism* (2nd ed.). New York: Van Nostrand Reinhold.

Getz, D. (2005b). *Event management and event tourism*. New York: Cognizant Communication Corporation.

Getz, D. (2007). *Event studies theory, research and policy for planned events*. Oxford: Butterworth-Heinemann.

Getz, D. (2008). Event tourism: Definition, evolution, and research. *Tourism Management*, *29*(3), 403–428.

Getz, D., Svensson, B., Peterssen, R., & Gunnervall, A. (2012). Hallmark events: Definition, goals and planning process. *International Journal of Event Management Research*, *7*(1/2), 47–67.

Goldblatt, J. J. (1990). *Special events: The art and science of celebration*. Milton: Wiley.

Graham Devlin Associates. (2001). *Festivals and the city – the Edinburgh festivals strategy*. Edinburgh: City of Edinburgh.

Hall, C. M. (1989). The definition and analysis of hallmark tourist events. *GeoJournal, 19*(3), 263–268.

Hall, C. M. (1992). *Hallmark tourist events: Impacts, management and planning*. London: Belhaven.

Holt, D. (2004). *How brands become icons: The principles of cultural branding*. Boston: Harvard Business School Publishing Corporation.

Mevlana'yı Anma Törenleri Şeb-i Arus Tescillendi. (2019, February 2). *Hürriyet*, Retrieved from http://www.hurriyet.com.tr/yerel-haberler/konya/mevlanayi-anma-toreni-seb-i-arus-tescillendi

Jago, L., & Shaw, R. (1998). Special events: A conceptual and differential framework. *Festival Management and Event Tourism*, *5*(1/2), 21–32.

Kızbaz, K. (2008). *Mevlana Felsefesi ve Türkiye'de Yapımı Tamamlanan Mevlana Belgesellerinin Karşılaştırmalı İncelemesi* (Master thesis). Istanbul University Social Sciences Institute, Istanbul, Turkey.

Lagos, E., Dolphin, A., & Kerlin, F. (2019). Designing and running overseas study tours. In S. Beeton, A. Morrison, *The Study of Food, Tourism, Hospitality and Events* (pp. 143–153). Springer: Singapore.

Levy, P. (2007). *Iconic events: Media, politics, and power in retelling history*. Lanham: Lexicon Books.

Marques, L. M. de M. T. (2011). "Cidades de eventos: O Caso de Lisboa" Congresso do Centenário do Turismo em Portugal, Lisboa.

Masterman, G. (2009). *Strategic sports event management olympic edition*. Amsterdam: Elsevier Butterworth.

Moscardo, G. (2007). Analyzing the role of festivals and events in regional development. *Event Management*, *11*(1–2), 23–32.

O'Sullivan, E., & Spangler, K. (1998). *Experience marketing: strategies for the new millennium*. Birmingham: Venture Publishing.

Pasanen, K., Taskinen, H., & Mikkonen, J. (2009). Impacts of cultural events in Eastern Finland–development of a Finnish event evaluation tool. *Scandinavian Journal of Hospitality and Tourism*, *9*(2–3), 112–129.

Ritchie, J. R. B. (1984). Assessing the impacts of hallmark events: Conceptual and research issues. *Journal of Travel Research*, *23*(1), 2–11.

Rumi. (n.d.). Retrieved from http://www.khamush.com/life.html

Şebi, Arus Şenliklerini 2000 Kişi İzledi. (n.d.). Retrieved from https://www.trthaber.com/haber/kultur-sanat/seb-i-arus-torenlerini-200-bin-kisi-izledi-399010.html.

Shone, A., and Parry, B. (2010). *Successful event management: A practical handbook*. Hampshire: Cengage Learning EMEA.

Silvers, J. R. (2004). *Professional event coordination*. Hoboken: John Wiley and Sons.

Tara-Lunga, M. O. (2012). Major special events: An interpretative literature review. *Management and Marketing*, *7*(4), 759–776.

Todd, L., Leask, A., & Ensor, J. (2017). Understanding primary stakeholders' multiple roles in hallmark event tourism management. *Tourism Managemen*t, *59*, 494–509.

Yeoman, I., Robertson, M., Ali-Knight, J., Drummond, S., & McMahon-Beattie, U. (2015). *Festival and events management: An international arts and culture perspective*. London: Routledge, Taylor & Francis Group.

Tirşe Erbaysal Filibeli, Sinan Aşçi, and Elif Cerrahoğlu

Chapter 14 Digital News Media as a Creative Industry: Tracking the Changes of Content Production

Convergence culture in virtue of creative industries lays bare a dramatic shift in the news industries. Such a culture of post-industrial journalism underpins how average individuals as their audiences look beyond the hype and have high expectations about the content in which material circumstances have been replaced with digital technologies. For this reason, news media as key actors in this convergence culture should be discussed by using both theoretical and practical implications on the integration of journalistic production, constraints of social media and fundraising, and audience expectations with convergence news making. Over recent years, how the growth of networked journalism has contributed to this shift is daily witnessed in a distinguished and sophisticated way, and this shift experienced within news media illustrates how the rise of network journalism has speeded up the changes of producing news stories.

Focusing on and thinking of digital media have become one of the unsubstituted needs for professionals in many fields of work; therefore, doing exploratory research is considered to be compulsory regarding a specific field and place. News media, for example, is one of the fields, which cannot resist technological developments. Following the emergent and technological adds-on in news media, both the professional environment and productions have come into prominence to be experienced, discussed, and evaluated from the perspectives of producers and consumers, also known as journalists and audience in this context.

Convergence culture (Jenkins, 2006, p. 2) refers to where old and the new media collide, where grassroots and corporate media intersect, and where the power of the media producer and the power of the media consumer interact in unpredictable ways. As understood from Jenkin's definition, convergence culture as a result of emerging technology would display old media and it is going to be more interactive in many ways. Convergence (Cambridge Online Dictionary, Retrieved on June 7, 2019) means the fact that two or more things or ideas become similar or come together. In other words, the word itself is transferred to the mass communication media such as television, radio, newspapers, or magazines which is necessary to use interactive technologies and involve several different media into one – which leads up to another term as "mix media." Bearing in mind that the medium is not the only channel like in the saying of McLuhan "Medium is the message," and medium could be anything. Hence, the more medium we have got, the more types of messages reveal.

With Web 2.0 technologies, journalism has become more interactive and immediate for both, the producers and consumers. For this reason, with reference to convergence culture and creativity, in this study, we focus on journalism-based creative industries. As every new technology has become an extension of our body (McLuhan, 1964), individuals who live in and experience the digital environment are getting more impatient to get the information they are looking for. That is why, content creators should work to keep up with the audience's expectations in terms of creativity and the fastness of transmitting the information.

Journalists as one of the content creators for mix media need to embrace "convergence" in regards to maintaining their jobs. According to Janet Kolodzy (2006, p.12), fewer individuals want to spend 30 minutes every morning with the daily newspaper or schedule to be home on time to watch a 30-minute network evening newscast. They all definitely go online and search for the filtered news, which means the kind of information they want to know and reach on the Internet. Kolodzy (2006) mentions that the audience nowadays is the one who wants journalism to be audience-centric, story-driven, too neutral, and professional. Following her ideas, it can be inferred that a convergence journalist should be also in the center of the values and skills, which traditional journalists hold – for instance, writing, reporting, producing, and disseminating. By taking all traditional skills and values into consideration to merge them with the new ones, journalists get many opportunities to choose the way they want to reach the audience and the audience wants to consume their productions.

This chapter also discusses how journalists and the audience are hand in hand, and how the lines between them are blurred. Axel Bruns (2005) puts forward the term "produsage" to refer to this blurring line. Regarding the processes of pre-, during, and post-production of the news content, the margins of the existing media sphere and the emerged one should be analyzed collaboratively by using the perspectives of professionals. To look beyond the process of news stories production regarding the alternative media in terms of ideation, narration, and presentation, we first try to put the debate on creative industries, sequential process of news, and fundraising 2.0 in context. We argue that the revived interest in journalism-based creative industries is the result of external and internal evolutions in journalism, technology, and their uses.

This study aims to reveal the contemporary distance between the orthodoxy of the newsroom and the culture of journalistic productions within a new framework in a dialectic attempt. For this reason, it explores the practical applications of convergence culture within creative industries from the perspective of media professionals who produce contents for digital platforms. To figure out how they struggle with the current economy-politic conditions in news media environment, a structured interview form has been prepared. Within this form, interviewees replied eight questions related to creativity-based actions in digital platforms from content types to content topics, from target audience to audience loyalty, and from fundraising to the future of news media. We got in contact with ten media professionals who have worked for different digital media platforms and produced different types of contents like podcasts, video news stories, and short documentaries. Only eight of them – working for T24, NLTR (NewsLabTurkey), Journo, Duvar, Medyapod, Medyascope, 140journos, and dokuz8 – accepted to take part in the research, and the answers of these media professionals were analyzed.

Creative Industries within and beyond Journalistic Pathways

Creativity in any aspect paves the way for coloring the contents, giving different opportunities to think of and focus on, and developing the components related to the real-life experiences of individuals. According to Cunningham (2002), creative industries are based on individual creativity, skill, and talent which are also involved in different kinds of industries holding a potential to create and carry out communicative actions, such as advertising, arts, design, architecture, music, television, radio, and performing arts. However, Cunningham (2002) focuses on the fields of academy, policy, and industry. Since knowledge and creating content play a huge role in the creative industries, such subcategories of creative industries consist of economic activities with information and knowledge.

Within different perspectives on the definition of creative industries as a term, we can infer that there are some samples to be considered as an effective representation of creative industries. As stated by Mercer (2009:186), Benedict Anderson defines the first "creative industry" dating from the fifteenth century and the invention of moveable type. Moveable types are considered as one of the cornerstones for spreading the word across the countries to contribute to individuals' lives by enabling them to get informed about what is happening all around the world. On this basis, helping individuals to get informed may seem equal to public broadcasting systems, and Cunningham (2002) stated that creative industries and public broadcasting systems are not the same in regard to globalism and nationalism. Creative industries are more global than public broadcasting because they are more about interactivity, convergence, customization, collaboration, and networks (Cunningham, 2002).

The elements mentioned by Cunningham to depict what creative industries are about have become prominent in order to understand the up-to-date systems of media and communication. To go in deep within media, communication, and creative industries, "convergence" is essential to refer to today's conditions of media fields because it creates another environment to experience a different culture. Convergence (Jenkins, 2006) refers to the management of technological, industrial, cultural, and social changes described by the people's action. In other words, convergence equally works with creative industries to what extent it is used. Convergence culture (Deuze, 2007) serves both as a mechanism to increase revenue and further the agenda of industry while at the same time enabling people – in terms of their identities as producers and consumers, professionals as well as amateurs – to enact some kind of agency regarding the omnipresent messages and commodities of this industry. Within this cultural aspect of convergence, it merges the components of mass communication outlets, such as print, television, and radio into the digital media platforms – even for interactive technologies.

Considering "convergence" defined by Cunningham and Turner (Hartley J. et al, 2013:36), it has three dimensions, which are technological, industry, and policy. The first type of convergence is the technological convergence that refers to enabling of the conversion and distribution of content across multiple formats and platforms. Smartphones, tablet computers, and AI (Artificial Intelligence) can be considered as effective instances for the daily usage and the consumption of technologically converged media items. The second one is industry convergence which means the merging of media and communication industries, basically for media conglomeration. Autonomous Vehicles, AgTech, and FinTech are the utmost important samples to discuss such types of convergence. The last type of convergence is policy-based, which is related to the regulation of changing industries. Policy objectives, policy instruments, and policy settings are decided and conducted within such industries that could show us the best applications for this type of convergence.

Interaction is put forward by scholars to mention how convergence and creative industries bring several components together for approaching media and communication both technically and collaboratively. By taking this idea into consideration, TV and film industries as examples of commercial industries date back to the 1970s and 1980s. However, there are four different cornerstones emphasized by Cunningham (2002):

- 1930s negative version;
- 1970s and 1980s reconceptualization of established commercial industries as cultural;
- applied arts practices (i.e. urban regeneration);
- the application of neo-classical economics to the arts.

These cornerstones depict that there are some effects of industrial movement throughout the formation and generation of cultural industries. The term "cultural industry" is first coined by Adorno and Horkheimer (Hartley J. et al, 2013, p. 78) as "an achievement of standardization and mass production, sacrificing whatever involved a distinction between the logic of the work and that of the social system." Following the cornerstones mentioned in Cunningham's work and the combinations discussed by different scholars, the main focus of this study is creative industries as cultural assets to media industry field, not only for content producers and platforms but also for the audience as an active participant in the process.

General findings in this study show that interviewees mostly identify the digital news industry as a creative industry. According to Interviewee 1 (140 Journos) in the simplest way, the media industry can be defined as the sector in which certain productions have been made to inform the society about the developments around them and make people comment what is going on all around them. On the other hand, s/he defines creative industries based upon production types, and explains that production is nurtured with technological innovations and how society adapts to these innovations.

Interviewee 8 (dokuz8) emphasizes that the media industry can be defined as a creative industry – in which media professionals transform information into the news by processing it within different kinds of digital tools – if we define the industry as the processing of raw materials. S/he adds that we put processed material at the end: in other words, the news in the market to catch the attention of the audience.

Interviewee 3 (Medyapod) states that new media technologies changed the communication habitat, and it affected the traditional news presentation formats. S/he underlines that journalists and broadcasters should have always been creative, and they should continue to be creative with the help of new technologies. S/he thinks that creativity is a must (sine qua non) for news media. To him/her, genres like the podcast, which democratize and decentralize production, can be identified as a sample in the creative media industry.

According to interviewee 4 (NLTR), media is the most creative industry in history. From the first newspaper to the radio, from the radio to television and eventually to the web, all forms of information are still being used for producing content and developed day by day. In addition to this, interviewee 5 (T24) points out that although journalism stands in a different position from other media sectors since it has to be considered as a public service; still it might be counted as a creative industry. S/he makes this assumption because of the change in the scope of journalism and the way it is handled making journalism more multi-discipliner.

Interviewee 1 indicates that 140 Journos might be considered as a part of creative industries since it puts both journalistic and advertising practices together as a media outlet. S/he says that conducting interviews with people according to the topic which they choose, data research, producing visual stories with a high aesthetic value, having a unique design culture, innovative use of social media are essential components of 140 Journos.

Interviewee 6 (Journo) says that broadcasting and publishing sectors are generally considered as creative industries. In terms of journalism, especially considering the vicious production practices in the mainstream in recent years, this creativity might be questioned. However, s/he states that it is also a creative activity considering the best practices of journalism.

Interviewee 8 emphasizes that journalism has been developed in parallel with the capitalist market. Within this scope, s/he explains how the news production process was transformed and became a creative industry in the needs of mass society. S/he says that dokuz8 as a news outlet was created as a reaction against industrialization; however, now dokuz8 is using most of the tools created as a part of this capitalist process for producing news. So, s/he states that the news-making process of dokuz8 has many creative features; for this reason, the way how dokuz8 makes news can be considered as an industrial production form.

Rethinking the Sequential Process of News Production within Creative Industries

Back in the late 19th and the early 20th centuries, what journalists were confronted with about producing and disseminating the content was a series of challenges based on gathering information and spreading the word to the masses. However, the buzzword which was started using to reveal and discuss major changes directly affecting the communication environment was Web 2.0. According to DiNucci's ideas on Web 2.0 (1999), the first glimmerings of Web 2.0 were beginning to appear, and we were just starting to see how that embryo might develop. This could be exemplified especially with newspapers' circulation and the trust in the mass media as an old version, which was in a steady decline and eroding. During these years, we have been experiencing to see the changes, and the challenges still remain to a certain degree because the debates on newspapers and journalism as a profession were regenerated in the past years with the help of new developments in changing media production and consumption patterns.

The changes in production and consumption patterns have been facilitated with digitization. In other words, technological convergence has changed the way, how news is found out, produced, and disseminated. The discussion in this chapter within this perspective is structured in two different and primary developments, the first of which is about changing professional experiences, and the second is developing several different genres by using the enhanced platforms regarding creativeness, fundraising, and spreading the words in formats. Based upon the first development in this field, the life cycle of such production may differ because it can be also boosted even with the production of audiences. That is why there is always a room for discussing how users and/or audiences act as professionals within these enhanced platforms working with Web 2.0 in a multi-directional way. The contents which are created by individuals are named after user-generated content (UGC) which contains both user collaboration and sharing. According to George and Scerri (2007), it occurs on a large scale of forms such as photographs, videos, podcasts, articles, and blogs. O'Reilly (Hermida and Thurman, 2008) states that new digital technologies empower users to develop, create, rate, and distribute internet content and applications.

In contrast to the expectations on creativity with the help of technological convergence into the news industry, David Domingo (2008) defines the news production as a generic process which consists of five different stages: (a) access and observation, (b) selection and filtering, (c) processing and editing, (d) distribution, and (e) interpretation. What Domingo (2008) provides the professional field is a cornerstone to understand what has been generally experienced during the production of news. However, there is another need in new models of news production, because journalists are getting involved in digitized profession cycle into production, presentation, distribution, delivery, and reactions as feedbacks through digital platforms where they have been working. For such a discussion, convergence is in the central point of digital news production and dissemination process within creative industries. That is why it is essential to understand how convergence equally works with divergence. The overall outcome and practices of professionals, markets, and technologies are merged and melted to generate various news media formats.

Since this contemporary convergent journalism has become widespread, not only the types of online journalism but also the types of output and the

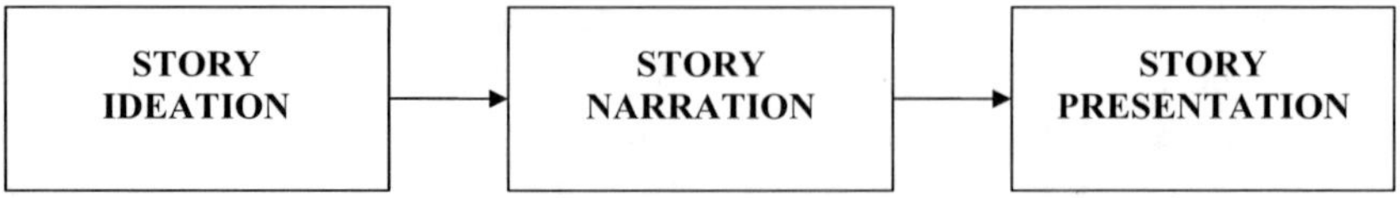

Fig. 14.1: Three components suggested by Hanitzsch and Hoxha (2014)

process have come into prominence to discuss and analyze in detail – in order to show the up-to-date basis by using Grounded Theory (Glaser and Strauss, 1967) built from the bottom-up through observations, notes, categories, and analysis of data. In Turkey's situation, typologies and models of contemporary journalistic works may be categorized with the help of international equivalents by beginning with the basic characteristics and specifications of works and coming up to a broader implication from there. Considering the international samples, INFOCORE (2014) Working Paper on "News Production: Theory and Conceptual Framework" reveals a set of components to decide on how generic influences on the news production process. As seen in the definition of "networked journalism" (Jarvis, 2006), professionals and amateurs work together to get the real story, link to each other across brands and old boundaries to share facts, questions, answers, ideas, and perspectives. In other words, this term aims to put the complex relationship forward, and it focuses on the process more than the product when compared to the other terms defining the contemporary journalistic styles. By getting all these ideas, a primitive version of "contemporary news production" framework (Hanitzsch and Hoxha, 2014) may be applied to the ones experienced in Turkey nowadays.

These three components in Fig. 14.1 refer to an interpretive framework by taking essential stages into consideration for the production of news. Based upon this retrospective analysis of news production – which consists of story framing, selection, emphasis, links/references, and presentation, people – as stated in Gillmor's work (quoted by Lasica, 2003) – are at the edges of the network and they have the ability to create their own news entries. This chapter opens up a new discussion on a new model by getting the practical experiences of journalists and content producers because this process does not end with presentation; however, news pieces definitely continue their life cycles into distribution to the audiences, productions completed by them, and the reactions of audiences to the news as an influence point on the future points and decisions.

Regarding the components of the news production process, our interviewees explain the whole process which they pass from determining the news topic to the publication step by step. Interviewee 1 specifies that observation, curiosity, and editorial consensus are the key components to choose topics for 140 Journos. 140 Journos' team produces video contents, visual and written stories with the motivation to understand Turkey. Members of 140 Journos propose the topics in which they are interested in the weekly editorial meeting. If the subject is accepted, it is scheduled and the preliminary research process starts. Following that, they determine subtopics and people who will be interviewed for which part of the video, and then they do interviews and features of the video; at the end, they pass through the last process called as "creative fiction stage." In this stage, the video is edited in detailed images and with the music, which is one of the most important elements of their video contents. They mainly focus on social issues, urban problems, politics in everyday life, current political developments, and Turkey's close political history.

Interviewee 2 says that in Duvar, they produce written, video, and multi-media news stories. When they produce contents, they pay attention to the accuracy and reliability of the work. S/he also indicates that they produce content in an impartial manner without judging any ideas, thoughts, or movements – which seems like one of the most important policies for Duvar.

Interviewee 6 says that they mostly give place to written news in Journo. However, they sometimes publish multi-media contents in different formats. In the future, they plan to have a podcast part. About the news topics, they take care of the ideas of their target audience. So, the wishes and the comments of their audience play an important role in determining news' topics.

In Medyapod, they especially produce podcasts, but also they publish written and multi-media news. In the near future, they plan to produce video contents and do live-broadcasting. Based on Interviewee 3's reflections on the choice of content topic, it can be said that the motivation for determining a subject matter might change from program to program and from programmer to another. S/he explains the mechanism behind the podcast titled ShortCAST, which is on digital culture and technology. They follow hot agenda and look into what is going on around them, and decide the topic. For instance, if there has been an event like the launch of Apple's new phone, they watch it and make a podcast about the event since it is a subject that everyone talks about. They just exchange their ideas in the recording and edit it very carefully.

Medyascope.tv basically is a platform mostly with video contents. The most important content type for Medyascope is the live-broadcasts which they produce in their studio. They also produce podcasts and written news. Interviewee 7 specifies that both local and international agenda affect their content production process as an internet-based news channel. Besides the agenda, they give places to stories related to lifestyle, art-culture, and sport. In Medyascope, they do an editorial meeting to decide content topics every morning, but they might add new topics and change the daily agenda regarding the latest news.

As a digital platform based on the topics of how to do journalism, NLTR works differently compared to the others. NewsLabTurkey aims to train and inform institutional and individual actors in the journalism industry in Turkey about journalistic practices and developments in the field. For this purpose, they have produced more than 150 contents under the specific categories as Newsroom, Tool Bag, Information Security, Business Models, Social Network, and Audience.

Interviewee 4 says that ongoing journalism debates all around the world, newly developed technologies for the use of journalists, emerging financial models in the journalism industry, sectoral and ethical issues, and original contents translated by experts form the main scope of NLTR. In this process, interviewee 4 specifies that they try to make both critical and innovative contributions to journalism in Turkey.

Interviewee 5 states that when they cover a news story in T24, they mostly choose their topics according to Turkey's agenda. S/he adds that it is hard for many journalists to devote a long time to produce content on different kinds of topics because of an environment where people talk about elections, political debates, diplomatic crises, and economic turmoil all the time.

Dokuz8 mostly brings out written news; additionally, they produce different types of contents such as video news or multi-media news which are sometimes based on data journalism, and they do live-broadcasting on the Internet. Interviewee 8 underlines that they produce news stories on specific data by using some visualization tools such as Infogram Flourish to tell the story with interactive maps. S/he also indicates that Turkey's agenda is very important when they determine their news' topics. For Dokuz8, the publication process differs according to the content type. If they gather news stories from volunteer citizen journalists, their professional news editors spend time to do fact-checking and then prepare it for being published with the reference to the volunteer citizen.

Without doubt, for a creative industry, the most important step is to gain audience loyalty to create a sustainable platform. To achieve this, they first have to determine the target audience and then develop some strategies to gain the trust of their audience. However, determining the target audience is hard for new digital platforms which especially produce specific contents like the podcast as Medyapod. According to Interviewee 3, podcast audience is still not identified in Turkey. However, they would like to enter into the life of individuals who spend a significant part of their day in public transport, who need to listen to something while working in their offices, who try to escape from the city mess, and who are with earphones while jogging in the evening. When they reach all these individuals and learn who listen to them more, they will be able to recognize their target audience and create strategies in marketing methods accordingly.

All interviewees bring up the importance of their audiences' reflections on their work. Interviewee 1 focuses on 140 Journos' target audiences' ages ranging from 18 to 34. 140 Journos broadcast by targeting individuals who effectively use digital media platforms like Youtube, Instagram, Facebook, Twitter, WhatsApp, and BluTV. To come together with their audiences, they have held some panels for the preview of their videos. In addition to this, 140 Journos' team works with the production process of the "Watch and Party" events for the Şokopop videos.

To interviewee 2, their target audiences are anyone who wants to reach the news. According to the interviewee, they have been able to take an important path for gaining audience loyalty even if they have been online for a short time.

Interviewee 3 specifies that their target audience is mostly full of active journalists and youth individuals who work in the communication sector. In addition to this specific target audience, they are aware of the fact that most listeners are interested in sports, technology, and politics. Interviewee 7 also highlights that they believe to be followed especially by young individuals. Besides, they think that the members of disadvantaged groups in the society follow them, and they also address the diplomatic community in Turkey with the help of their international publications.

According to Interviewee 4, journalists, media professionals, academics, and researchers, who are open to modernization and want to be more qualified, are involved in the general audience profile of NLTR. Not specific as seen in NLTR, interviewee 5 clarifies their audiences as the readers looking for news on the Internet and in the social media platforms. S/he specifies their audiences' educational background and ages as university grads and between 20 and 50 years old. According to interviewee 5, a considerable part of their readers follow specific journalists like Hasan Cemal, Mehmet Y. Yılmaz, and Oya Baydar who are contributors to T24.

Interviewee 8 points out that Dokuz8's target audience is citizens who are active in social platforms, citizen journalists, and journalists and journalism students in an extensive sense. Among these targeted audiences, local media organizations, alternative media companies, non-governmental organizations, non-profit organizations, and also trade unions and trade associations are parts of the target audience. Basically, Dokuz8 is a news source for anyone looking for alternative news. S/he adds that Dokuz8 systematically produces English content, and this aspect is increasingly getting recognized abroad by the audience who wants to keep up with what is happening in Turkey.

Fundraising in Social Media aka Fundraising 2.0

The Internet offers the journalists great opportunities to operate their own channels independently while the tools of which they have been making use have had a very ambiguous impact on journalistic autonomy. On the other hand, the production and reproduction of journalistic contents on the Internet drive the autonomy away because it also removes the traditional or current funding sources allowing journalists to experience independent journalism. Such a re-interpretation of autonomy points new and innovative ways by being in collaboration with the other components. The components related to the spread of new media have spurred the practices of a variety of computer-mediated non-profit phenomena.

Crowdfunding was defined by Schwienbacher and Larralde (2010) as "an open call, essentially through the Internet, for the provision of financial resources either in form of donation or in exchange for some form of reward and/or voting rights in order to support initiatives for specific purposes." This definition finds inspiration within concepts like micro-finance (Morduch, 1999) and crowdsourcing (Poetz and Schreier, 2012). However, it still stands for a unique category of fundraising which is defined (Retrieved on 05.05.2019, Cambridge Online Dictionary) as "the act of collecting or producing money for a particular purpose, especially for a charity." When these dictionary-based and traditional definitions are taken into consideration, we can easily infer that fundraising by using different methods allow founders of for-profit, cultural and social projects to request and look for funding from many individuals in return for future products. This seems like a novel method of digital or online giving. Ted Hart (2005) coined a term "ePhilanthropy" to define "the building and enhancing of relationships with volunteers and supporters of nonprofit organizations using the Internet to benefit a nonprofit organization." According to Bremner (1994), charitable giving is the act of giving money, resources, or time to an unrelated beneficiary which may be economic, social, cultural, or political need. Through a historical analysis perspective, five emergent fundraising structures were identified, namely religion-oriented, business-oriented, marketing-oriented, consumer-oriented, and for-profit-oriented (Saunders, 2013:141–148). Since these models do not represent a direct ordering for the needs and wants, the diversity and ever-developing complexity of several fundraising models are aimed to be provided in this chapter regarding how and why these bases have controlled and influenced the funding process over time in order to look at it in today's situation based on journalistic practices. The new fundraising potential is offered with the rise of Web 2.0; therefore, the traditional community fundraising should be revisited to be adapted to the online or digital environment.

Social networking sites, which some organizations or individuals create ties to other users, integrate formal social networks as experienced in Facebook, LinkedIn, or Twitter. That's why they are named after social networking sites because their primary goal is to combine features to enable two-way communication between organizations and its network of constituents (Lovejoy and Saxton, 2012; Waters et al., 2009). For not only basic communication environments but also the current financial situation, social networking sites continue to grow day by day to empower the communities digitally. So, it may remain essential that forward-thinking fundraisers continue to consider, investigate, and test the newly available online community fundraising opportunities now available if they are to be properly equipped for a healthy fundraising future. As it is understood, social networking sites or other websites like GoFundMe[1] or Patreon[2] have been adopted to provide social networking-driven charitable fundraising. Crowdfunding and/or fundraising remove gatekeepers in the environment of cultural production or journalism: in other words, it removes autonomy. It especially provides a direct relation and touches between the crowd and the producers.

The interviews carried out in this study aim to reveal the professionals' changing approach to more diversified and complex fundraising structures as an accelerator for a social change deeply and positively. Interviewee 3 mentions that Medyapod still has some problems about earning money from the content they create. They have made use of a Patreon donation account, and they have received less amount of money to supply their technical expenses. In addition to this, Medyascope and NLTR still continue to work on applications to stable the revenue model. Dokuz8 is an organization which focuses on several income revenues by taking mostly advantage of international fundings, and they plan to build a special structure for crowdfunding by improving audience loyalty.

Interviewee 6 expresses that Journo makes use of their own capital, but nowadays they have started using some funding tools, as well. On the other hand, interviewee 7 thinks that the capital structure of news media is still traditional in Turkey. S/he adds that media organizations have only an owner who thinks

1 https://www.gofundme.com/, GoFundMe is an American for profit crowdfunding platform.

2 https://www.patreon.com, Patreon is a crowdfunding membership platform based in USA.

that the media organizations are only commercial and for making money. For example, Medyascope's main income capacity is generated from advertisements.

According to interviewee 8, the main need for the sustainability of alternative media is to be supported by citizens. Thus, interviewee 1 discusses a different path in terms of crowdfunding and exemplifies how and why they have started crowdfunding with a burglary story which 140 Journos experienced in 2017. According to the interviewee's statement, employees in the organization thought about making a campaign for crowdfunding and they succeeded in it because it is related to audience loyalty. Interviewee on behalf of 140 Journos mentioned that they reached the needed amount of money which helped them supply all types of equipment which were robbed at their office. Unlike these examples, NLTR has been funded by international funding; that's why they are not involved in any crowdfunding process. In addition to this, interviewee 7 notes that Medyascope's main incomes are grants and donations which are publicly shared on the website.

Conclusion: Future Expectations on Newsrooms in the Age of Digital Production

Starting from these perspectives outside and inside the journalism profession discussed within creative industries, this study has looked at how such a contemporary distance between the newsrooms and newly settled culture in journalistic productions was revealed based on a new framework. The descriptions by the respective interviewees draw a clear picture which underpins the adoption of practical implications put by convergence culture and digitization. In this respect, the professional culture of journalism productions still favors a professional top-down approach, but there are ongoing and optimistic promises of an emerging participatory media culture as seen and experienced among the participants of this study.

Social networking platforms, as also shown in this study, have provided an opportunity for the new ways of raising and giving money, and brought both challenges and changes to the associated factors in the process of journalist productions. Considering these challenges and changes explained by the participants, it is confirmed that they started using some corporate techniques regarding the management of the foundation process, and developing up-to-date strategies to increase their productivity, efficiency, and profitability of news media.

Following all the ongoing processes in managing news media with the help of fundraising, the interviewees all agree on the fact that digitization and fundraising continue to play powerful roles in determining how to enter the matrix of journalistic production. Interviewee 1 confirms that the characteristics of social media platforms enable us to predict the future of content production on the Internet. Having had the preview of Instagram content on Twitter and then this feature being terminated, being able to post more photos and do live-broadcasting on Twitter or having Periscope as a new platform after Vine and Ustream were used less than previous years, copyright opportunities provided by YouTube, Facebook, and Twitter are specified as influencing factors of how 140 Journos decides on their own editorial policies.

Interviewee 6 specifically focuses on the restrictions given and shown by the consumers who are the most affecting actors on such industries. As interviewee 6 states from a social perspective, interviewee 8 also looks at how the life has been transformed. According to interviewee 8, the more social life is transformed with digitization, the quicker news media changes.

Interviewee 3 gives point to Medyapod's aims to create a new communication channel by making anyone heard in Turkey. S/he re-states that individuals' raw materials are enterprise and ideas in creative industries: therefore, creative industries in its infancy in Turkey are adopted by both producers and consumers. In contrast to this interviewee, interviewee 7 focuses on the future of creative industries technically: in other words, developments like augmented reality, immersion, and artificial intelligence are going to transform the media.

Interviewee 4 asserts that data-driven journalism, visual and multimedia contents, interactive graphics, the whole digital information and document sorting, and especially social media do groundworks for processing the news media in a fruitful way. The managerial actors, who are not always open to new ideas and transformation in media, play a crucial role according to interviewee 5. However, s/he still thinks that the media managed within traditional settings cannot resist the upcoming developments at all.

As understood from the perspectives of interviewees, digital systems and joint ventures to be used and applied in news companies or enterprises remain in its embryonic stages in Turkey. In this study, a journalism-based analysis of the structural changes through creative industries has enabled with the most-known practices to assess to what extent operational categories and a new model in news media have located the moments in the news production. In this perspective, media professionals who produce content for digital platforms must be creative enough not only for the production process, but also fund-raising. While they produce content, they should use all kinds of digital tools in order to catch attention of their target audience. Besides, they need to be accurate and trustworthy to gain audience loyalty. In addition to this, they should develop specific abilities to diffuse contents produced by them. However, only in this way, they can make use of crowdfunding tools successful and efficient unless they find international fundings and/or they can make profit from the advertisements. As a consequence, sine qua non features of news media as a sample of creative industry consist of high quality based on the content, its dissemination through and interaction with the audience, and lastly crowdfunding for making itself sustainable.

References

Bremner, RH. (1994) Giving charity and philanthropy in history. New Brunswick, NJ: Transaction Publisher.

Bruns, A. (2005). *Gatewatching. Collaborative online news production.* New York: Peter Lang.

Cunningham, S. (2002). From cultural to creative industries: Theory, industry and policy Implications. *Media International Australia Incorporating Culture and Policy*, *102*(1), 54–65.

Deuze, M. (2007). Convergence culture in the creative industries. *International Journal of Cultural Studies*, *10*(2), 243–263.

DiNucci, D. (1999). Fragmented future. *Print, 53*(4).

Domingo, D. (2008). Inventing online journalism: A constructivist approach to the development of online news. In C. Paterson & D. Domingo (Eds.), *Making online news. The ethnography of new media production* (pp. 15–28). New York: Peter Lang.

Glaser, B., & Strauss, A. (1967). *The discovery of grounded theory.* Chicago, IL: Aldine.

Hanitzsch, T., & Hoxha, A. (2014). News production: Theory and conceptual framework. Retrieved from http://www.infocore.eu/wp-content/uploads/2014/12/Theoretical-Framing_WP1_News-Productions.pdf

Hart, T., Greenfield, J. M., & Johnston, M. (2005). *Nonprofit internet strategies: Best practices for marketing, communications, and fundraising success*. Hoboken, NJ: John Wiley and Sons, Inc.

Hartley, J., Potts, J., Cunningham, S., Flew, T., Keane, M., & Banks, J. (2013). *SAGE key concepts series: Key concepts in creative industries*. London: SAGE Publications, Inc.

Jarvis, J. (2006, May 7). *Networked Journalism*, Retrieved from http://www.buzzmachine.com/2006/07/05/networked-journalism/

Jenkins, H. (2006). *June 19. Welcome to convergence culture*. Retrieved from http://henryjenkins.org/blog/2006/06/welcome_to_convergence_culture.html

Kolodzy, J. (2006). Convergence journalism: Writing and reporting across to news media. Lanham: Rowman & Littlefield.

Lasica, J.D. (2003). Whats is participatory journalism. Online Journalism Review, 7(08).

Lovejoy, K., & Saxton, G.D. (2012). Information, community, and action: How nonprofit organizations use social media. Journal of Computer Mediated Communication, 17(3), 337–353.

McLuhan, M. (1964). *Understanding media. The extensions of men*. New York: McGraw Hill.

Mercer, C. (2009). *Convergence, Creative Industries and Civil Society, Culture Unbound, 1*, 179–204.

Morduch, J. (1999). The microfinance promise. *Journal of Economic Literature*, 37, 1569.

Poetz, M., & Schreier, M. (2012). The value of crowdsourcing: Can users really compete with professionals in generating new product ideas?, *Journal of Product Innovation Management 29*, 245–256.

Saunders, S. G. (2013). The diversification of charities: From religion- oriented to for profit-oriented fundraising. *International Journal of Nonprofit and Voluntary Sector Marketing, 18*(2), 141–148.

Schwienbacher, A., & Larralde, B. (2010). Crowdfunding of small entrepreneurial ventures. *SSRN Electronic Journal*. Retrieved from https://papers.ssrn.com/sol3/papers.cfm?abstract_id=169918

Waters, R. D., Burnett, E., Lamm, A., & Lucas, J. (2009). Engaging stakeholders through social networking: How nonprofit organizations are using Facebook. Public relations review, 35(2), 102–106.

Güven Çatak, Cenk Köknar, and Ecehan Akan

Chapter 15 Virtual Reality as a Creative Industry and Its Progress in Turkey

Introduction

Virtual reality (VR) is a computer-generated experience, in which the users engage with a virtual world. VR presents an immersive experience to its users by delivering hi-tech auditory, visual feedback, and sometimes haptic feedback. In today's world, we usually imagine VR as a wearable headband that keeps the reality from the user's out of sight and allows the user to have an immersive experience within the virtual world. However, the VR technology changed its configurations repeatedly through history because of the technological advancements, and the scholars', developers' and artists' point of interest in the technology.

The VR technology itself is a consequence of creative design practices and inventions cumulatively. In 1793, painter Robert Barker held an exhibition for his panoramic paintings that can be considered as an immersive display (Benosman and Kang, 2001). Barker's panoramic painting exhibition was first of its kind. Later on, panoramic displays enriched with motion picture projectors as the technology advanced. For example, The Cinéorama in Paris Exposition which also includes circular display techniques Trans-Siberian Railway Panorama and the Mareorama that mimics motion by creating a journey using a painting on the way around (Uricchio, 2011). During the first half of the 19th century, a revolutionary invention behind today's 3D TV or VR happened: Stereoscope – it is an optical instrument that merges two images seen by each eye into one image (Brewster, 2012). According to Michael Gigante (1993), a comprehensive definition of the characterization of VR is the illusion of participation in a synthetic environment rather than external observation of such an environment. VR relies on three-dimensional (3D), stereoscopic, head-tracked displays, hand/body tracking, and binaural sound. VR is an immersive, multisensory experience. This extended definition of VR is also a road map of the history of VR. The synonyms of VR are virtual environments, microworlds, and virtual worlds.

Many researchers consider Sensorama as the first VR experience which was designed by Morton Heilig in 1962 (Regrebsubla, 2016). This device displays stereoscopic 3D images in a wide-angle view. The user places her head into the pocket to see the display that the pocket blocks the user's sight to make the experience more immersive. This device also has a fan-generated wind, stereo sound system, odor emitters, and moving chair to make the experience realistic and immersive.

The next three decades, the military, medical industry, and the automotive industry, of the United States shape the VR technology. However, the primary goal creating an alternative reality in a virtual world by providing auditory, visual, haptic, and smelling feedback remained the same. The most significant study that altered people's perception of VR is the first cubic immersive room, The CAVE is designed by Carolina Cruz-Neira, Daniel J. Sandin, and Thomas A, DeFanti (Cruz-Neira et al., 1993). This VR experience takes place in a cubic room in which the user experiences 3D images by using special glasses, and the graphics are accompanied by 3D audio as well. In The CAVE's setup, they used a physical space as a VR installation the first time instead of feeding images to the user by covering the user's head.

In the 1990s, Jonathan Waldern and W-Industries pioneered the consumer VR with Virtuality 1000 series which consists of Expality VR computer and Animette VR. The system provides a single virtual environment for multiple users. Jonathan Waldern publicized Virtuality Technology via a conference paper. A year later, in 1993, Consumer Electronics Show hosted Sega VR which has never been on the market officially. Nintendo's Virtual Boy came into existence in 1995, with a head-mounted display system similar to today's HMD technology (Garner, 2017). In 2012, after the Oculus Rift's Kickstarted campaign, VR hardware became commercially available, which was the pivotal point that led to the today's world in which VR headsets are used by PC, console and mobile phone users for entertainment, as well as, military, engineering, design, education, architecture, cultural heritage, and medical fields.

Although VR as technology has roughly a half-century history, there are 81 academic publications on this topic in Turkey: 60 master's thesis and 21 Ph.D. dissertations. The majority of researchers utilized and applied VR technologies on medical and educational fields, but there is also research on using VR in banking, architecture, cultural heritage, design, films, photography, gaming, as well as research that has been conducted to improve such as on haptic feedback, facial recognition, and usability. These researchers usually used VR as a supporting tool in the field of interest instead of working as a primary focus. Besides academia, there is a growing tech industry in Turkey, and over 20 companies use VR technologies in different fields.

In this chapter, the published academic works are listed chronologically to give a road map for the readers interested in academic work that has been done on VR technology and its applications in Turkey. Moreover, VR First BAU Lab and its contribution to academia shared briefly. Most importantly, the VR industry in Turkey is analyzed in detail to explore the utilization of the VR technology. Hence, the VR industry in Turkey and the United States and European countries compared by the industry professionals to reveal the similarities and differences. There are also a series of interviews conducted with Sami Hamid (VR Producer, Glitch Studios, personal communication, February 15, 2019), Yağız Hatay (Co-founder, Codemodeon, personal communication, March 1, 2019), Ahmet Burçin Gürbüz (Founder, Tasarım Atlas, personal communication, February 22, 2019), Ali C.Hantal (CEO, VRMasters, personal communication, March 20, 2019), Turhan Yiğitbaşı (Chief Technology Officer, Timelooper, personal communication, March 2, 2019), Tuğra Şahiner (CEO, WalkOVR, personal communication, February 28, 2019), and Alper Gökçer (Co-founder, Modern Innova, personal communication, February 20, 2019) to collect in-depth data about the businesses that work on the VR technology and its applications.

The Worldwide Status of Virtual Reality

At the beginning of millennium, the first decade is called "VR Winter". With a little interest in media, VR-related research has been done in laboratories all around the world. In the middle of the VR Winter, an HMD named Wide5 created by Mark Bolas (MxR Lab, University of Southern California) and Ian McDowall (Fakespace Labs), necessarily the HMD, provided 150 degrees of view which came handy in further VR research and pioneered perception of today's HMDs. Meanwhile, a former member of MxR Lab, Palmer Luckey started the famous Kickstarter campaign of Oculus Rift in 2012 (Jerald, 2015).

On the other hand, Crytek – a video game company that is located in Frankfurt, Germany – and Bahçeşehir University opened the first VR lab of Turkey in 2016, VR First. By paying attention to the VR market growth and the possibilities of improving this young technology, VR First provides a perfect space for developers, academics, and artists to improve the technology itself, and to experiment emerging usages of this technology in various fields such as spatial visualization, rehabilitation, gaming, and critical art practices. VR First also aims to empower the next generation developers and artists by providing an open workspace so that they can expand their knowledge, network, and can use the latest hi-tech hardware.

As the VR finally made itself known to the public, while Oculus Rift took its place in front of the individuals and accelerated the recognition of VR, Crytek – a video game company that is located in Frankfurt, Germany – initiated the VR First (VR1) global program which provides a perfect space for developers, academics, and artists to improve the technology itself, and to experiment emerging usages of this technology in various fields such as spatial visualization, rehabilitation, gaming, and critical art practices. The pilot laboratory released to the public located at Bahçeşehir University Galata Campus (Istanbul, Turkey). Moving forward to 2019, VR1 community has 50 laboratories including more than 700 academic networks. VR1 also aims to empower the next generation developers and artists by providing an open workspace so that they can expand their knowledge, network, and can use the latest hi-tech hardware. There is an increase of VR usage as a tool in various fields such as architecture, psychology, military to fulfill needs of field-related issues (e.g. Lohse et al., 2014; Wiederhold and Wiederhold, 2005). On another case, VR has become a useful advertising tool as it can be seen on EXPOs, AVMs, or in campaigns frequently. AR and VR satisfy the need of some in education to let children experience the facts or making the learning process fun.

On account of examining the 21st century of consumer VR, this chapter includes seven personally conducted interviews on VR with companies that have different scopes. Checking out the modern VR technology in consumer level, Yağız Hatay (Co-founder, Codemodeon), who has been working with VR since 2014, sums up the current status of VR usage worldwide:

> Although the high efforts and investments of tech giants such as Facebook, HTC, Sony and Samsung, VR have still been struggling to reach to the masses. On the other hand, enterprise-level usage of VR is rising. VR is often compared to AR and MR. Forecasts have been made numerous times in terms of the market size of these technologies in the upcoming years. Now, just by looking at the recent developments in the immersive technology landscape, I think that it is not really relevant to compare these terms with each other. We see that the immersive gadgets (headsets, etc.) have been evolving to serve as multipurpose hardware which can be used as a VR, AR or MR tool. That's for sure that these terms have different functionalities and offering different values but there are no solid boundaries between them. This is also why we have started to use a more flexible and inclusive term 'XR' (extended reality) to represent all forms of reality. (Interview with Yağız Hatay, March 1, 2019)

Similarly, Ahmet Burçin Gürbüz (Founder, Tasarım Atlas) gave a detailed explanation on this matter from three perspectives – available technology, people in the field, and economics:

> Currently there is an imbalance between the progress of the hardware and software in VR technologies. Available game engines, open source software, APIs, and so on present us with incredible opportunities where in comparison VR hardware including computers, network sub-structures, and HMDs cannot yet catch up. Not to underestimate where the progress has come from and especially where it is headed up to. So

> while there is so much chatter, news and marketing going on, in the end, this imbalance creates a situation where the end users get disappointed. But it is certainly valuable for the enterprise; for education and training, for marketing, for mental and physical health care. Which is also reflected in investments. Setting aside the investments on hardware, currently, the research and statistics state that investors are leaning to VR in enterprises. So it looks like we will continue B2B for a while more. One other thing that I appreciate is that the field is heavily open sourced, which supports the continuous chain of an end to end development. Where you leave off, I will continue with my perspective and where I leave off, they will. This is going to be the integral part that will grow the VR industry and global ecosystem. The industry is also full of curious people from all around the world who are enthusiastic and ambitious to progress and utilize this field of technology. (Interview with Ahmet Burçin Gürbüz, February 22, 2019)

The technology itself is quite old, yet its reach to consumers is relatively new; its future, as well as current status, is hard to portray. Still, VR is an industry well-grounded for several areas of utilization. In fact, Ali C.Hantal (CEO, VRMasters) emphasizes that by saying:

> VR has secured its place for gaming, professional training and simulations in the world. However, it has not met the industry's high expectations yet. This was the case for most of the new technologies in the past. When a new technology emerged, the first hype attracts huge attention and a good number of entrepreneurs as well as large corporations. Unfortunately, since the market and the industry can't settle in these first few years, some if not most of these ventures can't survive. It is the second and third wave that actually get lots of the survivors to the top. I believe we are at the verge of the second wave for VR in the world. (Interview with Ali C.Hantal, March 20, 2019)

According to Alper Gökçer (Co-founder, Modern Innova), VR gaming industry grows and B2B usage of VR increases worldwide. Turhan Yiğitbaşı (Chief Technology Officer, Timelooper) thinks VR enthusiasts, aside the technology, are today unable to get into people's daily lives. He claims that the majority of products on the market still consists of very short experiences for entertainment rather than functional. Additively Sami Hamid (VR Producer, Glitch Studios) notes:

> Consumer-focused virtual reality has gone through several years of inflated hyperbole led mainly by the media and large corporations and as of mid-2018 till present has been a gradual slowdown in terms of consumer confidence and general appeal by both the general public and developers alike as well as a drying up of investor capital. However although this might seem bleak it has been a natural and healthy process in streamlining the expectations of the industry as a whole and there has been a renewed focus by hardware and software manufacturers alike to push forward this technology over the next ten years while there is a continued exploration as to its viable industry and consumer applications. (Interview with Sami Hamid, February 15, 2019)

Comments on VR's current situation reveal the previous expectations. The current state of the VR does not meet these expectations thus, and VR is still waiting to reach its full potential. It is apparent in a reference to Gökçer (Co-founder, Modern Innova), Yiğitbaşı (Chief Technology Officer, Timelooper), and Hamid (VR Producer, Glitch Studios) that the VR market is smaller than the investors, developers, and entrepreneurs expected.

Virtual Reality Research and Projects in Turkey

Similar to the worldwide growing recognition of VR in Turkey, VR is beyond baby steps yet not completely mature. As its story told in a worldwide perspective, the first VR centered laboratory of Turkey opened to the public in 2016 by the cooperation of Bahçeşehir University and Crytek. VR1 BAU Lab Coordinator Kutsal Mustafaoğlu expressed that there are 16 VR and AR projects in development phase within the laboratory during the second quarter of 2019, among the projects in development phase, some of the commercial projects have investors behind, and some of the research projects conducted by Game Design Master of Arts students (personal communication, March 27, 2019).

In 2018, VR1 BAU Lab hosted two different sections of TUBITAK projects to increase recognition of VR in the educational field. The projects were organized by Övgü Öztürk Ergün, Güven Çatak, and Tufan Adıgüzel with the contributions of both project`s assistant coordinator Ecehan Akan and VR1 BAU Lab coordinator Kutsal Mustafaoğlu. TÜBİTAK 4004 Project "Öğrenciler için Sanal Gerçeklikle Tanışma, Gözlem ve Uygulama" was focused giving familiarity of VR to the teenagers aging between 13 and 18. 4005 Project "Öğretmen ve Akademisyenlerin Sanal Gerçeklik Teknolojileri ile Etkileşimli Buluşması" was focused on teachers (middle school and high school) and academicians all around Turkey. The projects reached out to hundreds of children and adults, and 59 teenagers and 99 adults not only experienced VR, but most importantly taught 101 courses on VR development; starting with what VR is, how to create educational content, basic Photoshop to digital communication tools, 3D modeling with Maya, and principles of 2D and 3D development using Unity. All the participants received an introduction about VR before the first three-hour-long class. Their VR experience was limited to selected VR games and environments on HTC Vive and Oculus Rift. Classes were designed for beginners, aimed to give the ability to manipulate tools at the basic level. Therefore, there was a predetermined course content; participants shaped an imaginary planet in an outer view during 3D Modelling class, and they manipulated the existing assets along with the outcomes of the whole program to create their own planets` inner design. The final VR experience for all the groups was taking a look of all planets in a galaxy view and teleport into a planet to move around and play mini-games added by instructors to improve the final products. After the end of their three-day-long VR adventure, participants were asked to create ideas on VR and participate in an idea contest. Furthermore, in a combined event for both projects held in BAU "VR Öğreniyoruz: Sektör Atölyeleri (We are learning VR: Sectorial Workshops)", the winners of the idea contest were announced in that event and awarded with VR1 BAU Lab access and mentorship.

In addition to the VR1 BAU laboratory activities, the increasing academic interest in VR can be seen via the increased number of Ph.D. dissertations; 10 dissertations were published between the years 2017 and 2018, while the total number of dissertations on VR is 21 (see Appendix).

Virtual Reality Industry Overview

Worldwide development

Güzbüz's (Founder, Tasarım Atlas) observation as an industry professional is:

> One of the major issues being able to stand and survive financially. Because VR is an emerging technology not evolved to its full potential, in addition to limited to none clientele, especially at the startup stages. One of the essentials is that I had to adjust was timing. For instance, I had a VR software development, targeting B2B which spawned late 2017, which also can be classified as RandD. With my team, we brought it up to the beta stage. We presented the project throughout 2018 to a large number of people of various professions and positions, including renowned futurists, investors, corporate business developers who all are also in our target client range. Our presentations for us became a sort of a focus group that spread over a year. The feedback that I got was great however one common point rose, which was essentially the world is not ready for the product yet. It became a great learning experience in terms of creating the right content at the right time for VR, in addition to how to actually create a client base from scratch. (Interview with Ahmet Burçin Gürbüz, February 22, 2019)

Yiğitbaşı (Chief Technology Officer, Timelooper) has remarked on the developmental issues and stated that it is possible to encounter a major problem with some technical aspects that none has encountered before, also points out that the device options are still very few, impractical, and expensive. Hantal (CEO, VRMasters) confirms the hardware-related issues and states the future expectations, especially the mobility issue of current bulky headsets that require computer to run. The standalone headsets such as Oculus Go and Mirage have been reported to lack both processing power and memory. Another issue that Hantal mentioned was the absence of haptics. He adds that today's VR equipment is like the mainframe computers 30 years ago, and soon we will see lighter and smaller standalone headsets with more processing power that will lead VR to conquer the markets. The hardware-related issues in terms of consumer expectation are also addressed by Hatay (Co-founder, Codemodeon) who highlights the need for standardization in the industry, explaining that VR still lacks movement and gesture recognition. He links up the standardization issue with regard to VR hardware market's fragmentation and thinks that supporting different HMDs and distributing content on different channels require additional effort and cost.

Considering all the interviews conducted and analyzed, it is possible to say that less reach to the hardware causes a decrease in the need for new content while the lack of new content causes less attraction in VR hardware. Şahiner (CEO, WalkOVR) says this loop can be broken down only by investments.

VR Industry in Turkey

Hantal (CEO, VRMasters) summarizes the current state of VR in Turkey as a success in adapting worldwide trends in VR technologies. He observes that the reality technologies will slowly replace the two-dimensional screens of today's world and open the way to fully immersive experiences, where there is a huge lack of content. He believes if Turkey can act quickly and start educating its youth on becoming content creators for this upcoming revolution, Turkey can become a leading nation providing the needed human capital to the world.

On the other hand, Hatay (Co-founder, Codemodeon) disagrees at Turkey's current adaptation rate with Hantal (CEO, VRMasters), as he finds Turkey's VR market immature. In his opinion, the VR community is still small, yet it is promising to see the support from some of the best Universities of the country which provide facilities and platforms that encourage individuals, teams, and students to create. He says it is possible to see forward-thinking companies that started using or experimenting with VR or AR; besides, the VR industry needs more of those brave companies to grow.

Gökçer (Co-founder, Modern Innova) and Gürbüz (Founder, Tasarım Atlas) came up with pretty close analyses over public expectation of VR as "fun and games". Gürbüz (Founder, Tasarım Atlas) remarks:

> It is here, present and visible to some extent. From a general public point of view, the tech is still mostly about 360 or 'fun and games' which is ok but builds limitations for creators. I love it when the public come across with some type of quality VR content and leave an immersive experience with amazement. Still, in terms of the general public, the

> number of people who are aware of VR's existence or its potential are quite low. From the people who have some type of idea, those who view VR tech as a new tool for games, are large in numbers. This is where we creators, developers step in. I personally do. I try at my best to introduce the technology, its current condition, its future projections and in total the potential, to individuals and to businesses in various sectors. In terms of the community of creators, I am encouraged by the fact that there are numerous developers and artists. The communication within the community in Turkey is not as high and dynamic as how it is in the global, in my observation. (Interview with Ahmet Burçin Gürbüz, February 22, 2019)

Besides the hardware limitations and growing community, VR experience still remains hard to reach for customers in daily life. According to Sami Hamid, who is a VR Producer at Glitch Studios, also the former VR1 BAU Lab Director:

> Like all countries across Europe, from the development perspective and leaders like BAU with their VR1 lab as well as community hubs helped mature a vibrant VR development community. However due to high prices on computer hardware coupled with an average low-income Turkey has suffered from a solid consumer uptake with VR being relegated to shopping malls and a handful of arcades charging premium prices for consumers who drop for a try. (Interview with Sami Hamid, February 15, 2019)

Through the aspects of industry professionals, the diagnosis on the immersive technologies, including VR and AR, is the insufficient recognition of its potential all over the world. Also, the economic pressure ongoing in Turkey, had been affecting the access for VR by users and even the companies.

Problems in Turkey

VR-related development still experiences basic issues all around the world. According to the comments and remarks of professionals, a list of challenges could be observed:

Limited access to the hardware

The difficulties of the development are not so different from the world, Gökçer (Co-founder, Modern Innova) states, however, access to the new hardware and early-bird products is a bit more difficult compared to some other regions of the world. Yiğitbaşı (Chief Technology Officer, Timelooper) gives a similar argument on the VR devices and accessories that are available in the U.S. and Europe and are not sold in Turkey. He finds it hindering for students and potential customers to have access to hardware as you need to fly there to get them or pay enormous shipping fee.

Lack of human resources

There also seems to be a lack of human resources, especially VR developers, as a consequence of brain drain. Yiğitbaşı (Chief Technology Officer, Timelooper) complains of this matter as opportunities in foreign companies luring new graduates that ultimately leads to lack of talented developers in Turkey's VR industry. Hatay (Co-founder, Codemodeon) also agrees that it is not easy to find VR developers.

Financial issues

Hamid's (VR Producer, Glitch Studios) statement explains it all:

> A proper infrastructure of financial support is sorely lacking. This seems to plague many nations with a poor entrepreneurial/startup infrastructure and in Turkey that is very obvious. VR from a consumer perspective still lacks enough of market penetration to make the development financially viable, while from industry applications there still seems to be a lack of maturity as to its various practical use cases beyond novelty/promotional applications. (Interview with Sami Hamid, February 15, 2019)

Another case is the lack of investments due to the lack of knowledge. Turkey's unstable economy keeps investors from risky investments which slow down the industry growth. As per Hantal's (CEO, VRMasters) opinion, Turkey's unstable economy has been the largest problem for VR until now. Unfortunately, many of the young entrepreneurs who started VR startups had to close doors since most of the potential clients in Turkey were trying to survive the hard conditions of the Turkish market. He also observes that companies do not invest in innovation or marketing strategies during hard economic times.

Recognition level of VR in Turkey

Gürbüz (Founder, Tasarım Atlas) summarizes the recognition issue regarding VR:

> In any other field, if you have a quality product and a good business network things progress in a pattern. In VR, as a developer, I not only reach out to a client base but also have to create it. I do not only have to promote my end product but the VR technology itself too. Specific to Turkey, setting aside the visionaries, our country is more of a 'trend follower' than a 'trend creator' when it comes to innovation. I have been reaching out to various businesses in Turkey for a good while now, to adopt VR technology including large corporate firms. One issue is that they would like to first see another and possibly a well-known, large revenue firm adopt and utilize any innovation than being the first one to do it. Another thing is that they mostly prefer to invest their budget to what they already do or use instead of adopting a new method. But I can gladly say that we

> have been steadily breaking this wall. (Interview with Ahmet Burçin Gürbüz, February 22, 2019)

Conclusion

Hatay (Co-founder, Codemodeon) argues on the decrease of popularity of the VR industry as a gaming and entertainment medium. He claims that the lack of high-quality content, expensive hardware, and the requirement of free physical space are the worldwide challenges that VR industry needs to face. If we add up the increase in AR content through smartphones, Pokémon Go, or Snapchat filters as indicators and if accessibility issues are solved, then the technology would come without any extra price to the individuals.

In the case of the VR industry, most industry professionals interviewed agree with Hatay (Co-founder, Codemodeon) in terms of the disadvantages of VR, the cooling down of the hype, and the positive future potential of popularity. As stated above, Hamid (VR Producer, Glitch Studios) concludes that there has been a general depression in the VR industry with an obvious decrease in popularity both from developers and the media.

Interviewees are also asked to express their opinion on VR's future as a creative industry in 10 years from now. Gürbüz (Founder, Tasarım Atlas) believes that VR will be contributing to the following fields more actively: education, health, architecture, design, e-commerce, agriculture, manufacturing, music, and entertainment. Hamid (VR Producer, Glitch Studios) has high hopes that he states in these words:

> I believe we will be seeing more human-oriented virtual reality applications. VR will be a powerful tool at bringing people together in a common space regardless of their geographic location. This will lend itself organically to applications such as distance learning, sales and business meetings, live performances and presentations, social entertainment. (Interview with Sami Hamid, February 15, 2019)

Yiğitbaşı (Chief Technology Officer, Timelooper) sums it up for all:

> As the devices get more comfortable available and affordable, the adoption rate will increase exponentially. I'm one of the believers that alternative reality glasses will replace our smartphones and will be a significant part of our daily lives. (Interview with Turhan Yiğitbaşı, March 2, 2019)

The industry professionals mostly point out similar aspects of VR industry worldwide and experienced slightly different issues in the Turkish VR industry. As VR covered the ground worldwide, we interpret from the common points spoken by the interviewees that it is a matter of time for VR industry to be recognized in Turkey. Noting that our interviews were limited to the number of seven, some working internationally, and practice on the similar fields of VR industry. The related issues in local industry are highly in focus – getting the hardware, financial troubles, the lack of human resources experienced in VR, and the technology's low recognition level among individual customers and investors. However, taking into account of today's VR industry and how it shaped its way in less than a decade, all interviewees are expecting a visible growth in the VR industry in Turkey.

The reported academic interest regarding VR is restricted to doctoral dissertations available in Council of Higher Education of Turkey (YÖK) Thesis Center and only five published papers/books are available on The Scientific and Technological Research Council of Turkey (TÜBİTAK) database. The chronological list demonstrates that number of dissertations is increasing as well as the interest in VR among future academics.

Appendix

Dissertations

Thesis No	Author	Year	Title(Original/Translation)	Subject
96700	Ayhan Karadayi	2000	Virtual reality model for Eastern Black Sea architectural archive	Architecture
210962	Barbaros Bostan	2007	Interaction in virtual reality	Science and Technology, Communication Sciences
260963	Elif Elçin Dereli	2010	The Comparison of the effects of virtual reality–based and task-oriented exercises on hand Functions in the upper extremity rehabilitation of the post stroke patients	Physical Medicine and Rehabilitation
295644	Nihal Kayapa	2011	Exploration of visualization traits in the perceptual differences between real and virtual reality environments	Architecture

Thesis No	Author	Year	Title(Original/Translation)	Subject
279715	Levent Çoruh	2011	Assessment of the effectiveness of virtual reality applications in art history course as a learning model (An example of Erciyes University Architecture and Fine Arts Faculties)	Education and Training, Fine Arts, Art History
322658	Erdal Devrim Aydin	2012	Improving spatial representation in 3D virtual environments: Building basic and connotative meanings	Science and Technology, Architecture
343092	Murat Ulubay	2013	Resilient features of re-emerging dyadic communication systems in an interactive virtual environment	Linguistics, Psychology, Communication Sciences
345249	Mesut Özonur	2013	The design of second life applications as virtual world and examining the effects of these applications on the learning of the students attending internet-based distance education in terms of different variables	Education and Training
329689	Gülsüm Çiğdem Çavdaroğlu	2013	Face recognition analysis by developing feature operators in virtual reality	Science and Technology, Geodesy and Photogrammetry
373029	Hakan Üstünel	2014	Force feedback haptic applications development in virtual reality environments for talented students' usage	Computer Engineering and Computer Science and Control, Science and Technology

(*continued on next page*)

Thesis No	Author	Year	Title(Original/Translation)	Subject
373028	Turhan Civelek	2014	Force feedback haptic applications development in virtual reality (VR) environment for high school students' usage in physics education	Computer Engineering and Computer Science and Control
477858	Ali Hussien Mary Kinani	2017	Improvements in robotic arm control based on computational intelligence and sliding mode control	Electrical and Electronics Engineering
473100	Zeynep Taçgin	2017	Development and evaluation of a virtual reality simulation to teach surgical sets used in the operating room	Education and Training, Health Education
496812	Şüle Biyik Bayram	2017	Effect of game-based virtual reality application on tracheostomy care learning of nursing students	Nursing
482732	Müberra Tanriverdi	2017	The effects of virtual reality exercises on balance in children with brain tumor	Physiotherapy and Rehabilitation
534242	Ulaş Güleç	2018	A virtual reality–based training environment designed for hands-on experience of software development	Computer Engineering and Computer Science and Control
520050	Mehmet Kösa	2018	Player acceptance and motivation for games with emerging technologies: A multi theory approach in virtual reality gaming and pervasive gaming contexts	Computer Engineering and Computer Science and Control, Science and Technology, Psychology

Thesis No	Author	Year	Title(Original/Translation)	Subject
515586	Rafet Durgut	2018	Development of physical therapy and rehabilitation application based on action recognition using by virtual reality	Computer Engineering and Computer Science and Control
509094	Tezel Yildirim Şahan	2018	Investigation of the effects of virtual reality on physiotherapy and rehabilitation outcomes on individuals with transtibial amputation	Physiotherapy and Rehabilitation
518389	Gülşen Taşkin	2018	The effects of virtual reality exergaming program on physical function, balance and pain in elderly participants with knee osteoarthritis	Sports
530442	Ebru Ağaoğlu Ercan	2018	Virtual reality, transformation of the concept of real truth and their reflections in popular culture	Philosophy, Radio and Television, Communication Sciences

References

Benosman, R., & Kang, S. B. (2001). A brief historical perspective on panorama. In R. Benosman et al. (Eds.), *Panoramic vision* (pp. 5–20). New York: Springer.

Brewster, D. (2012). *The stereoscope: Its history, theory, and construction, with its application to the fine and useful arts and to education*. Miami, FL: HardPress Pub.

Cruz-Neira, C., Sandin, D. J., & DeFanti, T. A. (1993). Surround-screen projection-based virtual reality: The design and implementation of the CAVE. *Proceedings of the 20th annual conference on computer graphics and interactive techniques* (pp. 135–142). ACM.

Garner, T. A. (2017). *Echoes of other worlds: Sound in virtual reality: Past, present and future*. Cham: Palgrave Macmillan.

Gigante, M. A. (1993). Virtual reality: Definitions, history and applications. In R. A. Earnshaw & H. Jones (Eds.), *Virtual reality systems* (pp. 3–14). London: Academic Press.

Jerald, J. (2015). *The Vr book: Human-centered design for Virtual Reality*. San Rafael: ACM; M&C, 27.

Lohse, K. R., Hilderman, C. G., Cheung, K. L., Tatla, S., and Van der Loos, H. M. (2014). Virtual reality therapy for adults post-stroke: A systematic review and meta-analysis exploring virtual environments and commercial games in therapy. *PloS One*, *9*(3), e93318.

Regrebsubla, N. (2016). *Determinants of diffusion of virtual reality*. Munich: GRIN Verlag.

Uricchio, W. (2011). A proper point of view: The panorama and some of its early media iterations. *Early Popular Visual Culture*, *9*(3), 225–238.

Wiederhold, B. K., & Wiederhold, M. D. (2005). *Virtual reality therapy for anxiety disorders: Advances in evaluation and treatment*. Washington, D.C.: American Psychological Association.

List of Figures

List of Tables

Notes on Contributors

Tolga Hepdinçler is Assistant Professor in Communication Design Department at Bahcesehir University. He received his Ph.D. on Film and Television from Ankara University and worked at the same university as a research assistant between 1998 and 2001. He also directed short documentaries and received nominations and awards in many festivals. He is currently teaching several undergraduate courses on photography and video production and graduate courses on visual culture and memory studies. His research interests include contemporary photography, art history, visual culture, and European film studies.

Şafak Şahin graduated from Anadolu University, Public Relations and Advertising Department. Şahin has completed his master's program in Advertising Brand Management of Bahçeşehir University. He completed his Ph.D. thesis titled "Personality Features, Creative Thinking Processes and Advertising Creativity Relation" in Bahçeşehir University, Department of Advertising and Public Relations. He was sales manager at Boyner Holding. He lectures on advertising, text writing, and creative communication in the Advertising Department.

Çakır Aker is currently working as Assistant Professor at Faculty of Communication, Department of Digital Game Design in Bahcesehir University, Turkey, and as the coordinator of Bahcesehir University Game Lab. He has a Ph.D. in Media and Communication Studies (2018) from Galatasaray University, an M.Sc (2010) from University of Pompeu Fabra, an M.B.A. (2008) from Bahcesehir University and a B.A. in Advertisement (2005) from Bahcesehir University. His research areas include gaming, interaction design, player experience, and user experience. Aker has working experience in advertising and teaching experience in the areas of interaction design, user/game experience, and gamification.

Güven Çatak is a professor and creative director working on game design, moving image, and new technologies. While studying architecture at İstanbul Technical University, he started to shoot short films and write critics in games magazines. His films *File of Mr. K* and *Down-Under* were screened at many festivals and won awards. He started his academic career at Bahçeşehir University (BAU) Visual Communication Design department. He took Moving Image and Game Design classes. At the same time he continued to write in *PC Gamer*, *Level* and *Oyungezer* magazines. He has Master's and Ph.D. degrees on computer games from Yıldız Technical University. Combining his media background and academic studies gave birth to "BUG" (2012). Started as a hub for the İstanbul indie game scene, BUG has become a platform for game design education. Still, he's working as an assistant professor at BAU and running the BUG components and its Game Design BA and MA programs.

Sercan Şengün is a researcher, teacher, and game designer, exploring phenomena at the intersections of video game studies, gamer communities, cultural informatics, virtual identities, and interactive narratives. He is currently Assistant Professor of Creative Technologies/Game Design at Illinois State University. In the past, he conducted research as a part of MIT CSAIL (Computer Science and Artificial Intelligence Laboratory), MIT ICE Lab (Imagination, Computation, and Expression Laboratory), and Hamad Bin Khalifa University's QCRI (Qatar Computing Research Institute), and taught graduate and undergraduate game design courses at Northeastern University, Bahcesehir University, and Istanbul Bilgi University.

Mustafa Feyyaz Sonbudak is an experienced designer in various design fields. He earned international recommendations for his design works and exhibits them at international art and design events. He is currently working on his Game Science and Design graduate degree at Northeastern University where he conducts research on subjects like gender bias in e-sports among others, and designs games. His recent games were showcased at PAX East 2019.

Barbaros Bostan is Associate Professor in the Digital Game Design department at the Bahcesehir University, Turkey. He has a Ph.D. in Information Systems (2007) from Marmara University, an M.B.A. (2003) from Yeditepe University, and a B.S. in Electronics and Communication Engineering (2001) from Istanbul Technical University. He worked as a postdoc researcher at IDM Institute, Games Lab of the National University of Singapore between 2008 and 2010. His research areas include computer games, presence, interactivity, gamer psychology, player motivations, and player profiling. Bostan has teaching experience in the areas of game history and analysis, storytelling in games, player psychology, research methods, and interactive narrative. He reviews journal articles and book chapters for various journals and publishers, local and international. He was the editor of *Gamer Psychology and Behavior* book published by Springer. He was also one of the section editors of *Encyclopedia of Computer Graphics and Games* published by Springer.

Ertuğrul Sungu after starting his university education and language studies in 2003 in Germany graduated from Haliç University, American Culture and Literature Department with high honour degree in 2012. After completing his postgraduate History Studies at Bilgi University, he started his Ph.D. at the Faculty of Communication at the same university. He continues to give lectures as a part-time instructor at Bilgi and Bahçeşehir University's Digital Game Design Departments. Besides his academic studies, he has been working as an editor and writer at LEVEL and Chip Online magazines since 2008. He is also the Turkish editor of the book series: *Guinness World Records Gamer's Edition: Everything You Need to Know About Game Records.*

Kaya Özkaracalar was born in 1968 in Istanbul. He received his undergraduate and graduate degrees on Political Science from Middle East Technical University in Ankara and his Ph.D. degree on Graphic Design & Arts from the Bilkent University in the same city. He was the editor of the quarterly *Geceyarısı Sineması* (1998–2004), Turkey's first journal concentrating on cine-fantastique. He has contributed to various publications in Turkey and abroad with film critiques and other writings on cinema. In 2015, he was elected to the Executive Board of Turkey's Film Critics Association (SİYAD) and is still serving on this board. He is the author of two books, *Gotik* (2005) and *Geceyarısı Filmleri* (2007) and has codirected several documentaries. Özkaracalar is teaching courses on world cinema and genre cinema at the Film and Television Department at Bahçeşehir Üniversity as full-time associate professor and is coordinator of the graduate program of Film and Television at the same university.

Tuna Tetik is a doctoral candidate at the Bahçeşehir University Cinema and Media Research program, and has directed a short film and a documentary that have both received awards.

Burcu Eker Akgöz is an associate professor in Public Relations at Bahçeşehir University, İstanbul. She earned her Ph.D. in Public Relations from Marmara University. She has started working as a research assistant at the Faculty of Communication in Bahçeşehir University in 2005. She is currently teaching several classes on Public Relations. Her areas of interest include event management, corporate culture, organizational commitment, crisis communication, and corporate social responsibility.

Elif Engin is an associate professor in Public Relations at Bahçeşehir University, İstanbul. She earned her Ph.D. in Public Relations from Marmara University. She has started working as a research assistant at the Faculty of Communication in Bahçeşehir University in 2001. She is currently teaching several classes on Public Relations. Her areas of interest include corporate storytelling and narrative, corporate social responsibility, corporate culture, and strategic public relations management.

Funda Kaya is currently a research assistant and a Ph.D. candidate in Bahcesehir University, Istanbul. After her corporate professional experience on marketing communications field, she decided to return to academia. She completed her two MA degrees in Film Studies (Bahcesehir University, İstanbul) and in Sociology (Bogazici University, İstanbul). Her research interests are in the area of visual culture, film studies, and gender studies.

Nilay Ulusoy is a professor at Bahcesehir University, Istanbul. She graduated from Marmara University's Communication Faculty in 1997. She finished Marmara University's Communication Sciences Master's Program in 2000 and her doctoral studies in 2006. In the same year she did research at National Center of Cinematography and the Moving Image (CNC) in Paris with a scholarship from the French Institute of Istanbul. She teaches courses on the history of narrative film (M.A. level), film theory, visual culture, and Turkish Cinema (Ph.D. level). Her fields of interest include language of fashion and Turkish Cinema history. She is the head of the Film and TV Department in Bahcesehir University.

Nazlı Eda Noyan is the founder head of Cartoon and Animation Department of Bahçeşehir University. She is the author and designer of 13 children's books; writer and director of awarded short animations "The Children of the Other Lands" and "A Cup of Turkish Coffee" (supported by ARTE and CNC); director of Istanbul Animation Festival Animist and founder of animasyonunkadinlari.org – an archive project for women of animation in Turkey.

Ömer Vatanarttıran received a MBA degree in Business Administration (İstanbul Bilgi University, 2007) and Ph.D. in Management and Organization (İstanbul Bilgi University, 2015). He teaches courses on Interpersonal Communication, Public Relations Ethics, and Media and Communication Theories in Bahçeşehir University. His professional experience includes voice acting, stage acting, television presenting, and event management.

Yahya Burak Tamer received his Electronics & Communication Engineering degree from Yıldız Technical University in 2001. He studied Sound Engineering & Design and received his M.A. and Ph.D. degrees in 2005 and 2012 from Istanbul Technical University, Advanced Studies in Music Department, Turkey. Burak Tamer's studies focus on interactive sound design and music production. Currently he is employed at Bahçeşehir University where he teaches courses on Sound Design, Interaction Design, Music Technologies and Production in the Communication Design department and Sound Technologies master's degree program. Tamer has been releasing music and performing live as an independent musician since 2006.

Barkın Engin received his M.A. and Ph.D. from Advanced Studies in Music program at Istanbul Technical University and recently works as a lecturer in Bahcesehir University Audio Technology Department. Engin has been also working as a sound engineer/designer for music and film productions since 2005. As one of the founding members of the bands Replikas & Reverie Falls On All, Engin has been performing live and releasing records since the late 1990s.

Ali Çağıl Ömerbaş is an assistant professor at Bahçeşehir University. He has recently completed his Ph.D. thesis on the power of understanding and gaming habits of Turkish video game players. His areas of interest include film and video game studies and popular culture.

İdil Kardemirlidağ Suher is a Professor of Public Relations Department at Bahcesehir University and head of the department since 2006. Suher teaches courses on public relations campaigns, public relations management, and strategy. Her research interests include "issue management" and "source credibility." She has worked in several research projects and gives seminars about "internal communication," "corporate reputation," and "persuasive communication."

Çisil Sohodol has been working in Public Relations Department in the Faculty of Communication at Bahcesehir University for 15 years. She received her master's and Ph.D. degrees on public relations at Ege University. Her researches and courses focus on Media Relations, Crisis Communication, and Theories of Public Relations.

Nilüfer Geysi is research assistant and Ph.D. candidate in Faculty of Communication at Bahcesehir University. She has completed her undergraduate degree on Public Relations and Advertising, and master's degree on Marketing Communication and Public Relations. Geysi's academic interests include corporate culture, globalization, and new media.

Tirşe Erbaysal Filibeli received her Ph.D. from Galatasaray University, Doctoral Program in Media and Communication Studies with her thesis focusing on "new social movements and peace journalism." She worked as special rapporteur for Hrant Dink Foundation, Asulis Discourse, Dialogue, Democracy Laboratory (2016). Since 2016, she has been working as a researcher in the country team of Turkey, of the Media Pluralism Monitor Project. She works as Assistant Professor at Bahçeşehir University, Department of New Media. She is the coeditor of the book titled *Journalism a 'Peacekeeping Agent' at the Time of Conflict*. She has many publications on contemporary issues in journalism and new media studies. Her recent research interests focus on algorithmic and digital manipulation, fact checking, "fake news" about minorities, and othering in post-truth era.

Sinan Aşçı received his Ph.D. in Media and Communication Studies with a thesis work mainly focusing on "cyberbullying and youth in Turkey" under the supervision of Prof. Dr. Michel Bourse from Galatasaray University (2018). Dr. Aşçı is an Assistant Professor in the Department of New Media at Bahçeşehir University, and he is working with an international research team as a PDRA and adjunct professor for SDI München. He has been teaching courses related to media studies at the associate and undergraduate level both in Turkey and Germany, providing his services as an editor and manuscript reviewer of peer-reviewed journals, and doing research on social media and cyberculture, digitization, digital journalism, and digital literacy.

Elif Cerrahoğlu completed her Bachelor's degree in Television Reporting and Programming at İstanbul Bilgi University (2015). She had 6 months education as an exchange student at European University of Madrid (2013). She is currently doing her master's degree in Film and Television at Bahcesehir University. Since May of 2017, she has been working as an administrative assistant in New Media Department at Bahcesehir University. Her research interests focus on new media technologies, virtual reality, and documentary film.

Cenk Köknar is a Ph.D. candidate in the School of Arts, Technology, and Emerging Communication at the University of Texas at Dallas. His main academic interests are play and game studies, digital media and culture, and user experience design. He is currently appointed as a research assistant in the Creative Automata Lab, in which he works as a researcher and game designer. He is also the collaborator of the Games Research Lab, Studio for Mediating Play, Fashioning Circuits, and Narrative Systems Research Lab and, in the past, taught undergraduate courses on game studies and video game development at the University of Texas at Dallas.

Ecehan Akan is a game designer and researcher on virtual reality and video games. She is currently a Research Assistant at Digital Game Design Department of Bahcesehir University, BUG Game Lab, and VR First BAU Lab. She is a graduate of B.Sc. Mechatronics Engineering, B.Sc. Electrical and Electronics Engineering, and M.A. Game Design. She conducts research on extended reality and games user experience subjects.